# The Medieval Culture of Disputation

THE MIDDLE AGES SERIES

Ruth Mazo Karras, Series Editor
Edward Peters, Founding Editor

A complete list of books in the series
is available from the publisher.

# The Medieval Culture of
# DISPUTATION

Pedagogy, Practice, and Performance

## Alex J. Novikoff

**PENN**

UNIVERSITY OF PENNSYLVANIA PRESS

PHILADELPHIA

Published by
University of Pennsylvania Press
Philadelphia, Pennsylvania 19104-4112
www.upenn.edu/pennpress

Printed in the United States of America on acid-free paper
10 9 8 7 6 5 4 3 2 1

Library of Congress Cataloging-in-Publication Data
Novikoff, Alex J.
   The medieval culture of disputation : pedagogy,
practice, and performance / Alex J. Novikoff.
— 1st ed.
      pages   cm — (The Middle Ages series)
   Includes bibliographical references and index.
   ISBN 978-0-8122-4538-7 (hardcover : alk. paper)
   1. Civilization, Medieval—12th century.
2. Civilization, Medieval—13th century.   3. Learning and
scholarship—Europe—History—Medieval, 500–1500.
4. Scholasticism—Europe—History—To 1500.
5. Academic disputations—Europe—History—To 1500.
6. Religious disputations—Europe—History—To 1500.
7. Debates and debating—Europe—History—To 1500.
8. Dialogue—History—To 1500.   I. Title.   II. Series:
Middle Ages series.
CB354.6.N68   2013
909′.1—dc23                                    2013012716

*For My Parents, Albert and Danièle*

# CONTENTS

# Introduction

Debate and argumentation are as ancient as civilization itself, but it is the argument of this book that the debates of scholastic authors offer particularly great insight into an essential habit of medieval thought and culture. The disciplinary divides of modern historiography have much to do with concealing its light. As a subject, these debates are treated seriously by philosophers and theologians interested in particular points of logic or doctrine, selectively by specialists of medieval learning who focus on particular authors or key ideas, and more rarely still by historians concerned with the wider cultural fabric of medieval society. Popular images of scholastic argumentation have only isolated the field further. From Renaissance humanists and luminaries in the age of reason to general assumptions today, these debates have routinely been condemned as medieval vestiges of an anti-intellectual world: pedantic at best, pointless at worst. The parody of scholastic debate finds its most familiar caricature in the proverbial question how many angels can dance on the head of a pin, a satire on medieval angelology (and scholasticism in general) that likewise seems to be early modern in origin. Our notions of modernity reaffirm this stereotype. In contemporary discourse, hardly a day goes by when we are not entreated to enter into dialogue with our wider community and to engage dialogically with our adversaries, ideals that are held up or at any rate understood to be the very antithesis of the medieval worldview.[1] Marginalized and often misunderstood, the history of dialogue and debate in the age of scholasticism is in need of a fresh assessment.

Many challenges remain to understanding the place of scholasticism in the broader culture of the High Middle Ages. A particular challenge is posed by the origins and development of disputation, the formalized debate techniques of the medieval university, whose existence is always assumed but whose impact beyond the academic environment has not been adequately explored. As a leading scholar of medieval rhetoric has put it, "the scholastic emphasis upon thesis, counterthesis, and listing of arguments must have had its effects on all kinds of discourse. It would be difficult to name a more pervasive influence with so little study given to its effect."[2] An especially vexed question is the relationship between the dialogue genre, a popular literary form in the twelfth century, and the dialectical methods of scholastic disputation. Giles Constable has stated the problem thus: "Dialogue and dialectic—the science of doubt as it has been called—played a fundamental part in the thought processes of the eleventh and twelfth centuries. It underlay the discipline of disputation that developed in the schools and was applied to almost every branch of intellectual inquiry."[3] Curiously, no scholar has yet pursued the history of dialogue and disputation along these other branches— what I shall call their cultural history. The centrality of scholastic disputation to medieval learning has never been doubted; the problem in charting its history is where to begin and in what direction to proceed. To date, the topic has more commonly been treated as a subsidiary and finite category of medieval logic in connection with individual "authors" or "schools," terms themselves that must be approached with caution in the scholastic period.[4]

Identifying disputation as a historical problem raises some fundamental questions. What precisely is the relation between the literary form of the dialogue and the scholastic practice of pedagogical debate? Can the formalized argumentation embodied in these dialogues and disputations (real or literary) shed light on deeper cultural mutations within medieval civilization? What impact does the institutionalization of disputation in the universities have on the surrounding literary, musical, and artistic culture? In sum, what is the cultural logic of disputation in the age of scholasticism? This book does not presume to provide definitive answers to these questions, but it does propose a more interdisciplinary and methodologically nuanced approach to a long recognized and often misrepresented feature of the medieval intellectual tradition. As I shall argue, scholastic disputation arose in the late eleventh century in connection with new developments in monastic learning, and over the course of the next two centuries it developed systematically and centrifugally from France and Italy to become a formative practice in the scholastic culture of medieval Europe, eventually transcending the frontier between private and public spheres and extending to multiple levels of society. Not only was the triumph of disputation one of the signal achievements of the medieval university curriculum, but its evolution and application beyond the confines of strictly academic circles (in debate poems and musical counterpoint, and most notably in the Christian confrontation with Jews and Judaism) suggest that the rise of medieval disputation can offer historians an instructive model of cultural history: specifically, it illustrates how dialogue escaped its literary origin and passed from an idea among few to a cultural practice among many.

## Methodology

The term "cultural history" is as elusive as it is seductive. Frequently invoked but rarely defined, cultural history in the early modern period is often identified with a combination of anthropological and historical approaches to understanding popular cultural traditions, using a variety of narrative texts or nonverbal forms of communication (public rituals, material texts, the body, and the like).[5] Among French historians, the study of medieval *mentalités* that flourished in the last third of the twentieth century was an attempt to access the shared ideas and worldviews of the medieval mind by investigating its cultural matrix, described by one cultural historian as a "historical anthropology of ideas."[6] Previous attempts at medieval cultural history have, therefore, often consisted of dissecting a single author or concept to get at the larger surrounding culture. What has not been pursued in sufficient detail is the evolution and diffusion of that most scholastic method itself— disputation—especially its extension into other, related spheres of cultural activity that did not immediately depend on the schools in which it first developed. This is not to say that the connection between scholastic and nonscholastic circles has gone entirely unnoticed. An important exception is Erwin Panofsky's short but provocative *Gothic Architecture and Scholasticism* (1951), which attempted to correlate the ordered and harmonious spaces of thirteenth-century cathedrals to the organizational structure of scholastic thought.[7] The spatial arrangement of the great cathedrals, Panofsky argued, derived from the systematic application of principles generated through scholastic reasoning, including the commentary and disputational formats characteristic of university schoolmen. A comparative model of a different sort led another scholar to suggest that elements of the scholastic method of the twelfth century were influenced by earlier Islamic colleges, which also gave prominence to a pro and contra form of argumentation, what is now sometimes referred to as the recursive method in scientific thought.[8] Intriguing as these parallels and potential connections are, my approach here is distinct. It is one thing to evoke loose parallels between thought and architecture or between two different cultural traditions; it is quite another to trace the organic evolution of an essential mode of analysis in a single culture. What this book offers is a culturally holistic approach to disputation itself, one of scholastic Europe's most recognizable features.

Studies of the medieval mind or the medieval "imagination" have been undertaken before, and in their most successful forms they have greatly enriched our understanding of medieval society by expanding intellectual and theological concepts into more culturally relevant categories.[9] In the case of disputation, however, one of the stumbling blocks to appreciating its cultural dimension is the tendency to freeze it in a moment in time rather than observe its evolution. Individual practitioners and instances of disputation have been studied, but rarely has there been a sustained consideration of the practice itself. When disputation is singled out for study, it is almost always in the context of the university curriculum and with scant regard for pre-university or extra-university manifestations. To uncover the formation of this essential habit of medieval culture, a more profitable approach will be to trace the development of disputation on the frontiers between private and public spheres and between learned and popular audiences. The crossing of these frontiers can best be observed when disciplinary boundaries are blurred and disputation is examined longitudinally across both time and place—the longue durée, to borrow a term from the economic historians of the Annales school. My goal, therefore, is to illustrate how an idea and a literary form originally limited to small intellectual circles in the late eleventh century evolved though multiple stages to become a cultural practice within the larger public sphere in the thirteenth.[10] It is in this sense that the study of scholastic disputation, long confined to technical discussions among specialists, offers historians a useful paradigm of cultural history.

In tracing the cultural history of disputation from learned to more popular audiences, this book additionally seeks to intervene in a current of contemporary historiography reassessing the nature of a medieval "public sphere," a concept most famously associated with the German philosopher Jürgen Habermas's analysis of seventeenth and eighteenth-century bourgeoisie.[11] Habermas's public sphere, as medievalists have rightly noted before, was largely based on a dismissive caricature of the Middle Ages and made no room for the existence of any public before the rise of coffeehouses, salons, print culture, and other features typically associated with the Enlightenment.[12] Responding either implicitly or explicitly to these assumptions, recent discussions of the premodern public have ranged widely, from the symbolic rituals of early medieval assembly politics to late medieval marketplaces, public intellectuals, and legal culture.[13] As will become clear in the chapters that follow, I employ the term "public sphere" to point to a division between the more cloistered and private world of monastic learning in the eleventh century and the more public, and indeed performative, sphere of university and extra-university disputations. In describing scholastic and public disputations in these terms, the final chapters of this study endorse performance as a useful category of historical analysis. One of the defining features of the medieval culture of disputation, I believe, is its passage from a philosophical and pedagogical ideal to a model of representational performance.

## Scope and Summary

This study is concerned with the intellectual and cultural world of the medieval West, chiefly between 1050 and 1300. To be sure, the phenomenon long known to medievalists as the "twelfth-century renaissance," now sometimes called the "long twelfth century," is widely acknowledged and has long been a topic of interest. This book specifically targets the return of the dialogue genre in the late eleventh and early twelfth centuries and the development of formal public disputations that followed. The chapters chart this evolution both chronologically and topically, with the deliberate ambition of not just joining but integrating disparate fields of medieval scholarship. Chapter 1 traces the early history of the dialogue genre in the West from its ancient Greek origins through the Early Middle Ages. Dialectic, rhetoric, and the circumstances of public disputation in the ancient world are described with a view to best appreciating the medieval continuities and departures from that tradition. Special attention is given to the role played by Augustine, who combated Manicheans through public disputation but also advocated an inner, spiritual dialogue with oneself and with God that ultimately helped lay the foundation for the medieval monastic world. During the first millennium of Christianity, many of the rudimentary typologies of the literary form were established, such as the monastic dialogue, the Jewish-Christian disputation, and the didactic student-teacher colloquy.

Chapter 2 focuses on the writings and influence of Anselm of Bec, whose emphasis on dialectical reasoning and the use of rational investigation were major influences in multiple areas of speculative theology. Through his teachings, writings, and authorial intentions Anselm inspired a new generation of writers who followed his lead in giving primacy to reason and dialogue as

tools for theological investigation and argumentation. Chapter 3 situates the
dialogue genre and scholastic disputation more broadly within the literate
culture of the twelfth-century renaissance. The intellectual innovations that
characterize the twelfth century and that include developments in historical
writing, epistolary writing, and verse must also be seen to include dialogue
and disputational writings as well. Subjects treated in these dialogues include
not only the older monastic themes of piety and spiritual awakening, but
increasingly they also deal with varieties of controversial issues such as relations between competing monastic orders, issues and limits of theological
interpretation, the role of new science, and competing Jewish and Christian
interpretations of the Bible.

Disputation might not have taken the direction that it did following the
generation of Peter Abelard and his contemporaries were it not for the recovery of a new source of authority in the emerging practice of disputation:
Aristotle's New Logic. Chapter 4 assesses the mid-twelfth-century recovery
of Aristotle's *Topics* and *Sophistical Refutations*, both of which offered guidance in the art of argumentation and debate. The enthusiastic recovery and
translation of these texts led commentators such as John of Salisbury to hail
Aristotle as the "drill master" of dialectic and to praise his *Topics* as a valuable
"weapon" in an aspiring student's arsenal of knowledge. Ranging from the
earliest evidence for Aristotle's influence, Adam of Balsham's *Ars disserendi*
(c. 1132), to the anonymous *Owl and the Nightingale* (thirteenth century), a
debate poem that includes a close articulation of Aristotle's methods and
procedures for argumentation, Aristotle's influence can be shown to have had
an abiding influence on the practice of disputation within scholastic circles
and in the medieval satirical imagination more generally.

Chapter 5 focuses on the institutionalization of disputation as a constituent element within the university curriculum and, more significantly, on
the permeation of the scholastic art of debate into the surrounding culture.
From the inception of the University of Paris, *disputatio* played a critical role
in training students how to argue and search for truth. A review of the basic
types of disputation offered in the university provides the launching point
for examining the assimilation of scholastic practices in other cultural spheres
not ordinarily considered by historians of the university: Notre Dame
polyphony and the emerging art of counterpoint, motets, and the musical
debate poems (*jeux-partis*) that were cultivated by the professional entertainers in Arras. Chapter 5 further goes on to document the absorption of disputation within the Dominican Order, for they above all recognized the value

of disputation in their goal of training itinerant preachers capable of debating with wayward heretics, Jews, and Muslims. In examining the scholastic, musical, and polemical applications of disputation, I argue for a deep mutation within medieval culture as disputation passed from private to public spheres and from classroom practice to public performance.

Chapter 6 looks at the polemical application of disputation in the Jewish-Christian debate from the anti-Jewish dialogues of the early twelfth century to the royal sponsorships of public disputations in the thirteenth. The exploration of the dramatic dialogue genre within the *Adversus Iudaeos* genre illustrates the absorption of dialectic and Anselmian thinking within a preexisting polemical tradition. While many scholars have speculated whether these dialogues were based on actual debates, I argue that the more relevant fact is that they *were* composed to dramatize an encounter, thus connecting the genre to the disputation exercises of the new scholastic milieu and the rise of liturgical drama. Scholastic, royal, and Dominican involvement in Jewish-Christian debates are examined throughout the thirteenth century, and particularly in the context of the Paris "Talmud Trial" of 1240 and the Barcelona disputation of 1263, both of which exemplify the performance of disputation in the age of scholasticism. A range of thirteenth-century vernacular anti-Jewish dialogues and contemporary iconographic depictions of Christians and Jews in dispute further show how scholastic disputation enhanced the power of polemic and established a normative cultural practice in the public sphere.

The concluding chapter offers a summative and suggestive assessment of the medieval culture of disputation. After considering some postmedieval reactions against scholastic disputation, I argue that there are five essential elements that form the medieval culture of disputation, and furthermore that this narrative framework offers a useful paradigm of cultural history. Ultimately, this book argues that the dialogue genre and scholastic disputation should be seen together as part of a broader cultural phenomenon that stresses the verbal and dramatic conflict of ideas as a vehicle of public persuasion and a path toward a deeper understanding of Christian truth. This culture of disputation would have a deep and lasting impact well beyond its medieval origins.

# CHAPTER I

# The Socratic Inheritance

An almost unavoidable pitfall in tracing the history of scholastic disputation is the inclination to begin in medias res, when the institutional structure of the medieval university is already firmly in place. While this chapter is a deliberate attempt to connect the age of scholasticism to an ancient tradition, the story of disputation in fact defies the quest for an obvious beginning. According to the latest theories in the cognitive sciences, the proclivity for debate and argumentation is so embedded in the human condition that it may actually result from the innate operations of the mind. This recent, and still controversial, position holds that human reason itself evolved for the purpose of winning arguments in the debating arena.[1] The "deep history" of disputation is well worth noting, even if the implications of these theories fall beyond the parameters of this study, for it is one of the arguments of this book that cultural practices cannot be divorced from habits of thought, especially in the medieval centuries when formal procedures for learning became institutionalized, publicized, and ultimately deployed in a variety of cultural forms still recognizable today.[2] A more firm point of departure for our purposes is the philosophical and literary tradition of dialogue that began in classical antiquity.[3] This chapter outlines the history of dialogue and disputation from their Socratic origins to the middle of the eleventh century, with particular focus on the cultural elements of a written and oral tradition that were filtered through Late Antiquity and refracted into the early centuries of the Middle Ages. The genesis and early development of formal philosophical dialogue are crucial because the medieval culture of disputation is both a reception to and a departure from that tradition.

Plato may have been the greatest student of Socrates, but he was not the first to commit to writing the learned and didactic conversations of his teacher. Diogenes Laertius (third century C.E.) reports that Zeno of Elea was claimed as the first writer of dialogues.[4] He also states that Aristotle in his lost dialogue *On Poets* named a certain, and otherwise unknown, Alexamenos of Teos as the originator of the genre, and in his *Poetics* (1447b11) Aristotle himself refers to the *Socratikoi logoi* ("Socratic Discourses" or "Conversations with Socrates") as an established literary genre. We also know of at least six other writers of dialogues during Plato's time.[5] The precise origin of ancient Greek dialogue is most likely unknowable. What seems certain is that Plato was the one who perfected the form and gave it its distinctive appeal. More interesting than the question of who invented the form is what exactly Plato hoped to achieve by recording philosophical thought in dialogue form.[6] The issue has long been a matter of some conjecture, as is the question of how faithful Plato really is in his depiction of Socrates and his ideas.[7] Some indication is given in Plato's so-called Seventh Epistle, which, occasional doubts of its authenticity aside, offers insight into his literary creativity and motives.[8] The letter was written when Plato was about seventy-four, and it is addressed to certain friends and associates of the recently assassinated Dion, a leading politician of Syracuse whom Plato had come to know in the Academy. The letter is biographically interesting because it offers a retrospective on Plato's early life and his decision to turn from politics to philosophy. About halfway through the letter, Plato launches into a lengthy discussion of the unsuitability of language as a medium for philosophy. Concepts such as the Good, the Beautiful, and the Just are beyond the expressive power of language, and, unlike other studies, philosophy cannot simply be expressed verbally (*hreton*).[9] This is not to say that language is useless in the instruction of philosophy, but rather that it has its limits and must be used appropriately. Plato explains that the sort of understanding necessitated by philosophy can be generated only "from living day by day with the matter itself, and many conversations (*sunousias*)" in its regard.[10] He goes on to state that it is the "most noble (*kallion*)" activity of the dialectician to implant "seeds of knowledge" in personal conversation and that, similarly, it is "entirely noble" to undertake insemination of this sort through written discourse as well. Since Plato's dialogues depict interactions of just this sort, the apparent implication is that philosophical knowledge is generated in conversations of the type exemplified in the dialogues themselves. According to one modern interpreter, these statements "suggest that Plato wrote in the form of dialogues in order to provide a dialectical context in which philosophical knowledge can take shape in the reader."[11] This, in fact, is a truism in the history of the

genre from ancient gardens to modern classrooms. Diogenes Laertius is again
helpful. He initially defines dialogue as "discourse consisting of a question
and answer on some philosophical or political subject."[12] He then further
distinguishes between two types of Platonic dialogues, the one adapted for
instruction and the other for inquiry. Amid further subdivisions of these two
types, some are then called dramatic, others narrative, and some are a mixture
of the two. The Middle Ages will offer continuity and departures from each
of these identified types.

One reason Socrates may not have written anything himself is because
of a conviction of the very inadequacy of language that Plato describes in
his Seventh Epistle. In Plato's *Gorgias* and *Phaedrus*, both dialogues treating
rhetoric, Socrates is portrayed as rejecting the written word as an effective
teaching method. Obviously Plato was somewhat less skeptical, though he
had his reservations as well. The reasons for this disparity of opinion between
teacher and student are probably best illustrated in the context of the changing attitudes toward writing in fourth-century Athens. Before Plato's day,
writing was considered as an aid to speaking rather than a substitute for it.
By Plato's time the position was changing, and during this transitional stage
the status of the *logos* became the subject of lively argument. There is evidence
during Plato's time of a controversy between the upholders of the spoken
word and the written word. For Plato's rival Isocrates, oratory itself became
a purely written medium, while Alcidamas took the opposing position and
maintained that speeches should not be written down at all but improvised
as the occasion demanded.[13] Plato's position may perhaps best be characterized as intermediary.

The issue of language—verbal communication and written word—is, as
we shall see, central to the medieval understanding of dialogue and disputation. Many of the ideas that would carry over from antiquity into the Middle
Ages would do so under the familiar rubrics of rhetoric and dialectic, disciplines not always separable and best summarized as the arts of persuasion
and good argumentation respectively. The early development of the study of
rhetoric is heavily indebted to Aristotle, whose *Rhetoric* was the first systematic (and most influential) study of the art of persuasion in the Hellenistic
period. According to ancient testimonies, Aristotle also wrote an early dialogue on rhetoric titled *Grullos*, in which he put forward the argument that
rhetoric cannot be an art (*techne*). Since this is precisely the position of the
*Gorgias*, the lost *Grullos* has traditionally been regarded as a sign of Aristotle's
early Platonism. In the first two books of *Rhetoric*, Aristotle presents two

tripartite divisions. The first division defines the three means of persuasion: speech can produce persuasion either through the character of the speaker, the emotional state of the listener, or the argument itself. The second division concerns the three species of public speech: deliberative if it takes place before an assembly; judicial if it takes place before a court; and epideictic if it either praises or blames someone. These divisions would influence nearly all subsequent classical discussions of language and rhetoric. The text of the *Rhetoric* received considerable attention after its translation into Latin by William of Moerbeke in the 1270s, but, paradoxically, it was not treated as a rhetorical text, despite the medieval fascination with the art of rhetoric. Instead, it was treated as a book of moral philosophy, being copied most often with Aristotle's *Ethics* or *Politics*.[14] By the thirteenth century, the scholastics had already built up a firm basis for applying logic and rhetoric, due in part to the reception of Aristotle's New Logic in the twelfth century.

The most important Aristotelian influence on medieval language came from the Latin translations of his *Topics* and *Sophistical Refutations*, both of which would influence the scholastic *disputatio* of the twelfth and thirteenth centuries, as we shall see in Chapter 4. In fact, it was Aristotle who was credited, beginning with Cicero, with first introducing the practice of *disputatio in utramque partem* (debate on both sides of the issue) in his Academy, a practice that reflects a definite dialectical shift from the Socratic method of arguing from only one side. In the *Topics*, Aristotle identifies strategies and techniques for constructing valid arguments in the course of a dispute; in the *Sophistical Refutations*, he deals with various fallacies connected with such argumentation. Though not in dialogue form, these works of dialectical reasoning still owe much to the "method of hypotheses" articulated in Plato's *Phaedo*.[15] Both works were translated by Boethius in the fifth century, thus assuring them at least a minimal readership during the early Middle Ages, and then again in the twelfth century when the complete corpus of Aristotle's logical works (the *Organon*) began its gradual but influential recovery into mainstream Latin education.

## Ciceronian Dialogue

The figure from antiquity who most impacted medieval language and rhetoric was Marcus Tullius Cicero (106–43 B.C.E.). His works were especially popular and authoritative in the twelfth century. A fluent reader of Greek and prolific writer of dialogues, Cicero was well acquainted with the corpus of Plato and Aristotle, mainly because the Roman educational system of the second century BCE had incorporated and absorbed Hellenistic methods of rhetorical instruction. He wrote seven rhetorical works, including *De inventione* (which was especially influential during the Middle Ages) but not including the anonymous *Rhetorica ad Herennium* (which was universally attributed to him until the Renaissance). In *De Inventione*, Cicero provides his clearest statements on rhetoric, which he defines as "eloquence based on the rules of art" designed to prepare speakers for the three types of orations named by Aristotle: deliberative, judicial, and epideictic (or demonstrative). Cicero also defines what he calls the "five parts of rhetoric": (1) invention (*inventio*), the discovery of valid or seemingly valid arguments that render one's cause plausible; (2) arrangement (*dispositio*), the distribution of arguments in the proper order; (3) style (*elocutio*), the fitting of proper language to the invented matter; (4) memory (*memoria*), the firm mental grasp of matter and words; and (5) delivery (*pronuntiatio*), the control of the voice and the body in a manner suitable to the dignity of the subject matter and style. These divisions directly or indirectly influenced all later writers on rhetoric and dialectic.

Cicero was the ancient orator par excellence, his legacy assured by both his orations and his manuals on the art of speaking. While strictly speaking less focused on matters of philosophy than his Greek predecessors, he was also well acquainted with the dialogue form and, as Malcolm Schofield has argued, in certain respects more original in his use of the genre even than Plato.[16] The fact that he never offered a systematic study or definition of dialogue is curious and may lead to the impression that he had a poor understanding of the genre or cared little for it. But it more likely stems from the fact that the art of social dialogue occupied an imprecise, albeit well-known, role in contemporary literary discourse. For, as he states in *De officiis*, "the power of speech in the attainment of propriety is great, and its function is twofold: the first is oratory; the second conversation . . . There are rules for oratory laid down by rhetoricians; there are none for conversation; and yet I do not know why there should not be."[17] Noting the lack of study given to conversation and the "informal discussions (*disputationibus*)" that provide for its ideal setting, Cicero proceeds to lay down some basic rules. The best models, he tells us, are the Socratics.

Cicero's dialogical works focus on the practice of rhetoric, but they are also varied in their setting and structure. *Brutus* features a critical discussion among friends over the history of oratory, with a special focus on the Attic and Asiatic styles. *De partitione oratoria* is a more simplistic but no less effective dialogue in which Cicero's son is imagined as a pupil asking appropriately leading questions of his expert father. And the lengthy *De oratore*, which Cicero himself states was modeled after the dialogues of Aristotle, develops one of the best-known discussions of style in Latin. In it, the experienced orators Marcus Antonius (the grandfather of the famous Mark Antony) and Lucius Licinius Crassus serve as the mouthpiece of Cicero as they engage in a wide-ranging conversation about all aspects of rhetoric with a number of younger orators. In *De oratore* especially, Cicero explains that the art of oratory has its roots in the ancient Greek, and mainly Aristotelian, give-and-take of philosophical dialectic. For Cicero, the perfection of this skill constitutes the essence of the consummate orator. As Crassus remarks, "If anyone comes forward who can, in the Aristotelian manner, put forward both sides on every subject, and can with knowledge of Aristotle's precepts develop two contrary speeches on every question . . . he is the true, the perfect, and the only orator."[18]

This emphasis on systematic expositions of opposing viewpoints for the attainment of good oratory is echoed in Book II of the *Tusculanae Disputationes*, where he writes to Brutus explaining the dialogical genesis of his philosophical and literary enterprise:

[I have always preferred] the rule of the Peripatetics and the Academy of discussing both sides of every question (*argumentum in utramque partem*), not only for the reason that in no other way did I think it possible for the probable truth to be discovered in each particular problem, but also because I found it gave the best practice in oratory. Aristotle first employed this method and later those who followed him. . . . I was induced by our friends to follow this practice, and in my house at Tusculum I thus employed the time at our disposal. Accordingly, after spending the morning in rhetorical exercises, we went in the afternoon, as on the day before, down to the Academy, and there a discussion took place which I do not present in narrative form, but as nearly as I can in the exact words of our actual discussion.[19]

For a philosophical position to be presented properly, it must be developed logically and systematically, but also with an elegant and full persuasiveness that constitutes what he goes on to call *perfecta philosophia*.[20] In drawing on the Greek commitment to dialectical engagement while refining the purpose and procedure of oratory, the Ciceronian dialogue may be described as hesitating between, or rather incorporating, both rhetoric and philosophy.[21] And therein lies Cicero's main contribution to the genre. For even if the construction of speeches on either side of the case was by Cicero's time well established, there is no evidence that the *literary* form of the philosophical dialogue-treatise pairing speeches *in contrarias partes* was the invention of anyone but Cicero himself.[22]

Cicero's contribution to the history of oratory has long been known, and the influence exerted by his dialogues on ancient and medieval rhetoric has been closely analyzed.[23] But Cicero's model of rhetoric and dialectic was not the only dialogical literary development of its time. Emerging simultaneously with the Ciceronian appropriation and development of the classical Greek dialogue was the question-and-answer dialogue, a genre that is often (and perhaps too quickly) dismissed as being unrelated to the more conversational dialogues of the Platonic type.[24] While Greek and Latin titles supply a variety of names for these question-and-answer dialogues, the earliest name appears to be *altercatio*, a term adopted from Roman legal argumentation. Originally it referred to a part of the argumentation in which a summary of the facts set forth in the course of a trial was made by the plaintiff and the defendant in the form of a rapid give-and-take examination and retort. A term frequently encountered in Greek titles is *aporiai* ("difficulties"), a word originally employed in Homeric exegesis but later adopted by patristic and Byzantine authors. Just as in Homeric exegesis and criticism, problems both real and imaginary were raised and settled by the critics under that designation, so the Christian fathers found difficulties in the interpretation of the Scriptures and sought to solve them.[25] *Dialuseis, dialogos*, and *kephalaia* ("heads") are also popular titles for question-and-answer dialogues in the later Byzantine period. Another term, *quaestiones et responsiones* or simply *quaestiones*, became especially popular in patristic writings as church fathers sought to answer questions and resolve problems raised by the study of the Bible.

The variety in appellations for these question-and-answer dialogues contributes to the difficulty in assigning a precise origin for this particular genre, but they appear to go back to the second century.[26] The genre flourished in the first few centuries of the first millennium when the pagan philosophical and dialectical tradition merged with early Christian doctrine. There are many surviving examples of these secular and religious question-and-answer dialogues. An especially popular one from this period is the late second-century *Altercatio Hadriani Augusti et Epicteti Philosophi*, which features the learned emperor Hadrian interrogating the philosopher Epictetus on a wide variety of topics. Hadrian was known to have sought out philosophers as often as possible. He had a particular interest in understanding the different philosophical schools, as evidenced by his recorded correspondence with his adopted mother Plotina on the succession of the school of the Epicureans. He also met with representatives of the different faiths, as evidenced by the various Hebrew Midrashim detailing his dealings with rabbis. Most important, the *Altercatio* is a question-and-answer dialogue that went on to have many versions (including a shorter *Disputatio Adriani Augusti et Epicteti Philosophi*) in various languages and with many manuscripts. It was subsequently excerpted without the names of the interlocutors into other dialogues, including Alcuin of York's (d. 804) *Disputatio Pippini*, and it is cited or quoted by various Carolingian authors. A late preface to the text provided a source for the thirteenth-century Provençal version of the dialogue *Enfant Sage*, which appears in various forms in forty or fifty manuscript versions in various languages during the late Middle Ages.[27]

Many authors of the Roman Empire nevertheless continued to look to Plato and Cicero for inspiration. The historian Tacitus responded to the vanishing Ciceronian tradition in his *Dialogus de oratoribus* (c. 102). Set in the 70s C.E., the dialogue paid homage to the Ciceronian model while simultaneously lamenting the contemporary decline of rhetorical eloquence, the blame for which he placed squarely on the shoulders of the empire's erosion of political freedom.[28] In his *Sympotic Questions*, the Greek historian Plutarch also looked backward to a more halcyon time by promoting the characteristic form of Greek philosophical identity: he presents debates both about the proper way to conduct a symposium and about the suitable topics for conversation within a symposium, all while deprecating excessive disputatiousness. Lucian of Samosata was a rhetorician by trade who wrote satiric dialogues dealing with ancient mythology and contemporary philosophers. The dialogue, therefore, could serve to preserve and engage with the ideals of a bygone age. In the following centuries, the rise of Christianity, conditioned by the confluence of ancient Jewish traditions and classical Greek traditions, brought about the most significant shift in the culture history of the dialogue.

## The Early Christian Background

The study of the Bible "as literature" is nothing new. Genre studies are not only commonplace but also fashionable, and scholars of religion are right to warn against disassociating the narrative from its deep religious and cultural context. There are, however, several points worth highlighting. Dialogue as a form of "verbalized action" is central in biblical narrative, and it is skillfully employed to enliven the continuous prose. The biblical writers repeatedly use dialogue not merely to define political positions with stylized clarity but also to delineate unfolding relations, nuances of character, and attitude. It has been noted that much of this dialogue is itself a liturgical form rooted in the responsorial patterns of temple worship.[29] After all, the midrashic collections that have come down to us are structured as conversations rather than as systematic expositions.[30] The same hermeneutic tendencies can also be said of the rabbis themselves. As Gerald Bruns writes, "their relationship to the text was always social and dialogical, and even when confined to the house of study (*beit midrash*) it was never merely formalist or analytical. They saw themselves in dialogue with each other and with generations of wise men."[31] Certain passages of the Bible may have been especially influential in offering literary models of dialogue. The book of Job, in particular, is constructed as a series of dialogues between Job and his friends, Eliphaz, Bildad, and Zophar. The first of five poetical books of the Bible, Job was a constant source for medieval ethical ideas and poetical inspiration.[32] The story in Luke 2:41–52 of Jesus disputing with the elders in the temple at the precocious age of twelve is not only a famous and frequently depicted scene in the life of Jesus, it is in fact the *only* biblical passage that provides an account of Jesus' boyhood.

Doubtless it was Christianity's theological roots in ancient Judaism that led to the most serious and enduring of religious confrontations, appropriately termed the Jewish-Christian debate. Early Christianity's struggle for self-assertion amid its debt to ancient Jewish liturgical practices and its appropriation of Jewish Scripture led to a genre of works that has long been subsumed under the ancient title *Adversus Iudaeos*.[33] It would be difficult to overemphasize the importance of this polemical genre to early, and indeed later, Christianity. As Jaroslav Pelikan succinctly put it, "virtually every major Christian writer of the first five centuries either composed a treatise in opposition to Judaism or made this issue a dominant theme in a treatise devoted to some other subject."[34] While many of these anti-Jewish works took the form of a treatise or letter written for a particular occasion, an important set of texts took the literary form of a dialogue, often purporting to be the record of an actual encounter. The most famous of these recorded debates is Justin Martyr's *Dialogue with Trypho* (c. 160).[35] Trypho was an important rabbi whom the historian Eusebius describes as "the best known Jew of that time," a description that he may have borrowed from the introduction to the dialogue, now lost.[36] Scholars generally agree that Justin's work represents the literary form of an actual exchange between himself and the rabbi Trypho in the city of Ephesus, but that it was composed many years after the fact and reflects the author's hindsight on the debate.[37] The dialogue features the two men in amicable conversation about the Jewish people and their place in history, and about Jesus and whether he was the promised Messiah. A principal question is whether the deity of Christ can be reconciled with the uncompromising monotheism of Scripture. Because of the civility of the exchange and the fact that the two men part as friends, historians have commended the work for its "courteousness and fairness."[38] But Justin's *Dialogue* equally represents a growing body of literature that actively sought to discredit the continuing validity of Jewish law and to demonstrate the truth of Christianity, in dramatized dialogical form.

Justin's *Dialogue* may have been occasioned by an actual encounter in the streets of Ephesus, but the delay in recording the conversation leads one to suspect that, in committing the exchange to writing, Justin included a few good lines that he wished he had thought of at the time. Certainly, many of the later works purporting to be the result of an actual encounter were more literary than anything else. "The dialogue with Judaism became a literary conceit," writes Pelikan, "in which the question of the uniqueness of Christianity in comparison with Judaism became an occasion for a literary exposition of Christian doctrine for a non-Jewish audience of Christian readers."[39] Other early Christian dialogues of the *Adversus Iudaeos* genre that likewise assume the literary form of a dialogue include the *Dialogue of Jason and Papiscus*, attributed to Aristo; Origen's *Contra Celsum*; the related dialogues *Athanasius and Zachaeus* and *Timothy and Aquila* (fourth–fifth centuries); Evagrius of Gaul's *Altercatio Simonis et Theophili*; and the *Disputation of Sergius the Stylite Against the Jew*.[40] A full analysis of anti-Jewish dialogues in a scholastic context will be given in Chapter 6.

The popularity of these religious dialogues should not only be seen as part of early Christianity's theological struggle for self-definition but also in light of the public discussions that are alleged to have occurred between Christians and Jews. Public debate was, after all, a common enough occurrence in the Greco-Roman world of Late Antiquity and a constituent element in the preservation of social order.[41] Obviously, not all these public confrontations resulted in a literary dialogue that dramatized the event; only some did. There are also the accounts of alleged disputations between Christians and Jews that served to bolster the faith, much like the miracle stories of saints with which there is considerable overlap. These disputations were not necessarily recorded in dialogue form. At least seven such accounts from the fourth and fifth centuries survive, including two that centered on the figure of Constantine's mother Helen.[42] The earlier of these two ostensibly occurred in Rome in 314/315 and it is preserved in the *Actus Silvestri*.[43] The legend states that, following Constantine's conversion to Christianity, Helen wrote telling him that he ought rather to have become a Jew. This made him uncertain, and he arranged a disputation between representatives of the two faiths to settle the matter. The parties met at the home of Constantine, and the debate began between Bishop Sylvester and twelve rabbis sent by the high priest of the Jews. Constantine served as adjudicator with two pagan philosophers by his side. The principal Jewish spokesman performed a miracle by dashing a bull to the ground by whispering in its ear the Hebrew name of God. Sylvester outperforms the Jew when he restores the bull to life by calling on the name of Jesus. Following this miraculous display of Christian powers, the two philosophers are converted, together with more than three thousand Jews, Helen, her sons, daughters, and chamberlains.

A later account of a public discussion is set in the land of Yemen and recorded in the *Vita* of Bishop Gergentius (c. 480).[44] Abraamius, the Christian king of the Himyarites, is said to command the conversion of his subjects on pain of death. The Jews, hoping to win him to their faith, petition for a public disputation with Bishop Gergentius. The debate takes place in the presence of the king, the court, and the principal men of the kingdom. It lasts for four days. On the fourth and final day, Jesus Christ reveals himself in his glory, and the Jews are converted. These and numerous other accounts of debates between Jews and Christians underline an important point: it is not only the superiority of Christianity over Judaism that early Christian authors wish to demonstrate but also the act of demonstrating this publicly and in the presence of Jews themselves. Thus, even if many of these accounts belong to the more general typology of miracle stories, the phenomenon of a public disputation between Jews and Christians was deemed sufficiently important to merit a privileged place in accounts that are not presented as dialogues as such. This fluidity between literary dialogue and public disputation is a perennial problem in the history of the genre, more notable still in the context of the twelfth and thirteenth centuries, and has been the cause of considerable confusion as to whether one should speak of a literary invention or a social practice. Both, it is argued here, are constitutive of the medieval culture of disputation.

Disputations between Jews and Christians, either real or alleged, are certainly not the only known form of public debates in Late Antiquity. While difficult to define in the abstract, the form of the debate was clearly an important manifestation of Greco-Roman beliefs concerning persuasion and proof more generally. This spirit of competitive strife, or "agon" as it was called, was at its highest during the Platonist philosophical groups of the late third and fourth centuries, precisely the period when orthodox Christianity emerged as a dominant theological (and philosophical) force. Dialectical disputation in the circles of Plotinus, Porphyry, and Iamblichus allowed the agon to intrude into the philosophical life and enabled junior philosophers to claim excellence by competing openly with their elders. The *Vitae philosophorum et sophistarum* of Eunapius of Sardis and other late fourth-century works illustrate the role played by disputation in the social and intellectual stratification of these competing philosophical coteries. Early Christians simply adopted the practice from their pagan neighbors. Especially after Constantine's legalization of Christianity (313), public disputations were used to combat paganism and competing Christian heresies. Naturally, this application of public disputation developed over a period of time and in several stages. A glimpse of this process can be seen in the debates between orthodox Christians and the Manicheans. Early on, Manicheans employed public debates to challenge opposing religious and philosophical views, particularly beliefs about the origins of evil. Disputation quickly became an integral factor in the spread and success of Manichean doctrines. Both Manichean and anti-Manichean texts attest to Mani and his followers debating in Egypt, Gaza, Mesopotamia, and Roman North Africa. As the Manichean movement attempted to spread to the Roman Christian communities, it was the bishops who, through public debate, provided the most effective rebuttals. The most famous example of this was Bishop Augustine of Hippo's successful refutation of Manichean doctrines in public disputations. His open and very public displays of learning against pernicious enemies of the church helped solidify his prominence as the most effective expositor of orthodox doctrine of his time. As Richard Lim has argued, Pseudo-Mark the Deacon's the *Vita Porphyrii* and the anti-Manichean writings of Augustine demonstrate how the rising power of local bishops was consolidated and strengthened via formal debates with Manicheans, debates deliberately staged to forestall the more diffuse and intimate forms of suasion that had brought the Manicheans their

initial success.[45] The debates between "orthodox" Christians and Manicheans, in turn, led to a body of Christian *Adversus Manichaeos* literature which,
like its anti-Jewish counterpart, helped fix normative orthodox and heretical
identities and, consequently, precluded spontaneous disputation between
ordinary orthodox Christians and Manichean dissenters. This body of polemical literature, some of it dialogical, some of it not, lasted for centuries. In
John of Damascus's *Dialogos contra Manichaeos*, one finds what Lim calls
a "template debate" between two interlocutors referred to simply as "the
Orthodox" and "the Manichean."[46] Writing in the first half of the eighth
century, John was also the earliest Christian writer to concern himself at any
length and in a systematic way with Islam.[47] In later centuries when these
other authors and their works were less read, the image of Augustine as the
Christian apologist against heresy furnished scholastics with a ready model of
disputation (see Figure 1).

The Manichean heresy was not the only challenge to orthodoxy that
played out in public debates. Figures such as Aetius the Syrian and Eunomius
the Cappadocian, called Anomoeans by their detractors because they allegedly believed the essences of the Father and Son to be dissimilar, were widely
feared by contemporaries as public debaters precisely because of their rhetorical skill in constructing sophisms and syllogistic chains. In drawing on the
logic of their Platonist forebears, these two men championed the intellectual
and social claims of competitive disputation and, in doing so, profited from
the channels of social mobility recently opened to men of talent within the
context of fourth-century imperial Christianity.[48] Like the Manicheans, their
theological disputes brought to the fore important disagreements over ideals,
social order, and the construction of authority in the Christian community.

The competitive individualistic debate that was once valued by pagan
philosophers and early Christian polemicists became, over the course of the
fourth and fifth centuries, increasingly supplanted by individual and commu-
nal authority within the church. As the social world of Byzantine Christianity
became increasingly stable in its theological positions, the silent but powerful
holy man gradually replaced the dialectician, and disputation was limited in
favor of consensus and hierarchy.[49] Disputation was officially ruled out at the
Council of Aquileia in 381. Ambrose of Milan is reported by his Arian adversaries as having delivered a short tirade on the bane of dialectical sophistry in
which he roundly denounced his rivals' facility with disputation.[50] Disputation was further marginalized at the later councils of Ephesus in 431 and
Chalcedon in 451. From then on, "the sway of the *logos* [verbal debate] in

Figure 1. A disputation between Saint Augustine and Faustus the Manichean. School of
Mont St. Michel, Normandy. Early thirteenth century. Bibliothèque Municipale,
Avranches, MS 90, fol. 1. Erich Lessing / Art Resource NY.

formal councils was eclipsed by consensual procedures that centered on written evidence read aloud by *notarii* and episcopal *sententiae* reacting to those
documents."[51] It would be a gross and unfair exaggeration to imagine that
public debate ceased to function within the church after these councils. There
is certainly evidence for interfaith debates at court. The seventh-century *Vitae
patrum Emeritensium*, for instance, contains a story of a debate between a
Catholic bishop and an Arian bishop in the presence of judges appointed by
the Visigothic king, and it is the public rhetorical skills of the Catholic bishop
that are emphasized.[52] Nevertheless, as authority began to be gathered, cen-
tralized, and transformed into a distinct hierarchy, the role of public disputation decreased markedly from the social standing it once had. What did
continue and evolve in new directions was the literary form of the dialogue.
Here again, Augustine would prove to be its most original contributor.

## Augustine and Boethius: Two Models of Dialogue

The cultural transition that historians now call Late Antiquity was instrumental in braiding disputation, dialogue, and Christian devotion into a single
strand. Augustine's career is as central to this evolution as it is to the evolution of Christian theology more generally. In addition to his public debates
with Manicheans, the bishop of Hippo also wrote three dialogues while at
his residence at Cassiciacum: *Contra Academicos*, *De beata vita*, and *De ordine*.
Along with his *Soliloquia,* these dialogues are his earliest extant writings,
and as such have received sustained interest among scholars interested in the
evolution of his thinking.[53] One of the many points of contention concerning
these dialogues is their historicity: that is, the degree to which they reflect
actual conversations. Augustine himself states that they do, but that is no
guarantee since, as we have seen, it is a literary ploy that pervades the genre.
As a result, two competing camps of interpretation have arisen: one maintains
that the dialogues are merely touched-up renditions of philosophical discussions held at Cassiciacum, while the other asserts that they are literary fictions
that derive mainly from Augustine's fertile imagination.[54] Given the extensive
classical traditions of both dialogue and public disputation and given Augustine's early Neoplatonism, perhaps it is safe to state that it was something of
each. A more interesting question is what precisely Augustine intended to
convey in these dialogues. For one, they are controversial in their subject
matter. In presenting his earliest ideas in dialogue form, Augustine could

reproduce not only the discussions he alleged took place but, more important, the inner tensions of his nascent philosophy. As Henry Chadwick explains, "the literary convention of the dialogue form enabled [Augustine] to state difficulties with which he himself was still wrestling, and which he could discuss with a thoughtful elite."[55]

Augustine's use of dialogue, like his disputations with the Manicheans, stems directly from his concern for dialectic, including what it consists of and how it should be applied. Yet Augustine did not articulate a unified vision of what the subject entailed. So, while he does state in *Contra Academicos* (3.13.29) that he knows more about dialectic than any other part of philosophy, his overall conception carries different nuances in different works. In *Contra Academicos*, dialectic is defined, in passing, as the knowledge of the truth (*scientia veritatis*); in the anti-Donatist work *Contra Cresconium*, dialectic is referred to as the skill of disputing (*peritia disputandi*); and in *De ordine*, dialectic is placed between grammar and rhetoric in the sequence of the *ordo disciplinarum*. In his early work *Soliloquia*, in which the author is featured in conversation with a teacher named Ratio ("reason"), Augustine never uses the word "dialectic," but his Socratic inheritance is clear when he writes that there is no better way of searching for truth than by questioning and answering.[56] The pedagogic and dramatic issues that arise in the *Soliloquia* are given even fuller expression in Augustine's later dialogue *De magistro*, a text that likewise involves clarifying the techniques of disputation, articulating the personae of master and student, and taking language itself, written and spoken, as a principal theme. Augustine's use of dialogue and dialectic, in turn, led to another original development, one that would affect the literary and devotional practices for the duration of the Middle Ages: meditative reading and self-knowledge.[57]

The first explicit mention of a new meditative approach to truth is supplied in the *Soliloquia*, where Ratio praises the method of question and answer (*interrogando et respondendo*) but notes that only in silence can such a method be carried out. Indeed, this method explains the title of the work: "Think of the very reason we have chosen this type of conversation. I want them to be called 'Soliloquies' because we are talking with ourselves alone. The title is new and perhaps it is rather harsh, but suitable enough, I think, for the situation it wishes to highlight."[58] The importance of this self-conscious exploration cannot be overstated. For in directing inwardly his exercise of dialectic, Augustine consciously "invented a genre whose achievement was to internalize the process of dialogue by writing fictions of the mind in conversation with itself."[59] The culmination of this internal dialogue in search of Christian truth and self-knowledge would of course be the *Confessiones*, a work of monumental importance to medieval and modern sensibilities of self-reflection.[60] This is not to deny the oral activity of reading. As Paul Saenger has shown, our notion of silent reading owes its origins to the scribal techniques that developed later in the Middle Ages.[61] But it does reinforce the transition from public to private realms of speculative dialogue.

One of the first to employ Augustine's meditative theory of reading while preserving the literary form of the dialogue was the Roman statesman, scholar, and philosopher Anicius Manlius Boethius (c. 480–524). Boethius's life and writings have long been regarded as symbolizing the transition from Late Antique world to the Middle Ages. The paradigm is no less valid in the context of his engagement with dialogue. Boethius famously made it his lifetime project to "translate and comment upon all of Plato's dialogues and put them into Latin form," a project he also famously did not live to complete.[62] What he did accomplish, while awaiting his execution under house arrest, was the *Consolatio philosophiae*, a timeless classic that is at once profoundly original and at the same time heavily indebted to Cicero and Augustine and other philosophies such as Stoicism and Neoplatonism.[63] The plot of the *Consolatio* is well known: in a vision, Lady Philosophy approaches Boethius, and the two discuss how to come to terms with evil, freedom, and providence. Visionary experience and philosophical dialogue combine to provide Boethius and his readers a rationally satisfying explanation for the tribulations he and other virtuous citizens must endure.[64] The *Consolatio* is often and justifiably heralded as the supreme masterpiece of Boethius's imaginative intellect, but it should also be noted that his earliest known work, a commentary on Porphyry's *Isagoge*, was also a dialogue. Though this student-teacher colloquy lacks the literary grace and philosophical depth of his later (indeed final) work, it remains, according to Seth Lerer, "deeply significant that Boethius opens and closes his intellectual career with dialogues."[65] Indeed, in his commentary on Porphyry's *Isagoge*, and to an extent in the prefaces to his theological tracts that preserve the dialogue format, one can chart how Boethius transitions from the more ancient practice of recording open conversations or debates to the Augustinian practice of internalized conversations. "Like Augustine," Lerer observes, "Boethius focuses on the necessary silence in which such mental disputations must transpire. In addition, he self-consciously reflects on the problems of transcribing these imaginary colloquies, and the prefaces [to the theological tracts] look back over the tradition of the literary dialogue, while at the same time foretelling the problems of

reading and writing which the prisoner confronts at the *Consolatio*'s opening."[66] In some sense, Boethius can be seen as drawing his meditative inspiration from Augustine, his literary influence from Cicero and Plato (as well as
Augustine), and his philosophical insights from within. Boethius was the last
figure of that transitional time between antiquity and the Middle Ages for
whom knowledge of the classical Greek heritage merged with a unique literary form to produce a work aimed at instructing the doubtful in matters of
great importance.[67]

Like Boethius, Gregory the Great (590–604) was born into the highest
echelons of Roman society, was given a classical education, and played a
pivotal role in the transition from Late Antiquity to the medieval world.
Though his familiarity with Greek was certainly less than that of Boethius,
he rose to the highest position in Christian society not because of the knowledge he possessed but because of what he envisioned as essential training
for the fledgling flock of Roman Christians. His *Dialogi* were composed
in the early years of his pontificate and were intended to educate Christians
in the important figures of the faith.[68] In keeping with the late antique form
of the dialogue, the work consists of a lengthy conversation between Gregory
and his companion Peter the Deacon. In this regard its didactic element
differs little from the question-and-answer dialogue of the classical tradition.
But Gregory also draws on the contemplative mood inaugurated by Augustine and continued by Boethius. He opens thus: "In my grief I retired to a
quiet spot congenial to my mood. . . . I sat there for a long time in silence
and was deeply dejected when my dear son, the deacon Peter, came in."[69]
Although less widely circulated than his frequently copied *Moralia in Job*, the
*Dialogi* quickly became a staple of a good Christian education. Because of
the prominent place assigned to Benedict of Nursia in the *Dialogi*, Christians
with little direct access to earlier works could appreciate through Gregory's
writings the life and ideals of Saint Benedict. Gregory's great achievement,
then, in the *Dialogi* as well as in his other works, was to simplify and present
for a popular audience much of Augustine's thought and to integrate something of the spirituality of the Eastern tradition with that of the West in a
way that balanced the active and the contemplative in the Christian life.

## Dialogue and Disputation in the Carolingian World

The world of the Carolingian renaissance brought a revival of classical learning; the literary and pedagogical use of dialogue is symptomatic of this intellectual rebirth.[70] Charlemagne (r. 768–814) made it his program to stimulate

learning and literacy at his court and throughout the Frankish kingdom.[71] There was none more important to this program than the Northumbrian scholar Alcuin whom Charlemagne, in 781, invited to take up residence at the royal palace under the title "Master of the Palace School."[72] At the imperial capital of Aachen, Alcuin trained a generation of scholars, many of whom rose to important ecclesiastical and governmental positions, and, from there, he exerted influence to the cause of learning. Alcuin's supreme merit as a figurehead of the ninth-century renaissance in learning was as a reformer and educator, and it is to these causes that he devoted much of his writings. His pedagogical works include *Ars grammatica, De orthographia, De rhetorica et virtute, De dialectica, Disputatio Pippini,* and an astronomical treatise titled *De cursu et saltu lunae ac bissexto.* Four of these works take the form of a dialogue (the treatises on orthography and astronomy are the exceptions). Revealing something of the classroom setting, the *Ars grammatica* features Alcuin in conversation with his students, while the *Disputatio Pippini* (which draws heavily from the second-century *Disputatio* between Hadrian and Epictetus discussed above) is presented as a conversation between Alcuin and Charlemagne's son. The works on rhetoric and dialectic, perhaps because they treat more advanced subjects, are set as dialogues between Alcuin and the emperor Charlemagne himself. For the most part, these dialogues are compilations of ideas drawn together from the work of earlier scholars. *De dialectica,* for instance, is based on works by Cassiodorus, Boethius, Cicero, Marius Victorinus, Julius Victor, Quintilian, and Pseudo-Augustine. In the dialogue, Alcuin arrives at a basic but essential distinction: he distinguishes rhetoric as the art of disputation on practical matters and dialectic as the art of disputation on theoretical matters, namely, theology.[73] The distinction was not entirely new, but, in composing dialogues about, among other things, the very art of disputation, Alcuin was successful in reinstating the ancient practice of debate as central to the learning of his times.

Very few other dialogues are known from the ninth century. An anonymous *Interrogationes et responsiones* on the book of Genesis and Paschasius Radbertus's life of Abbot Wala of Corbie *Epitaphium Arsenii,* each stem from the circle of scholars associated with Alcuin.[74] The anonymous *Scolica enchiriadis* is a three-part treatise on music that reflects at once the influence of Boethius and Cassiadorus, the Carolingian interest in grammar, and the concern for the training and education of singers engaged in daily worship.[75] Its literary form, and some of the ideas in the treatise, is believed to come from either Augustine's *De musica* or Fortunatianus's *Rhetorica,* both dialogues in circulation during the ninth century.[76]

The revival of dialectic in the Carolingian age should not be underestimated, even if its continuity into the eleventh and twelfth centuries is hard
to establish. The most important monument to Carolingian learning is also
a dialogue: the *Periphyseon* by John Scotus Eriugena, completed around 867.
It consists of a lengthy dialogue in five books between an anonymous Teacher
(*nutritor*) and his Student (*alumnus*). It is a compendium of all knowledge
presented within a Neoplatonic cosmology of the procession and return of
all things from the divine One.[77] In the course of his work, Scotus goes
significantly beyond anything taught in Alcuin's circle, drawing on both
Latin and Greek works of Late Antiquity to produce what is effectively the
first practical attempt in the medieval West to unite philosophy and theology
in a single oeuvre. An Irishman by birth, John Scotus was employed for a
time at the court of Charles the Bald, hence marking him as a scholar of the
Carolingian court, but he is also known to have been associated with ecclesiastical centers such as Reims, Laon, Soissons, and Compigne. He is widely
regarded as the most outstanding thinker in the Latin West in the centuries
between Boethius and Anselm. The structure of the dialogue strongly resembles the student-teacher framework found in Alcuin's dialogues and many
other dialogues of this period, but it is not the genre's originality or lack
thereof that should catch our attention. The prevalence of dialogue among
the chief thinkers of the Carolingian age reminds us that literary form and
pedagogy are always closely related and that with the revival of active learning
comes an inherent move toward a more interactive verbal exchange. This
seems to be especially reflected in the pedagogical dialogues of Alcuin and
John Scotus, which each echo the oral practices of classroom instruction.

Not directly connected with the Carolingian renaissance but from the
same period are the Old English colloquies of the ninth and tenth centuries.
The most famous of these are the poetical dialogues of *Solomon and Saturn*,
once believed to be two versions of the same poem but now recognized as
distinct works.[78] Dating from the ninth or tenth centuries, these poems
descend from the eastern legends of King Solomon, and each feature the
Hebrew king debating with an interlocutor. Despite the common tradition,
the subject matter of these two dialogues differs considerably, both from each
other and from their ancient source. In the first Solomon-Saturn dialogue,
Saturn seeks to be persuaded of the virtue of the Pater Noster and receives
the requested information from Solomon, whose erudite reply on matters
of faith constitutes nearly three-fourths of the poem.[79] The second of the
Solomon-Saturn dialogues is the more superior in terms of its literary power.
It features a debate between Solomon and Saturn, and, more akin to the

recorded debates of antiquity, the author of this dialogue reports in the introduction that the words are the record of a high debate heard in person.
Saturn is here not merely the recipient of instruction but an expositor of
difficult riddles, all of which Solomon answers to his satisfaction.[80] In both
dialogues, Solomon represents the Judeo-Christian tradition triumphant over
the pagan wisdom of Saturn. The importance of the Solomon and Saturn
dialogues for later times resides principally in its connection to the very popular, more irreverent Latin dialogue *Solomon et Marcolfus*, in which the figure
of Saturn is replaced with a character named Marcolf who replies in merry
and often scatological fashion to the serious proverbs of Solomon.[81] Of this
latter variant of the *Solomon and Saturn* poem, many Latin and vernacular
versions are found in the twelfth, thirteenth, and fourteenth centuries.

The renaissance of learning associated with the Carolingian court is often
said to have come to an end soon after the empire broke up in the late
ninth century. There is, however, evidence for the continued cultivation of
pedagogical dialogue within certain circles. One finds an anonymous
eleventh-century musical handbook (*Enchiridion musices*) in the form of a
student-teacher dialogue, Berno of Reichenau's short *Dialogus* between a
monk and himself concerning the Christian calendar, and various Latin colloquies on grammar from tenth-century Britain that follow the standard
teacher-student form ideally suited to the classroom setting.[82] The study of
dialectic is more nebulous, but the logic schools of Abbo of Fleury and
Notker Labeo of St. Gall show that it was studied.[83] As is so often the case,
controversy provides a stimulus for cultivating debate and putting the tools
of argumentation into action. The so-called Cadaver Synod of 897 offers a
good illustration of this. In what is truly one of the most bizarre episodes of
papal history, Pope Stephen VI exhumed the body of his deceased predecessor Formosus (r. 891–96), dressed him in the papal vestments, and placed
him on trial for a variety of charges, the most important being the validity of
his pontificate. The synod declared the decrees of Formosus invalid and
required those who had been ordained by him to submit to reordination or
cease the exercise of their offices on pain of excommunication. We would
know little of this episode were it not for some controversialists who saw fit
to argue in defense of the accused. One such author was Auxilius Presbyter—
his very name a pseudonym meaning "helper" or "defender." He had been
ordained by Pope Fomosus himself but wrote in response to the reenactment
of the synod's decrees by Pope Sergius III in 911. One strategy of his polemic
was to compose works in which he reimagined the proceedings of the synodal

debate. The very headings of his works—*Tractatus qui infensor et defensor dicitur* and *Liber cuiusdem requirentis et respondentis*—reveal the importance of literary debate, and each of these works reads like trial records presenting arguments for and against the main protagonist.[84] Eugenius Vulgaris was a friend of Auxilius and a fellow defender of the late Pope Formosus. He also challenged the election of Pope Sergius in a dialogue dedicated to Peter the Deacon, arguing that only a deserving man can ever truly be pope.[85] His rhetoric may have been useful to the Ottonian emperors, for a copy of this treatise survives in the Bamberg State Library.[86] On the whole, these works are hardly literary achievements, but the continued use of public debate within the early medieval church suggests that some element of rhetorical and disputative argumentation never disappeared from the structure of ecclesiastical institutions. Early medieval ecclesiastical debates should therefore not be underestimated, even if our understanding of the nature of these debates remains highly dependent on the imaginative polemicists who recorded them. A few other dialogues on contentious topics might additionally be signaled. Ratherius of Verona (d. 974) advocated the controversial Eucharistic teachings of Paschasius Radbertus in an imaginary confessional dialogue.[87] An anonymous *Altercatio* between Church and Synagogue written sometime in the middle of the tenth century revisited the familiar issues of the Christian-Jewish debate, but drawing heavily from Augustine.[88] In all these instances, the dialogue in question was written in response to (or more properly in support of) a contested issue. Nor were these minor incidents or isolated examples. Pope Sergius had Eugenius incarcerated at Monte Cassino in response to the circulation of his polemical writings.[89] In Ratherius's case, the dialogue he composed provoked substantial opposition, and he had to defend himself in a letter in which he upheld the doctrine of transubstantiation, though without materially advancing the development of the dogma. The anti-Jewish *Altercatio* was copied many times over in later centuries. Pedagogy, polemic, and doctrine—these themes were topics that would be taken up anew by monastic scholars who had access to greater libraries and expanding classrooms.

## Dialogue and Disputation in the Eleventh Century

The first indications of a new trajectory in dialogue and disputation begin to gather force in the middle of the eleventh century. Especially relevant is Peter

Damian (1007–72), a figure who more than anyone from his time anticipates the "academic" circles in which dialogue and disputation will thrive. Peter was born in Ravenna and educated at the monastic school at Faenza and then at the cathedral school at Parma.[90] On completing his studies in the liberal arts, he became a secular master and, according to his biographer John of Lodi, earned both wealth and a reputation among his students from his teaching.[91] In about 1035, he decided to become a monk. Abandoning the life of professional teaching, he entered the monastery of Fonte Avellana located at the foot of Mt. Catria in the Apennines. There his teaching abilities were recognized, and he was transferred by the Order to Pomposa, where the monks apparently stood in need of a good schoolmaster. It is there that Damian wrote his first work, an anti-Jewish dialogue titled *Antilogus contra Judaeos*. The work, along with a letter, is addressed to a nobleman Honestus who had written to Peter requesting arguments that could be used against the Jews. Peter responds with a discussion, based on Scripture, of the Trinity of persons in one divine substance; of the divinity and humanity of Christ, the Messiah, who has already come into this world; and finally, of many other topics Jews customarily raise against Christians: "My dear friend," Peter begins, "by our brother Leo you recently sent word to me, begging that I should write something for you to use in silencing, with reasoned arguments (*rationalibus argumentis*), the Jews who debate with you; and that when entering a controversy concerning Christ, you could win your case with the clearest testimony from Scripture."[92] The stress that Peter places on "reasoned arguments" and "debate" provides tantalizing hints of the nature of the discussions that Jews and Christians could be expected to have had in the eleventh century. Records of epistolary exchanges from this period are known, but were Jews and Christians truly disputing in public?[93] Or is Peter simply livening up the dialogue by suggesting an air of veracity? It is a familiar problem, and any answer will necessarily be highly conjectural. We shall return to this problem in later chapters. What can be noted, however, is that Peter's phrasing also signals an important shift in focus within the genre of *Adversus Iudaeos* literature. The particular reliance on reason (*ratio*) as an instrument of persuasion moves beyond the mere repetition of arguments that had characterized the anti-Jewish dialogues and treatises of the early Middle Ages, and it looks forward to a next generation of writers who, beginning with Anselm and his circle, will make the most of rational argumentation as a weapon of verbal discussions.[94]

Peter Damian's *Antilogus* (the title is recent) follows his discussion of Scripture. In contrast with earlier dialogues that simply launch into questions and responses, Peter offers a brief preamble articulating the purpose of the work:

> But now let us have a brief discourse in dialogue form (*dialogo brevis inter nos*), using questions and answers, on certain ceremonies about which you often inquire in great detail, and in your wordy circumlocutions bring suit in these matters; so that when all shall be to your satisfaction, you will be compelled either to agree that you have lost, or to depart in confusion because of your shameful disbelief.[95]

Peter's attempt to provide reasoned arguments for a debate with Jews is prefaced by an explicit indication that the dialogue form will best illustrate the path to victory in that encounter. This too will become central to the Anselmian approach. The question of which exerted a greater influence on Peter's approach, his cathedral school training or earlier models of Jewish-Christian dialogue, is difficult to determine. At Pomposa, Peter had access to a library containing the works of many of the fathers and doctors of the church, including Jerome, Augustine, Ambrose, Gregory Nazianzen, John Chrysostom, Cassiodorus, Bede, Isidore of Seville, Paschasius Radbertus, Lanfranc, and others.[96] Since Peter's arguments over the Incarnation, the Trinity, circumcision, and other issues of Jewish-Christian differences are hardly new, the dialogue might be (and has been) easily dismissed as simply reissuing earlier arguments in a new context. Yet his prologue and other elements of his literary output suggest that Peter instead be seen as indicative of a new generation of dialecticians.

Peter Damian maintained an extensive correspondence with some of the most eminent figures of his day, including popes, bishops, abbots, and noblemen, and he was on several occasions charged with missions to settle local disputes. His most famous work, *De divina omnipotentia*, has been described as a critical departure point for medieval and postmedieval discussions of divine omnipotence.[97] Some twenty years and eighty-eight letters after his epistolary response to Honestus, Peter undertook to resolve another debate through fictitious dialogue. From 1061 to 1064, there were two claimants to the Holy See. After the death of Pope Nicholas II in July 1061, the cardinals met under the direction of Hildebrand (the future Gregory VII) and on

September 30 they elected Alexander II, a leader of the reform party. Less than a month after Alexander's election, an assembly of German and Lombard bishops and notables opposed to the reform movement convened and elected the bishop of Parma, Cadalus, who assumed the name of Honorius II. Peter Damian wrote two letters to this antipope condemning him for his actions. The second of these, Letter 89 in Kurt Reindel's critical edition of the letters, was written after Honorius and his supporters brazenly engaged in battle with papal forces.[98] Responding to these actions, Peter attacks the antipope with every weapon in his rhetorical arsenal, and this includes his *Disceptatio synodalis*, a dialogue purporting to be a synodal procès-verbal between the imperial counsel (*Regius advocatus*), representing Honorius, and the defense attorney for the Roman church (*Defensor Romanae aecclesiae*), representing Alexander.[99] Given current events, it was evidently written to influence the forthcoming synod to be held in Augsburg in October 1062, where the schism between the pope and antipope would hopefully be resolved. The fictitious hearing in the form of a dialogue allowed Damian to explore in depth the significance of the Papal Election Decree of 1059 and to explain his own position on the relationship between church and state in this period. In a somewhat surprising reversal of tone, Peter has the adjudicator conclude with a plea for harmony, "so that the human race, which under both aspects of its nature is ruled by these two powers, should never again, God forbid, be torn apart, as was recently achieved by Cadalus."[100] The work drew no response from Honorius. When the synod of Augsburg finally did meet, a long argument by Peter Damian was read aloud and is believed to have influenced the eventual decision in favor of Alexander II. Honorius was excommunicated, but, despite a further condemnation at a synod in 1064, he remained defiant until his death in 1072.

Peter Damian used his early training and talents as a rhetorician to address many pressing issues of his day. Perhaps no two issues of the mid-eleventh century were as important to theologians as church reform and the Jewish-Christian debate, and it is on precisely these issues that Peter composed his dialogues. Peter may have been skeptical of the new interest in dialectic, but he was clearly a skilled debater, and he also understood the power of persuasion via literary form.[101] Peter Damian represents continuity with the past in the controversial circumstances occasioning dialogues but novelty in his transition from a teaching career to a powerful church theologian. Many authors and pedagogues would follow Peter's lead and combine an academic background in the *trivium* with an emerging art of disputation.

The rise of disputation over the next several generations played a central role in producing one of medieval Europe's greatest contribution to Western intellectual history: scholasticism and the universities.

## Toward Anselm

The medieval dialogue is a direct outgrowth of its classical form. From Platonic philosophy, Aristotelian logic, and Ciceronian rhetoric, Christian authors inherited key models of literary dialogue and argumentation. The works of these ancient authors, in combination with biblical examples of dialogue and a classical tradition of public disputation, were absorbed into early medieval culture via the works of Augustine and Boethius. Augustine, in particular, played a decisive role because he excelled in public disputation while simultaneously introducing a more meditative and contemplative model of inner spiritual dialogue. As the social position of public disputation declined in the fifth and sixth centuries, Augustine's monastic model of inner dialogue continued. Of course, other ancient models of dialogue and disputation never disappeared entirely, as the Carolingian revival of dialectic illustrates. A wide variety of topics were reflected in late antique and Carolingian dialogues, ranging from lengthy works of philosophy and theology to brief classroom question-and-answer colloquies on the rudiments of Latin grammar. The ability of the dialogue to function as pedagogy and as polemic was an essential reason for its enduring success from ancient to medieval times.

An especially recurrent topic is the Jewish-Christian debate. The centrality of this debate to Christian theology and self-identity makes it one of the largest subgenres of medieval dialogue writing. To be sure, there are a great many treatises of the *Adversus Iudaeos* genre that are not dialogues, and a full examination of Christian attitudes toward Jews at any moment in time must necessarily consider the full range of these other works. Yet the popularity of the dialogue form needs to be accounted for, and it is only when viewed alongside other ancient classical traditions of dialogue and disputation that its literary, rhetorical, and cultural dimensions can be appreciated. The Jewish-Christian debate well illustrates that the literary form of the dialogue and the social act of disputation cannot, and should not, be separated entirely. This very overlap, or borderland, between literary form and social practice provides a useful segue to exploring to the world of monastic pedagogy in the age of Anselm of Bec.

# CHAPTER 2

# Anselm, Dialogue, and the Rise
# of Scholastic Disputation

The Italian-born Lanfranc of Pavia (c. 1005–89) and his more illustrious pupil and compatriot Anselm of Bec (c. 1033–1109) have long been considered pivotal figures in the theological and especially philosophical developments of the late eleventh century. Long ago dubbed the "father of scholasticism"[1] on account of his attempts to harmonize reason and faith, Anselm has occasioned increasing scrutiny in recent years as scholars have begun to target the cultural and pedagogical (as opposed to strictly philosophical) role of Anselm and his milieu in the early stages of the twelfth-century renaissance.[2] In a particularly stimulating interdisciplinary exploration of the cognitive relation between builders and their craft and masters and theirs, Charles M. Radding and William W. Clark have advanced an intriguing model suggesting that theologians and Romanesque builders of the eleventh and twelfth centuries were part of a larger transformative development in which thinkers and artisans developed new methods for solving new problems; these new methods, in turn, transformed practitioners of a craft into members of new and distinct disciplines.[3] The verdict is still out on the precise nature of those important developments, but especially vexing is the question of the abbey of Bec's importance and influence under Lanfranc and Anselm during these changing times. As a leading scholar of Anselm has recently put it, "The character of the school of Bec emerges as a riddle to be solved. What was its focus, what did its teachers teach, and how long did it last?"[4] Recent studies have modified Richard Southern's portrayal of the curriculum of Anselm's school at Bec as largely devoted to monastic ideals and demonstrated that history and law were also studied, that a good number of students went on to become able administrators, and that Anselm may even have unwittingly contributed to the rise of courtly love.[5]Much of the fog surrounding the authorial publication and dissemination of Anselm's writings has now been cleared by Richard Sharpe's meticulous analysis in "Anselm as Author," revealing a careful and more deliberate editorial planning on Anselm's part than previously recognized.[6] However, even amid the gathering attention directed toward these figures and their cultural context, it is the most basic and obvious feature of Lanfranc's and Anselm's written record that has been the most undeservedly neglected: their use of dialogue and its correlation to the early development of scholastic disputation. To be sure, the revival of dialectic in the eleventh century and especially in the twelfth has long been known and rather well charted, particularly with regard to the growth of theology as an academic discipline.[7] What follows is a somewhat more focused line of inquiry. Looking beyond the well-trodden ground of Anselm's philosophy and theology and instead examining his pedagogical innovations, this chapter explores Anselm's contribution to the development of literary dialogue and to the origins of the scholastic *disputatio*.[8] Anselm's influence as a prolific author of dialogues can especially be observed in a younger generation of writers and thinkers who studied with him or directly sought to imitate his style and whose oeuvres need also to be considered. By examining the circle of Lanfranc and Anselm, the methods embodied by their teachings, and the writings they produced, this chapter aims to show that the scholastic dialectical methods, later so prominent in medieval universities, have their origins within the general milieu of monastic learning. More specifically, these methods will be shown to have their origins in Lanfranc's and Anselm's engagement with dialogue and disputation at the school of Bec.

## Lanfranc of Pavia

Lanfranc's biography, what little we know of it, echoes with the timeless qualities of an intellectual success story. He was born in a town in northern Italy, lost his parents at an early age, and in his youth traveled north in search of greater educational and professional opportunities.[9] There is some evidence that Lanfranc was already a successful disputant in the law courts in his native region of Lombardy, though it is difficult to know precisely what that entailed.[10] The Ottonian influence on the region also assured him of an education in the liberal arts before he left for France in the early 1030s, one perhaps inclusive of what Stephen Jaeger has described as the "charismatic pedagogy" of the cathedral schools.[11] His eventual arrival in Normandy is not altogether surprising, given that Pavia itself lay on the pilgrimage route to Rome and, when still in Italy, he would have seen pilgrims traveling both to and from Normandy and England.[12] One tradition tells of his having heard Berengar of Tours incognito, but left already convinced of the unsoundness of his teaching.[13] Apocryphal or not, the story foretells the later disputes that would elevate Lanfranc's teachings to the high stage of papal and international politics.

Lanfranc settled at the newly founded monastery of Bec in Normandy, where he proved himself a competent and devoted member of the community. He was speedily appointed prior (c. 1045), giving him oversight of both the internal and the external affairs of Bec. On account of his rising reputation as a teacher and the need to raise money for the development of the abbey, Lanfranc began to admit outside students who were not destined to remain in the monastic milieu.[14] An early student at the monastic school of Bec was Gilbert Crispin, a future abbot of Westminster, who described the "clerks, sons of dukes, and the most celebrated masters of the schools of Latin learning" who came flocking to Lanfranc, attracted by the reputation of the place.[15] At a tense moment during the investiture conflict in 1059, even Pope Nicholas II sent for Lanfranc's help, praising Lanfranc for his skills and reputation as a master of rhetoric and dialectic.[16] And that indefatigable observer and chronicler of ecclesiastical history Orderic Vitalis lavished praise on Lanfranc's abilities, saying that "by intellect and learning Lanfranc would have won the applause of Herodian in grammar, Aristotle in dialectic, Cicero in rhetoric, Augustine, Jerome, and the other commentators on the Old and New Testaments in scriptural studies."[17] Both during his lifetime and afterward, Lanfranc was a teacher whose verbal skills were highly regarded and widely prized.

Lanfranc's success also earned him his detractors. During his years as prior of Bec, he became involved in a feud with Berengar of Tours over the exact nature of the Eucharist.[18] Berengar initiated the dispute by suggesting that the miracle of the sacrament represented a spiritual and not material transformation. The sources for his unorthodox views were two similarly titled works written by two monks at the famed Carolingian monastery of Corbie in the ninth century.[19] Berengar adopted the view of the later author, Ratramnus (whose views Berengar believed came from John Scotus), that saw the Eucharistic elements as sacred signs that betokened an inner reality communicated to the recipient's soul, not the historical body of Christ. As early as 1049, the content of Berengar's teaching was provoking suspicion. In a letter to the king of France, Theoduin of Liège expressed concern that Berengar was saying that the historical body and blood of Christ were not present in the Eucharist and, further, that he was questioning the very efficaciousness of the sacraments.[20] That same year, Berengar wrote to Lanfranc challenging his orthodoxy, ostensibly because Lanfranc had condemned the Eucharistic view of John Scotus. Berengar did not just question Lanfranc's position; he challenged him to a public debate, "if an opportunity should arise for us," so that he might hear for himself what Lanfranc believed. Berengar heightened the wager by allowing Lanfranc the pleasure of assembling "whomever you may wish as competent judges or as hearers."[21] Pope Leo IX, who was then in the midst of a campaign aimed at reforming the church, made the issue public when he summoned the two opponents to a council in 1050. There Lanfranc ably defended himself, and by doing so augmented his prestige, while the pronouncements of the absent Berengar were condemned. At Tours, however, Berengar continued to teach and publicize his views. Further councils at Vercelli, Brionne, and Rome were convened in an effort to stamp out Berengar's heresy.[22] At these occasions, Lanfranc was able to use his dialectical skills and elevate to a new level the emerging art of disputation. "In the most learned disputations (*profundissimis disputationibus*)," Orderic Vitalis later wrote, Lanfranc "publicly worsted Berengar at Rome and Tours, forcing him to pronounce anathema on all heresy and to profess the true faith in writing."[23] The intricacies and details of this much-discussed theological debate do not concern us here, but, broadly speaking, Lanfranc employed dialectic to a greater extent than Berengar, who relied more strictly on the tools of grammar.[24] Lanfranc also argued his position by making use of the account of the physical universe elaborated in Aristotle's *Categories*, which had become known in the Latin West in the schools of northern France in the tenth century.[25] Significantly, one of Lanfranc's most influential works resulted from this prolonged dispute: an epistolary dialogue titled *De corpore et sanguine Domini*.[26] Addressed to Berengar, whom Lanfranc decries as "an enemy of the Catholic Church," the work was written sometime in the early 1060s, after Lanfranc left Bec for Caen.[27]

The exact reasons for the work's composition remain vague. Lanfranc seems to have written it on his own initiative to controvert Berengar's teaching and as a rejoinder to Berengar's derogation of apostolic authority.[28] A statement in the opening chapter suggests that, before writing, Lanfranc had wished to engage "in a more secretive debate (*clandestinis disputationibus*)" with Berengar, as had taken place in Brionne, but that Berengar refused.[29] There is no evidence from Berengar's side to corroborate this assertion. Surely, Berengar's defeat and humiliation by the multiple councils that condemned him meant that no further debate was necessary. Yet the controversy originally erupted, we recall, when, in a letter, Berengar challenged Lanfranc to a public debate. Perhaps Lanfranc, in leaving a written record of his victory over Berengar, decided to return the favor. The prefatory statement would, therefore, be rhetorical, like the fictitious, but plausible, dialogue between Lanfranc and Berengar that follows. What seems clear is that the literary framework of the anti-Berengarian polemic was a direct result of the prolonged dispute and would-be disputations between the two adversaries. In that regard, it bears a curious resemblance to the *Disceptatio sinodalis* of Lanfranc's contemporary Peter Damian (discussed in Chapter 1, and importantly also of north Italian origin and training). There is, of course, an important distinction: whereas Peter's polemic was composed for a specific occasion and quickly became obsolete, Lanfranc's epistolary dialogue on the Eucharist enjoyed great popularity in the years following his death. Its posthumous success helped influence what would shortly come to be known as the doctrine of transubstantiation, and it remained an oft-cited text throughout the Middle Ages.[30] It is a striking fact that two contemporary theologians of north Italian origin should deliberately cast their polemics in the form of a dialogue in an age just prior to the scholastic debates of the twelfth century, for it is precisely this spirit of pro and contra that will predominate in the later *quaestiones disputatae*.

Some of the enduring success of Lanfranc's anti-Berengarian dialogue clearly had to do with its argumentation and literary form. Guitmund of Aversa, a former student of Lanfranc's and a member of Pope Gregory's reform circle, later composed a treatise that likewise targeted the unorthodox views of Berengar.[31] Titled *De corporis et sanguinis Christi veritate in Eucharistia*, this treatise quotes several passages from Lanfranc's polemic and reasserts many aspects of the doctrine that had been developing to counter Berengar.[32] Not coincidentally, it also assumes the form of a dialogue, here between Guitmund and another monk named Roger. The format of the dialogue eventually breaks down when Guitmund launches excitedly into a lengthy explanation of the miracle and meaning of the Eucharist and draws on Augustine for authority in backing his statements. However, the strong reliance on proving his points according to reason ("*ratione*") and via debate

(Guitmund refers to the beginning of "disputationis nostrae" as following the example of Augustine) is evidence enough that a spirit of rational dialogue was becoming a preferred medium for arguing about theology. This shift is significant because both reason (*ratio*) and debate (*disputatio*) would, in the course of the twelfth century, become hallmarks of the scholastic method.

Lanfranc's contribution to dialogue and disputation is not restricted to his debate with Berengar and the epistolary dialogue on the Eucharist that the controversy provoked. Close analysis of the text of his commentaries, particularly his commentary on St. Paul, reveals the broader scope of his educational and dialogical advances.[33] Written at an early stage in his career, perhaps shortly after his conversion to the monastic life and when he was still newly acquainted with patristic sources and theology, the commentary text itself indicates its use as a teaching guide. In the commentary, a question-and-answer format is developed around Paul and his opponents. Lanfranc repeatedly interjects phrases such as "it is as if someone said (*quasi quis diceret*)" to help the reader reconstruct the debate between Paul and his opponents. Evidently, Lanfranc viewed the progression of Paul's argument as a series of answers to questions, as if readers had in their possession the written account of one side of the dialogue between Paul and his questioners.[34] Someone asks Paul a question, and Paul answers. Prior to about 1050, this fusion of dialectical procedure with Scripture within a commentary was not common.

Lanfranc's exegetical method of glossing Paul is significant in at least two respects: it reflects an important development in the medieval understanding of Scriptures and simultaneously captures the classroom setting of an eleventh-century monastic school. Ann Collins's study of the manuscripts and glosses of Lanfranc's Pauline commentary yields some pertinent conclusions: "Dialogue was central to the commentary's format and to Lanfranc's method. The glossed format operated as a type of dialogue with the primary text. Two voices, Lanfranc's and Paul's, contributed to the reader's (or listener's) comprehension of the text's meaning. But essentially, Lanfranc's attention to the element of debate between Paul, his opponents, and his audience, indicates something about the rules and methods followed in Lanfranc's classroom."[35] Disputation in the classroom for the purpose of understanding was as important to Lanfranc's hermeneutics as were his public debates (and epistolary disputation) with his academic rival and theological foe Berengar. A younger contemporary of Lanfranc, Sigebert of Gembloux, admiringly describes the manner in which Lanfranc explicated the apostle Paul "according to the laws of dialectic (*secundum leges dialecticae*)."[36] It was precisely this combined study of arts and theology that gave Lanfranc and the monastery of Bec its reputation (*fama*) across Europe in the late eleventh century.[37] And it was precisely this endeavor, with even greater attention to the power of dialogue and disputation in a classroom setting, that allowed Anselm to achieve his theological, philosophical, and pedagogical success.

## Anselm: The Early Years

Anselm, first of Aosta, then Bec, and finally Canterbury, is the critical hinge on whom many aspects of late eleventh-century intellectual life turned. Like Peter Damian and Lanfranc a generation earlier, Anselm was born in Italy, orphaned young, and undertook a journey north in search of greater educational opportunities. Like Lanfranc, he was clearly exposed to some form of secular learning in his native region, for Orderic Vitalis tells us that Anselm arrived at Bec "laden with the gold and treasures of Egypt—that is the learning of secular philosophers."[38] After wandering for several years in Burgundy, Anselm settled in 1059 at the new abbey of Bec in Normandy, where he, too, was attracted by the teaching reputation of Lanfranc.[39] His conversion to the monastic life thus coincides approximately with Lanfranc's controversy with Berengar. Curiously, Anselm never wrote about his teacher's handling of the Eucharistic debate, although, in his *Cur Deus homo* nearly forty years later, he followed Lanfranc's early lead and offered the first explicit reference to Aristotle in a theological work. Most importantly, when Anselm arrived at Bec in 1059, "he became part of an intellectual scene full of debate and conflict," an important aspect of which was occupied by rival methods of employing grammar and dialectic in theological arguments.[40] This overall intellectual climate, as Richard Southern and Pierre Riché each rightly noted some years ago, deeply influenced Anselm's intellectual development.[41] To explain how exactly this climate translated to Anselm's method and legacy is the task at hand.

When Lanfranc eventually left for the monastery at Caen, later to become archbishop of Canterbury, Anselm succeeded him as head of the school. As prior of Bec, Anselm read widely the works of the church fathers, particularly Augustine, and he continued to expand the library's holdings. His first work, the *Monologion*, reflects a close reading of Augustine's *De Trinitate*. Anselm describes the work as a *meditatio* on the divine being. But

by "meditation" Anselm specifically meant the inner dialogue and deliberation that were characteristic of Augustine's spirituality:

> Some of my brothers have persisted in asking me to give them an
> example of meditation, by writing down some thoughts on the
> divine essence and other related matters, which I have communi-
> cated to them in my regular discussions (*colloquia*). They asked that
> nothing should be put forward on the authority of Scripture, and in
> this I have consulted their wishes, rather than my own capacity or
> the nature of the subject. They also asked that whatever conclusion
> was reached in the course of each investigation should be expressed
> in plain language with intelligible arguments and simple disputation
> (*simplicique disputatione*), so that the necessary conclusions and clear
> truth of the matter would be clearly expressed.[42]

These opening words in the prologue to the *Monologion* point to what will
quickly become recurring features of Anselm's method of inquiry: dialogue
and disputation. These, along with an unprecedented commitment to demonstrating Christian truth by reason alone (*sola ratione*), formed the critical
elements in Anselm's pedagogical innovations at Bec's "enigmatic" school.[43]
Anselm later explained his simultaneous reliance on and departure from
Augustine along similar lines in a letter to Lanfranc:

> It was my intention throughout the whole of this disputation (*dispu-
> tationem*) to assert nothing that could not be immediately defended
> either from canonical writers or from the words of St. Augustine.
> And however often I look over what I have written, I cannot see
> that I have asserted anything other than this. Indeed, no reasoning
> of my own, however conclusive it seemed, would have persuaded
> me to be the first to presume to say those things that you have
> copied from my work in your letter nor several other things besides.
> St. Augustine proved these points in the great discussions in his *De
> Trinitate*, so that I, having as it were uncovered them in my shorter
> chain of argument, say them on his authority.[44]

Anselm did not listen to his former teacher's criticisms that he should cite
his authorities more explicitly, and this further distanced the two men.[45]
These words also point to some more profound lessons that Anselm extracted

from his close reading of Augustine.[46] Even a work cast in the form of a meditation was, for Anselm as it was for Augustine, a dialogue with oneself. Anselm was indeed indebted to Augustine, and for Lanfranc that fact necessitated additional references. From Anselm's perspective, all further reflections on the matter of the divine being, even if originally stimulated by a reading of Augustine, were the result of an inner dialogue (or disputation as he calls it) and did not merit any citation beyond the bare essentials. Very much like his commitment to proving Christian doctrine *sola ratione*, Anselm was also venturing to demonstrate his propositions (indeed, most of his philosophy) by means of inner disputation alone.

Anselm's exploration into the dialogical process of learning grew steadily following his initial meditations, and this development needs to be seen in the context of his teaching and administrative responsibilities. One of Anselm's decisions as prior following Lanfranc's departure for Caen was apparently to discontinue the practice of admitting the local nobility, although it is important to stress that this did not mean an immediate end to the admittance of outside students. Indeed, the assumption that the school reverted to being a strictly internal establishment for the monks of Bec is partly what has led previous scholars to presume the short-lived nature of the school and thrown them off the scent of Anselm's more sustained and widespread pedagogical innovations.[47] Rather, there must have been a gradual process whereby eventually most of the students became monks instead of laymen, for Orderic Vitalis tells us that both clerics "and laymen came to sit at the feet of the renowned philosopher."[48] This diversity in the kinds of students who came to Bec, as I shall show below, was intimately connected with Anselm's development of the teaching program students and monks at the monastic school underwent.

Anselm's method of instruction, as far as it can be reconstructed from his writings and those of the monks who knew him, was to hold a Socratic form of debate with his pupils in which the participants in the dispute argue out the issues.[49] Evidence for this comes from his theological and philosophical works that are cast in the form of a dialogue between master and pupil. To be sure, the dialogue genre extends back to antiquity, and it was used effectively (as a weapon of polemic) by Lanfranc and by Lanfranc's north Italian contemporary Peter Damian, but over his career Anselm went on to write more dialogues than any Latin Christian author since Augustine.[50] No fewer than seven works of Anselm take the literary form of a dialogue, as well as several others attributed to him but of dubious authenticity.[51] *De grammatico* is the earliest

(c. 1060–63) of these dialogues and concerns not grammar in the sense that the title implies, but the section in Aristotle's *Categories* that deals with substance—the same section that provided the philosophical basis for Lanfranc's reply to Berengar.[52] Anselm's purpose was, of course, much different from that of his teacher: he hoped to offer an introduction to the acts of speech and judgment that are the subject matter of all logic. As such, it is the only one of Anselm's works that does not treat a theological question.[53] Like his later works, there is nothing overtly disputational—that is, confrontational—about the work, although the student (*discipulus*) does display his mental and rhetorical acumen in a less than reverent manner: "Do not be quick to contradict what I am going to say," the student interjects in the early lines of the discussion, "but allow me to bring my speech to its conclusion, and then either approve it or improve it."[54] The discussion over Aristotle's syllogisms comes to a close when the teacher in the dialogue applauds the student's progress but warns him against the power wielded by other dialecticians:

> Since you know how vigorously the dialecticians (*dialectici*) contend, in our day, with the problem you have proposed, I do not want you to cling so tightly to the points we have made that you would hold to them with stubborn persistence even if by weightier arguments someone else could destroy them and could prove something different. But should this destruction occur, you would not deny that at least our disputing (*disputandi nobis*) has benefited us in the practice of argumentation.[55]

The student of *De grammatico* (as well as the lesson he learns) is quite unlike the students found in Anselm's later works. One plausible reason for this, Richard Southern has suggested, may be that the work was written for, or to reflect, the sort of pupils who were not yet monks but who were sent to Bec to learn dialectic rather than theology before Anselm ended the external policy of the school.[56] If that is the case, one can well understand why Anselm might have preferred to exclude the less reverent secular student portrayed in *De grammatico* from the more pious and devoted monks of the later dialogues. The form and content of Anselm's dialogues may, therefore, serve as windows onto the current issues that engaged him in discussions with his students. In fact, Anselm's biographer Eadmer seems to confirm this when he states that the treatise was written in the form of a disputation with a disciple ("cum discipulo . . . disputantem") precisely because he was dealing with the questions of dialectic.[57]

Anselm continued to adhere to the dialogue form in *De veritate*, *De libertate*, and *De casu diaboli*, a trilogy that he intended to be copied and read in that order.[58] Much more compliant and open to instruction are the "student" interlocutors of these dialogues: "If I cannot do anything else," the student in *De veritate* humbly states, "I will at least help by being a good listener."[59] The general form of investigation in these three dialogues is the same: a student presents issues in need of clarification to the teacher, who then patiently explains them. The titles of these works are less at odds with the subject matter than in *De grammatico*: *De veritate* deals with various conceptions of truth, *De libertate* with freedom of choice and its relation to sin and grace, and *De casu diaboli* with the status of the devil and the differences between good and evil angels. In none of these works is a name given to the student or teacher; the student throughout remains an anonymous pupil in search of greater understanding of the Christian faith. Although it has been established that these three philosophical dialogues were written after *De grammatico*, it is also clear that Anselm conceived of all these dialogues in connection with a student's education. Indeed, in the preface to the three philosophical dialogues Anselm states as much:

> At different times in the past I wrote three treatises pertaining to the study of Sacred Scripture. They are similar in having been written following the question-and-answer form (*interrogationem et responsionem*) with the person inquiring designated as "the Student," and the person answering, "the Teacher." I wrote a fourth work in a similar style, which begins with the words "De grammatico" and which is not without use to those who need to be introduced to dialectic, but because it pertains to a different study from these three, I do not wish to number it with them. . . . Although I did not compose these treatises one right after the other, nevertheless their subject matter (*materia*) and their similarity in the disputational form (*similitudo disputationis*) require that they be written together as a unit and in the order in which I have listed them.[60]

Anselm is explicit in calling attention to the fact that his didactic writings, even if not necessarily treating the same subject, are conjoined by their literary form and purpose; they all belong to the same stated educational and intellectual program. In 1078 Anselm was promoted from prior to abbot of the monastery of Bec, a position he held for the next fifteen years. His biographer Eadmer stresses the administrative burdens that befell Anselm during his tenure as abbot and consequently says nothing about his literary productivity during these years, but Richard Sharpe has recently reaffirmed that it was most likely during this fifteen-year period that Anselm composed (or least drafted) his first four dialogues.[61] In 1093 Anselm was selected to succeed, once again, his former teacher Lanfranc, this time as archbishop of Canterbury. The move, like Lanfranc's appointment before him, was a clear result of the closer ties between Normandy and England following the 1066 conquest. Anselm, however, did not wish to leave Bec and accepted the position only after making his reluctance known. The obstinacy of William Rufus and the pressure placed on Anselm by the initiatives of Pope Urban II meant controversy for the newly appointed archbishop. Unable and unwilling to break his allegiance to Pope Urban II for King Rufus, who supported the antipope, Anselm soon found himself a political exile seeking protection at the papal court.[62] There he completed his magisterial *Cur Deus homo* (c. 1098), a work that, as its title suggests, seeks to explain why an all-powerful and perfect God became human.[63] Undoubtedly the most famous of his dialogues, *Cur Deus homo* is Anselm's only work to name the student, Boso, who is in dialogue with him.[64] The first chapter, quoted below in its entirety, also exposes Anselm's purpose in explaining Christian doctrine through dialogue:

> I have often and most earnestly been requested by many, both in person and by letter, that I hand down in writing the proofs of a certain doctrine of our faith which I am accustomed to give to those who make inquiry; for they say that these proofs please them, and they regard them as satisfactory. They make their request not in order to approach faith by way of reason (*per rationem*), but in order that they may be pleased by understanding and contemplating those things that they believe and so that they may as best as possible always be prepared to convince anyone who demands of them an explanation for that hope which is in us. Unbelievers habitually raise this problem against us and ridicule Christian simplicity as absurd. Many believers also ponder this in their hearts. And so the following problem comes about: for what reason and on the basis of what necessity did God become a man, and by his death (as we believe and affirm) restore life to the world, when he could have done this

by means of some other being, angelic or human, or merely by his will? Not only learned men but also many unlearned men ask about this problem and seek to know its solution. Many individuals therefore persist in asking that this problem be handled; and in spite of the fact that the investigation seems very difficult, the solution is intelligible to everyone and is commendable because of the usefulness and elegance of the reasoning. Therefore, even though the holy Fathers have said what ought to be sufficient, I will nevertheless endeavor to show to those who inquire what God has seen fit to disclose to me about this topic. And since those things that are investigated by the method of question and answer (*interrogationem et responsionem investigantur*) are clearer and more acceptable to many minds, especially slower minds, I will take as my fellow disputant (*disputantem*) the one who has been urging me on more insistently than any other, so that in the following manner Boso may question and Anselm reply.[65]

Anselm is in fact engaging in multiple dialogues, not one. The first, the theological justification for the work, is Anselm's attempt to provide a rationally sustainable answer about the faith of Christians to the doubts and accusations of unbelievers, and Christians as well. (Whether these unbelievers include Jews and Muslims or are restricted to pagans and heretics is a matter of some scholarly dispute.)[66] The second dialogue, which can be seen as both a pretext for the first and an example of his method of inquiry, is the alleged conversation Anselm undertook with his philosophically astute student Boso. In the earlier dialogues, the nameless participants play only a very subordinate part in the development of the argument. "Boso's part in the *Cur Deus Homo*," Southern remarks, "is quite different: the central argument of the whole work, in its first formulation, is put into his mouth."[67] Boso himself, and his brother, had come to Anselm in search of answers to their "perplexae quaestiones."[68] Through Boso, Anselm was effectively conversing with representatives of the newly organized secular schools in northern France, Laon chief among them. Indeed, there is considerable evidence that Anselm's statements in *Cur Deus homo* reflect an engagement with the skepticism of contemporary masters.[69] Especially intriguing is Anselm's stated belief that the method of question and answer will prove effective even for persons of slower minds, in contrast to chapter 2 of the *Rule of St. Benedict*, which advocated teaching by words only for receptive monks and by example for the duller ones.[70] Who exactly are these slower-minded individuals of whom Anselm speaks? How does this statement fit into Anselm's larger project of theology and instruction? How did this Socratic method of investigation impact the writings of his students and followers? These questions go to the heart of the Anselmian contribution to dialogue and disputation in the late eleventh century and can only be fully answered by considering other works of Anselm, including the works attributed to him, and the works of his students.

## Anselm: Teacher and Debater

Eadmer reports that Anselm in his *Proslogion* was searching for a single irrefutable proof of the existence of God, one that would be more convincing still than the "chain of many arguments" he had developed in his *Monologion*.[71] This ambitious theological endeavor, which resulted in his celebrated ontological proof of the existence of God, did not meet with universal approval. Gaunilo, a monk from neighboring Marmoutier, responded to Anselm's arguments with an equally famous rebuttal, foreshadowing, according to some, the Kantian refutation of the ontological argument some seven centuries later.[72] Writing to Anselm "on behalf of the Fool" (for in the *Proslogion* Anselm postulated that only a fool could not see his reasoning), Gaunilo challenged the single-argument proof for the existence of God.[73] Gaunilo's critique did not result in any dialogue per se, from Gaunilo or Anselm, but the intellectual debate did provoke a detailed and no less original reply from Anselm. "Since my arguments are not attacked by the Fool, against whom I directed my treatise," Anselm writes, "but by an intelligent and orthodox Christian on behalf of the Fool, it will suffice to reply to the orthodox Christian."[74] The resulting supplement, which Anselm later insisted accompany the circulation of his *Proslogion*, was a point-by-point response to Gaunilo's criticisms. In the response, Anselm presented a philosophical or theological issue and then expounded upon it until the issue was considered settled. Central, again, to Anselm's rebuttal is the idea that reason, debate, and proper argumentation will prevail on his side: "Let those who have even a minimal knowledge of debate and argumentation (*disputandi argumentandique*) come to my defense. For is it reasonable (*rationabile est*) for someone to deny what he understands because it is said to be identical with that which he denies because he does not understand?"[75] In retrospect, this work must be seen as an early example of the scholastic method of investigation later embodied in the twelfth-century *quaestiones* and thirteenth-century *summae*. Anselm never abandoned the meditative procedure of investigation (and inner dialogue) he had first laid out in his *Monologion*, but the reply to Gaunilo does belong to Anselm's broader theory of argumentation, one that would prove especially popular in the burgeoning secular schools in northern France.

Anselm is most frequently discussed in connection with his ontological proof of the existence of God (a term made popular by Kant in the eighteenth century) and his original application of reason to demonstrating the truths of Christian doctrine. But no less important to his thought was the potency of intellectual debate, both literary and real. In addition to his didactic treatises written in dialogue form, Anselm clearly regarded disputation as an integral component of his philosophy and methodology. A consideration of his vocabulary helps illustrate this point. In the corpus of his writings, Anselm employed the verb "disputare" and its accompanying noun forms on more than forty occasions.[76] While the meaning of this term clearly varies from a simple "discussion" or "conversation" to a more intense "dispute" or "debate," there is a clear parallel between the form of his writings and the vocabulary he employs. As innovative as *what* Anselm was teaching was the *method* by which he taught. From his earliest meditation to his last letters, with several real debates in between, Anselm consistently referred to his rational investigations and dialectical argumentations in terms of a "disputatio." Not surprisingly, then, the effects of this dialectical procedure stood out to all who met Anselm in person, particularly those who learned from him. There is hardly anything clearer in the contemporary reports about Anselm than his need to develop his thoughts by talking: the monk "Gundulf listened to him at Bec, Guibert of Nogent listened to him on his visits to Flay, Eadmer at Canterbury, and they all said the same thing—his talk was irresistible."[77] Everyone wanted him to talk and to dispute, leaving no difficulties unraveled and no student unconvinced. Anselm's biographer stresses that "everyone therefore who could enjoy his conversation was glad to do so, for on any subject they wished he had heavenly counsel ready for them." Even William the Conqueror, "stiff and terrifying" to everyone around him, was made amiable in his personal encounters with the abbot of Bec, "so that to everyone's surprise he seemed an altogether different man when Anselm was present."[78] The charismatic pedagogy that Stephen Jaeger has identified for the Ottonian courts of this period would seem to be very much a part of Anselm's character.

Richard Southern, in his otherwise magisterial studies of Anselm, tended to minimize both Lanfranc's influence on this particular method of philosophical investigation and the overall influence exerted by Anselm's predilection for rational dialogue.[79] But that is a serious underestimation of an important cultural mutation that Southern was, in fact, among the first to recognize. Once again, Orderic Vitalis proves a worthy commentator; in an oft-quoted but often underappreciated passage of his *Historia Ecclesiastica*, he describes with amazement the achievements of both Lanfranc and Anselm:

> A great store of learning in both the liberal arts and theology was assembled by Lanfranc in the abbey of Bec, and magnificently increased by Anselm so that the school sent out many distinguished scholars and also prudent pilots and spiritual charioteers who have been entrusted by divine providence with holding the reins of the churches in the arena of this world. So by good custom the monks of Bec are so devoted to the study of letters, so eager to solve theological problems and compose edifying treatises, that almost all of them seem to be philosophers; and by association with them, even with those who pass as illiterates and are called rustics (*rustici*) at Bec, the most erudite doctors can learn things to their advantage.[80]

Orderic is not merely praising the learning that resided at the school at Bec; he is praising how learning was undertaken (that is, it was active, not passive) and the fact that it was diffused. Even illiterate peasants ("rustici") carried forth into the world a spirit of philosophy that could be attained nowhere else. A dearth of contemporary evidence prevents one from knowing more about the day-to-day activities of Anselm's teachings, but if the comments of Orderic Vitalis and the testimonials of Anselm's students are any indication, a liberal education with a focus on debate and philosophical inquiry was more pronounced at Bec than at perhaps any other monastic or cathedral school of the time. While many later illustrations portray Anselm as the saintly theologian divorced from his everyday surroundings, a twelfth-century British manuscript illuminator saw it fitting to depict Anselm the teacher in accordance with his charismatic reputation: in the company of fellow monks, holding a Tau, and engaged in a discussion over his books (Figure 2).

If there is no doubt about the authenticity of Anselm's above-mentioned works, there is doubt about the authenticity of several later works that have

Figure 2. Master Anselm in conversation with fellow monks, giving them books. Upper
half: Anselm, as archbishop of Canterbury 1093–1109, presenting books to Countess
Matilda of Tuscany. Twelfth century. Oxford, Bodleian Library, MS Auct. D.2.6, fol.
185v. Used by permission.

long been assigned to him and whose authorship is now frequently given as
"Pseudo-Anselm." Because they circulated under Anselm's name and were
considered representative of his thought by his immediate and later followers,
they merit some consideration.[81] This is especially the case because they also
happen to take the literary form of a dialogue or disputation. Four works fall
into this category. *De custodia interioris hominis*, formerly believed to be part
of a treatise ascribed to Hugh of St. Victor, is a short dialogue on the spiritual
realities of the faith with an emphasis on God and the certainty of his existence.[82] It contains the allegory of the soul and its forces, the four cardinal
virtues guarding it, and the messengers Fear and Love narrating their vision

of heaven and hell.[83] An untitled "monastic dialogue" between a Benedictine monk and Christ on the spiritual virtues of poverty also circulated under the authorship of Anselm, as did the much later (possibly Franciscan) *Dialogus Beatae Mariae et Anselmi de Passione Domini*, which purports to record a revelation to Anselm in which the Virgin herself answered the saint's queries on the events of the Passion.[84] Finally, the work that bears the closest resemblance to Anselm's hand, even if its authorship remains uncertain, is the *Disputatio inter Christianum et Gentilem*.[85] This disputation between a Christian and a pagan (synonymous with "gentile") on the Incarnation is clearly modeled on Anselm's *Cur Deus homo*, only here the pagan opens the dialogue by specifically inquiring after the rationale of the Incarnation.[86] His tacit acceptance of God and the Incarnation coupled with his explicit rejection of the authority of the Bible creates difficulty in assigning a specific religious or nonreligious affiliation to this "gentile." As Anna Sapir Abulafia remarks, "It is almost as if our author has not yet quite made up his mind whether his Pagan will be Boso or one of the *infideles* Boso represents."[87] Over the course of the discussion, the Christian urges the pagan to accede to faith, if only temporarily, so that he may be able to understand. Pseudo-Anselm thus uses Anselm's axiom of belief as a way to understand (*credo ut intelligam*), but he also goes further. As the discussion turns to the question of why a God-man had to be born of a virgin, and of his divinity more generally, the Christian insists that these truths are plain and visible to any "rational being." In confronting the problem of how to convert an unbeliever to faith, the Christian is going significantly beyond the limits set by Anselm. As Abulafia again notes, "Pseudo-Anselm is not urging belief so that knowledge can be imparted; he is using knowledge as a weapon to force someone to believe."[88]

There is more. In at least one version of this *disputatio*, the characters' headings actually change midway through the dialogue from "Christianus" and "Gentilis" to "Magister" and "Discipulus."[89] This shift in nomenclature is surely not haphazard. It is supported by a transitional moment in their conversation. Immediately after the gentile recognizes and admits his error ("fateor me hoc usque errasse"), the Christian confidently assures his fellow disputant that the Lord "will open himself up to us because we ask questions, as long as we in turn patiently follow the questions and kind answers (*interrogando et beniuole respondendo*) provided by the authority of Holy Scripture, just as we might follow a father's lead."[90] The dialogue reads like the climactic scene of a screenplay: "I ask you, Father," Fidelis (formerly Gentilis) humbly responds, "that you now not treat me like an outsider, but that with you as teacher and me as student you instruct me, as a father instructs his son, to become closer to my salvation."[91] The turning moment (indeed conversionary moment) in the non-Christian's attitude toward Christian truth is thus highlighted by a sudden transition from codisputant (one who disputes with or against the representative of Christianity) to "faithful" student (one who asks questions in search of answers). His conversion to Christianity toward the end of the dialogue, for there was by this point no reasonable alternative but to convert, is crystallized by his proclamation that he cannot fathom how anyone could remain an unbeliever. And, thus, via form and content, the didactic lesson imparted by the teacher to his student is clear.

The dialogues attributed to Anselm differ from each other in their subject matter and in the tone of their discussions, but they all present a central and persuasive aspect in the Anselmian approach to thinking about faith: namely, it is through conversation, interrogation, indeed disputation that a more accessible explanation of doctrine can be articulated and achieved. In point of fact, it matters less who the interlocutors in the dialogue actually are than what intellectual positions they stand for and what emerges from their discussions.[92] If these points are made anonymously in works purporting to be by Anselm, they are equally evident in the writings of Anselm's known disciples.[93] The best known among them are Gilbert Crispin, a former student at Bec, and Honorius Augustodunensis, an important disseminator of Anselm's thought, both writers of innovative and influential dialogues.[94]

## Gilbert Crispin

Gilbert Crispin (c. 1045–1117) came from a noble Norman family. From a very early age, he was associated with the monastery of Bec, where his family had close ties. There he came under the tutelage of both Lanfranc and Anselm. When Lanfranc was made archbishop of Canterbury, Gilbert was called upon to become the fourth abbot of Westminster. Gilbert is the author of treatises on monasticism, the Eucharist, and simony, and of a *vita* of Abbot Herluin (the founder of Bec), all of which reveal the liberal arts training he acquired as a monk at Bec. His most famous work is his *Disputatio Iudei et Christiani*, composed most likely in 1092 or 1093.[95] Whereas nearly all Gilbert's other works are extant in only one manuscript, the *Disputatio* survives in over thirty manuscripts, of which twenty date from the twelfth century.[96]

By Gilbert's time the *Adversus Iudaeos* genre of writings had been in continuous existence for nearly a millennium, and from a theological and exegetical perspective Gilbert contributed nothing original to that long-standing tradition of polemic. A large selection of the *Disputatio* deals with the validity of Mosaic law, the Incarnation, the coming of the Messiah, and the propriety of using images like the crucifix to adorn churches.[97] These topics were all familiar themes of the Jewish-Christian controversy. The Christian levels the familiar accusations of Jews' misreading Scripture that had been made countless times before, and the content of the Jew's argument is fully in line with the arguments contained in other Jewish-Christian disputations and Jewish biblical exegesis. Why the extraordinary popularity of Gilbert's disputation? Naturally, the main attraction of the work must be sought in where it differs from previous attempts at the same *Adversus Iudaeos* genre.

A unique feature of Gilbert's enterprise is the space allotted to the Jew in the discussion. Unlike earlier examples of Jewish-Christian disputations, the Jew is allowed to speak at length both in defense of his own position and in opposition to the arguments of the Christian. A possible source for this seemingly balanced discussion is Gilbert's assertion that the disputation is the result of an actual conversation that he had had in London with a Jewish merchant from Mainz. Some have challenged that such a conversation ever took place, suggesting that the work is instead a creation of Gilbert's literary imagination, but Gilbert's most recent editor maintains that some version of the recorded disputation did actually take place.[98] Gilbert's intentions in the work are implicitly and explicitly professed in the dedicatory lines to his teacher Anselm:

> I send to your fatherly prudence a little book I recently wrote that puts in writing what a certain Jew said when disputing with me (*mecum disputans*) in defense of his law against our faith and what I replied to his objections in favor of our faith. I do not know where he was born, but he was educated in Mainz, and he was well versed even in our law and literature and had a mind practiced in Scriptures. He came to see me for business since for certain things I was very necessary to him. Whenever we came together, we would soon begin talking in a friendly spirit about Scriptures and our faith. One day, God granted both him and me greater leisure than usual, and we began questioning each other (*inter nos questionari*), as was our custom. Because his objections were consequent and logical, and

since he explained with equal consequence his former objections, while my reply met his objections toe to toe and by his confession seemed equally supported by the testimony of Scriptures, some of those who were present requested that I preserve our little debate (*nostram disceptatiunculam*) so that they may be of use to others in the future.[99]

The mention that this Jew was experienced in Jewish-Christian disputations is, if the statement can be taken at face value, a very early indication that disputations of the sort witnessed in later centuries were already beginning to take shape in the eleventh century.[100] Rhetorically, the preamble also serves to set the bar high for the Christian. When he scores points against the Jew in the disputation that ensues, he is not merely voicing what is already known to Christians; he is also outdisputing a talented representative of the opposite side. One statement that is readily confirmed is "the friendly spirit (*amico animo*)" of their debate, for even though the Jew does (in some manuscript versions) eventually convert at the end—like Pseudo-Anselm's disputation, there is no reasonable alternative at the end—a certain level of mutual respect is maintained throughout. The politeness of their exchanges, which is not generally a common feature of anti-Jewish disputational writings, may indeed, as has been suggested, be a sign of the original conversation on which the work is based. It may equally be a consequence of the Anselmian approach to arriving at truth through open dialogue. In a sense, the same problem of derivation that presents itself with Justin Martyr's second-century *Dialogue with Trypho*, which was purportedly the result of an actual exchange, resurfaces with Gilbert Crispin. Here, however, there is a markedly different context with which to work. Scholars have long known that much of Gilbert's writings display the mark of his teachers Herluin, Lanfanc, and Anselm, and that training helped prepare him for the difficult task of maintaining the noble ideals of Bec in the wholly dissimilar surroundings of royal Westminster.[101] Specifically, Richard Southern has highlighted the relation between Gilbert's *Disputatio Iudei et Christiani* and Anselm's *Cur Deus homo*, positing that Gilbert's encounters with Jews played a role in Anselm's formulation of the Jewish opposition and that Anselm in turn provided some of Gilbert's ideas on the Incarnation.[102] Certainly the reason-based discussion of why God became man in Gilbert's *Disputatio* is a nod to Anselm. But there is also in Gilbert's oeuvre the distinct flavor of Anselm's question-and-answer method, and one cannot but wonder whether Gilbert was writing in view of the same "slower-minded" persons who had compelled Anselm to adopt the dialogue form.

The disputation between a Jew and a Christian was followed by another disputation, the *Disputatio Christiani cum Gentili*.[103] This disputation tells the story of Gilbert's attending a secret meeting of "philosophers" in London where he became involved in a debate with a pagan.[104] Like the opponent in *Cur Deus homo*, the "gentile" of this disputation is unwilling to accept either Jewish or Christian law. The Christian, in turn, agrees to proceed according to the dictates of reason (*ratio*) rather than biblical authority. The discussion that ensues, however, falls considerably short of the announced goal.[105] First, the gentile himself retreats from his earlier position and states that they each know the sacred texts of the other. Second, and perhaps on account of this fact, the Christian invokes Anselm's logic and implores the gentile to "submit to faith for a little while, for, in yielding to faith, you may come to understanding."[106] The remaining debate focuses largely on the proper interpretation of biblical evidence, and it is on this basis that some commentators have seen in the gentile a "rational Jew" or even a Muslim.[107]

Gilbert Crispin devoted considerable place in his writings to religious controversy, but he also wrote three other dialogues dealing with more purely Christian themes. Here, too, the Anselmian influence is present. A dialogue on the fall of Satan, *De angelo perdito*, constitutes the work that is theologically closest to Anselm. Its resemblance to Anselm's *De casu diaboli* is evident in the very beginning where Gilbert's unnamed questioner asks how it came about that Satan did not "stand fast in the truth" (John 8:44). In other passages, it seems likely that Gilbert is articulating points Anselm made in his teaching at Bec but that did not find their way into his finished works. Their meetings at Westminster in 1086 and 1092/93, when Anselm was a guest of Gilbert's, may have also contributed to the development of Gilbert's writings on the devil. "Whether or not Anselm brought Gilbert a copy of the *De Casu Diaboli*," G. R. Evans explains, "it is clear that his recollections of the schoolroom at Bec were vividly revived by his conversations with Anselm."[108] A later treatise on the Holy Spirit, *De Spiritu Sancto*, is cast in the form of a dialogue between a teacher (*Magister*) and student (*Discipulus*). Here the similarities to Anselm's writings are fewer, the work's main reliance being on Augustine. Gilbert did, however, send the finished work to Anselm, accompanied by a letter requesting that he resolve the final question raised by the *Discipulus*, namely, whether the Son only was made man.[109] No response from Anselm survives, but Gilbert's gesture is paradigmatic of the intellectual exchange that shaped both of their works. The third theological dialogue, *De altaris sacramento*, treats the thorny issue of the Eucharist, which Lanfanc had disputed with Berengar and which Anselm had avoided altogether.[110]

## Honorius Augustodunensis

The figure of Honorius Augustodunensis (c. 1070–c. 1140) is as enigmatic as he is important and overlooked. Among the many unknowns in his life are his place of birth, his location of study, and the source of his eponym (Autun, Canterbury, Augsburg, Regensburg, and Aosta have all been suggested).[111] Some have conjectured, mainly on the basis of his adherence to John Scotus Eriugena's cosmology and Anselm's theology, that he was of Insular origin, but that theory cannot be verified and must remain doubtful. A more recent hypothesis suggests that Honorius (originally Henricus) might have come originally from Aosta, a member of the same minor nobility of Savoy as Anselm.[112] What does seem clear is that he lived and wrote in England for a considerable period of time, some of it in Anselm's Canterbury, before relocating to Regensburg sometime before 1130. There he became a Benedictine monk and joined with the circles of reformers that included such notables as Rupert of Deutz (himself the author of an anti-Jewish dialogue). During his years in Regensburg, Honorius played a critical role in disseminating to a German audience the ideas, methods, and reforming ideals of Anselm.[113] During his life and for centuries afterwards, Honorius was one of the most deeply influential writers in the West.[114]

Honorius is silent about nearly all aspects of his autobiography, except one: his authorship. In his own last-named treatise, the *De luminaribus ecclesiae*, Honorius proudly claims authorship of twenty-two "by no means despicable" works.[115] The quantity of his output is equaled by its diversity; it includes reformist, polemical, liturgical, cosmological, didactic, and exegetical treatises. No fewer than five of his works assume the form of a dialogue.[116] At least five other works, also in dialogue form, are possibly his as well.[117] Each of Honorius's works is deserving of its own attention, and in some cases badly needing an editor, but several of his dialogues are particularly useful in tracing the use of the form for didactic purposes. Standing in a class of its own is the *Elucidarium*, also sometimes referred to as the *Dialogus de summa totius Christianae theologiae*.[118] It is the first of Honorius's many writings.[119]

Cast in the form of a dialogue between master and student, the *Elucidarium* was translated into all the vernacular languages of the medieval West and survives in well over three hundred medieval manuscripts, making it "arguably the most revealing and important of all of Honorius's writings."[120] Certainly, it was the most widely read. The length, structure, and literary form of the work recall the Anselmian style: "I have often been asked by a fellow student to explain certain little questions" is how Honorius begins the prologue.[121] Like Anselm, Honorius opens with a short introduction in which he explains the circumstances of the work and sets out his intentions, a practice that extends to his exegetical commentaries as well.[122] By composing this work, Honorius continues, he hopes "to leave for posterity (*transmittere posteritati*)" questions that have already been "debated (*disputata*)" orally and that, when read, will prove useful and pleasing to others and to God. The work is didactic and dogmatic, intended to set out in simple terms for a less-than-advanced reader all the important principles of the Christian faith. In this sense, the work is encyclopedic as well.

A similar explication precedes a later, longer, and more philosophically profound work by Honorius, the *Clavis physicae*. This work was composed in the form of a dialogue between student and teacher, Honorius divulges, "because to the greatest philosophers, such as Socrates, Plato, and Cicero, not to mention our own Augustine and Boethius, it seemed to be the teaching method that offered the most power when introducing a subject."[123] Given that Honorius had almost certainly not read Plato but knew him only secondhand, it is striking how conscious he and Anselm before him are of their appropriation of the Socratic method. The *Clavis physicae* is one of Honorius's cosmological treatises, and it takes as its subject an explication (some will say simplification) of John Scotus Eriugena's *Periphyseon* (860s), also a dialogue.[124]

Three other dialogues between master and pupil, the *Libellus octo quaestionum*, the *Scala Coeli major*, and the *Cognitio vitae*, as well as several other treatises not in the form of a dialogue, also draw heavily from the philosophy of Eriugena. Formerly ascribed to Augustine, the *Cognitio vitae* is particularly interesting for its relation to Anselm's thought and method. Based largely on Anselm's *Monologion*, it follows Anselm in his logical proof of the existence of God, in the importance placed on "the light of right reason," and in the relationship between teacher and student. Here the work is actually constructed as a discourse between master and pupil. In answer to the pupil's question of why some students are slower to learn ("quaedam [animae] tardior est ad discendum"), when all minds have the same nature (again recalling Anselm's prefatory remarks in *Cur Deus homo*), Honorius used the familiar metaphor of the sealing wax and candle.[125] The wax represents the malleable material of the mind, which needs study, training, and the flame of truth for it to be impressed. The metaphor of the wax seal is a very old one—that other great writer of dialogues, Plato, described the mind as like a block of wax that would take the impression of our perceptions and thoughts. Honorius, however, seems to have inherited his understanding from his teacher Anselm, who used it in one of his letters; according to Eadmer, Anselm likened the malleability of a young man, neither too young nor too old, to a piece of wax that is neither too soft nor too hard.[126] The metaphor of the seal and the wax struck a chord with many medieval authors, and, as Brigitte Bedos-Rezak has shown, seals came to occupy important social and symbolic functions at precisely this time in the intellectual development of medieval Europe.[127] It can be found in a number of twelfth-century authors, including Honorius's contemporary Hugh of St. Victor, who said that our imitation of the saints is the imprinting of their lives in us just as a seal molds the wax on which it is pressed.[128] Honorius uses this opportunity to articulate his own pedagogical creed, one that employs the spirit of investigative philosophy instilled in him by Anselm in order to go beyond the more inward rationale of his teacher, explaining that, in matters of instruction, the teacher who is outside the student's mind can only plant and water the seeds of knowledge. It is truth dwelling within the mind that creates wisdom.[129]

Wax seals and instructional dialogue are more than fleeting moments of compositional insight for Honorius (or Anselm). A further illustration of Honorius's debt to his teacher Anselm, as well as his departure from him, can be observed in another work that likewise turns on the metaphor of the seal, his *Sigillum Sanctae Mariae*, a commentary on the Song of Songs from a Marian perspective that was composed sometime in the first decade of the twelfth century and probably while Honorius was still a resident in England (and possibly while Anselm was exiled from Canterbury, 1103–7).[130] In good Anselmian fashion, the questions that motivated the composition of the work are explained in the prologue as originating in Honorius's students: grateful for the illumination shown them in the earlier *Elucidarium*, the "assembly of students" beg their master to undertake a new work that explains why certain texts are read on the feast of Mary "although they do not pertain to her at all."[131] This deceptively simple question, Rachel Fulton has argued, "was no less than revolutionary," for what they were asking for in effect was the reasoning behind the liturgy. And what Honorius proposed, contrary to the tradition of the fathers such as Gregory the Great and Bede, was to read the Song of Songs "as a dialogue not between Christ and the soul or Christ and the Church but, rather, between Christ and his Mother."[132] Fulton has also suggested that Honorius was writing in response to questions suggested to him in part by the prayers of Anselm and that these questions had their roots in devotional, rather than primarily exegetical, concerns.[133] Here again, I should like to emphasize that Honorius's method rests on an original understanding of dialogue within the commentary tradition and that his inspiration for blending prayer and dialogue under the umbrella metaphor of a wax seal appears to derive from Anselm. Indeed, Honorius's Marian and dialogical reading of the Song of Songs evokes Anselm's devotionally original meditations and his own dialogue *Cur Deus homo*, which Honorius explicitly refers to in the *Sigillum*. The resulting commentary can be seen as a drama unfolding in two acts, as Honorius endeavors to make the conversation between the Queen of Heaven and her celestial bridegroom audible while at the same time exciting a devotion to her by recollecting for his audience her role at the Judgment (and thus terrifying his readers enough so that they would pay attention and pray for her intercession).[134] In the fourth and final scene of this drama, Mary is found to be pleading on behalf of "her people," the Jews, as they approach the seat of Judgment.[135] Christ assures her, "If she [Synagoga] be a wall, let us build upon it," and the Virgin promises, "I will be a wall for them."[136] The scene is somewhat surprising, for Jews figure as villains in a number of the miracle stories that were, already in Honorius's lifetime, making their way into the more popular collections. Yet concerns for Jewish objections to Christianity, and in particular the Incarnation, were precisely the topic of (live) debate that had concerned Anselm and another student, Gilbert Crispin, in the latter's conversations with the Jew from Mainz. Fulton states, "There is little doubt that [Anselm] was well aware of the arguments that Jews of his day brought forward against this most Christian doctrine, if not from conversations with Jewish scholars himself . . . , then most definitely from conversations with his friend Gilbert Crispin."[137] If contemporary Jews insisted that the doctrine of the Incarnation was nothing short of an insult to God and that the height of that insult was that God had confined himself within a woman's womb, then to defend Mary's purity as both virgin and mother was to champion the idea that God might deign to become human and that he did so literally through a woman. This point had even greater contemporary resonance in the area where Honorius would spend a good portion of his career (Regensburg), as so many Jews had recently perished at the hands of the crusaders in 1096 for refusing to convert and accept baptism. In a work not a dialogue but deeply dialogical, Honorius effectively braids the different strands that I have traced through the teachings of Anselm: deep devotion expressed through conversation and dialogue, an exegetical method that uses dialogue (and in this instance a Marian reading of the Song of Songs) to explain to students the deeper meanings of the liturgy, and a heightened awareness of the Jewish objections to Christian doctrines such as the Incarnation that were the topics of current debate.

## Conclusions

The second half of the eleventh century witnessed profound changes in the institutional and intellectual landscape of western Christendom. Major forces in these changes were the figures of Lanfranc and Anselm. Lanfranc's participation, indeed his central role, in the controversy over the Eucharist brought him fame as one of the leading dialecticians of his time and led him to write an influential dialogue, a cleverly constructed polemic that sets in writing the sort of theological disputation that was current during the eleventh-century ecclesiastical reform. As an educator at Bec and commentator on Paul, Lanfranc developed early on a technique for merging exegesis with dialogue. The disputational quality of his Pauline glosses can be seen as an early glimpse into the scholastic (one might say protoscholastic, for the secular schools of the twelfth century had yet to appear) methods of learning that would be developed most immediately by Anselm, and most famously by the generation of Abelard, for whom irreverent disputation was the very source of so many of his calamities.[138] Lanfranc's mentorship of Anselm was for this reason central to the eleventh-century development of theology and philosophy. As prior and abbot of Bec, Anselm developed further than anyone before a method of engaging students through verbal interrogation and literary dialogue. His productivity in the latter regard was instrumental in spreading his novel ideas and methods across Europe, an accomplishment that was helped in no small measure by his students Gilbert Crispin and Honorius Augustodunensis and by the anonymous author(s) Pseudo-Anselm, whose immensely popular dialogues are testaments to Anselm's success. In addition to his much-emphasized reliance on reason and logic, Anselm's contribution to medieval thought and writing can clearly be seen in his revival and reworking of a dialogical/disputational quality of inner meditation. The problem of unbelievers that had confronted Augustine and that had led him to debate publicly with Manicheans and to write treatises (some of them in dialogue form) to counterattack their challenges was raised again in the writings of Anselm and Gilbert, but now with the challenges posed by pagans, unnamed heretics, and especially Jews. This controversy continued to generate an abundance of literature and later produced actual debates (public disputations) between Christians and Jews, as we shall see in Chapter 6. Thus, by the time of Anselm's death, the seeds for an arena of academic and religious dispute were widely sown. It is revealing that the most widely circulated texts of Anselm, Gilbert, and Honorius were each written in dialogue form. All three writers, and Lanfranc, too, valued rational investigation, dialogue, and disputation as a successful strategy for arriving at (and demonstrating) Christian truth. It is this arena of educative dialogue and intellectual dispute that the next generation of thinkers, teachers, and debaters inherited and out of which grew, in time, the methods and practices most emblematic of the medieval university.

CHAPTER 3

# Scholastic Practices of the
# Twelfth-Century Renaissance

The twelfth-century attitude toward classical learning and literature is often summed up by the memorable words of Bernard of Chartres, who is quoted by his disciple John of Salisbury as saying that "we are like dwarves standing on the shoulders of giants: we see more and farther than our predecessors not because we have sharper vision or greater height, but because we are raised up and borne aloft on their gigantic stature."[1] This proclamation of new insight framed by a conscious indebtedness to the past elegantly sums up the relation between old and new in the "twelfth-century renaissance," a concept most famously articulated, though not invented, by Charles Homer Haskins (1870–1937).[2] The dual nature of this renaissance is especially worth emphasizing, for no less important than the recovery and translation of ancient texts were a number of intellectual and institutional developments that can only accurately be described as distinctly new.[3] Among the most familiar of these are a transition from oral to written record, the flowering of vernacular literature, the proliferation of cathedral schools and private masters, the formation of classical canon law, and the emergence of theology as a formal branch of learning more important still than the seven liberal arts inherited from antiquity.[4] Regardless of whether the term "renaissance" is the most appropriate or not, and various alternatives have been suggested, there can be little doubt that this was an age conditioned by new learning and by new methods of organizing and distributing that learning.[5]

In charting the rise of a culture of disputation over the course of the twelfth century, it will be well to appreciate at the outset that disputation itself reflects both rebirth and novelty. On the one hand, the dialogue as a form of meditation and reflection persists, as do the familiar question-and-answer colloquies, while, on the other, a more thoroughly "scholastic" milieu emerged in the twelfth century in which more argumentative and disputative forms of communication thrived. Despite the vociferous rhetoric of contemporary personalities, a great deal of fluidity existed between these circles, and any rigid distinction between monastic and scholastic practices must, therefore, be resisted. In the previous two chapters, authors were examined chronologically in order to observe the decline of ancient philosophical dialogue and its reemergence out of monastic pedagogy. In this chapter, it will be helpful to proceed thematically in order to sample the range of intellectual inquiry that occasioned both literary dialogues and scholastic disputation, placing these two interrelated expressions first within a changing institutional context and then against the broader panorama of the twelfth century's creative impulses.

## New Schools and New Learning

By the close of the eleventh century, an increasing number of schools and masters in northern Europe were attracting students to the study of the liberal arts and theology.[6] Three kinds of schools can be distinguished around the turn of the twelfth century. The first and most common of these were the monastic schools, such as Bec, made famous by the teachings of Lanfranc and Anselm, and the abbey of St. Victor in Paris, which maintained a distinguished line of scholars from its founder William of Champeaux (fl. 1070–1121) to Walter of St. Victor (d. after 1180). Second, there were the cathedral schools such as Laon, Notre Dame, Reims, and Chartres, which likewise flourished when they could boast powerful and charismatic teachers.[7] Bernard of Chartres (c. 1060–c. 1124), to follow from the opening quotation, was known as the "Socrates of Gaul" on account of his learned classes, his wit and wisdom, and his ability to engage his students in a conversational manner (*collatio*) befitting their abilities.[8] Further afield, the cathedral schools of Bamberg and Würzburg were important centers of study as early as the eleventh century.[9] A third kind of school, less frequent and more ephemeral than the first two, was a private school individually established by a successful master. Peter Abelard did this more than once. While most of these schools were in northern Europe, mention should also be made of Toledo, where a distinguished and multiconfessional group of scholars copied, translated, and studied the philosophical and mathematical works from Greek and Arabic, translations that later travelled north and deeply impacted the schools and scholars in France and England.[10] Despite the diversity of these establishments and the differing interests and positions adopted by the various masters and their followers, the institutional character and overall environment of these schools were becoming distinctly "academic" in the modern sense of the term.[11] There was overlap in the subjects that were taught, exchange in the student and teacher personnel among these schools, and a general set of educative methods that everywhere prevailed. Nothing reflected this new period of learning more than the renewed focus on the seven liberal arts, depictions of which would grace the sculptures of cathedrals and the pages of illuminated manuscripts from the twelfth century onward (Figure 3).[12]

The division of the seven liberal arts was a classification that the scholars of the new schools consciously inherited from Boethius. His works of theology, philosophy, and logic were staples of the curriculum throughout the Middle Ages, but perhaps especially so at the turn of the twelfth century because of this renewed attention to the arts within these new schools. While there is ample evidence for the study of all the seven liberal arts, it was the language arts of the *trivium* (grammar, rhetoric, and dialectic) that most impacted the study of theology (a term also invented by Boethius, though this was not widely known at the time). The necessity of grammar as a basis of study was never under question, although it too seems to have been examined anew by various groups of thinkers (including Anselm) starting in the late eleventh century. The evidence for the teaching of rhetoric at this time is often difficult to interpret, but John O. Ward and others have argued convincingly for its study among the new schools of the early twelfth century.[13] Logic (or dialectic as it was more frequently called) is naturally the discipline that most contributed to the development of debate as a theory and practice. Overall, the turn of the twelfth century was marked by continuity in both the logical curriculum and its cathedral school setting, a curriculum composed primarily by Boethius's translation of Aristotle's *Categories* and *On Interpretation* (the so-called Old Logic), the *Isagoge* by Porphyry, and four works by Boethius himself. However, these texts were increasingly provoking new questions about the role of language itself, especially among the private masters who had greater range of freedom in the direction of their thought. This new "language-focused" logic departed from the concerns of earlier logicians and, in turn, produced distinct schools of thought as to the relation between words and things, most famously memorialized in the clash among

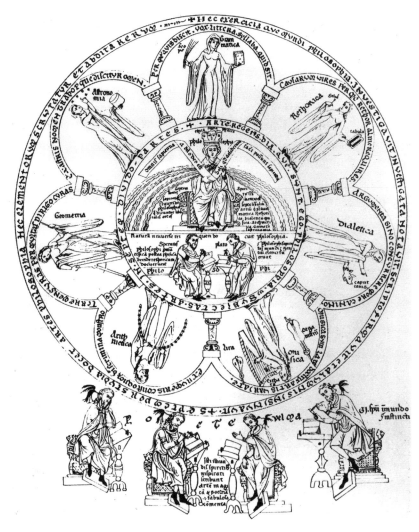

Figure 3. Personification of the Seven Liberal Arts. Logic had a privileged place in the medieval curriculum. In the middle an enthroned Philosophy is crowned by the faces of *ethica*, *logica* (the centerpiece), and *phisica*. She presides over Socrates and Plato, who are in the act of writing. The banner in her hand asserts the divine origins of all wisdom: "All wisdom is from the Lord God" (*Omnis sapientia a Domino Deo est*); and the freedom that comes with learning: "Only the wise are able to do what they desire" (*Soli quod desiderant facere possunt sapientes*). From the twelfth-century *Hortus deliciarum* by Herrad of Hohenbourg, now destroyed. Bridgeman Art Library, New York.

nominalists, realists, and vocalists (a sort of midway position between the first two ultimately espoused by Peter Abelard).[14] Many anonymous or unattributed commentaries on these texts have now been identified as critical to this new focus, but fundamental problems in sorting out the narrative of early twelfth-century logic remain. The business of knowing which text to associate with which school and which author to associate with which commentary remains one of the riskiest and most delicate tasks in medieval philosophy.[15] The highly technical nature of their chronology and attribution must be left to the experts. In focusing on the trees, however, it is important not to lose sight of the forest. The practice of disputation is a case in point, for it concerns not just the texts relative to the arts curriculum, but how teaching was conducted in the first place. Once again, it is the pedagogy of literary dialogue that informs our appreciation of classroom disputation within this new academic milieu. Its form and function must be evaluated.

## The Dialogue as Literary Genre

The clearest evidence that the dialogue genre underwent a regeneration during the period of the twelfth-century renaissance (for present purposes, c. 1075–1200) is numbers: fewer than ten dialogues can be counted in the century prior to Anselm of Canterbury's writings at Bec (1080s), but over eighty exist from Anselm's time to the close of the twelfth century.[16] These dates are admittedly arbitrary; the numbers are not. The authors of these dialogues and disputations are among the most important writers and thinkers of the twelfth century: Odo of Tournai, Rupert of Deutz, Hugh of St. Victor, Anselm of Havelberg, Aelred of Rievaulx, Adelard of Bath, Peter Alfonsi, Peter Abelard, Walter of Châtillon, Andreas Capellanus, Joachim of Fiore, and many others, including several anonymous authors. The quantity of dialogues written in the generations following Anselm and his circle reflects the success of new methods of writing and argumentation—the scholastic method, so called because of its association with the schools of the late eleventh and twelfth centuries.[17] In some sense, these figures are hardly surprising, since alongside the resurgence in dialogues there can, and should, be placed a concomitant growth in a number of other literary enterprises, such as letter writing, poetry, commentaries and glosses, sentences, and even history writing.[18] These genres offer points of comparison with, and important distinctions from, the dialogue.

Epistolary and verse writing have long histories. Their popularity from the early twelfth century onward gave rise to the *ars dictaminis* and the *ars poetriae*, instruction in the art of letter writing and verse writing, respectively. These became staples of the new liberal arts training.[19] In the twelfth century, the epistolary genre also yielded systematic and structured letter collections, and these could be at once intimate and entirely public. As John Cotts has recently argued for Peter of Blois, a clerical letter collection could comprise a diverse and dynamic textual community of school-trained intellectuals. More than a mere collection of letters between parties, the content and form of Peter's letter collection reveal the delicate coordination of professional, educational, and spiritual concerns of his broader public.[20] The commentary tradition is also ancient and emerges out of early Christian exegesis. From about 1100, it became increasingly connected to the rediscovery of ancient texts, for, in addition to commentaries on Scripture, twelfth-century authors also devoted much attention to commenting on Boethius, Porphyry, and Aristotle.[21] Closely related and difficult to distinguish from the commentaries are the glosses that likewise flourished in the twelfth century.[22] Glosses often resulted from a master's lectures given at a cathedral or monastic school.[23] Chronicles, foundation legends, and history writing more generally owe their success to the growth in literacy during this period, an emerging sense of a historical awareness, and the desire (perhaps need) to preserve in writing events and individuals deemed important to a specific place or country.[24] The Norman military achievements of the eleventh century and the crusades of the twelfth provided chroniclers with much to write about. Yet, unlike these important forms, whose purposes and audience are often more apparent if not explicit, there is no immediate explanation for the dialogue genre's sudden popularity during the last quarter of the eleventh century and the duration of the twelfth. No *ars dialogi* or *ars dialogica* as such existed during the Middle Ages comparable to the more familiar *ars dictaminis* or *ars poetriae*. Most of Plato's dialogues remained unknown and untranslated until their enthusiastic discovery (and recovery) by the humanists of the Quattrocento, and so could not have served as direct models.[25] And most twelfth-century dialogues or written disputations did not designate an intended recipient or audience, although some were indeed prefaced with an address. What did develop and eventually formalize in the schools and universities of the twelfth century was the practice, and later theory, of disputation.[26]

## Pedagogical Dialogue and Disputation

Many dialogues of the twelfth century follow in form and function the patterns established in the eleventh century and before. The theological nature of the dialogues of Anselm and his followers can readily be seen, later in the century, in Aelred of Rievaulx's *De spirituali amicitia* (c. 1158–63) and his *Dialogus de anima* (c. 1160) and Joachim of Fiore's *Dialogi de prescientia Dei et predestinatione electorum* (c. 1183–84). The Anselmian pedagogical influence extends to Latin dialogues that do not treat theological subjects.[27] In Conrad of Hirsau's (c. 1070–c.1150) *Dialogus super auctores*, for example, a teacher instructs an inquisitive pupil on how to approach and understand the works of twenty-one classical authors, among them Prudentius, Horace, Ovid, Homer, and Virgil.[28] This early contribution to the *accessus ad auctores* genre echoes in its opening paragraph the didactic program encountered in Anselm's dialogues, only here it is the student who opens the conversation, saying "the style of this long-awaited discourse must be carefully controlled so that the debtor discharges his debt more fully than is demanded of him. For thus, on the one hand, the teacher is better able to exercise his goodwill, while on the other, the slower partner, that is the learner, who is in dire need, is helped."[29] There is no mistaking the deliberate choice in proceeding to learn through dialogue, as the form once again aims to benefit persons of "slower" minds. Perhaps reflecting the educational opportunities of the early twelfth century, the pupil also cautions against the vainer reasons for deepening his training: "I am not so much jealous of your reputation (*fama*), which you have won by imparting sound teaching, as eager for my own advantage, being anxious to perfect my eloquence or my talent."[30] In another work by Conrad of Hirsau, the *Dialogus de mundi contemptu vel amore*, reason (*ratio*) and philosophical argumentation play a critical role in the dialogue between a monk and a cleric as they debate the sins of the world. The prologue to the *Dialogus* announces that the discussion will proceed through "alternating reasons" (*rationibus alternis*), giving a very scholastic flavor to an otherwise quite monastic work.[31]

Conrad of Hirsau is one of a number of contemporary authors whose original dialogues, new in content more so than form, offer intriguing glimpses into an increasingly oral and dialogic approach toward learning. The inquisitive student in search of answers can also be found in the dialogues of Adelard of Bath, whose *De eodem et diverso* and *Questiones naturales* offer detailed descriptions of the science and philosophy Adelard acquired on his travels to eastern lands and his encounter with Greek and Arab learning.[32] There is a playful and strikingly amicable tenor about these dialogues, for in both these works Adelard presents himself in conversation with his nephew, whose badgering questions, criticism, and curiosity of his uncle's travels abroad form the pretext for the ensuing discussions. While there is no sense of a debate beyond a friendly and affectionate discussion, it is curious that Adelard refers to the discussion in *Questiones naturales* as a "disputatio" and ends *De eodem et diverso* asking his nephew to "judge for yourself whether I have disputed rightly (*utrum recte disputaverim*)."[33] These two works (and a third dialogue with his nephew on hawking) are in form and structure rather straightforward examples of the student-teacher dialogue encountered earlier. What is novel and seemingly Anselmian is his vocabulary. So what does Adelard intend by "disputatio"?

In the opening exchange in *Questiones naturales*, Adelard reminds his nephew that seven years ago he and some other students had been sent to acquire learning in French schools (*in Gallicis studiis*) with a certain man of high reputation. Northern France in the early twelfth century boasted several centers of learning conceivably alluded to by Adelard where famous personalities and a commitment to the liberal arts (and especially dialectic) attracted students from near and far. Chartres and Laon are possible candidates.[34] So could be Bec, which, as we have already seen, produced a number of teachers of high reputation who taught through dialogue. The dialogue form that Adelard deliberately employs may itself reflect the dialectical procedures of these "French schools," just as his emphasis on reason (*ratio*) is clearly in line with the new currents in early twelfth-century thought.[35] Elsewhere, Adelard shows an even more deliberate sense of awareness in his choice of the dialogue form. In the dedicatory letter prefacing *De eodem et diverso*, Adelard instructs Bishop William of Syracuse "to prune away what is redundant and to rearrange what is badly ordered."[36] The speeches offered in the work are not mere recordings of an earlier conversation but seem intended for quotation and use in future debates about ancient learning. We might say that the dialogue was constructed as a sort of guidebook for future engagements in the topic. Similar motivations lie behind Adelard's verse introduction to *De avibus tractatus*, where he says to his nephew that anyone who is interested in the subject of hawking "and has this disputation in hand" can become expert.[37] "Disputation" must, therefore, mean something more than just a friendly but informed conversation, for Adelard seems to be referring both to the subject matter (hawking) and the method for imparting that subject (debate). It is precisely this relation between the dialogue as a literary form and disputation as a social practice, still flexible in Adelard's day, which will develop into something more stable over the succeeding decades. The level of controversy implied by the term "disputatio" will likewise gain precision as harder and riskier questions will be asked and rougher personalities will join the fray.

## The Reemergence of Public Debate

A transitional figure in the relation between dialogue and disputation is the Benedictine Abbot Rupert of Deutz (c. 1075–1129), the most prolific author of the twelfth century and a staunch defender of traditional monasticism.[38] In his effort to controvert what he saw as the intrusion of dialectic into the sphere of theological study, Rupert engaged in public disputes at Liège, Laon, and Châlons-sur-Marnes.[39] The topics of debate differed from one disputation to the next, but Rupert did not shrink from opportunities to face off with his adversaries who dismissed him on account of his ignorance of dialectic. One of Rupert's greatest enemies during these years was Anselm of Laon, with whom he never was able to dispute in person; he had to settle for other masters from Anselm's school. Rupert proudly recounts his combative position several years later in his apologetically written commentary on the Benedictine rule (c. 1125). He went to France, he says, in order to engage in a mighty battle of disputation (*praelium disputationis*) with those famous masters whose authority was always held over and against him.[40] Portraying himself as seated on a paltry ass, with only a servant boy to accompany him, Rupert combines the imagery of a lone protector of the faith with the vocabulary of feudal combat as he described his expedition to join battle (*ad conflictum*) in distant cities in France where a large band of masters and students, not unlike a sizeable army (*quasi non paruus exercitus*), met him in order to hear his arguments and defeat them. The fact that Rupert employed such colorful imagery is more than just rhetorical flourish. Peter Abelard used much the same language in his own autobiographical apology, the *Historia calamitatum*: "I preferred the weapons of dialectic to all the other teachings of philosophy, and armed with these I chose the conflicts of disputation (*conflictus pretuli disputationum*) instead of the trophies of war."[41] Abelard, of course, actually did come from knightly background and, when in Paris, he strove to use the tools of logic and the methods of dialectic in precisely the manner to which Rupert objected.

Not all instances of disputation emanated from classroom pedagogy or academic rivalry. A comparable description of disputation is given, but with a different purpose, by Herman-Judah (d. 1181), the Rhineland Jew turned Premonstratensian canon. His *Opusculum de conversione sua* is a rare (and still controversial) specimen of medieval autobiography.[42] In the second chapter of the *Opusculum*, when still a Jew, Herman states that the intense conversations (*confabulationibus*) that he heard among clerics compelled him to inquire into the sacraments of the Church. Listening in on these conversations led Herman to challenge the leading cleric of the day, Rupert of Deutz, to a public disputation: "He was subtle in temperament, learned in eloquence, and most accomplished in sacred as well as in human letters. I saw him and invited him to do battle in disputation (*ad disputationis invito conflictum*)."[43] Herman is not immediately converted by his alleged disputation with Rupert—it is the pious prayers of two women who finally bring about his conversion—but disputation remains a theme of his progression toward Christianity until finally he takes on the role of disputing his former coreligionists as a representative of Christianity. Thus, within a fifteen-year period (c. 1120–1135) three separate accounts describe open conflicts of disputation (two of them involving Rupert). The implication here is not that these texts are necessarily interrelated or that one author was echoing another (although the choice of Rupert as disputant in the *Opusculum* may well have to do with Rupert's self-described reputation for debate), but rather that these years represent above all a transitional moment in the growing intensity and importance of disputation as a method of argumentation and a weapon of polemic.

Rupert composed two dialogues in addition to his memorials of disputation and his countless exegetical commentaries. Not surprisingly, they both confirm his disputative reputation. The first of these dialogues, the *Altercatio monachi et clerici* (c. 1120–22), is a short debate between a monk and cleric over the right of monks to preach and teach publicly in the church.[44] It is both his best-known work and one of the most widely read of all the religious disputes that were written during this period.[45] In a refutation of this work written during the 1150s, the Premonstratensian Philip of Harvengt alleged that the *Altercatio* was based on an actual debate between Rupert and a cleric, but that Rupert had manipulated its outcome when composing it so as to make himself the victor.[46] To what extent the work reflects this alleged encounter we may never know, but the choice of form for its final presentation is undoubtedly deliberate. Rupert's second dialogue, the *Anulus sive Dialogus inter Christianum et Iudaeum* (1126), is even more interesting for its relation to disputation and debate during this critical decade.[47] Like so many of the other works of the Jewish-Christian controversy that take the literary form of a dialogue, the *Anulus* (Ring) features a Christian disputing with a Jew over the correct interpretation of Scripture. Among the topics that receive attention are Christian accusations of Jewish carnality and Jewish accusations of Christian idolatry. However, unlike a number of other Jewish-Christian dialogues, the *Anulus* does not purport to be the recorded account of an actual exchange. On the contrary, Rupert opens the *Anulus* by stating that Rudolph of St. Trond, a close friend of Rupert exiled in Cologne, commissioned the work. Rudolph in his own writings says that, while living in Cologne, he had frequently engaged in conversations and amicable discussions with local Jews, becoming so trusted by them that even their women were permitted to go and converse with him. It is noteworthy that this is the same Jewish community, and at the same approximate time, that Herman in his *Opusculum* professes to be from and where discussions he heard among Christian clerics prompted him to inquire further.[48] Rupert's *Anulus* is, thus, specifically written with future discussions in mind. Once again, we shall take note of the authorial intent, for, in the prologue to the work (which Rupert characterizes as a *disputatio*), he says that he has composed a work in the form of a dialogue so that it unfolds as a duel (*ut sub dialogo totum duellum procedat*) in the lone battles (*monomachia*) that Christians must wage against Jews.[49] Rupert further explains that such a work will be of use to the young soldier (*tirunculus*) who will need appropriate quotations from Scripture and all the other reasons (*omni ratione*) as he goes forth into battle (*conflictum*). This explicit combination of polemical intent and literary form certainly suggests that the concept of disputation carries a more forceful purpose for Rupert of Deutz than it had for earlier generations, but it is even more noteworthy for offering an explicit indication of why it as written in the form it was. The dialogue-disputation between Jew and Christian was not written as a record of an earlier debate but as an aide for future ones. This was already implied in the dialogues of Anselm and Adelard, but it becomes too frequent in the writings of Rupert and those who follow him to be read simply as a transcript of earlier debates. What we are starting to see is a move toward deliberate, preparatory debate beyond the classroom and into the broader culture at large, a theme that will be taken up at greater length in Chapters 5 and 6.

Rupert is exemplary of a new feudal-like deployment of combative disputation beyond the classroom, but the monastic pursuit of theological debate must not be ignored either, for it is also changing in the face of a new and disputative generation. This is notably the case with Hugh of St. Victor (c. 1096–1141), the most prolific and influential of the canons of St. Victor in Paris and one of the most important masters of the early twelfth century.[50] His celebrated *Didascalicon* (c. 1128) is a guide to the medieval arts and an elementary encyclopedia for approaching God and Christ, in which Hugh avoided controversial subjects and focused on what he took to be commonplaces of Catholic Christianity.[51] Considering the space allotted to the proper methods of teaching and learning the arts, it might seem surprising that Hugh does not devote a chapter to the practice of disputation itself. On the other hand, he readily concedes that "logical knowledge" (the fourth division of knowledge in Book I) is responsible for the art of speaking correctly and disputing effectively (*quae recte loquendi et acute disputandi scientiam praestat*).[52] His one genuine reference to academic disputation is made in passing and rather routinely:

> Later, when you have studied the arts and come to know by disputation and comparison (*disputando et conferendo*) what the proper concern of each of them is, then, at this stage, it will be fitting for you to bring the principles of each other's to bear upon all the others, and, by comparative and back-and-forth examination of the arts, to investigate the things in them which you did not well understand before.[53]

Hugh takes for granted the process of disputation (and back-and-forth examination), but as an element of logical analysis within the rigors of a monastic education. As he sees it, these arts are essential to full Christian understanding and are the only means of ensuring a command of the text adequate to justify using it as a basis for theological interpretation and the study of Scripture's allegorical sense.[54] But this use of disputation within the context of allegory and the *quadrivium* would seem a far cry from the debates of Rupert and Abelard. Was Hugh not also alarmed by the aggressively disputatious paths pursued his contemporaries? The later (and less studied) *Epitome Dindimi in Philosophiam* shows that he was. Framed as a dialogue between Sosthenes and Indaletius, one of two dialogues by Hugh that employ these characters (the other being *De Grammatica*), the *Epitome* offers a focused discussion (he calls it a *colloquium*) between a master and teacher on how philosophy has been corrupted by more modern practitioners of disputation. "In former times," Dindimus explains to his attentive pupil Sosthenes,

> seekers who did not know how to philosophize disputed about phi-
> losophy. Now another generation has succeeded them, and these do
> not even know for sure how one ought to conduct a dispute about
> philosophy. They have gone one step back from those who were
> already backward enough, in order to learn how to dispute about
> disputation, and they cannot figure out where to classify the very
> disputations about which they dispute. For if philosophy is an art,
> and to dispute about philosophy is an art, to what art do we leave it
> to dispute about disputations?[55]

Dindimus's warning to his student suggests that the rise and intrusion of disputation in the orderly world of learning did indeed trouble the Victorines. Hugh was certainly not alone in condemning excessive disputatiousness, but, in presenting his attack on scholastic disputation in the familiar form of a student-teacher dialogue, the *Epitome* nicely illustrates the pedagogical and subversive functions of the genre, again reminding us that a primary concern of twelfth-century authors is not *that* debate is taking place but *how* it should take place and for what purposes.

Hugh wrote other dialogues that take aim at contemporary society. In *De vanitate mundi* Reason and Soul meet to converse about problems that have arisen as a consequence of new trends in learning. Unnecessary disputations are once again in the background of this didactic dialogue. Soul thus says to Reason, "although what you say is much against my opinion, it could be that I am deceived, and that what you say is true. I want, therefore, to listen rather than to dispute."[56] What follows is a poignant critique of contemporary schoolroom practices. Reason pushes Soul to observe the world around them, and Soul responds:

> I can see a place of learning, full of pupils. There is a great throng,
> and I pick out men of different ages there, boys, lads, young men

and old, with differing pursuits as well. Some are learning to school their still unskilled tongues to new elements of speech and the formation of unfamiliar words, some are trying to learn the inflexions of words by first listening to their regular forms and their cases, and then putting them together and committing them to memory by repeating them over and over again. Others again, who with yet keener and livelier zest, seem to dispute on graver matters and try to trip each other with sophistry.[57]

One cannot help but hear the language-based logic of Peter Abelard murmuring in the background. The fact that scholastic disputation should feature so prominently in a dialogue on the vanities of the world tells us a great deal, not least about an emerging self-conscious distinction between monastic and scholastic pedagogical approaches. Another work by Hugh, *De arrha animae* (often translated as the *Soliloquy on the Earnest Money of the Soul*), is a spiritual dialogue that upholds the monastic commitment to disciplined, nondisputatious learning. It is framed as a friendly conversation (*amica confabulatione*) between Hugh and his own soul and is essentially a meditation upon the divine benevolence.[58] Written in the last years of his life (1139 seems most probable), it enjoyed a tremendous success, perhaps because of the very simplicity of its message.[59] In the tradition of Augustine and Anselm, Hugh understands and articulates the dialogic quality of meditation as a passageway to the deeper recesses of human emotions, "that you may learn where you should seek true love and how you ought to arouse in your hearts a desire for heavenly joys by zeal in spiritual meditations."[60] Hugh's exceptional range of works show how the inner spiritual dialogue that had survived from Augustine's day could join with a deeply mystical focus on love, all the while employing the philosophical arts as tools toward achieving that interiority. In the monastic tradition, two groups of theologians in the twelfth century initiated and conducted a movement of theological speculation on love: the Victorine school embodied by the writings of Hugh of St. Victor and the Cistercian school epitomized by Bernard of Clairvaux and William of St. Thierry.[61] In their efforts to redirect the spiritual concerns of their contemporaries, all three authors would have their turn critiquing the scholastic methods of their day, and this meant disputation. Hugh's critique was basically conservative and came in the form of the didactic, spiritual dialogue. The Cistercian critique would be ad hominem and public, a fitting reaction to twelfth-century Europe's most disputatious character.

## Peter Abelard and Disputation

Any discussion of the centrality of disputation in the twelfth century inevitably centers on that most charismatic and irredeemable figure, Peter Abelard (c. 1079–1142). Of the many adjectives that have been imputed to him, "disputatious" seems especially well merited. His own declarations in the beginning of his autobiographical *Historia calamitatum* invite the epithet: "I began traveling across several provinces disputing, like a true peripatetic philosopher, wherever I heard that the study of my chosen art most flourished."[62] Trading the court of Mars for the bosom of Minerva, he tells us in one of his most memorable turn of phrases, he relinquished the weapons and trophies of war to do battle in disputation (*conflictus pretuli disputationum*). That Abelard was argumentative, short-tempered, and even bellicose toward his intellectual rivals is a characterization that even Abelard would unlikely have contested.[63] The contumacious qualities of his tumultuous twelfth-century career have figured prominently in assessments of him by medieval and modern interpreters alike.[64] Yet the literalness of his disputatious career should not be given over entirely to the figurative image of a brilliant but cantankerous scholar who perpetually ran afoul of the authorities. Too often, the consequences of his actions and the sheer forcefulness of his personality have clouded our appreciation of his particular place in the development of scholastic disputation. It is his role as disputant, often relegated to a means to an end and not treated as a pedagogical practice itself, which forms the basis of the present discussion.

Abelard is no stranger to academic scrutiny.[65] The controversy he attracted because of his theological and nominalist positions, the peripatetic career he led as a private master in northern France, and the vivid details of his forbidden love affair with his pupil Heloise have sustained his reputation from medieval to modern times as the leading thinker, teacher, and paramour of the twelfth century—to say nothing of the ongoing debate concerning his putative coauthorship of the controversial *Epistola duorum amantium*.[66] He has long been heralded as a pioneer of the so-called "scholastic method" that pitted opposing arguments or conflicting statements against one another, that is, pro and contra.[67] For this, it is common to point to his *Sic et non* where he famously placed opposing and seemingly incompatible statements from scriptural and patristic authorities side by side, much to the consternation of ecclesiastical authorities such as Bernard of Clairvaux.[68] In the preface to this work, Abelard articulates his famous dictum that "by doubting we come to question, and by questioning we arrive at truth," a phrase that is sometimes confused for an expression of theological uncertainty or skepticism.[69] More likely, the conflicting texts were presented in a systematic fashion to stimulate reflection and debate on the points at issue.

Abelard is also the author of a celebrated dialogue, the *Collationes*, sometimes misleadingly retitled the *Dialogue Between a Christian, a Philosopher, and Jew*. While the literary merits of the work have not gone unnoticed (it in fact consists of two dialogues set in a dream: the first between the Philosopher and a Jew and the second between that same Philosopher and the Christian), the *Collationes* has traditionally been examined in either the context of his ethical writings or in the context of Jewish-Christian relations, both areas in which Abelard made original contributions.[70] The enigmatic dialogue is, nevertheless, fully consistent with his overall hermeneutical strategy, for, as he says in the preface, "no debate is so frivolous that it does not teach us something."[71] The virtue of *disputatio* is a recurrent theme as the dialogue progresses from theological to ethical considerations. A second dialogue is the short *Soliloquium*, in which he presents an imaginary dialogue between his two selves, "Peter" and "Abelard."[72] Unlike Augustine's *Soliloquia*, on which it is loosely modeled, Abelard does not offer an examination of his self but instead presents a theoretical conversation on the love of wisdom and the meaning of the name of Christ.[73] In both dialogues, an even exchange between the participants is imagined—that is, they do not purport to be real encounters—and the reader is showed the dialectical path to deeper truth. The *Sic et non*, the *Collationes*, and the *Soliloquium* all reveal something of Abelard's propensity for philosophical debate and critical inquiry, but the crux of Abelard's contribution to the emerging art of disputation neither begins nor ends with these celebrated works.[74] To best appreciate Abelard's overall engagement with scholastic disputation, it is necessary to take stock of his other writings as well, to consider his always deliberate choice of language, and to situate his writings and vocabulary in the wider intellectual context of his contemporaries and adversaries.

It is well known that Abelard thought very highly of his intellectual abilities. It is especially his ability to out-perform his opponents in classroom and public disputation that he chooses to emphasize in his moralizing autobiography. When forced to leave Paris early in his career because of one master's jealousy, Abelard set up a school in Melun where he built his fame as a teacher of dialectic: "Consequently my self-confidence rose still higher, and I hurried to transfer my school to Corbeil, a town closer to Paris, so that I could assault him through more frequent encounters in disputation."[75] Disputation provided Abelard with an instrument of revenge, but it could also serve him as he went on the offensive. When Abelard famously contested his teacher William of Champeaux on the question of universals some years later, it was "in the course of our debates" (*disputationum nostrarum*) that he was able to force William to modify his position, thus humiliating him and destroying his reputation.[76] This belligerent display of dialectical skill contributed to his notoriety and would prove to be a pattern in his career. A later disagreement with another former teacher, Roscelin of Compiègne, over the nature of the Trinity, and specifically over an early version of Abelard's theological treatise, the *Theologia summi boni* (c. 1118), led to a condemnation at the Council of Soissons in 1121, the first of two ecclesiastical condemnations in his career. Roscelin did not live to see his former student turned opponent condemned and his book burnt, but, in the years leading up to the council, Abelard attempted to settle the matter in the manner he knew best: through public disputation. Sometime prior to the Council of Soissons, Abelard sent a letter to Bishop Gilbert and the clergy of Paris (now known as Epistle 14) requesting that a public debate be organized in front of witnesses, the intent of which, presumably, was to secure victory and inflict another humiliation in a verbal contest.[77] This time the ploy did not work out in Abelard's favor, since Gilbert considered the dispute too serious a matter for his diocese and remitted it to the papal legate, who promptly put Abelard, and Abelard alone, on trial at Soissons.[78]

If Abelard was so predisposed to debating his teachers, it must follow that this is how he conducted himself in his classroom. The first part of his teaching career (c. 1102–17) was almost exclusively devoted to the study of logic, when he was a private master successively at Melun, Corbeil, and Mount Sainte Geneviève, culminating in his appointment as master of the cathedral school of Notre Dame in Paris. The content of his lectures during these early years is preserved in his detailed logical works as well as in some unattributed twelfth-century commentaries on the Old Logic that likewise seem to preserve the records of Abelard's teachings.[79] Four logical treatises survive whose attribution to Abelard is certain: the *Logica ingredientibus*, the *Dialectica* (a lengthy textbook that scholars now date to c. 1116–18), the *Tractatus de intellectibus*, and the *Logica nostrorum petitioni*.[80] The opening line of the fourth of these works announces its purpose clearly: "At the request of my fellows (*nostrorum petitioni socii*) I have undertaken the labor of writing logic, and in accord with their wishes I shall expound what I have taught about logic."[81] The logic that Abelard was concerned with is what we would today classify as ontology or philosophical semantics. In what is presumed to be the first of these four works, the "Logic for Beginners," Abelard defines logic as the art of judging and discriminating between valid and invalid arguments or inferences. The ancient theory of topics, as transmitted by Boethius's *De topicis differentiis*, had been concerned with finding rhetorically convincing rather than irrefutable arguments. Abelard wishes to use the theory to explore the conditions for logically valid reasoning in all its forms. He does not restrict inferences to syllogisms, but instead is interested in a more general notion of consequence, a problem grounded in his reading of Boethius. The fundamental problem for Abelard is identifying the conditions under which one proposition follows from another.

The *Dialectica* offers the lengthiest and most complete treatment of logical consequences. The novelty of his arguments has been much analyzed. Interspersed within the work are numerous polemical references to the statements of his contemporaries that would seem to derive from the argumentative form of oral disputations. Here, for instance, is an attack on his former teacher William of Champeaux on infinitizing expressions:

> It is customary to ask why Aristotle did not mention infinite expressions here, since such expressions are often formed. . . . Some hold that Aristotle is concerned here only to demonstrate the formation of simple assertions. Others will in no way concede that an expression may be infinitized, with whom, I recall (*memini*), master V. agreed. And indeed he denied this not so much with respect to sense as with respect to the nature of the construction. You will find his weak and false account of the conjunction of words in his *Glossulis super periermenias.*[82]

Many passages of the *Dialectica* evoke the statements, the beliefs, and the positions of others who spoke (*decebat*) or whom Abelard heard or remembered (*memini*). They hearken back to the debates of his student days while simultaneously suggesting an oral delivery in the form of questions and answers characteristic of a teacher's disputation. Throughout the treatise, a position held by one disputant is shown, through a series of formal steps, to entail an obviously false conclusion. The designation "textbook" frequently given to this work belies the fact that this was equally a work of polemic. The prologue to the fourth and final book of the *Dialectica* is, among other things, an explicit defense against "the malicious new charge concerning my writing on logic which has been made against me by those who are envious of me," a clear reference to his earlier logical works and an accusation that is also central to his autobiography.[83]

There are other reasons to suspect that the *Dialectica* preserves his classroom debates, or at any rate his notes on these debates. There are inconsistencies in the arrangement of material. At one point Abelard makes reference to a position mentioned above (*ut supra meminimus*) when there has, in fact, been no allusion to this position before then. At another point, he makes reference to indirect and direct contraries as if the distinction had been explained, which it is not until later.[84] And on at least one occasion, he refers back to his earliest "introduction" on logic as an "altercation" (*altercatione*), again underlying the oral and disputative delivery of his teachings.[85]

There is still the question of what Abelard's classroom looked and sounded like. The *Dialectica* and his other logical commentaries preserve his own formal logic by means of enumerating the positions that he sought to defeat, but they do not give much sense of how his disputations may have unfolded in the classroom. Perhaps the most explicit evocation of the give-and-take of Abelard's classroom is given not in Abelard's works but in the hagiographical *Vita prima Gosvini* (c. 1173) that vividly describes how St. Goswin of Anchin (d. 1166) disputed with Abelard during his teaching days at Mount Sainte Geneviève (c. 1110). The *Vita* was written down by a fellow monk who knew Goswin personally, and it recounts how Goswin studied grammar and dialectic in his native Douai, moved to Paris to attend the classes of several erudite scholars (*quamplures eruditissimi*), and then returned to his native city. There, disillusioned by the academic lifestyle, he converted to the monastic life. The description of Paris in the age of Abelard reads like a formal rebuttal to the *Dialectica*:

> At that time Peter Abelard, having gathered around him many students, was leading a public school [that is, open to other religious orders] in the cloister of Sainte Geneviève. His knowledge was well tested and his eloquence sublime, but he was the inventor of strange and unheard of things and asserted entirely novel claims, and in order to establish his own theories he set out to disprove what others had proved. Thus he came to be hated by those of saner mind, and just as he turned his hand against everyone, so everyone took up arms against him. He said what no one had before him presumed to

say and amazed everyone. So when the absurdity of his inventions came to the notice of those who were involved in teaching in Paris, they were first stunned, then gripped with a great zeal to confute his falsities, and began to ask one another who among them would undertake the business of disputing him (*ex eis aduersus eum disputandi negitium subiturus*).[86]

The fact that the account stresses both the novelty of Abelard's teachings and the need for him to be dismantled through disputation makes it all the more tantalizing that Goswin's biographer is giving us a deliberate counterthesis to Abelard's autobiography. On account of his talent and readiness for the task, Goswin is chosen by his companions to take up the challenge of disputing Abelard. First, however, he receives advice from Master Jocelin, the future bishop of Soissons. Jocelin opposes the idea of a confrontation telling Goswin that Abelard is "not a debater but a sophist" (*disputatorem non esse, sed cauillatorem*) and that he "acts more like a jester than a doctor" (*agere ioculatoris quam doctoris*).[87] The terminology calls attention to the farcical element of debate. If an anonymous logical commentary from the early twelfth does reflect Abelard's classroom discussions, as some scholars believe, then its vernacular jokes and vulgar language would confirm his reputation for classroom amusement.[88] Despite his respect for Jocelin and his advice, Goswin sets out in youthful exuberance to Abelard's school, taking several of his companions with him. The encounter that follows makes for one of the most compelling episodes in twelfth-century intellectual history:

> Upon arriving at the place of combat, in other words the entryway to his [Abelard's] school, he found him lecturing and inculcating his novelties to his students. As soon as he was there he began to speak, and he [Abelard] gave him scornful looks. A warrior from his youth, and seeing that the newcomer was just starting to grow a beard, he disdained him in his heart, no less than the Philistine did David. He [Goswin] was indeed of fair and handsome appearance, though of moderate height and weight. But the egotist was forced to respond to his pressing assailant: "Keep quiet and be careful not to disturb the course of my lesson (*lectionis*)." But he had not come there to be quiet and so he fiercely persisted. Meanwhile his adversary, holding him in disdain, paid no attention to the words that were being uttered, judging it undignified that so great a professor should

answer to such a puny youth. But he was judging him on appearance, finding him contemptible on account of his age, and he did not take notice of the perceptive intelligence of his heart. But his disciples knew this young man well, and, so that he would not fail to give an answer, told him that he [Goswin] was a sharp debater supported by great learning (*disputatorem acutum et multum ei scientae suffragari*), and that it was not dishonorable to take on the business of disputing someone like him, whereas it was most dishonorable to continue refusing. "So let him speak up," said [Abelard], "if he has something to say." Speaking his mind, he [Goswin] asserted propositions so competently that they exuded neither levity nor garrulous verbosity, and on account of their depth they drew the attention of all who were listening: the one assumed, the other affirmed, the former unable to respond to the affirmations of the latter. As those games of sophistry were shut off by the one who knew nothing of these cunning tricks, he [Abelard] was finally forced to admit that he was not in accord with reason.[89]

The *Vita* of Goswin would seem to be not only a rebuttal of Abelard's self-image but a most revealing glimpse into the confrontational character of early twelfth-century teaching. Of course, the content of the disputation is never actually given. Either this is because it eluded the hagiographer or, more likely, because it was deemed unimportant to the narrative, which after all goes on to stress Goswin's turn away from the vainglories of the classroom and toward the solitude of monastic life. What is clear, if the account is taken at face value, is that Abelard's classroom sessions (*lectiones*) were just as disputational as any other facet of his turbulent life. The *Vita* goes on to describe the saintly life that Goswin led as a monk at Anchin and the illustrious personalities that he shared company with, including two popes and Bernard of Clairvaux.

Abelard's most serious battle was with the Cistercian reformer Bernard of Clairvaux (1090–1153) and his powerful entourage, most notably William of St. Thierry. The numerous events and points of contention that punctuated Abelard's increasingly hostile relationship with the church have been told many times before.[90] What needs emphasis is the manner in which disputation literally, and literarily, framed this conflict. Sometime between 1138 and 1139, William of St. Thierry contacted Bernard to solicit his aid in reprimanding Abelard for asserting what he believed to be doctrinal errors. As an abbot in Reims and a former cathedral school student, William would have long been aware of Abelard and his teachings. It has even been suggested that William and Abelard met while students at Laon, although this cannot be confirmed.[91] In any event, it was following his conversion to the Cistercian order around 1134 or 1135 that William first became preoccupied with Abelard's teachings, and particularly his disputatious method of handling Scripture. His course of action was to compose a treatise detailing the heresies of which Abelard was guilty. The result was the *Disputatio adversus Petrum Abaelardum*—the title is significant—and it was sent to both the bishop of Chartres and Bernard of Clairvaux. Accompanying the *Disputatio* was a letter requesting that action be taken against Abelard and copies of two of Abelard's book, his *Theologia* and his *Liber sententiarum*, the records of his teachings. While William was above all concerned with the theological and doctrinal positions that Abelard was allegedly disseminating to his captive audiences, it is also clear that he was disturbed by Abelard's method of shamelessly questioning authorities and pointing out existing contradictions among them, a method exemplified by his *Sic et non*, to which William also makes reference.[92] "Truly that man," William wrote of Abelard, "loves to question everything, wants to dispute everything, divine as well as secular."[93] Not to be ignored is William's own strategy to controvert Abelard. In composing his *Disputatio*, William adopted the very method of argument and counterargument, thus giving Abelard, mutatis mutandis, a taste of his own medicine. Offending passages from Abelard's writings are quoted and followed by opposing passages from Scripture and church authorities. This, of course, is precisely the method that Abelard used in his *Sic et non*, and, judging from Abelard's logical works, it seems reasonable to assume this was also the pedagogical method recorded in his *Liber sententiarum*.[94]

If William thought it clever to use Abelard's disputational method against him, he was not alone. Thomas of Morigny, also a former friend of Abelard, lists fourteen heresies supposedly perpetrated by Abelard in his own *Capitula haeresum XIV*, which includes quotations from the same works cited by William of St. Thierry.[95] Like William, Thomas also eschews the straight format of the treatise and proceeds by supplying counterarguments to the statements of Abelard. Whether Bernard commissioned the work from Thomas after having received William's *Disputatio* and copies of Abelard's books or whether Thomas wrote his list independently remains uncertain. What is known is that Bernard drew heavily from both these works in drafting his own letter to the papal curia condemning Abelard. Yet another work attacking Abelard, probably also by Thomas of Morigny, can be included among the polemical tracts that use the title and procedures of scholastic disputation. Written within a year after the trial of Sens (1141), this *Disputatio catholicorum patrum adversus dogmata Petri Abaelardi* took aim at Abelard's own postcouncil *Apologia* and the third version of his theological treatise, the *Theologia scholarium*.[96] Here Thomas, if he was indeed the author, was less interested in reviewing Abelard's doctrinal and methodological errors. He sought instead to show through argument and counterargument that Abelard's *Apologia* was an unconvincing attempt to demonstrate his orthodoxy and that (most damningly of all) he had treated the attributes of God not catholically but philosophically (*non tam catholice quam philosophice*). Like William of St Thierry before him, Thomas of Morigny is employing the same strategy of quoting Abelard's sources against him, the same literary formula of composing a disputation, and the same essential commitment to making full use of the tools of rhetoric and dialectic in a polemical assault. These anti-Abelardian disputations are decidedly not original in their conception or execution; they are noteworthy precisely because they signal the pervasive use of scholastic *disputatio* even among those who seek to limit its use. As such, they remind us that it is the improper application of disputation that is being objected to rather than the employment of dialectical reasoning itself.

Bernard of Clairvaux was the central figure in the literary and ecclesiastical campaign against Abelard, particularly during the second half of Abelard's career. Although Bernard had known of Abelard for some time, his correspondence and subsequent meetings with William of St. Thierry seem to mark the turning point in his efforts to silence him.[97] What is more, the ensuing controversy that led to Abelard's condemnation at Sens in 1141 had apparently as much to do with Abelard's overall approach to knowledge of faith, an approach that placed logic and disputation at its center, as with the doctrinal mistakes Abelard was accused of committing.[98] Bernard's first step was to alert the archbishop of Sens and the bishop of Paris in the hope that an order would be issued preventing Abelard from teaching. Neither official, however, was willing to intervene in the matter. Bernard then wrote a long and now famous letter-treatise to the papal curia detailing Abelard's errors, but this proved scarcely more effective, since Abelard's supporters included members of the papal curia itself.[99] True to form, and in a nearly exact repetition of the earlier incident at Soissons in 1121, it was Abelard who escalated the affair by writing to Rome in the hope of setting up a public disputation, in Abelard's mind the ideal opportunity for the two adversaries to confront one another and one in which Abelard must surely, and no doubt correctly, have seen himself as the clear favorite.[100]

There were good reasons for Abelard to play to the masses. The many students he had won over in the intervening years would surely have produced for him a solid base of support, as the *Vita* of Goswin suggests. The desire for the encounter to be a public event is repeated in a letter addressed "to his most beloved comrades" that Abelard circulated in the run-up to Sens and in which he requests their presence at the eventual encounter.[101] It is hard to know from this letter alone what exactly Abelard expected from this meeting. His earlier attempt to produce a similar encounter had, of course, failed. Nevertheless, the desire for his students and friends to be present suggests some level of active participation from the crowd and the public nature of this would-be debate anticipates the performance elements of the quodlibetical debates that do indeed grow out of this scholastic environment, as we shall see in Chapter 5. Other sources make similar implications. It was a chief complaint of the bishops of France in their letter to Pope Innocent II that "throughout France, in cities, villages and castles, the doctrine of the Trinity is being argued about not only by scholars and within the schools, but casually (*triviatim*), by everyone."[102]

Bernard declined to go up against Abelard in such a setting, positioning sacred truth as the antithesis of bellicose argumentation. "I refused," Bernard explains in another letter to Pope Innocent, "because I am but a child in this sort of warfare and he is a man habituated to it from his youth, and because I believed it an unworthy deed to bring faith into the arena of controversy, resting as it does on sure and immutable truth."[103] Bernard knew, or knew well of, Abelard's debating abilities, and he was ready to admit that he was not up to the task of disputing with the leading master in Paris, who was also several years his senior.[104] Bernard was also making explicit for the first time his position that disputation represents an inappropriate method of instruction in the study of Christian doctrine. On this point there is no reason to believe that Bernard's discomfort began with the controversy over Abelard or ended with the latter's condemnation at Sens. Jacques de Vitry (c. 1160–1240) in one of his sermons to scholars tells a story about Bernard's shock on hearing his first scholastic disputation in Paris.[105] This shock need not necessarily suggest the radical dichotomy between scholastic and monastic circles that is often used to differentiate the two men and their circles. Suspicious intrigue might be more exact, for, in one of his early treatises, *De gradibus humilitatis et superbiae* (c. 1125), Bernard had actually attempted to proceed using the fashionable disputation of scholastic reasoning, and the result was hardly successful. Bernard did not pause to verify the quotation on which he based his argument. "I tried to prove the whole sequence of disputation from the basis of a false quotation," he later explained, surely with some embarrassment.[106] Realizing his error, Bernard wrote a *Retractatio* that was to be placed in front of the work in all future copies. This failed attempt to construct an argument along scholastic lines may well have been in the back of Bernard's mind when he preempted the debate by delivering his objections to the bishops the night before, in addition to his resistance to debating matters of faith on principle. The encounter therefore never took place, and at Sens in May 1141 Abelard was condemned to silence all the same.[107]

Abelard's career was punctuated with successful and unconsummated attempts at public disputation, but did Abelard himself have a coherent vision of the value and purpose of disputation? In the prefaces to the *Sic et non* and the *Collationes*, Abelard clearly indicates that there is great value in questioning and debating because it allows one to perceive a greater truth, although in neither case is the final solution given. In his *Dialectica* he claims that dialectic is the discipline "to which all judgment of truth and falsehood is subject" and that it holds "the leadership of all philosophy and the governance of all teaching."[108] An obvious and inherent danger in the way he applies dialectic against his enemies is that the establishment of "truth" itself will be conditioned by the debaters themselves rather than by doctrine. It is a charge he would face multiple times in his career. Abelard's most deliberate statement on the value of open debate instead comes from one of the most polemical treatises that emanated from his characteristically poisonous quill.[109] Coyly addressed "to an ignoramus in Dialectic"—little imagination is required to guess at the unidentified recipient(s)—Epistle 13 offers a passionate defense of logical disputation and a blistering attack against such a person who could be so ignorant as to misunderstand its true aims. Dated by most scholars to between 1130 and 1132, the broadside would seem to anticipate his reentry into academic life in Paris (c. 1132) after a hiatus of over ten years.[110] For perhaps just that reason, it contains the most detailed explanation of Abelard's theory of disputation. "Certain teachers of our own time," he opens thunderously, "since they cannot attain the capacity of dialectical reasoning, curse it in such a way that they reckon all its teachings to be sophisms and deceptions rather than consider them to be forms of reason."[111] The accusation that Abelard alludes to is familiar and has already been encountered in the writings of his contemporaries. Abelard aims to show not only that the art of dialectic is not contrary to sacred Scripture but also that it is in fact explicitly endorsed by the church fathers. First among his *auctoritates* is Augustine, and he quotes from both *De ordine* (2.13) and *De doctrina Christiana* (2.31) on the utility of disputation and particularly its ability to delve into and resolve the various questions that arise from the study of Scripture.[112] The distinction between dialectic and sophistry, Abelard maintains, is that the former consists of the truth of reasoning, while the latter consists of the appearance of such truth.[113] Second among his *auctoritates* is "the very prince of the Peripatetics," Aristotle himself. Abelard invokes the *Sophistical Refutations* as a treatise on the art of dialectic, but he is unable to cite from the text itself, most probably because the text was not yet available to him in its entirety and his knowledge of its content was still secondhand.[114] Further citations from Augustine and Jerome center on the necessity to combat falsehoods and heresy, for "the doctors of the Church themselves also remind us to train in disputations (*in disputationibus exercere*) against this plague."[115] Maintaining that the training in dialectic offers much more than mere academic exercise for sharpening the mind and insisting that it possesses true value for the diligent faithful, Abelard draws a remarkable conclusion: "For we are not equipped to rebut the attacks of heretics or of any infidels whatsoever, unless we are able to unravel their disputations and to rebut their sophisms with true reasoning. . . . when we have refuted those sophists in this disputation, we will display ourselves as dialecticians, and we will be truer disciples of Christ."[116]

Again resorting to offense as his best defense, Abelard essentially reverses the accusations that disputation and sophistry are useless deceptions indistinguishable from one another by maintaining the unique value of disputation. Mastery of disputation, it would seem, produces nothing less than true Christian knowledge. This statement pushes significantly further his general claims about the superiority of dialectic made in the prologue to the fourth tract of his *Dialectica*. Moreover, Abelard appears to be advancing an idea not heard since Late Antiquity, namely, that disputation has a value in promoting orthodox belief against heretics and infidels. "To come to the point," Abelard says with more than a hint of aggravation, "who would not know the art of disputation (*artem disputandi*), by which term it is established that dialecticians as well as sophists are known without distinction?"[117] Both the utility and the definable scope of disputation are to Abelard self-evident. He uses the words *ars* and *scientia* interchangeably.

Several things are striking in Abelard's tendentious yet shrewdly constructed letter to an ignoramus in dialectic. While he articulates the merits of
logic in his longer opus *Dialectica*, and quotes Augustine on the value of
disputation elsewhere in his theological works, the apologetic tenor of this
letter reminds us that it is *method* as much as *content* that he so wishes to
defend. In referencing but not quoting from Aristotle's New Logic when
searching for authorities to rely on, Abelard shows himself to be on the cusp
of a new chapter in the intellectual and cultural history of disputation, for
the texts that are not yet available to him will in fact be widely used by the
following generation of schoolmen (like John of Salisbury, discussed in Chapter 4) for whom disputation will need less defending but more defining.[118]
The missionary purpose that he cites in the letter for mastering disputation
may serve him rhetorically in his epistolary counteroffensive, but it also anticipates the Dominican use of disputation in the thirteenth century when mendicant preachers went from town to town disputing openly with heretics and
made disputation a formal component of their training exercises.

If Abelard's letter is primarily concerned with defending the merits of
disputation on theological grounds, he is also attuned to its distinct relevance
on another topic of great currency in the early twelfth century: the Jewish
question.[119] While often overlooked by scholars interested in Abelard's ideas
about the Jews, the final paragraphs of his letter clearly orient disputation in
the direction of the Jewish-Christian controversy:

> To come to the point, who could not know that even the Lord Jesus
> Christ himself refuted the Jews in repeated disputations (*crebris dis-
> putationibus*) and crushed their slanders in writing as well as in rea-
> soning (*tam scripto quam ratione*), that he increased the faith very
> much not only by the power of miracles but also by the strength of
> words? . . . Since, however, miraculous signs have now run short,
> one means of combat remains to us against any people who contra-
> dict us: that we may overcome with words, because we cannot do so
> through deeds.[120]

It may be more than coincidence that the date of this letter (c. 1131) is roughly
contemporary with his *Collationes* (now placed between 1127 and 1132).[121]
Both give careful consideration to the Jewish-Christian debate, and both
underscore the fact that in the twelfth century it was precisely that: a debate,

both literally and metaphorically a disputation. Many Jewish-Christian dialogues were written in the twelfth century, and many of them under the explicit rubric of a *disputatio*.[122] Obvious though it may be, this point is worth emphasizing. What population could be more directly implicated by the dialogical and disputational format of logical argumentation than the very neighboring communities who likewise profess adherence to God's law, are themselves the living letters of that law (in Augustine's words), and yet refuse to accept the very premise of Christian doctrine?[123] Since Jesus himself disputed with Jews and miraculous signs now are few, Abelard concludes, it is fully consistent that this same classroom exercise that probes for deeper truth be applied to incredulous Jews. This move toward a public demonstration of error through disputation will have immense consequences for long-term Jewish-Christian relations, as we shall see in Chapter 6.

The wholesale merits of disputation for Abelard, therefore, are three: it promotes a greater understanding of Scripture and of the Christian faith as warranted by the fathers; it equips one for rebuttals against heretics and infidels; and, because miraculous signs can no longer be counted on, it serves as an essential weapon in debating with Jews, the Christian dialogical "other" par excellence. This final point can be further refined in light of the *Collationes*, which echoes via a dream vision the theoretical basis for disputing with Jews and Christians. The virtue of disputation above and beyond the presentation of authorities is explicitly made by the Christian in his *collatio* with the Philosopher, and with language that anticipates the university curriculum: "Debate, both about texts and about views, makes itself a part of every discipline, and in every clash of disputation (*in quolibet disputationis conflictu*) truth established by reasoning is more solid than the display of authority."[124] Elsewhere Abelard notes that the discipline of disputation (*disputationis disciplina*) is of great value for every sort of question that has to be delved into arising from Scripture. The idea that disputation will serve different ends depending on their contexts is underscored in the second dialogue of the *Collationes*, where the Christian says to the Philosopher that they must conduct their dispute differently from the way he and his fellow Christian colleagues would dispute together.[125] The Christian and the Philosopher of the *Collationes* both agree that there is nothing to be gained by squabbling in a childish and uncivil shouting match: "Our concern is entirely that of enquiring for the truth . . . from time to time, it is permitted to grant what is false for the sake of going on with the argument."[126] And so, throughout the opus,

Abelard returns to the form and function of disputation, matching theory with practice in the literary form of a dialogue.

Several related conclusions emerge from Abelard's involvement with disputation. First, he consistently projected disputation onto his intellectual battles. By this we do not simply mean that he belligerently fought to assert his interpretations over others; he memorializes his clashes with his former teachers in the context of classroom debates, and he twice strove to set up public disputations with Bernard of Clairvaux, positioning his *sic* to Bernard's *non*. Second, Abelard's originality in regard to medieval *disputatio* and the scholastic method needs to be restated. He was neither the originator of scholastic disputations nor a promoter of modern skepticism. To the contrary, Abelard thrived and failed in an age of widespread disputes, was himself the target of at least two literary *disputationes*, and had a firm sense that disputation could powerfully effect a Christian's grasp of the truth and an unbeliever's grasp of Christianity. As such, Abelard articulates the essence of his agenda in places where we perhaps least expect it: not in the preface to his *Sic et non*, which relates more properly to the notion of discordant harmonies, nor in his treatise *Dialectica*, which discusses problems of language and logic, but in his later letter to an ignoramus in dialectic and in his *Collationes*, which offer theoretical and practical applications of the techniques for disputation. To be sure, the *Collationes* is ultimately concerned with ethical matters (notably how to achieve the highest good), but this is only arrived at following a shrewd orchestration of the "art" or "discipline" of disputation in which all sides can be heard and evaluated. The absence of a final conclusion may be accounted for because it was intended to be completed at a later date, as its recent editors suggest, but it may equally have been intended that way so as to emphasize the principle that arguments (rather than conclusions) promote true knowledge. Finally, Abelard's engagement with nonbelievers can be further refined. Abelard clearly views disputation as a valuable weapon when confronting infidels, heretics, and Jews, for it can serve polemically and persuasively to demonstrate actively religious falsehood. This is fully consistent with Abelard's chief authority, Augustine, who triumphed in both his antiheretical disputations and in his authorship of dialogues. Abelard may well have seen himself as a new Augustine: master rhetorician and dialectician, unrivaled disputant in the classroom, dutiful expositor of Christian theology, and champion of a philosophical Christianity in the face of heretics, unconverted Jews, and unlettered ignoramuses.

## The Revival of Roman Law

Abelard is paradigmatic of a new intellectual scene in which dialectic and classroom disputation emerged as the characteristic form of intellectual exchange. It is important to stress that his role as the most famous itinerant debater of his day was not only impossible one century earlier, but probably not possible one century later either, when the institutional structure of the university would have limited his ability to navigate between formal and informal institutions. A crucial parallel context for examining the rise of disputation in twelfth-century schools is the revival of Roman law, which occurred first in northern Italy and eventually in France as well. Because the systematic study of law often centered on a question-and-answer format to legal disputes and the harmonizing of conflicting interpretations, the canonists and lawyers who pioneered this revival offer an equally important preuniversity context for examining the scholastic practice of disputation.

A venerable scholarly tradition holds that the revival of Roman law began with the founding of a "law school" at Bologna at the turn of the twelfth century by a certain Irnerius (c. 1055–c. 1130).[127] The extent of Irnerius's school at Bologna has, however, been challenged, notably by Anders Winroth's demonstration that Gratian's *Decretum* was, in fact, the product of later accretions (c. 1150) to an original text.[128] This discovery carries the implication that much of the early tradition of jurisprudence in Bologna has been exaggerated and that any law school properly speaking originated not before the 1130s. In other words, developments in the study of law were subsequent to many of the developments in theology and the liberal arts. Nevertheless, there are good reasons to view the revival of Roman law in parallel to the earliest innovations of the twelfth-century renaissance. Even if the systematic teaching of Roman law did not begin before the middle decades of the twelfth century, it is also clear that the recovery of the juristic learning embodied in Justinian's sixth-century *Digest* came as an especially powerful, "almost intoxicating," revelation to Western jurists in the late eleventh century.[129] The ramifications of this recovery were far-reaching. Much like the recovery of Aristotle's New Logic would transform medieval logic, the intricacy and ingenuity of the legal reasoning in the *Digest* attracted and transformed the minds of those who were familiar with legal problems. From the significant portions of the *Digest* that were made available, medieval jurists learned how to frame sophisticated legal arguments, how to manipulate legal categories, how to analyze problems, and how to find solutions to apparently contradictory opinions.[130] Naturally enough, the systematic study of canon law often centered on a question-and-answer format to legal disputes and the harmonizing of conflicting interpretations.[131] In time, the *quaestiones disputatae* of the glossators (or commentators) of the law would become an established genre within the legal literature.[132] The dialectical procedures of the lawyers, thus, need to be seen alongside the parallel developments in theology, regardless of exactly how early they began.

A significant figure in promoting the new methods for reconciling conflicting texts was Bishop Ivo of Chartres (d. 1115), a contemporary of Anselm. His treatise on legal interpretation and his collection of church law, the *Panormia*, were many years ago hailed for having anticipated the methods of scholasticism in part because he explicitly acknowledged the problem of contradictory texts.[133] Recent scholarship on Ivo has modified this portrait: his sole authorship of the *Panormia* is no longer certain, and his method of handling contradictory texts is now being examined in a more theological and more local—less judicial and less papal—context.[134] In any event, the preface to the *Panormia* (c. 1095) opens with a prologue that was frequently copied in the twelfth century as a separate treatise under the title "Of the Consonance of Canons" (*De consonantia canonum*).[135] One of the most widely diffused canonical collections of the first half of the twelfth century, this prologue has been called "a milestone in the history of the art of interpretation" for transferring certain principles of biblical and rhetorical hermeneutics to the field of the sacred canons, principles that were to prove of considerable consequence both to scholastic theology and to the nascent canonical science of the twelfth century.[136] As a former student of Lanfranc at the Norman abbey of Bec, Ivo's application of dialectics to the legal tradition surely owes something to the same pioneering circle of Lanfranc and Anselm. Ivo's continuators, and especially the "Four Doctors" associated with Bologna, developed the method of probing contrasting opinions further and "initiated a culture of juristic debate that was to become an integral part of medieval learning."[137] From simple antinomies in the sources to hypothetical cases, from real difficulties in interpreting a legal term to the didactic device of formulating statements as questions, the *quaestiones* of the glossators offer broad examples of the application of dialectic in the field of law.[138] They were sometimes clad in the dress of a Socratic dialogue, sometimes presented as a more elementary question-and-answer catechism, and sometimes made into the structural elements of a *summa*, like the frequently copied *Summa decretalium quaestionum* by Honorius of Richmond (late 1100s).

The most famous canonical collection of the twelfth-century, by an elusive master known to us simply as Gratian, displays the centrality of this approach in the very title he gave his work: *Concordia discordantium canonum* (Harmony of Discordant Canons).[139] The structural resemblance to Abelard's *Sic et non*, where seemingly conflicting statements of the church fathers are placed side by side, has long intrigued scholars, even if the precise relation between the two authors remains uncertain.[140] The presumption had long been that theological argumentation preceded legal argumentation. In the early twentieth century, legal historians were hard pressed to place the influence in the direction from law to theology.[141] Building on Winroth's conclusions, the latest manuscript analysis once again argues the reverse.[142] The causal influence may never be solved, nor need it be, for what is at issue is the very spread of a culture of disputation not restricted to a single area of inquiry but rather pervading the ideas, texts, and culture of the entire period. As Stephan Kuttner rightly cautioned, "It was a mistaken question, based on a search for 'influences' where the reality was that of an intellectual climate which became apparent at the same time but in different ways north, west, and south, wherever the need for organizing knowledge in a comprehensive, rational manner was felt."[143]

The regular and systematic application of *disputatio* in legal circles comes from the middle decades of the twelfth century, precisely when cathedral schools, private masters, and the renewed study of dialectic were flourishing in France. These glosses were primarily directed toward harmonizing conflicting references, constituting the so-called *solutiones contrarium* that eventually characterized the questions of the decretists.[144] These *quaestiones disputatae* of the twelfth-century glossators are direct products of the dialectical procedures that accompanied the study of law and theology.[145] In all its diverse manifestations, the *quaestio* was at first indissolubly bound to the text (scriptural, patristic, or glossarial), which formed an integral part of the *lectio* or exposition of the master. At first these questions, or problems, when they were written down were intended to accompany the text. This is the case, for instance, with Robert of Melun's *Quaestiones de divina pagina* (c. 1145).[146] At some point in the middle decades of the twelfth century, the desire to collect together and to systematize the results of such inquiries led to the publication of collections of *quaestiones* isolated from, yet still dependent on, the texts that gave rise to them. Such were the *quaestiones* of Odo of Soissons who taught at Paris c. 1164, and such, reduced to greater order and system, were the deeply influential *Sententiae* of Peter Lombard completed shortly after

1150 at Paris, which most likely also had their origin in the classroom setting
of questions and disputations on biblical passages.[147] Peter's *Sententiae* borrow from Gratian's *Decretum*, and his method of positing and harmonizing
conflicting authorities shows the definite influence of Ivo of Chartres's canon
law collection and Abelard's *Sic et Non*. Peter Lombard was also a former
student of Abelard.

Several generations of scholarship have thrown much light on these various *quaestiones*. Although the border line between the different forms of these
questions is not always easy to draw, and perhaps ought not to be imposed,
it was the expert opinion of Stephan Kuttner that these questions had their
origin in the practical exercises of disputation in the classroom.[148] As with
the theological circles, a certain amount of fluidity between pedagogy and
literary form seems likely. From the time of the second generation of Roman
law glossators, these disputed questions became a standard supplement to the
regular reading (*lectio*) of the law texts. Taking place under the master's direction and intended as a supplement to the purely theoretical lectures and
glosses, these early disputations connected theory to practice. In the words of
Hermann Kantorowicz, they were "the chief link between the written law of
Justinian and its application in the contemporary courts of justice."[149] The
earliest known collection of these disputed questions is the so-called *Stemma
Bulgaricum*, which seems to have been formed in Bologna in the time of the
glossator Bulgarus (c. 1115–c. 1166), from whom the collection derives its
name.[150] Whether Bulgarus can legitimately be credited with being the "originator" of the *quaestio disputata*, his *Stemma* and the similar collections made
by Martinus Gosia, Hugo de Portaravennate, and Jacobus de Borraigne (collectively known as the Four Doctors) bear the hallmark of actual disputations
held before a presiding master who in each case decided on the claims. The
structure of these *quaestiones* bears an incipient resemblance to the disputations that would later become fixed in the university curriculum.[151] The master formulated a case (*casus*) and the problem (*quaestio*), and both were made
known to the students some days before the disputation was to take place
(generally once a week). The *reportator*, an authorized pupil, copied case and
problem on parchment and took down more or less correct notes of the
disputation (*argumenta*) by his fellow students and the solution (*determinatio,
definitio*) of the master. He noted the references to all the sources that were
cited during the disputation in the two lateral margins of the *casus* and
sketched the solution (sometimes incorrectly) in a few words at the bottom,
generally, but not always, mentioning the names of the master in the third

person. He then edited these rough notes, adding sometimes a title and an exordium (for example, referring to the school of Bulgarus) at the beginning and supplementary or critical remarks of his own after the solution, often recognizable by the use of the first person (that is, "it seems to me . . .").

These dialectical procedures extend beyond the *quaestiones disputatae* of the Four Doctors. The glossator Rogerius (c. 1158) instituted in the study of civil law the discursive dialogue form containing questions in which the speakers engaging in debate often had allegorical names. His *Enodationes quaestionum* consists of a debate between Rogerius and Jurisprudentia, the one demanding, the other giving the solution of the apparent contradiction.[152] The characters of Rogerius and Jurisprudentia recur in two other works by Rogerius: *Quaestiones super Institutis* and *De praescriptionibus*. The conscious decision to frame his composition as an allegorical dialogue is underscored in the preface to the second of these dialogues where Rogerius says—in language reminiscent of Anselm and Abelard—that it is through the method of questions and opposing arguments (*questionum modos et adversariorum allegationes*) that one may perceive the right solutions.[153] Rogerius's students repeated the style of representing legal disputes in dialogue form: In Placentinus's *Quaestiones de iuris subtilitatibus*, the debate is between two unnamed litigators, Auditor and Interpres. Pillius, a student of Placentinus, wrote a legal dialogue titled *Libellus disputatorius*. More examples could be listed, but the pattern is both clear and familiar. Much like Anselm's students repeated and further developed the theological dialogue, succeeding generations of glossators saw in the *quaestio disputata* and the lawyerly dialogue a form ideally suited to the presentation of legal arguments, and one that naturally reproduced the dialectic exercises of the classroom. Searching for influences between scholastic circles in France and legal circles in Italy is therefore not only impossible (Anselm and Lanfranc, we recall, both came from northern Italy), but misses the essential point: a culture of disputation was emerging in the twelfth century that blurred oral and written forms of communication and that pervaded all disciplines that were grounded in classroom exercises.

## The Drama of Disputation: Anselm of Havelberg

One does not need to be teacher in a classroom of theology or law to appreciate and replicate the pedagogical value of disputation. The inseparable nature of literary dialogue and public debate can be observed in the career and writings of Bishop Anselm of Havelberg (c. 1095–1158), whose works bring into view the Mediterranean and especially Greek-speaking world of the twelfth century. His *Antikeimenon* (c. 1149) reproduces in dialogue form two debates that allegedly occurred in Constantinople in 1136 between Anselm and a Greek Orthodox archbishop from Nicomedia named Nicetas.[154] Not surprisingly, Anselm's arguments occupy the lion's share of the work, and the Greek disputant concedes defeat after every important argument. In this way the work is quite in step with the polemical flavor of the many contemporary anti-Jewish dialogues that have as their main purpose a clear and present demonstration of the triumph of Christianity. Nevertheless, the connection between the work's literary form and the scholastic—indeed, dialogical—methods of the mid-twelfth century invite reflection.

Anselm was a canon of the young Premonstratensian order and a protégé of its founder Norbert of Xanten (d. 1134). He was an ardent defender of the new reformed life against the criticisms of men like Rupert of Deutz. His polemical *Epistola apologetica* was a vigorous defense of the belief that a canon held the highest position on the hierarchy of spiritual lives, the very subject that had prompted Rupert to pen his *Altercatio* several years earlier. Anselm was also an able administrator and a skilled diplomat in the service of emperors Conrad III and Frederick Barbarossa and an emissary for Pope Eugenius III during the Second Crusade, so he was well acquainted with both the educated elite and the political currents of the day. It is in this context and against this background that the *Antikeimenon*, as well as Anselm's other works, must be read.[155]

A close reading of the *Antikeimenon* reveals important clues connecting the disputational culture we have been describing and the dialogue genre to which it is so obviously belongs. While scholars have long been intrigued by Anselm's account of the Constantinopolitan disputation, the recorded exchanges between Anselm and his Greek interlocutor occupy only the second part of a larger work. Preceding the dialogue is a history of the faithful, *De una forma credendi* (On the Single Form of Believing),[156] which addresses the concerns of his brethren about the proliferation of new religious orders, but which he paired together with the written version of the disputation specifically requested by Pope Eugenius.[157] These seemingly separate works are connected not only by virtue of having been included together in a dedication to the pope (and thereby offered to a larger audience under the umbrella of papal sanction) but also by a broader pedagogical approach that will lead readers from one level of understanding to the next.[158] Central in this regard is Anselm's concern to provide arguments of value for disputing eventual critics.

Anselm addresses Pope Eugenius in the prologue stating that he has written *De una forma credendi* because he was plagued by questions about the variety of religious lives in the church and that, during his time in Constantinople as legate, he used to dispute religious matters with the Greeks "sometimes in private, sometimes in public."[159] The formal disputation that resulted from his conversations was with "the most learned and venerable Archbishop Nicetas" because he was the first of a board of twelve Greek theologians (*didascalos*) to whom all difficult theological questions were brought. Anselm describes him as a man "well schooled in Greek scholarship and endowed with a distinguished eloquence of speech and self-assured in its use."[160] In announcing the historical context that produced these works and recording his winning arguments, Anselm is providing a manual for his brethren (in disputes with both monastic opponents of the new orders first and in confrontations with Greek orthodox Christians next) and also implying that his success over Nicetas was no minor affair—a public victory that surely deserved to be shared and celebrated. Like Gilbert Crispin's praise for his Jewish opponent in the alleged London disputation, the bar is set high in order to emphasize the magnitude of the achievement. And like Saint Anselm in his dialogue with Boso, this Anselm recognizes that his choice of genre (*sub dialogo*) is helpful to others more intellectually modest than he. Those who stand to benefit from the *Antikeimenon* are "the humble few who, not having such a nimble ability to learn something quickly, are perhaps going to read these things gladly that they may both more truly understand those things which the Greeks say and, to some extent, discover here those things which can be said to them in return."[161] These remarks echo Saint Anselm's stated purpose in the prologue to *Cur Deus homo* of writing out his dialogue with Boso for the benefit of "slower minds." It should be noted that St. Anselm had himself taken on the challenge of refuting the Greeks at the Council of Bari (1098) where, in his biographer's words, Anselm was persuaded by the pope to confute the Greeks in a "rational and catholic disputation" (*rationalis atque catholica disputatio*).[162] The product of that encounter was *De processione spiritus sancti*, a treatise not in dialogue form but a work that was likely available to Anselm of Havelberg during his student days at Laon.[163] As one scholar who has compared the two Anselms explains, "the principal difference between the ways in which the two scholars went about

their task seems to have lain in the fact that Anselm of Canterbury had almost
certainly not held formal discussions with advocates of the Greek viewpoint,
while Anselm of Havelberg did so most conscientiously and at some
length."[164] The implied similarities are equally worth emphasizing: both
Anselms introduced the drama of dialectic into their pedagogical writings,
making dialogue a centerpiece of their engagement with theological
controversy.

The general prologue sets the stage for the two works that follow.
Inserted in between *De una forma credendi* and the *Antikeimenon* proper is a
proem which, though easily ignored, offers a very precise description of the
sort of disputation Anselm had in mind:

> Since among the [Greeks], Archbishop [Nicetas] was noble in his
> devout bearing, sharpest in his ability, most learned in the study of
> Greek letters, most eloquent in speech, and most cautious in giving
> and receiving answers, he neglected none of these things whether in
> a disputation (*disputatione*) or in a quiet deliberation which seemed
> capable of being turned to the advantage of his opinion and the
> destruction of ours; and this was especially the case since he was at
> the time the leader among the twelve elect *didascalos*, who by custom
> preside over the schools of the Greeks. And he was elected by them
> to the task of going up against me in our disputation
> (*disputationis*).[165]

In repeating Nicetas's talents as a disputer and the high esteem that he
commanded among his fellow Greeks, the proem posits an unmistakably
oppositional relationship between the two parties. The Latin subtitle to
the *Antikeimenon*—*Liber contrapositorum*—emphasizes that very opposition
while also evoking the very scholastic idea of pitting truths against falsehoods.
The insertion of the proem after the treatise on religious life and before the
debate itself is just as important. The brothers to whom the first part of the
work was addressed are now implicitly being led from disputing matters of
religious devotion with other Latin Christians to the arguably more serious
task of facing an Eastern Christian whom Rome considered schismatic. In
the first work, these brothers were given justifying arguments in the form of
a treatise; in the second, they are shown by example the successful procedures
for engaging and winning a debate. For this reason, it is unlikely that the
dialogue that ensues is an accurate rendition of the 1136 disputation, even if

that was the impression Anselm wished to convey, and indeed has conveyed to some of his modern readers.[166] But it has been shown that many quotations from Western theological sources find their way into Anselm's speeches and that a passage from his earlier *Epistola apologetica* is actually placed in the mouth of Nicetas, all tell-tale signs that this is a carefully constructed work and not a mere transcript.[167]

The disputation as it exists in Anselm's rendition was carried out respectfully and even amicably. This is no mere formality, since many of Anselm's points depend on this fact. The circumstances surrounding the formal encounter are vividly described and the location for the first of the two debates is set near Hagia Irene.[168] The seats are arranged facing each other; court officials, judges, translators, and notaries are present; and a silence of anticipation pervades the crowd of onlookers.[169] Some Latins were present besides Anselm, of whom he names three as having a good knowledge of Greek: James of Venice, Burgundius of Pisa, and Moses of Pergamon. It is of some curiosity that the contemporary translator of Aristotle's *Topics* and *Sophistical Refutations*, James of Venice, was on hand to witness the debate, though as far as we can tell not present here to perform his skill as translator. Of these three others, Moses (undoubtedly Jewish) was chosen to be interpreter. At this point, Anselm states his humble purpose: "Reverend fathers, I did not come in search of a quarrel. . . . I came to inquire about and understand the faith, yours and mine, most especially because it pleases you."[170] The drama of the moment is thus combined with Anselm's willingness to provide answers to his Greek audience. Nicetas, too, speaks in favor of an open and amicable exchange. Truth will be arrived at much sooner, he says, "than, if in our eagerness to conquer, we dispute arrogantly."[171] These pleasantries, like the laudatory dedication to Pope Eugenius, are mostly formulaic, but they also move in the direction of a more representational understanding of the nature of speech acts. Anselm's articulation of the virtues of public disputation seize on precisely this point:

> we give or receive similitudes in the fashion of theatrical representa-
> tions (*similitudines scenicas*), not because they capture the pure truth
> of things but because they conduct the spirit of the listener to a
> better understanding of things; and it often happens that, by such a
> method of instruction, that which is not understood because of its
> highly elevated nature can be understood.[172]

Once again, the pedagogical—and specifically dramatic—value of debate is emphasized, and the literary form of the dialogue becomes embedded in a more acute understanding of the theatrical nature of argumentation.[173] Paul Zumthor has suggested that the power of the medieval dialogue derived from its theatricality, its ability to render a teacher present to a reader, and this would seem to be an especially apt assessment of Anselm's goals.[174] For these reasons, the form and function of the *Antikeimenon* connect especially well to the larger twelfth-century scholastic culture of disputation, while at the same time anticipating the performative elements of representational debate that will be explored in the following chapters.

## Disputation in Paris c. 1200

The rise of scholastic disputation during the early twelfth century transcends a single subject (theology, law, science) or a single geographical location. The hub of this new learning, however, was northern France, both because of its great concentration of schools and scholars and because this would be the center for the study and absorption of ancient philosophical works c. 1150–1250. Before proceeding to the recovery of Aristotle's New Logic, it will be helpful to return briefly to the scholastic scene in Paris in the late twelfth century to observe just how central disputation had become to the elemental practices of scholastic education.

Peter the Chanter of Notre Dame (d. 1197) was one of many masters active in Paris during the last quarter of the twelfth century, particularly important because his circle reveals a rich network of scholars during a transformative period in the history of scholastic education. As the choirmaster and second-ranking dignitary of the cathedral chapter of Notre Dame, Peter was at the center of a wide (and wide-ranging) circle that included Robert of Courson, Jacques de Vitry, Stephen Langton, Alain of Lille, and the future Pope Innocent III.[175] On several occasions, the Chanter was employed by the papacy to settle disputes, including defending the legacy of Thomas Becket at a debate in Paris sometime in the early 1170s.[176] His seminal and most copied work, a manual of ethics titled *Verbum adbreviatum* (c. 1192), contains a famous description of the functions of a theologian. Without any sense that an apology might be necessary, Peter places disputation squarely within the duties of theological study:

The training of Holy Scripture consists of three exercises: reading (*lectio*), disputing (*disputatio*) and preaching (*predicatio*) against which prolixity is the enemy, the mother of oblivion, and the step-mother of memory. First, reading is laid down like the basement and foundation for what follows, so that from this source all support is derived by the other two exercises. Secondly, the structure or walls of disputation are put in place for, as Gregory says, nothing is fully understood or faithfully preached unless first chewed or ground by the tooth of disputation. Thirdly the roof of preaching is erected so that he who hears says "I came" and thus the crowd draws the crowd. One should preach after, not before, the reading of Holy Scripture and the investigation of doubtful matters. The Christian religion truly consists of faith and good conduct of which reading and disputation pertain to faith and preaching to conduct.[177]

This oft-cited quotation is perhaps more important for what we already know than for any original statement relating to late twelfth-century learning. The metaphor of chewing in order to comprehend, attributed to a venerable authority for good measure, conveys the active and deliberative process of learning, rather like the modern sense of talking something through. Only here, it segues to a clear and final missionary goal. Bracketed by the already well-defined process of *lectio* and the soon-to-be universal art of *praedicatio*, disputation is, for the first time, explicitly incorporated into the everyday scholastic practices of the medieval curriculum.[178]

Further context for situating this passage may be supplied from another work of the Chanter's long ignored by medievalists, *De tropis loquendi*. In the best study of this text to date, Luisa Valente has demonstrated that the Chanter was far more than just a theologian devoted to sacramental questions.[179] He was also an exegetical theologian who eagerly applied the latest analytical tools derived from logic, rhetoric, and speculative grammar to the explication of biblical passages containing ambiguous or polysemous terms. In contrast to masters of the verbal *artes*, the Chanter was less interested in the technicalities of the arts than with how they help exegetes understand Scripture.[180] His metaphor for the duties of a theologian, more descriptive than prescriptive, was part and parcel of that larger, exegetical program that was shared by some members of his circle. The best surviving image of the Chanter depicts him in dialogue with his equally influential contemporary

Alain of Lille, whose own unique mystical philosophy blended Aristotelian logic with Neoplatonic philosophy (Figure 4).

The Chanter's description of disputation was not all praise. Like many others, he was well aware of the dangers inherent in disputation, and he cautioned against its abuse. He opens his discussion in the *Verbum adbreviatum* by distinguishing three kinds of questions found in theological disputation: those that are useless because they treat neither faith nor morals should be eliminated immediately, those that are useful and clear are unnecessary, and those that are useful and difficult should be discussed with modesty and without wrangling.[181] The virtue of disputation thus lies in its ability to wrest meaning from questions that are both difficult and important. In support of his position, Peter compiles a list of biblical examples (and some citations from Seneca) to serve as an analogy for how theologians waste their time entertaining useless questions. He does not indicate exactly what these foolish and useless questions are, but he does specify what unwanted results can come from fruitless questioning: division among theologians and heresy. This last concern seems to have been shared by several others of Peter's circle, several of whom warned students and clergymen not to engage in public disputations with Jews or heretics, for the orthodox preacher could not hope to compete with heretics' teaching, which lured reprobates eager to escape penance through the Cathar doctrine of the *consolamentum*. Writing from Paris in the 1190s, Peter of Blois also warned that, "as a result of illicit and careless debates a virulent crop of heresies runs wild."[182]

As a master in Paris, Peter practiced the methods of disputation in his own school, and this can be gleaned from his writings. His theological work *Summa de sacramentis* consists entirely of *quaestiones*, which, as we have already noted, were often written renditions of the dialectical exercises conducted in the classroom.[183] Since, as he tells us, nothing can be fully understood unless first prepared by "the tooth of disputation," Peter turns in chapter three of the *Verbum adbreviatum* to offering positive advice on how disputations should be conducted. To avoid the dangers associated with useless questioning (*inutilitate questionum*) Peter urges his fellow theologians to fashion their debates not into altercations (*altercationes*), but into conversations (*collationes*) that yield a common inquiry after truth. Calm deliberation should be the order of the day, not heated debates. Such "conversations" recall the monastic tradition of pedagogical dialogue that was intended to provide students with a practical guidance to religion and ethics.[184] The distinction Peter draws, shared by many of his contemporaries, illustrates the

Figure 4. Master Peter the Chanter (right) in dialogue with Master Alain of Lille (d. 1202). Manuscript from the Abbey of Ottoburen (1228–1246). British Library, MS ADD. 19767, fol. 217. Used by permission.

degree to which masters in Paris were still grappling with academic procedural techniques and their problem of definition. Peter offers some examples
of what he means by the deliberation associated with a *collatio*. He draws his
examples from ancient law, Roman law, and the life of Aristotle. The example
from Aristotle is an anecdote of a student who did not have the patience to
wait as instructed until the following day to answer a question. With youthful
exuberance, the disciple offered an immediate solution, only to discover that
it was wrong. The moral of the story reinforces the metaphor that only when
the readings have been properly "chewed" can a full understanding be
claimed. The citation from Aristotle is secondhand, for there is no direct
reference in Peter's work to the New Logic. It is precisely the contribution of
Aristotle's logic in catalyzing scholastic disputation that the following chapter
seeks to uncover.

The twelfth century produced great intellectual ferment on many fronts.
New methods of teaching, charismatic personalities, and a great variety of
written works define this intellectual renaissance. Among the most salient
features in the making of scholastic culture are an explosion of dialogues, the
development of the *quaestio disputata*, and the rise of public and classroom
disputations. Rather than seeing these elements as wholly distinct or attempt-
ing to draw causal connections among them, their relationship might perhaps
better be depicted by an image of concentric circles, each delimiting one area
in unique fashion while all having a common focal point. Individually and
collectively they demonstrate a profound transition from the silent and cloistered learning of the early Middle Ages to what I have called a culture of
disputation. Surely there is something deeper than a metaphorical "discourse
of opposites" that one scholar has highlighted as a symbolic element in the
rhetoric of the twelfth century.[185] In the generations from Adelard of Bath to
Peter the Chanter, there is an unmistakable shift in meaning and use of
*disputatio* from the more simple spiritual conversation or investigation of
prior generations to the more intense debates of the scholastic world—
debates about new questions, debates about old questions, indeed, debates
about the very usefulness of debating. The terms and methods of analysis
gain greater meaning as well as greater precision during the twelfth century,
and many of the dialogues, classroom practices, and accounts of disputation
reflect those changes. Henri de Lubac made a poignant remark about this
intellectual shift years ago: "while monastic 'lectio' tended, and is always
inclined to tend, toward meditation and prayer, scholastic 'lectio' tends
toward the question and the disputation. It is directed toward a kind of

disputation which, although it is not absolutely new, monopolizes the meaning of this word more and more. What we have here again is a fact of language that can serve as an emblem of the evolution which is in progress."[186] Having charted the linguistic and academic contours of that evolution, it is time to consider one of the most decisive elements in the rise of scholastic disputation: the reception of Aristotle's New Logic. The broad influence that Aristotle exerted on the medieval culture of disputation will be assessed though a combination of logical and poetical works, allowing for a more holistic appreciation of scholastic thought's penetration into the wider culture.

# CHAPTER 4

# Aristotle and the Logic of Debate

The rise of scholastic disputation within legal and theological circles might have remained a minor byproduct of the new schools and scholars of the twelfth century had it not been for the recovery of Aristotle's *Topics* and *Sophistical Refutations*, works that dealt directly with the dialectical process of forming and refuting arguments. The translation and transmission of this New Logic in the middle of the twelfth century had a profound impact on the development of scholastic disputation, lending authority and guidance to the practice most characteristic of the medieval schoolmen. This chapter examines the reception of Aristotle's New Logic within and beyond the schools of the twelfth and thirteenth centuries with a view to understanding how his strategies for debate and techniques of logical argumentation were read, assimilated, and satirized within an emerging culture of disputation.

The writings of Aristotle were made available in the Latin West in three clearly distinguishable waves of translation. The first wave broke on the late Roman world and is attributable almost in its entirety to the efforts of Boethius. His translations of Aristotle's treatises on logic and his adaptations of various other works on logic and rhetoric in the sixth century opened the door for early medieval knowledge and interest in ancient logic and philosophy. The second wave commenced in the twelfth century with the gradual translation of the full corpus of Aristotle's logical works, an enterprise that lasted well into the thirteenth century and that eventually included his treatises on medicine, astrology, natural science, and politics. The third wave of translations began in the late fifteenth century and concentrated on the texts of Aristotle's works themselves rather than on the coordination and classification of the sciences. This produced, above all, new editions of the Greek text accompanied by new Latin and vernacular translations and commentaries.

The second wave of translations that began early in the twelfth century catalyzed the scholastic practice of disputation.[1] Certainly, logic was studied in the centuries between Boethius and the retranslation of Aristotle's New Logic. There were outstanding schools of logic at the end of the tenth century at St. Gallen under Notker Labeo and at Fleury under Abbo. Unlike the abbey of Bec, however, these monastic schools do not appear to have had a broad impact on the outside world. What little we know of their disciples show few traces of having influenced the thought and culture around them. There was also a considerable movement in language-based logic at the turn of twelfth century, as we saw in chapter 3, but this was mostly focused on the texts of the Old Logic as transmitted through Boethius. Thus, even the logic of Peter Abelard, who was undoubtedly the most original logician of the twelfth century, fell out of favor shortly after his death, although this is not to say that he did not have a school of followers. David Luscombe and Yukio Iwakuma, among others, have shown that he did.[2] It was not Abelard's condemnation to silence that dissuaded the continuity of his logical advances or those of his contemporaries. Rather, it was the arrival onto the scene of a new corpus of Aristotelian texts that helped transform the curriculum, eventually impacting a broad range of cultural practices far beyond the schools in which logic was taught. To assess the cultural significance of this impact, once described as the "greatest innovatory force" in the study of the *trivium*, it is first necessary to appreciate the range of evidence available.[3]

The evidence for our knowledge of the reception of Aristotle's works is of several kinds.[4] First, there are the manuscript copies of Aristotle, the scholarly study of which began in 1819 with the publication of Amable Jourdain's *Recherches critiques sur l'âge et l'origine des traductions latines d'Aristote* and culminated in the twentieth century with the project to edit the complete corpus of the translations under the auspices of the Union Académique Internationale and continues with the "Aristoteles latinus" volumes containing critical editions of the translations. Second, there are the glosses preserved in the manuscripts, which provide demonstrative evidence of their being read and studied.[5] This area is the one most in need of further study since there exist twelfth- and thirteenth-century unedited glosses from northern France and specifically from the abbey of Mont Saint-Michel that preserve some of the oldest known Latin glosses on Aristotle's New Logic.[6] Third, there are the university documents, at first banning the study of Aristotle but later (March 1255) prescribing them as part of the educational curriculum. Fourth, there are the hundreds of surviving commentaries, often called *quaestiones* because of the questions that Aristotle's works raised for medieval authors, along with other aids to study such as compendia and collections of extracts. Fifth, and most crucially from a cultural historical perspective, there are the numerous references to Aristotle and Aristotelian logic by medieval authors, some of whom were active within the schools and universities, many of whom were not.

## The Early Reception of Aristotle's New Logic

Aristotle's announced purpose in the *Topics* is to provide an art of argumentation.[7] His intention was to codify the Socratic style of arguing into an art, the possession of which will make a person adept at the sort of dialectical disputation popularized by Socrates. To be a formidable arguer of the Socratic sort, Aristotle believes, the most important skill required is facility in the discovery of arguments, and the majority of the *Topics* is devoted to the method for finding arguments useful in dialectical disputations.[8] What exactly a "Topic" is for Aristotle and what exactly is the method that the *Topics* are supposed to be based on are technical issues that have long exercised the attention of logicians. In one sense, an Aristotelian Topic is primarily a strategy of argumentation and secondarily a principle supporting the crucial inference in the argument generated by such a strategy.[9] It is especially the notion of argumentation as strategy that fascinated the first commentators of the twelfth century.

An early witness to the importance of Aristotle's New Logic for medieval disputation is Adam of Balsham. His treatise *Ars disserendi* of about 1132 (most often translated as the *Art of Discourse*, but *Art of Argumentative Reasoning* is also possible) survives incomplete and exists in two recensions, the second one appearing with important changes under the title *Dialectica Alexandri*, probably out of association with Adam's most illustrious follower in the second half of the twelfth century, Alexander Neckham. Little is known about Adam's life other than that his family was of French extraction and that he owned some land in his native Balsham near Cambridge, but over his career he shared company with some of the most prominent personalities in Paris. Adam most likely taught for some time near the Petit Pont that crossed the Seine in Paris (Adam Parvipontanus is his other appellation).[10] He testified against Gilbert de la Porrée in 1147 shortly after being appointed canon of Paris, and in March 1148 he was present along with Peter Lombard, Thierry of Chartres, and several other masters at the Council of Reims where Gilbert's doctrines were discussed.[11] John of Salisbury, also from southern England, met Adam probably between 1136 and 1138 in Paris, and frequented him in later years, before 1148, discussing many problems with him, "apparently as a younger man discusses with more learned and wiser friends, exchanging books."[12] John describes Adam as "our peripatetic Englishman (*noster ille Anglus Peripateticus Adam*)" and records his gratitude at having learned "a great deal from his explanations," although he also says of Adam's writing that he gets so involved in verbal intricacies that his exposition is of little use.[13] Indeed, it is probably the highly technical nature of the treatise that has caused it to be so often ignored in modern scholarship, even though it represents, as its modern editor states, the first time that "Aristotle's *Topics* and *Sophistici Elenchi* were put into contribution [*sic*] in an original treatise by a Latin writing author."[14] It is not possible to reconstruct the exact nature of the relationship between John of Salisbury and Adam (John insists that he was never a formal student of Adam), but one theme that concerns them both is the influence of Aristotelian logic on the practice of discourse, and especially the art of disputation.

Adam's treatise is that of a forward-looking pedagogue interested in the practical application of newly available texts. He thinks that the language of the logic textbooks is antiquated and that the present revival of Aristotelian dialectic will change the understanding and practice of debate. According to Adam, others before him had written about the art of discourse, but nobody had discovered and expounded the whole of it in a comprehensible manner. With fresh translations of Aristotle's New Logic in hand, and a considerable reliance on the logic of Boethius as well, Adam undertakes to produce a handbook containing all that is essential for mastering the discipline. The currency of academic disputes and the lack of any formal rules governing their procedure are cited as being one of his motivations for writing the treatise: "There was not yet the custom of disputing, for then there was only the beginning, nor as yet an art of disputing, for one ought to dispute before an art can be made of it, and what the art should be about comes before the art itself."[15] Accordingly, Adam's focus is with the discourse in the form of questions and answers, for it is from *enuntio* and *interrogatio* that the principles of discourse are to be found. He cannot yet make a pronouncement on the art of disputation per se because the practice of debate is still in its infancy, and art comes from practice, not vice-versa. Much of the treatise is consequently devoted to practical methods for discussing fallacies. Obscurities and ambiguities in speech are to be avoided, or exposed when they are encountered. Adam gives rules and advice about how to detect equivocations and other defects of speech. These are not theoretical discussions but a direct attempt to merge language and logic in the public practice of discourse (*disserendi*). Anyone who desires to become a master of this "art" must become familiar with the traps inherent in language into which the unwary can fall or which can be consciously set by an opponent.[16] It is Adam's anticipation that the study of Aristotle and the continued practice of debate will produce a more fixed and developed art.

The fullest and most significant discussion of Aristotle's New Logic in the context of scholastic circles is from John of Salisbury (d. 1180), who picks up where his friend Adam of Balsham left off. John may not have been a student of Adam, but he was a student of Abelard, and he had a fine ear for the scholastic developments of his age. He is especially attuned to the increasingly popular method of classroom disputations and provides an unparalleled testimony to the unfolding effects that these new works of Aristotle were exerting on current methods of teaching, even if he most likely knew the *Topics* only in its Boethian translation.[17] After all, John was a cleric and a bishop rather than a master. His *Metalogicon* (1159) is dedicated to Thomas Becket and comprises a defense of the verbal and logical arts of the *trivium* against the charges of the pseudonymous Cornificius and his fellow opponents of a liberal arts education (a slightly more judicious variant on a rhetorical ploy already encountered in Abelard's Letter Thirteen). As with Abelard, it is not difficult to supply an image of the type of opponent John had in mind, as there were many authors who followed Bernard of Clairvaux and William of St. Thierry in denouncing the corrosive effects of scholastic disputation. The Benedictine monk Peter of Celle, for example, wrote to John warning him of the perils of Paris, where masters were seldom attached to an organized community and taught free from restriction, where disputation had replaced traditional methods of instruction, and where the curriculum could be as fleeting as the desires of students.[18] Hoping to draw John to his monastery in Reims, Peter contrasted the tranquility of the monastic surrounding to the noise and clamor of the schools: "There no book is bought, no master of scribes is employed; there is no circumvention of disputations, no entanglement of sophistries; there is a clear conclusion of all questions, a complete understanding of universal reasons and proofs. There life confers more than reading, simplicity is more profitable than sophistry."[19] Peter of Celle's words evoke the contemporary rhetoric contrasting the order and tranquility of monastic life with the disputatious environment of schools.

Critics like Peter of Celle did not convince John; he neither joined a monastery nor abandoned his dedication to upholding the liberal arts. But he was a reformer, and, in the recovery of Aristotelian texts and ideas, John saw both danger and possibility. In addition to offering a detailed account of what a scholastic education should consist of, John also reveals the growing divide among scholars over the utility of the newly translated logical works of Aristotle, an issue that had not confronted Hugh of St. Victor writing a generation earlier.[20] John praises the advances made by his former teachers, among them Abelard and Thierry of Chartres, but he also goes significantly beyond them by carefully considering Aristotelian logic in connection to the rules of scholastic disputation. Logic in its narrower sense, John explains, is "the science of argumentative reasoning."[21] Its excesses and abuses result from the improper application of Aristotelian ideas among contemporary masters:

> I must observe that, very often, many of them seem to be wrangling over words, rather than disputing about facts. Nonetheless, there is nothing that is less appropriate for a professor of this art [of logic], since such procedure ill befits a serious man. As Aristotle declares [in Book I of the *Topics*], "to dispute in this wise over a word is utterly abhorrent in dialectic, unless it be the sole possible way in which a proposition may be discussed."[22]

John wishes that classroom disputation would rid itself of unnecessary verbiage and return to the systematic logic it aimed to uphold. A similar plea was invoked later in the twelfth century by the satirist Walter of Châtillon, who complained in one of his poems that "scholars have become idle and unfruitful; they learn only in order to say 'I have disputed'."[23] John would agree, but it is reform, not satire, that he seeks to achieve. Even amid the unrefined, off-topic, and prideful disputers of the schools, the very practice of stylized debate that stems from Aristotle produces some important advantages:

> This evil [of immoderate disputation] sometimes has a certain [incidental] utility. Those who are made accustomed to frequent disputation on all sorts of topics, provided this training is kept within

bounds, may thus obtain a well-stocked vocabulary, fluent speech, and retentive memory, in addition to mental subtlety. For the mind is improved by consistent exercise.[24]

John goes to pains to find the appropriate middle ground, in part because of an ardent belief, no doubt instilled in him during his student days, that the correct use of language is an aid for the hidden truth of things. The true danger is that "once we go beyond the proper limits, everything works in reverse, and excessive subtlety devours utility."[25]

One of the primary objectives of the *Metalogicon* is to remove the obstacles that impede the progress of learning. To this end, John is not solely interested in the logical implications of Aristotle's *Topics*. The question of genera and species, and of universals, is also addressed, and he offers a running commentary on the education and personalities of other masters of his day. His uneasy relations with many of his former associates has led John of Salisbury to be dubbed the "best of students and worst of pupils," an appellation that could surely be given to many twelfth-century personalities.[26] Yet John returns time and again to Aristotle's work for its relevance to contemporary logical theory, and especially the practice of scholastic disputation. Chapter 10 in Book III of the *Metalogicon* is expressly devoted to the "usefulness" (*utilitate*) of Book VIII of the *Topics*, which addresses the methods of verbal reasoning. Seizing on the now familiar metaphor of disputation as a form of verbal combat, John explains how Aristotle can best prepare the young scholastic:

> In military matters, a commanding officer must first see that his
> army is properly supplied with arms and other military
> equipment. . . . In like manner, the contriver of the science of rea-
> soning [that is, Aristotle], the drill-master of those who profess to
> be logicians, has in the foregoing books, as it were, provided the
> means of disputation (*instrumenta disputandi*), and stacked in the
> arena arms for the use of his students. This he has done by explain-
> ing the meanings of uncombined words and clarifying the nature of
> propositions and topics. His next step is to show his disciples how
> they may use these instruments, and somehow to teach them the art
> of engaging in [argumentative] combat. As if to set the members of

the contestants in motion, he shows them how to propose and
answer questions, as well as how to prove and evade.[27]

John's explication of Aristotle was clearly meant to guide students (perhaps
masters, too) in the art of disputation as well as in its proper application.
Others of his generation who opposed dialectic wholesale might well have
found cause to disagree with his assessment, but therein lies the subtlety of his
defense. For John there is no mistaking Aristotle's relevance to contemporary
masters; the return of the New Logic was catalyzing the practice most characteristic of the schools of his day, and the one most problematic for upholders
of the monastic attitude toward learning: disputation.

The recovery of Aristotle's *Topics* in the mid-twelfth century marks a
significant moment in the formative development of scholastic disputation.
While knowledge of the later, and better documented, university *disputatio*
is necessary for a full appreciation of this contribution, John of Salisbury
himself makes note in the *Metalogicon* of the dramatic changes brought about
by the Aristotelian impact. "If what [Book VIII] teaches is both borne in
mind and correctly observed," he observes, "it contributes more to the science of argumentative reasoning (*ratio disserendi*) than practically all the
works on dialectic that our modern predecessors were accustomed to teach
in the schools."[28] If Bernard of Chartres and his generation were dwarves
perched on the shoulders of giants, John and his generation are themselves
sitting on the shoulders of those dwarves because of their access to Aristotle's
New Logic. John proceeds to examine point by point the ways in which Book
VIII of Aristotle's *Topics* can, and should, serve as a textbook for scholars
involved in deploying the methods of disputation.[29] This aspect of logic constitutes the centerpiece of John's defense of the *trivium* as a whole, and it is
well worth noting that his focus on the practical rules of disputation as outlined in Book VIII of Aristotle's *Topics* is the second lengthiest chapter in the
entire *Metalogicon*.

An apparent paradox of the *Metalogicon* is that John pours scorn on the
artificiality of contemporary logic and praises literary style and the quest for
lucidity, all while offering a highly technical discussion of logical training.[30]
One resolution of this paradox has been to see John both as a critic and a
humanist, a defender and a reformer of scholastic practices. This is how John
survives in most assessments of his place in the twelfth-century renaissance,
and there is much truth to that image. It must also be acknowledged that

disputation itself posed an essential paradox: it trained students in the art of thinking constructively, while it opened the door to the destructive vices verbosity, sophistry, and pride. The recovery of Aristotle's logical texts did not quell that paradox. On the contrary, it provided authority and an enhanced vocabulary for a new generation of masters.

## Everard of Ypres

The absorption of Aristotelian texts led authors to become increasingly sensitive to the storehouse of knowledge that both he and the Greek world possessed. John of Salisbury fused two Greek words (*meta* and *logos*) to create his neologism of a title, *Metalogicon*. The scholastic and canonist Everard of Ypres used the Greek character "Ratius" (Reason) to expound on the teachings of his mentor Gilbert of Poitiers in his *Dialogus Ratii et Everardi* written sometime between 1191 and 1198 toward the end of a long life.[31] The cultural positioning of this text heavily depends on the scholastic fascination with Aristotelian logic in which it is grounded.

Everard was born around 1120 in the Flemish town of Ypres. He was a student of Gilbert of Poitiers, studying the liberal arts first at Chartres and then following his teacher to Paris where he took classes in dialectic and theology.[32] Gilbert, who himself studied at Laon, was a major proponent of the *quaestio* technique. According to Gilbert's teachings, a *quaestio* consisted of an affirmation and a negation that contradicts it, each of which seems to be true.[33] Since contradictories cannot be true, the *quaestio* is to be resolved by showing how two statements are ambiguous and, insofar as they are true, not contradictory. Everard's studies with Gilbert had a profound impact on his written works, and this is clearly visible in the *Dialogus*. Everard remained a faithful and loyal student of his master when Bernard of Clairvaux placed Gilbert on trial for heresy at the Council of Reims (1148) when Gilbert was bishop of Poitiers. Gilbert was eventually cleared of all charges.[34] Everard remained with Gilbert until the latter's death in 1154. During the next forty years Everard spent time teaching law and the liberal arts in Paris, but also as a monk at the Benedictine abbey of Clairvaux, a curious choice given his association with Gilbert of Poitiers.[35] His years at Clairvaux would appear to have been toward the end of his life, so one may speculate that his affiliation with Gilbert (and his teachings) in an atmosphere of adherents loyal to Bernard of Clairvaux was a motivation to compose his defense of his teacher, even though many years had passed since the trial of 1148. Indeed, the council seems not to have faded entirely from general memory, for, as late as 1189, Bernard's secretary from the Council of Reims was asked to send a report on the council to the cardinal of Albano.[36]

The *Dialogus* features two theologians, Everardus, a Latin, and Ratius, a Greek, engaged in a discussion over the ideas of Gilbert of Poitiers, including the very doctrines that originally had him placed on trial. In an unusual role reversal for twelfth-century dialogues, Ratius argues in defense of Gilbert, while Everardus plays the part of a Cistercian monk skeptical of Gilbert's ideas. By using Ratius as his mouthpiece, Everard the author actually goes so far as to project his relationship with Gilbert onto his fictional character: Ratius claims to be a devoted student of Gilbert who followed him from Chartres to Paris and remained with him until his last days as bishop of Poitiers.[37] Because Everard used his own persona opposite Ratius, one cannot help associating the literary framework with Gilbert's *quaestio* technique of using the seemingly contrary position to prove the thesis. The two monks in the dialogue are not only friends, but, we are told, they were also students together at Paris. This past relationship is invoked early on in the debate and helps establish the generally amicable discourse that persists throughout the dialogue, punctured with some jokes and the occasional rudeness. A noticeable feature of the *Dialogus* is its similarity with other dialogues of the twelfth century that likewise show a friendly and open exchange between mutually respectful characters.

The discussion begins in proximity to a monastery. Everardus is walking about, meditating on the monastic life, when his Athenian friend Ratius interrupts him with the playful suggestion that his meditation is getting him nowhere. Everardus is eager to discuss his thoughts with Ratius and to be instructed by him, "since I know that you taught at the Areopagus."[38] Unfortunately Everardus hears the bells calling him to service and he must cut their encounter short, but with the promise that their conversation will continue. Ratius, meanwhile, reassures Everardus that he will wait. It is at this point that Everard the author reveals his first motivation for holding a discussion. While walking away, Everardus says to himself, "I will tell him everything I think of the monks, no matter what order they belong to or what habit they wear. I will talk to him frankly, not in order to put others down but in order to get over my doubt."[39] A frank discussion will, thus, afford Everardus (the character and one may presume the author as well) a chance to articulate his thoughts and overcome his uncertainties. The chiming of the bells is another curious feature of the work. Throughout the dialogue, the characters move about within the vicinity of the monastery; sometimes they sit on the grassy hillside, other times they shelter under a roof to be protected from the rain foreseen the previous evening, but they always remain close enough to the monastery to hear its bells. Everard apparently thought that the unity of place created by the bells was the best symbolic setting for an open discussion.[40]

The opening scene of the *Dialogus* shares much in common with the culture of debate evidenced in other dialogues of the twelfth century. Like Anselm of Havelberg's *Antikeimenon*, there is a strong emphasis on the dramatic backdrop to the conversation. The intellectual merits of the Greek spokesman are quickly established, and a sense of open and fair exchange sets the tenor for the dialogue that ensues. If the disputants in the dialogue do not correspond to real persons, they do sit comfortably within a familiar cast of ancient and twelfth-century characters: an Athenian scholar trained in dialectic who finds himself in France debating with a representative of Western monastic theology. Here, however, the Greek scholar stands for reason and wisdom (his mother, significantly, is named Ratio and his sister, who urged him to study in France, Sophia). Among the other similarities of these works, both Everard's *Dialogus* and Anselm's *Antikeimenon* were sent with dedicatory letters to the reigning pope, both include a debate with the author as one of the participants, and both include a supplementary letter from an unnamed brother commenting on the dialogue as well as the letter to the pope.[41] The *Dialogus* and the *Antikeimenon* have the additional similarity of both beginning with reflections on the divisive issue of competing monastic orders: Anselm preceded his debate with a separate work on the subject, *De una forma credendi*, while Everard uses the theme to launch into a broader discussion about Gilbert.

The value of Everard's dialogue as a window onto the form and function of medieval dialogue has been noted before. In a detailed study of the text, Peter von Moos has connected the *Dialogus* to a more general theory of dialogue inherited through classical sources but developed in the twelfth century and exemplified in the verbal exchanges between Everardus and Ratius.[42] The patterns of discourse present in the dialogue suggest that there are broader issues of conversation and communication that typify a "dialogic culture" of the late twelfth century.[43] The scholastic method, for instance, proves a strong undercurrent in the speeches of both Everardus and Ratius. "I see now that you are full of rage," Everardus says to an irritated Ratius almost prepared to abandon their talks. "That is indeed the ways of teachers:

when they are up against a wall by the questions put to them and they are unable to answer them they cut short and become irritated. A learned teacher, on the other hand, rejoices at the opportunity to solve the problems, for it is in contradictions that wisdom is practiced."[44] Everard of Ypres, a theologian trained in dialectic, conceals his sympathies by having his monastic counterpart in the dialogue chastise Ratius for lacking the sophistication of a true *magister*. But Ratius is in fact of the same opinion. Defending Gilbert's inquiries into the Trinitarian mystery, he too voices criticism of the uneducated along much the same lines: "And this is what I have often said when the occasion arose, 'Some monks, who are educated but not sufficiently trained in the scholastic method (*scholis exercitati*), simply transcribe in their books what they find expressed in the writings of the orthodox Fathers. But how these things are to be understood they neither know nor bother to learn from those who do know'."[45] Together Everardus and Ratius record their criticisms of those who shun the scholastic approach, all while maintaining their conversation about the man they both hold in great esteem: Gilbert of Poitiers.

What of Aristotle? In Book VIII of the *Topics* (and elsewhere in the *Sophistical Refutations*), Aristotle suggests that dialecticians employ several different methods of debate to catch the adversary by surprise, including off-topic and even irrelevant questions. Everard seems to be projecting these techniques onto his interlocutors, who jump from one topic of conversation to another. Discussion over Gilbert's theology is interspersed with some very unconnected questions: "does patience come from the suppression of anger or vengeance?"[46] "Does a rightful owner have the right to retake by force something of his that was stolen?"[47] "Is an ironic fib the same thing as a lie?"[48] The comparison between anger and vengeance, however unconnected to the other questions, is hardly random. It is taken directly from Book VIII of the *Topics*. These "quodlibetical questions," von Moos observes, "have precisely the preparatory character that Aristotle in Book VIII of the *Topics* assigns as subterfuges allowing the principal subject to be replaced by problems and definitions that are related only in appearance, but in fact serve to throw sand in the eyes of the adversary."[49] The ultimate purpose of the debate is perhaps best summed up in the words of Ratius, who complains teasingly to his friend Everardus that he must bring together the double duty of instructing (*officium docendi*) and argumentative reasoning (*officium disserendi*).[50] Ratius thus conceives of debate as fulfilling both pedagogical and scholastic purposes, of educating the unlearned and of disputing with equals in search of deeper understanding.[51] In this way the *Dialogus* provides a scholastic counterexample to the accusation of pedantic disputation highlighted by the satirists. Von Moos is right to ascribe this work to a "dialogic culture" of the twelfth century, but its importance transcends the literary. Everard of Ypres offers not just a paradigm of medieval dialogue, of which there are multiple typologies, but also a connecting tissue in the evolution and application of debating techniques more broadly. By reviewing the *quaestiones* of his teacher Gilbert of Poitiers, employing an Athenian personification of reason as a sparring partner, placing the dialogue in the context of a French monastery, and drawing on models supplied by Aristotle's New Logic, Everard elegantly illustrates the expanding theater of literary dialogue and the scholastic absorption of Aristotelian logic within the schools of France. This pattern holds true from the very literary form of the work down to the questions that are raised and then refuted.

## The Satire of Disputation

Comedy and satire have always been powerful instruments in exposing the excesses and perceived flaws of contemporary society. The early days of scholasticism were no different. For the satirists of the twelfth and thirteenth centuries, the fascination with Aristotle and the logic chopping of the schools naturally provided a feeding ground for parody and allegory. A lament over the decline of learning pervades so much of the writings of twelfth-century satirists that C. Stephen Jaeger has called back into question the very notion of a "renaissance" in an age suffused with pessimism.[52] The argument is alluring, but are not prophets of doom endemic to all periods of creative advancement? Leaving aside the reliability of contemporary judgments, it is telling that Aristotelian logic should loom especially large amid these critiques.

If the early twelfth century spawned resurgence in theological, spiritual, and didactic dialogues, the second half of the twelfth century saw a flurry of satirical dialogues and debate poetry. These trends may well be correlated. Often it was the cultural context of academic disputation proper that was mocked by these satirists. The northern French poet Vital of Blois was among the first to satirize the dialectical education of the schools in his comic dialogue *Geta* (c. 1150).[53] In this classic twelfth-century comedy, Vital appropriates the plot of Plautus's Roman comedy *Amphitruo*, in which Jupiter seduces Alcmena, the beautiful wife of the general Amphitryon, who is away on campaign, by disguising himself as the absent general, while Mercury feigns the identity of the general's servant.[54] In Vital's *Geta*, however, Amphitryon is not a general at war but a scholar studying logic in Athens (symbolic of Paris) and his servant Geta accompanies Amphitryon to Athens with even greater hopes of achieving fame as a logician. But unlike the conclusion of Plautus's comedy, in which the general eventually realizes what has happened in his absence, both Amphitryon and Geta are thoroughly fooled by Alcmena's denial of the affair, even in the face of an abundance of inculpating evidence. Their studies in logic have stripped them entirely of any common sense, and this seems to be a central point of the comedy. Bemoaning his difficult life as the poor servant of a poor scholar, Geta consoles himself saying, "as a reward for my troubles I carry home wonderful sophisms and can even prove that a man is an ass."[55] His pretentious claims to logical analysis and circular reasoning lead him to doubt his own identity when he is confronted by Mercury, who claims to be the real Geta: "Perhaps the arts have made me Plato. I am not Geta and cannot be called Geta; if I am not Geta, I ought not to be called Geta. . . . Alas, I am nothing."[56] The voice of reason amid the confusion of the whole affair finally comes from a second servant, Birria, who is thankful that he stayed in the kitchen and did not accompany his master to these mind-warping schools. "Greece [that is, Paris] received these men sane and sent them away crazy," he says, for "dialectic does make men insane."[57] The image of Parisian scholastics losing sense of reality because they are mired in hairsplitting logic would be a favorite theme for centuries to come.

The anonymous dialogue *In sublimi solio* is a clever satire between a rich cleric and a poor scholar. The two representatives bring their debate before the wise king Solomon, a dramatic setup that resembles the dream vision of Abelard's *Collationes*, in which Abelard is judge of two conversations, and the historical backdrop of Yehuda Halevi's *Kuzari*, in which the king of the Khazar people hosts representatives of the three monotheistic religions before adopting Judaism. The setting of the court of Solomon has additional parallels to the irreverent *Solomon and Marcolf* dialogue, whose Latin prose tradition probably took shape around 1200. Here, however, it is the art of discourse in the service of faith and learning that is up for discussion, rather than the brash dichotomy and scatological one-liners hurled between Solomon and Marcolf. The scholar admonishes the priest for his corruption, while the priest ridicules the scholar for the fruitlessness of his labors. "You do not know what you should preach in church," the scholar defensively exclaims. "You fill the pews but do not know how to speak. We scholars know what you ought to do. But you, full of avarice, do not even know how to say Mass."[58] A central theme of the dialogue is the importance of verbal reasoning as a mode of communication. The priest only further embarrasses himself by his response: "I, a wealthy man, do not envy the miserable scholar, since I know that no honor is given to him. But I have prebends and preside at the altar. I have power and prestige." The reciprocal accusations and mutual self-flattery of the two discussants form the satire of this work, as both characters emerge diminished in the nobleness of their cause. At the end of the encounter, Solomon pronounces the scholar to be in the right, an indication perhaps of where the author's sympathies lie.

In another late twelfth-century dialogue, *Hora nona sabbati* (also anonymous), a priest and a scholar are once again featured in a contest over who is more virtuous.[59] The debate begins when the scholar interrupts the priest and criticizes his sermon. Finding fault with the priest's grammar and logic (an invocation of the *trivium*), the scholar initially has nothing to critique in the substance of the sermon. As in Vital of Blois's *Geta* and *In sublimi solio*, the scholar of *Hora nona sabbati* speaks in favor of the intellectual merits that accompany the life of a poor scholar. He is depicted richly dressed and accompanied by a servant weighed down with the pagan books of Aristotle, Socrates, and Plato. Rapidly the debate degenerates into a litany of reciprocal accusations regarding sexual immorality and personal misconduct. Only the ringing of the gongs for Vespers shields the priest from answering some particularly embarrassing charges, and he is literally saved by the bell (perhaps the ninth hour referred to in the title). The priest in this debate, however, is not so reticent or incompetent in matters of dialectic. In a move unthinkable several generations earlier, the priest challenges the scholar to continue the debate in public with the provision that the loser be left to the mercy of the congregation (one is reminded of Rupert's earlier debates with scholastics or Abelard's challenge to Bernard of Clairvaux). As the standard-bearer for good speech and clear reasoning, the scholar naturally agrees, but he is outwitted by the priest who skillfully arranges for the unsuspecting scholar to sing a solo verse admitting defeat during the responses of Vespers. As per the agreement, the congregation attacks the beguiled logician, who barely escapes with his life. Both the scholar and the priest are subject to satirical humiliation in this dialogue, but here the priest initiates the public disputation and promptly outmaneuvers the overconfident logician for all to see. As a parody of the schools, the logician serves to show the risks posed by those whose training in the secular arts have filled them with pride and ambition and yet pretentiously claim that they deserve advancement because of their superior learning.

Logic and scholastic disputation were assuredly favorite topics of satire before the formal institutionalization of the university. In *De natura rerum,* Alexander Neckham (d. 1217) wrote a long chapter on the seven liberal arts in which he sharply satirized the craze for dialectical disputations at Paris and deplored the decline of interest in literature. Gerald of Wales likewise pointed out that an undue emphasis on dialectics was in large measure the cause of the decline of ancient literature. Criticisms about the overbearing role of logic in the arts can be detected from the twelfth century straight through the humanists of the fifteenth century and beyond, often by writers well acquainted with the inner workings of scholastic learning.[60] Perhaps the most animated satire of the arts to emerge during the first generation after the formation of the University of Paris was the allegorical *Bataille des VII arts* (The Battle of the Seven Arts) by the northern French trouvère Henri d'Andeli. In this work of the second quarter of the thirteenth century, the grammatical tradition of Orleans is set against the dominance of Aristotelian logic in Paris, and the poem takes an almost elegiac perspective on the decline of *belles lettres* in the face of the leviathan of Paris and its narrowly specialized arts faculty.[61] "Paris and Orleans are at odds," the poem opens. "Do you know the reason for the discord? / It is because they differ about learning" (lines 1–5).[62] A boastful and presumptuous Logic gathers her forces on a hill outside Paris, perhaps Saint Geneviève, ready to march out against Orleans. The army consists of the *trivium* and the *quadrivium,* philosophy, theology, necromancy and astrology, canon and civil law, and various named masters of Paris. The assembled crowd is placed under the leadership of Pierre de Courtenai, "a very learned logician" (line 51). The army of Grammar gathers her forces amid the grain fields outside Orleans. Her forces consist of a long list of ancient and contemporary sources, from Priscian and Donatus to Walter of Châtillon and Bernard Silvestris, a veritable encyclopedia of classical and classicizing literary texts as they would have been known to an early thirteenth-century clerk. Now there is clearly a problem with D'Andeli's notion of the liberal arts, for grammar would ordinarily be part of the *trivium,* rather than waging war against it. Indeed, the poem is calling our attention to this point. The scholarly seven, once side by side in the curriculum, in the poetry of allegories and the prose of encyclopedias, and in the statues and illuminations of the arts (cf. Figure 3), have been torn apart by the prideful ascendancy of Parisian logic. A mighty battle ensues, and the academic contest of a century is packed into vivid hours.

The imagery offered in this poem is unfailingly evocative and memorable. Mounted on his horse, Aristotle violently initiates an attack on Priscian, who is defended by his nephews Sir Graecismus and Doctrinale (two grammar textbooks of the early thirteenth century). A tussle ensues, and Aristotle is unhorsed. Priscian, his nephews, and their companions then seize the counteroffensive and try to bludgeon his eyes out when *Sophistical Refutations*, the *Topics*, and various other logical works and authors of the past come to Aristotle's rescue. Other passages evoke the schools of Paris more directly. There is mention of an Englishman named Gauthier (Walter) who holds disputation on the little bridge in Paris (*L'Englois qui lut sor Petit Pont*), and who comes to the aid of Astronomy (lines 398–404). No identification of this Walter has ever been made, or probably ever will be made, since our poet appears to have confused the logical school of Adam of Balsham (Parvipontanus) of a century earlier with some unidentified astronomer of his own day.[63]

More intriguing still is the apparent reference to Philip the Chancellor, head of the University of Paris from 1218 to 1236. Early in the battle, before any action takes place, we learn that "Madame Exalted Science" (that is, Theology) leaves the arts to fight among themselves because she does not, in fact, care about their dispute. Her retreat from the scene of battle provides the occasion for invoking the leading scholastic master in Paris:

> Methinks she went to Paris
> To drink the wines of her cellar,
> According to the advice of the chancellor,
> In whom she had the greatest confidence
> For he was the best clerk in the Isle de France;
> But in one way he considered her foolish,
> That when she holds disputations in his schools
> She abandons strict theological questions
> And trumpets philosophy.
> As for the arts students, they care for naught
> Except to read the books of nature.   (lines 82–92)[64]

The strong likelihood that the chancellor in question is Philip the Chancellor was made long ago by Paul Meyer, who also pointed out d'Andeli's authorship of the *Dit du chancelier Philippe*, a eulogizing poem of 266 lines in which the chancellor's patronage is associated with jongleurs, chansons, and vielle playing.[65] We shall return to the imprint of scholasticism on his motets in the following chapter. In this passage, however, it is Theology's abandonment of proper debates in the name of philosophy to which the Chancellor, "the best clerk in the Isle de France," objects. It is only a passing remark, but given the close association between the two men, it naturally begs the question if there is anything in Philip's oeuvre that might be pointed to as a source for this reference. As chancellor of the university, he was a prolific giver of sermons. Here are some criticisms he raises in one of them:

> At one time, when each *magister* taught independently and when the name of the university was unknown, there were more lectures and disputations and more interest in scholarly things. Now, however, when you have joined yourselves together in a university, lectures and disputations have become less frequent; everything is done hastily, little is learnt, and the time needed for study is wasted in meetings and discussions. While the elders debate in their meetings and enact statutes, the young ones organize villainous plots and plan their nocturnal attacks.[66]

The two statements are admittedly not identical, but the connection, nevertheless, seems justified. Both the poem and the sermon look back to better days before the excessive specialization of the arts. Both lament the disappearance of proper learning that is (or was) the function of scholastic disputation. And, most curious of all, both evoke the violence incited by institutionalized learning.

The broader significance of satire now comes into focus. The recovery of Aristotle's New Logic had a profound influence on the teaching practices of the schools. It impacted not only how masters thought about logic but what they did with it as well, and it is this second element that the satirists found amusing or objectionable or both. It was, of course, a serious matter, as Abelard learned the hard way, but it is precisely the unsettling application of disputative logic that was targeted by the poets who championed the overshadowed disciplines of the *trivium* (grammar and rhetoric). The representation of disputation and the liberal arts is well illustrated by a fifteenth-century relief of Plato and Aristotle from the Duomo in Florence (Figure 5; compare with Figure 3). Wherever one turned, it seems, disputation could be found, heard, or seen. And this is the point, for the culture of disputation involved not one arena of disputation, but many, and, like the shards of a broken pot, its remains are scattered across the cultural landscape. The logic of Aristotle was never far away. For a final example of vernacular debate poetry, we turn to one of the most extraordinary and elusive works produced during Aristotle's absorption into the world of scholastic learning.

## The Owl and the Nightingale

Within the venerable corpus of vernacular debate poetry, there is none more extraordinary and unique than *The Owl and the Nightingale*, a Middle English poem that has traditionally been dated to between 1189 and 1216 on the basis of an apparent reference to a recently deceased King Henry (Henry II died in 1189; his grandson Henry III acceded in 1216). The possibility that the king in question may have been Henry III (d. 1272) has never been ruled out and would place the work considerably later.[67] The latest lexical study of the poem in fact favors the later date, and, for reasons that will become clearer, so shall I.[68] While discussions of this debate poem have often been confined to the world of Middle English literary history, the content and framework of this particular debate merit serious consideration in the context of scholastic disputation and the formalization of the university curriculum. In particular, the verbal contest undertaken by the two birds resonates with the procedures of debate exposed in Aristotle's New Logic and the institutionalization of scholastic learning already alluded to in the *Battle of the Seven Arts*.

The poem is written in rhymed octosyllabic couplets and features two talking birds, an owl and a nightingale, in a humorous but sometimes acrimonious debate over who can sing the best. When the serious Owl is about to lose her temper and physically threatens the cheerful Nightingale, the birds decide on a verbal contest to be judged by a certain Nicholas of Guildford living in Portesham, Dorset, whom some modern critics have taken to be the author of the poem.[69] During the debate, they touch on a very wide array of contemporary topics: foreknowledge, music, confession, papal missions, ethics and morals, happy marriage, adultery, and many more. In the end, the birds set out to meet the judge, whose verdict remains concealed even at the end of the poem, thus preserving an air of irresolution.[70] The robust humor and exuberance of the poem, its idiomatic and colloquial language, its breadth of subject matter, and its fluency and stylistic control have long

Figure 5. Plato and Aristotle in dispute. Relief from the series of the Liberal Arts at the Campanile of the Duomo in Florence by Lucca della Robbia the Elder, 1437–1439. Museo dell'Opera del Duomo, Florence. Scala / Art Resource NY.

earned *The Owl and the Nightingale* the admiration of scholars: "a marvel of literary art before our medieval art was born."[71] While its rhetorical and allegorical complexity is without precedent in Middle English literature, there is much that is still uncertain about the exact meaning of the figures found in the poem.[72] Over the years, the two birds have been interpreted as standing for various contrasts within different medieval institutions (religious/secular), classes (clergy/nobility), and cultures (English/French), as well as dramatic expressions of two fundamentally different attitudes to life (the one pious and pessimistic and the other irreverent and optimistic).[73] Of the many different historical figures that have been proposed, at least one commentator has suggested that the debate between two birds metaphorically stand for Abelard and Bernard of Clairvaux.[74] The lack of any real clues as to the larger symbolic significance of the two birds (if in fact there is one) forbids any firm conclusions, much as the absence of any comparable examples in Middle English poetry prior or contemporary to it has baffled attempts to locate the appropriate literary context.[75] In fact, our very inability to assign to the two birds characters of strictly definable significance may itself be a clue to broader significance, for the author (or authors) may not have chosen to show us a debate between particular personages or institutions, but to show us debate itself. After all, much of the poem's subject matter is of a frivolous and inconsequential nature. And if an unresolved verbal debate with a care for logical argumentation is all that the modern reader has to go by, then James J. Murphy was surely right in pointing to the more general developments in scholastic culture and its "environment of discourse" as the relevant literary-historical context for understanding the poetic debate.[76] More particularly, Murphy suggested that the argumentative, dialectical framework supplied by Aristotelian logical discourse is replicated in the lively debate between the two birds. Few interpreters of scholasticism and the medieval reception of ancient logic have followed Murphy's lead, but these suggestions merit revisiting in light of the present discussion concerning the place of Aristotle's *Topics* in the culture of disputation.

The Owl and the Nightingale, or *Altercatio inter filomenam & bubonem* as the Latinized rubric of the Middle English poem reads in one of the two surviving manuscripts, opens with an anonymous narrator describing the experience of overhearing a huge debate, a controversy that was fierce and ferocious and furious (*stif & starc & strong* reads the alliterative collocation).[77] The humorous but acrimonious nature of their dispute includes quarrels over the relative merits of their song and an exchange of insults regarding their appearances (ll. 69–80). The hot-tempered Nightingale is responsible for escalating the tension of the encounter. Repelled by the Owl's "mutant" looks, the Nightingale professes herself incapable of singing on account of the Owl's presence and explains that she would rather spit than sing (lines 33–41). The Owl, in turn, scolds the Nightingale for making such threats and rebukes her for remaining concealed under the cover of darkness as she insults her appearance. Agreeing to settle their dispute not through petty quarreling but through a third party, the two birds search for an adjudicator who will render a fair decision: "Even though we don't agree with each other, we can better plead our cases in decent language with propriety and decorum, than with bickering and fighting" (lines 180–86). The whole premise of the poetic debate, therefore, is the contestants' agreement to fight with words and not physical weapons, an honorable and perhaps even logical progression for the build-up of the poetical debate, but one that especially resonates with the tenor of scholastic disputation and legal procedure.[78] The primacy of verbal and logical reasoning over physical strength has already been encountered in a number of earlier twelfth-century dialogues and accounts of disputations. It was specifically endorsed by John of Salisbury in the very chapter of the *Metalogicon* devoted to the usefulness of Book VIII of Aristotle's *Topics*: "Since dialectic is carried on between two persons, this book [of Aristotle] teaches the matched contestants whom it trains and provides with reasons and topics, to handle their proper weapons and engage in verbal rather than physical conflict."[79] The idea that the author of the poem was in some way connected to the world of institutionalized learning is implied by the fact that the named arbiter, Nicholas of Guildford, is referred to by the very scholastic title of "Master."

In fact, a number of passages relating to the verbal debate between the two birds echo, or rather mimic, scholastic exercises in disputation. The Nightingale focuses particularly on the Owl's nocturnal behavior, suggesting that the Owl's weakness lies in her inability to see clearly by day. In a lengthy reply, the Owl responds with a litany of counterexamples, including a comment about the Nightingale's unfounded verbosity: "You're called 'nightingale', and it would be better to call you 'nightingabble', for you've got far too much to say" (lines 255–58). As a counter example to her supposed faulty daytime seeing, the Owl points out that a hare likewise skulks away all day and yet can see perfectly fine when the hounds come after him (lines 376–79). The Owl, in other words, is pointing out the absurdity of the Nightingale's argument: a nocturnal existence does not necessarily imply an inability to see clearly during the day. These and other rebuttals put the Nightingale firmly on the defensive and force her to realize the better arguments advanced by the Owl: "The Nightingale turned this over in her mind and thought for a long time what she could say after that, for she could not could refute what the Owl had said to her, since she had spoken both truth and sense" (lines

391–96). It would be difficult to argue that the Nightingale is losing the debate or that the Owl is necessarily winning. Yet the poet has expressly highlighted the juncture in the contest, it would seem, more for the purpose of calling attention to the dialectical traps set up by the two contestants than for judging the rightness of their positions. Appropriately enough, the Nightingale's concern now is with the danger of making a tactical mistake: "Now she regretted that she had allowed the debate to progress so far and was afraid that her answer might not come out right. But nevertheless, she spoke confidently, for it's prudent to be assertive and put up a brave front against one's enemy, so as not to abandon the matter out of cowardice. Indeed, he will grow bold if you run away, but he'll run away himself if you don't let up" (lines 396–407). Having been put on the defensive because of an apparent weakness in her position, the Nightingale is certainly not about to concede defeat, and, perhaps paradoxically, it is her bravery rather than her arguments that permit the debate to proceed. This may seem like a pleasant excuse for the poem to continue, but Aristotle in Book VIII of the *Topics* (159a) also takes up the very same issues of arguing from a position of weakness:

> With regard to the giving of answers, we must first define what is the business of a good answerer, as of a good questioner. The business of the questioner is so to develop the argument as to make the answerer utter the most extravagant paradoxes that necessarily follow because of his thesis: while that of the answerer is to make it appear that it is not he who is responsible for the absurdity or paradox, but only his thesis: for one may, perhaps, distinguish between the mistake of taking up a wrong thesis to start with, and that of not maintaining it properly, when once it has been taken up.[80]

It does seem that the poet has appropriated in some fashion the strategies of Aristotelian logic, for both the questioner (the Owl) and answerer (the Nightingale) are replicating these steps. Here it is important to remember that Aristotle's guidelines are meant to guide all forms of argumentation, irrespective of subject matter. If our poet is indeed regurgitating this text, then the recourse to valid strategies of argumentation suggests that the procedural logic of their debate is ultimately more relevant than the content of the debate itself. The frivolous positions advanced by the two birds are thus precisely what they seem: unimportant chatter, a parody of the serious stuff one might encounter in a theological debate. The *Vita* of Goswin discussed in Chapter 3, let us recall, said nothing of the substance of his debate with Abelard, but it did indulge in the procedures and the performance of the encounter.

Perhaps the most deliberate connection to Aristotelian logic is when the Nightingale is confronted with the problem of how to answer the Owl's speech accusing her of a useless existence (lines 549–658). The Owl puts forth eight distinct arguments and follows them with the taunting suggestion that she might as well quit. The Nightingale is clearly frazzled: "At these words the Nightingale was almost completely at a loss what to say and eagerly racked her brains to see if she could think of anything else she could do apart from singing that might be helpful to other creatures" (lines 659–65). The Nightingale does eventually collect her thoughts and she ponders the problem of how to respond in a moment of crisis. The resulting reflections show more than passing familiarity with the opening of Book VIII of Aristotle's *Topics* dealing with the problem of choosing a reply. "The Nightingale had well employed her mind on a strategy. Even in difficult and narrow straits, she had considered her tactics thoroughly, and had found a good answer even in these tough circumstances" (lines 701–6). Given the close association of Book VIII with an institutionalized form of dialectical exchange, all this can be seen as a very specific point in a round of gymnastic dialectic. When the Nightingale has concluded her remarks, the Owl retorts with an accusation of sophistry: "'Hang on! Hang on!' said the Owl, 'You're going about this with trickery (*swikelede*). You're talking such lies, that everything you say seems to be the truth. All your words are so slick, so specious and casuistical, that anyone who hears them thinks that you're telling the truth" (lines 837–44). Aristotle had dealt with issues relating to false arguments in the *Topics* but treated the subject head on in his *Sophistical Refutations*, which dealt with, as he explains in the opening lines of the treatise, "what appear to be refutations but are really fallacies instead" (164a).[81] Aristotle had listed the four classes of arguments in dialogue form (didactic, dialectical, examination-arguments, and contentious arguments), and all four seem to have echoes in the increasingly aggravated debate between the two birds. At one point, the birds get so frustrated with each other that the verbal debate nearly turns physical: "The Owl was angry and eager for a quarrel" (lines 1043–44); "At these points the Nightingale would have fought with sword and spearpoint had she been a male, but since she couldn't do any better, she fought with her wise tongue instead" (lines 1067–72). The threat of physical attack may at first seem like a playful insertion of the poet for comic or dramatic effect, but, as we noted above, John of Salisbury commented on this very dimension of disputation in his gloss on Aristotelian logic. Here, then, is how Aristotle frames the dilemma in Book VIII of the *Topics* (161a):

> For often the failure to carry through the argument correctly in discussion is due to the person questioned, because he will not grant the steps of which a correct argument might have been made against his position. . . . Accordingly, it sometimes becomes necessary to attack the speaker and not his position, when the answerer lies in wait for the points that are contrary to the questioner and becomes abusive as well: when people lose their tempers in this way, their argument becomes a contest, not a discussion.[82]

Aristotle's point here suits the debate poem well: the verbal contest between the birds, at first mere insults, then a reasoned debate, and finally an outright conflict that loses sight of its dialectical purpose, illustrates the range of logical arguments, fallacies, and emotions that naturally arise in the course of a disputation. In the end, procedure trumps the threat of violence. A third bird, the Wren, intervenes and advises the disputants to fly off as agreed to Portesham in Dorset where Master Nicholas of Guildford will offer a verdict on the debate; he will, to use the scholastic language of the universities, offer a *determinatio*. No verdict, though, is ever returned, and the poem concludes as briskly as it began. The reader, once again, is left without the anticipated conclusion and we are instead left to our own devices to arrive at the most logical conclusion ourselves.

Having established the dialectical underpinnings of this poem, the question of its dating can now be revisited, however speculatively this must be done. As mentioned, the editorial consensus has long been that the deceased king in question is Henry II, a presumption ostensibly supported by the claim that one of the manuscripts containing the poem dates from the mid-thirteenth century (that is, before the death of Henry III). But the dating of this manuscript is no longer as certain as it once was. There are, on the other hand, important internal linguistic features of the poem that suggest a later date. In particular, the poem contains a batch of words that the historical dictionaries tell us appear here for the first time (for example *afoled, alegge, bataile, carter, dahet, facum, huing, ipeint, kukeweld, plait, plaiding, stable*).[83]

After *The Owl and the Nightingale*, the next dictionary entries start clustering from c. 1290 onward. Were the poem to be dated between 1189 and 1216, we would need to believe that no attestations of these words were recorded for up to three generations after their initial appearance. Moreover, we know nothing about the readership of this poem until the early fourteenth century. Alan Fletcher has advanced the hypothesis that the first known reader of the poem was likely the Dominican friar Robert Holcot (d. 1349), on the basis of an apparent reference to the quarreling protagonists of the poem in his *Moralitates*. If late thirteenth-century Guildford really was the poem's geohistorical epicenter, then a cultural formation answering that of the poem was available in only one place, and it did not exist in Guildford until 1276, when a royal foundation of Dominican friars was established. Mendicant friars, as we shall soon see, were great mediators to the laity in their sermons and disputations of the scholastic doctrine of contraries (*solutiones contrariorum*), and they were well represented in the universities beginning in the middle of the thirteenth century. William of Ockham, for instance, was an Oxford-trained Franciscan friar whose dialogues and disputed questions exerted a profound influence on Holcot. While no one is suggesting that either Holcot or Ockham was the author of *The Owl and the Nightingale*, there are good reasons to speculate that their intellectual environment was quite similar to the one that produced the poem. This environment was conditioned above all by regular training in the scholastic exercise of the *disputatio*. The format for such *disputationes* is well known. A teacher would assign one of his pupils, a senior student, plus one or more juniors, the task of disputing an issue. The senior student would have the duty to defend some particular thesis—for instance, that the world was created in time or, for that matter, that the world was not created in time. The thesis would be attacked, and the opposite thesis would be presented by the others. The master would then settle the dispute, trying to bring out what was true in what had been said by the first student and what was sound in the criticisms made by the other students.

Accepting, then, that the poem centers on inherent parody of dialectical games as mediated through Aristotelian logic, its value as a cultural artifact would seem more closely tied to a scholastic environment conditioned by the institutionalization of dialectical argumentation than to a comment on any one aspect of medieval society. The poem has more in common, for instance, with the learned genesis and lay audience of the *Bataille des VII arts* (c. 1236–48), which certainly allegorized the takeover of Aristotelian logic in the schools. "As the superlative example of Middle English debate literature,"

Alan Fletcher writes, "and as a part of the social consequence of its superlative achievement, *The Owl and the Nightingale* denaturalized and renaturalized debate as a constitutive cultural force, and connected its author and his community with the exhilarating and dangerous truth that the Truth lay in their hands."[84] The cultural force in question was the deep meditation on Aristotelian logic that began in the twelfth century and crossed the threshold from intellectual circles to more popular audiences in the thirteenth. This process is evident in the satires and poetry that absorbed strategies of logical argumentation and deployed them to entertainment and even comedic effect. Having examined the profound impact exerted by the recovery of Aristotle's New Logic, it remains to be shown how the practice of disputation became institutionalized as a basic function of the thirteenth-century classroom. In continuing to look expansively rather than restrictedly at the cultural dimensions of scholasticism, special focus will be given in the following chapter to the music, performance, and iconography associated with the cultivation of scholastic methods; in other words, the *art* of disputation.

# The Institutionalization of Disputation: Universities, Polyphony, and Preaching

The first half of the thirteenth century marks the full development of scholastic disputation and the efflorescence of scholastic culture more generally. Many elements of this golden age of medieval civilization are well known, including the preeminence of Paris as a center of learning, government, Gothic architecture, and art.[1] The broad fundamentals of this period will therefore be assumed rather than retold. However, two of the most distinct developments during this period—the rise of universities and the formation of the mendicant orders—were especially important in providing formal and institutional settings for the practice of disputation. The institutionalization of learning that took place in urban universities populated by an international body of students and teachers and the rise of noncloistered mendicant preachers who actively crossed the threshold between monastic and scholastic learning produced a cultural dissemination of the techniques of debate and argumentation that transcended the more limited circles of "intellectuals" of the twelfth century. The rise to prominence of an order devoted to preaching and disputing beyond the parish church, the Dominican Order, is of crucial relevance to the spread of scholastic disputation. This chapter charts the evolution of disputation both within the university curriculum and beyond it, in areas of activity not ordinarily considered by historians of scholasticism. Particular consideration will be given to the contrapuntal musical developments that emerge from the scholastic circles associated with the University of Paris and the musical *jeux-partis* (debate poems) associated with thirteenth-century Arras. In considering how an essential feature of scholastic culture transcended the structure and organization of the medieval university, this chapter further illustrates the process by which the practice and performance of disputation reached audiences not directly trained in the schools and universities.

Universities emerged as corporations of masters and students under papal sanction and, in their early years, were referred to as *studia generale*. Institutionally, they were autonomous entities that were allowed to confer the license to teach (*licentia docendi*). They operated under their own system of jurisdiction and enjoyed other privileges as well. This autonomy brought a new and lasting structure to the educational methods associated with a liberal arts education, a legacy of medieval history that has often and deservedly been told before.[2] The institutionalization of disputation within the structure of university education made systematic for the first time the dialectical procedures of education already developed in the learned circles of the early and middle decades of the twelfth century. The very idea of asking questions about theology became formalized, absorbed, and expressed in branches of learning and performance that had not previously been explicitly concerned with debate. The consequences of this transformation were profound, both at the time and in the long term. The institutionalization of debate in the form of the university *disputatio* became the hallmark of scholastic education and a central element of the academic training in all subjects (including medicine and law), as well as an important feature in Dominican schools where students were trained in the art of effective preaching. As a method of instruction, university disputations lasted well beyond the Middle Ages and survived into the seventeenth and eighteenth centuries, before finally exiting the academic curriculum amid the Scientific Revolution's challenge to scholastic learning.[3] Although no longer formally practiced since the eighteenth century, the essentials of the medieval disputation still persist in the form of the textual dissertation and the *viva voce* defense.[4]

## The Proto-University Masters

The Paris theologian and social reformer Peter the Chanter has already been cited for describing the function of theologians as consisting of reading (*lectio*), disputing (*disputatio*), and preaching (*praedicatio*). Stephen Langton (fl. 1187–1216) was one of several members of Peter's influential circle of masters at Paris. His activities as a glossator of Scripture and author of *quaestiones* likewise illustrate the early formalization of academic practices.[5] At a time when the *lectio* and the *disputatio* and the intermediary *quaestio* were still difficult to distinguish from one another, Stephen saw in the disputation a freedom in the use of terms that did not exist in the lecture. His commentary on Hosea 2:16 sets forth the nuance:

> Some people in no sense concede that the Father, Son, and Holy
> Spirit are three omnipotents. For this they cite that part of Jerome's
> gloss. Thus we know that one can fall into heresy when terms are
> put forth by themselves and out of order. We say that this is under-
> stood about the words of profane novelty. Neither is it to be allowed
> in lectures that there are three omnipotents; but in disputations it
> may be allowed for 'omnipotent' to be taken as an adjective.[6]

The possibility of discussing the term *omnipotens* adjectivally or substantively suggests that it was not allowed in the more factually based lecture. It was mandatory that the master be concerned with the *materia subiecta* and the truth of the propositions contained in the text—propositions that were addressed as the text itself required. But the possibility of handling the term in its other forms was allowed in the disputation, for there discussion followed from the conditions established at the beginning of the proposition. The actual truth or falsity of the proposition, in other words, was irrelevant; one deduced conclusions based on the consistency of the discourse. This rhetorical approach opens the possibility for multiple interpretations on topics about which there traditionally had not been, nor could be, any room for discussion. Obviously, this is not entirely new—it is precisely this reasoning that led critics of the preceding generations like Bernard of Clairvaux to declare such debating to be dangerous and even scandalous—but Stephen's comments would seem to indicate and even assume that disputation was already at the turn of the twelfth century an activity distinct from the lecture.

Another clue for piecing together the development and institutionalization of disputation in this early phase comes from the anonymous author of an early thirteenth-century tract on the nature of sophistic debate. Here the dual rewards of holding a disputation are stressed:

> The purpose of disputations is twofold (*duplex est finis disputant-
> ium*), and according to this twofold end, the disputation itself is also
> twofold. The first purpose is to acquire knowledge or faith of things
> simply. Disputation of this kind concerns things of belief simply

and without condition. Hence, those disputing in this type of disputation pursue the truth of things. The other goal is the exercise, or
what is to be exercised. Disputation, however, for this purpose is
not about things believed simply, but concerns things believed con-
ditionally (*sub conditione*). Hence, those disputing in this type of
disputation do not pursue the truth of things in and of themselves,
but the truth of things that they possess under a condition.[7]

Disputation involves the pursuit of truth, but not just the universal truth
that is contained in Scripture. The truth that is the goal of disputation is a
pursuit of knowledge valid under the given conditions, an exercise in logic
and hermeneutics. If this anonymous comment can be taken as testimony to
the activity of disputation itself, then its message should not be missed: students participating in the classroom disputations of the universities are being
introduced to the dangerous but exhilarating truth that "the truth" lies in
their hands.

Theoretical discussions of disputation are good indicators of the increasing prevalence of the practice. As Adam of Balsham wrote, "one ought to
dispute before an art can be made of it."[8] The struggle to define an emerging
practice characterizes the rise of scholastic disputation in the early university.
More than the theory of debate, it is the practical use of disputation in the
classroom setting that comes of age around the turn of the thirteenth century.
Among the earliest examples of disputations held for the benefit of bachelors
and students are the *Quaestiones disputatae* of Simon of Tournai, a master
in Paris from c. 1165–1201, who in his youth had attended the classes (and
disputations) of the lawyers in Bologna.[9] Dating from the last decade of the
twelfth century, on the eve of the formal recognition of the University of
Paris, Simon's *Quaestiones* consist of 102 disputations containing 371 individual questions dealing with a wide, but standard, array of topics relating to
Christian theology, including the Trinity, Christological problems, original
sin, the morality of human actions, virtues and vices, and the sacraments.[10]
Details about the conduct of these disputations are few, since the *Quaestiones*
are intended as reports on the discussions that took place for the benefit of
others not present. Within these disputed questions, some sense of the events
can, nevertheless, be discerned. We learn, for example, that the audience
consisted not only of students but the entire teaching personnel as well.
Master Simon, seated in his chair (*Symon sedet*), directed the discussions by
introducing the questions of the day, supplying the necessary authorities

(*auctoritates*), responding to objections, and finally offering the solution.[11] The number of questions to be disputed varied from one day to the next, and sometimes Simon had to remind his audience that a certain topic has already been discussed (*alibi discussum est*).[12] At other times, he interrupted the disputation to postpone further discussion until another day (*alias tractatibur et decidetur*).[13] If the fact that these disputations were recorded for posterity is not evidence enough of Simon's popularity as a debater, we also have the testimony of the English chronicler Matthew Paris (d. 1259), who pauses in his wide-ranging *Chronica majora* to tell us that even the largest lecture hall (*amplissimum palatium*) could scarcely contain the crowd of students that flocked to hear Simon. For if Simon lectured well, Matthew writes, he disputed even better (*legit igitur subtiliter valde et subtilius disputavit*).[14] Other figures of note in the Paris of King Philip II Augustus (r. 1179–1223) confirm this reputation: Henry of Brussels, Gerald of Wales, and Thomas of Cantimpré each remarked on how many students Simon seems to attract with his disputations, speaking scornfully of his inordinate pride.[15] Not since the days of Peter Abelard had the disputations of a lecturer in theology provoked such sentiments of admiration, contempt, and even jealousy.

Simon's pedagogical success must be measured against his concern about the increasing popularity of disputation. Like John of Salisbury earlier in the twelfth century, Simon had some serious reservations about his academic contemporaries, their lust for glory, and the abuses of learning that pervaded Parisian society. "The studies of sacred letters among us are fallen into the workshop of confusion," Simon writes in a letter c. 1200 addressed to the pope, "while both disciples applaud novelties alone and masters watch out for glory rather than learning."[16] The fashionable new literary genres that accompany the developing arts of the *lectio* and *disputatio* are especially of concern to Simon, who complains that masters "everywhere compose new and recent *summulae* and commentaries, by which they attract, detain, and deceive their hearers, as if the works of the holy fathers were not still sufficient . . . [and] contrary to the scared canons there is public disputation as to the incomprehensible deity."[17] Evidently Simon does not consider his own reputation as a lecturer and disputer a threat. With biting sarcasm and the imagery of a university climate that transcends time, Simon's litany of complaints amount to this:

> Faculties called liberal having lost their pristine liberty are sunk in
> such servitude that adolescents with long hair impudently usurp

their professorships, and beardless youths sit in the seat of their
seniors, and those who don't yet know how to be disciples strive to
be named master. And they write their *summulae* moistened with
drool and dribble but unseasoned with the salt of philosophers.[18]

Once again, the voice of the critics provides us with some of the best detail
concerning educational life at this critical juncture in scholastic culture.
Simon's address to the pontiff (it is unknown whether the letter is addressed
to Celestine III or Innocent III) is more than another harsh criticism of
contemporary academic climate of the sort already encountered over the
course of the twelfth century; it is a direct appeal for papal involvement in
the educational affairs of the Paris schools: "All these things, father, call for
the hand of apostolic correction, that the disorder in teaching, learning, and
disputing may be reduced to due form by your authority."[19] Simon is
requesting that the pope intervene in regulating the teaching methods and
educational climate that are, as he contends, getting plainly out of hand. It
was precisely such regulation on the part of the papal legate Robert of Courson in 1215 that provided the first extant statutes for the University of Paris,
the document and year traditionally cited for first establishing a governing
body of masters recognized by the papacy and possessing the authority to
issue the *licentia docendi*.

Simon of Tournai's *Quaestiones* are among the earliest disputations that
record the presence of an *opponens*, a bachelor who furnishes arguments
against the thesis. Although never named, these students served a vital role in
the orchestration of these disputations, since the objections they raise elicit
the finer and final solutions (*solutio*) of the master himself. The crucial next
step in the institutionalization of the *quaestio disputata* will be the official
establishment of the university and the university curriculum, without which
the formal scholastic disputation could never have flourished as it did.


## Universities Take Shape


Bologna has long claimed to be the university with the earliest foundation
date.[20] Like many other universities, the term *studium generale* did not begin
to be used until well into the thirteenth century. In fact, most aspects of the
early University of Bologna were dominated by the activities of the students
who poured into the city and coalesced into guild-like organizations called

*universitates* (corporations) followed by their place of origin.[21] This was the prototype of the organizations that were later to be called *nationes* (nations). Building on the northern Italian tradition of legal studies, Bologna rapidly became preeminent for its law faculty. Yet, despite the earlier tradition of the *quaestiones disputatae* of the glossators, which continued well into the thirteenth century, Bologna did not in its early years become closely associated with the institutionalization of disputation. This would happen later, part of the general influence that the French and English universities were having on universities elsewhere in Europe. Once again, the Paris schools provided the greatest center of activity for the practice and systematization of the academic *disputatio*.

Scholars agree that the University of Paris grew rather than was founded.[22] Many of the intellectual and even structural components of what would become the University of Paris were already firmly in place by the end of the twelfth century, including a lively controversy over the place of disputation in the lecture halls.[23] A bloody brawl between town and gown in 1200 prompted King Philip II, who was afraid that masters and students would leave Paris for more peaceful surroundings, to issue letters patent that stated, with marked emphasis, that all crimes committed by students from this time on were to be tried by an ecclesiastical court and that this right should be confirmed on oath by the population of the city of Paris. The most convenient *terminus post quem* for discussing the formal activities of the University of Paris is 1215, when statutes promulgated for the masters and scholars of Paris by cardinal legate Robert of Courson gave papal recognition to the corporation of masters and students (*universitas magistrorum et scholarium*) and aimed to regulate various procedures associated with the education of students.[24] The content of these statutes reflects the climate of opinion that saw a need to reform the schools in Paris. Among its stipulations, the statutes of 1215 laid down teaching programs and procedure (including appropriate days and times for lecturing and disputing), regulated academic custom at official gatherings and clothing and occasions for mourning, confirmed the rules for examinations for the *licentia docendi* (fixed two years before by agreement between the *universitas* and the chancellor), set the minimum age for lecturing in the arts at twenty-one and for lecturing in theology at thirty-five, and repeated that masters should exercise jurisdiction over scholars.[25] As Stephen Ferruolo has stressed, these statutes are the earliest *extant* regulations of the University of Paris, and as such constitute the first surviving rules of any university. Though important, they do not necessarily constitute actions that are entirely new or original. Several years earlier, for example, young masters had deviated from established norms concerning dress codes, the scheduling of lectures and disputations, and attendance at the funeral of deceased colleagues. As a result, masters from the faculties of arts, theology, and canon law had together elected eight deputies to formulate the first set of regulations for the schools.[26] The faculties had also agreed that all the masters in Paris would be required to submit themselves to these regulations by oath in order to continue teaching. These earlier regulations do not survive, but we know about them because, in 1208–9, Pope Innocent III issued the decree *Ex litteris vestre* recognizing the right of the Paris masters to reinstate a certain "Master G" who had previously been expelled from the university for refusing to swear to abide by these regulations.[27] One thing that seems obvious is that the statutes governing the academic customs and procedures at Paris arose out of the need to regulate the activities of scholars and students. This also explains in part why the statutes of 1215 were issued when they were. Robert of Courson had once been a master at Paris and a member of the circle of scholars surrounding Peter the Chanter. In fact, Robert was a former student of Peter the Chanter, and many of his *quaestiones* survive as evidence of his own lectures and disputations and demonstrate a considerable debt to his teacher in both subject and method.[28] As the chief representative for the pope who was preparing for the Lateran Council to the be held in Rome later that year, Robert of Courson was in the ideal position to work in cooperation with the Paris masters who had, for several years, been organizing and trying to regulate their own affairs. Additionally, Pope Innocent III was himself an alumnus of the schools at Paris.[29] The Paris statutes of 1215 were, therefore, not a systematic set of rules imposed upon the university by an external authority, but a much needed set of guidelines drawn up because of the influence of a group of masters who were willing to cooperate with a former master turned papal legate and establish procedures and policies in writing that would thenceforth be enforced independently by the university.

Why the schools of Paris should be the first to receive written statutes governing their educational procedures and social functions is a question that strikes at the heart of the continuity between the intellectual innovations of the twelfth century and the formal institutionalization of those advances in the thirteenth. As the political capital of the Capetian monarchy, Paris enjoyed several fortuitous advantages, including the proximity of ambitious kings, the distance of sympathetic popes, and especially the well-informed and active support of learned bishops and chancellors.[30] Paris also had the

dual advantage in 1215 of receiving as papal legate a former master who understood the inner workings of the Paris schools and could sympathize with the
prevailing sentiment, vividly expressed by Simon of Tournai, that there
needed to be ecclesiastical involvement to bring about reform. Thus began,
de jure, the medieval university. Over the next several decades the *disputatio*
flourished in its new institutional home and formed an essential ingredient
in the basic organization of academic learning.[31]

## Types of University Disputation

The development of the formal practice of disputation in Paris has been
traced in the faculty of arts, notably by Olga Weijers, as well as in the faculties
of advanced learning: theology, medicine, and canon law.[32] Instruction at the
bachelor level was given in the *trivium* and the *quadrivium*, with particular
emphasis on dialectic. A student could proceed to one of the three higher
faculties (theology being the most prestigious) in pursuit of a master's or
doctorate only after successful completion of the first degree. Historians of
the medieval university generally distinguish between several different forms
of disputations in the period following 1215.[33] The *disputatio ordinaria* was
held at regular intervals, usually in the morning, for the benefit of bachelors
and students.[34] It was presided over by a master who announced beforehand
the question that would be asked. A bachelor, the *opponens*, supplied arguments against the thesis, while another, the *respondens*, attempted to answer
the objections that were raised and to demonstrate their weakness.[35] Typically, the master gave a summing up or *determinatio* at the end, but not in
all cases, and sometimes not at the time of the disputation, but rather at a
later date.[36] The questions dealt with during any one disputation were usually
related to the same problem or type of problem, and the exercise was public
in the sense that it was open to bachelors and students from different schools,
in contrast to the (less well-documented) *disputatio privata*, which the presiding master held in his own school and only for his own pupils.[37] Visual
depictions of university disputations are few, but a particularly exceptional
one from a manuscript produced in Paris around 1250 gives a good sense of
the oral and performative nature of the practice (Figure 6). The text itself is
a copy of a twelfth-century commentary on Aristotle's *Nicomachean Ethics*,
but the iconography clearly belongs to the thirteenth-century scholastic environment and shows scholastic masters debating Aristotle's definition of happiness in the presence of engaged and inquisitive students.[38]

Figure 6. University masters engage in scholastic disputation over the Aristotelian definition of happiness. Note the presence and participation of students, who clutch their books. Mid-thirteenth-century Parisian copy of a commentary on Aristotle's *Nicomachean Ethics* by Eustratius (c. 1120), Greek bishop of Nicea. National Library of Sweden, MS Va 3, fol. 205v. Used by permission.

In a short time, a second kind of disputation, the *disputatio de quolibet*, gained currency in the university curriculum.[39] Once thought to owe its genesis to Thomas Aquinas, the quodlibet made its appearance sometime in the second quarter of the thirteenth century shortly before Aquinas joined the faculty of theology at Paris.[40] In contrast to the ordinary disputation, which focused on specific topics announced beforehand and which was held for the benefit of students and faculty only, questions posed at these disputations were offered *de quolibet* (about anything at all) and could cover any number of subjects, ranging across theology, metaphysics, canon law, and medicine. The initiative for the subjects debated lay with the audience, and the disputing master never knew beforehand what questions would be asked. Less frequent than the private disputations, these quodlibetical disputations generally took place in the Latin Quarter's rue du Fouarre (*vicus straminis*) and only during Advent and Lent. Most especially, they were open to the general public and attracted a diverse, even international audience.[41] Masters and scholars from other schools might attend. All kinds of ecclesiastics and prelates, and even civil authorities might have been present—indeed, all the "intellectuals" of the time who were attracted by skirmishes of this kind and who had a desire to ask questions and oppose arguments.[42] All other activities at the university ceased when these quodlibetical disputations took place, thus ensuring maximum representation from among the university ranks. So great was the popularity of disputing that, by the later thirteenth and early fourteenth century, the art and practice of debate evolved into newer forms, such as the *disputationibus de sophismatibus* and the *ars obligatoria*.[43] The precise nature of these debating exercises has long been difficult to determine with certainty, no doubt because they were principally oral activities that did not lead to written forms, although some rulebooks for the later Middle Ages do survive.[44]

The early history of the quodlibetical disputations is most interesting from a cultural historical perspective. In addition to the fact that they quickly become a staple of the university calendar and spread beyond the faculty of theology in Paris where they began, there are other reasons these ritualized spectacles should have been so popular. Jody Enders has rightly observed that the public gatherings at quodlibetical disputations share much in common with the forms of dramatic performance that are documented during this era and that also tended to efface distinctions between actor and audience, spectacle and daily life, ritual and representation.[45] The theatricality and indeed the entertainment value of these university events would not have been lost on a bustling Parisian audience that was witness to novelties in dramatic performance, innovations in polyphonic music (much of it emanating from the school of Notre Dame), and the growing popularity of a new genre of debate poems that featured human or anthropomorphic characters disputing on a multitude of topics, such as we have already seen in Chapter 4.[46] The role of theatrical activity in public life during these decades provides a useful counterpoint to developments within learned circles. As Carol Symes has demonstrated in the urban context of Arras, performance practice in the thirteenth century was not merely a mirror of society but a social and political sphere that engendered the exchange of information and ideas and served as a vibrant medium for debate, deliberation, and dispute.[47] It is not the place here to explore the complicated elements that elevated theater to a position of prominence in medieval culture, but the relevance of drama and performance to the general appeal of the quodlibet is significant. The staging of dialectical exchanges open for public consumption, and in the presence of a diverse and international audience, offers an intellectual corollary to theater's evolution into (and creation of) a public sphere. Thus, if the first half of the thirteenth century were formative decades for the institutionalization of learning, it was also a period in which one must locate the further spread and dissemination of the culture of disputation inherited from the twelfth century. Many disputations along with their determinations survive from the second half of the thirteenth century onward. All the famous masters associated with the universities have left records of their disputations and arguments in the form of quodlibetical questions or sentences.[48] They constitute a literary genre unto themselves and a valuable source for assessing the university's most pronounced contribution to the medieval culture of disputation.

Because the *disputatio de quolibet* could cover any topic at all and was done in the presence of a larger than usual crowd, it is easy to imagine how this particular forum could provide the venue in which reputations were won or lost. The ostentatious atmosphere that had elicited a plea for order by Simon of Tournai is the source of yet another characterization by Haimeric de Vari, chancellor of the University of Paris in the mid-thirteenth century, who compared the scholastic disputation to cock fights (*combats de coqs*): "one cock challenges another, its feathers bristling. . . . It is the same thing today with our professors . . . pecking and clawing at each other."[49] The Dominican encyclopedist Vincent of Beauvais (fl. 1250–64) was in substantial agreement with his contemporary Haimeric, stating, "the

contentious disputation of mature and modest men is repugnant and cen-
surable. And today, hardly one out of many thousands can be found who is
modest in disputing, but all are contending, and struggling, and disturbing
rather than elucidating the truth."[50] Perhaps the harshest words came from
the influential Franciscan philosopher William of Ockham (d. 1347), himself the author of important quodlibetical questions, who described the disputants of his day as "barking dogs" and lashed out against the "detestable
presumption" of certain contemporaries who arrogate to themselves the
title of master and tear to pieces "every view dissenting from their own
dogmas."[51] Peter Abelard, one must imagine, would have felt very much
at home in the theatrical and pride-driven environment of quodlibetical
disputations, or what the Averroist philosopher in Paris Jean de Jandun
(d. 1328) called, in very Abelardian vocabulary, the "intellectual contest"
(*intellectualia certamina*) of the theological faculties.[52]

The university disputation was, thus, inherently competitive and combative, in Walter's Ong's term, agonistic.[53] The drama and suspense of the
disputational process, as well as the sublime aura of a renowned teacher, led
one fourteenth-century sermon writer to fictionalize a disputation *in scholis*
between Albert the Great and the devil disguised as a student (*in forma unius
scholaris*).[54] In this fictitious scenario, Albert is standing at the podium disputing with the full collectivity of masters and students on hand, confident that
no man nor "even some kind of angel could conclude against him," when
the devil walks into the classroom disguised as a young boy. Initially, the
devil demolishes his opponent with three arguments of such great depth that
Albert neither understood nor knew how to respond. He left the day's session
on the losing end, pondering how to respond at their next meeting. Albert is
described as pacing about in his cell at night meditating on the arguments of
his opponent when suddenly a voice cries out to him, "ecce medium argu-
menti," revealing the truth of how to frame his argument. The clarity of the
argument now apparent, Albert returns to the disputation on the following
day, and truth triumphs over falsehood for everyone to behold. The moral of
the story, one is led to believe, is not just the victory of right reasoning but
also the public display of that reasoning.

Not everyone viewed Albert's heroic nocturnal solution to a disputation
in such miraculous terms. Old criticisms about the uselessness, frivolity, and
general inappropriateness of theological debate remained. One anonymous
thirteenth-century writer characterized the thriving disputational form as little more than time-wasting "wars of words":

> In those days, many questions were raised and disputed in the quod-
> libet; nor do I have any doubt that many are useless and frivolous,
> contributing in no way to the edification of faith or morals, but
> rather to their subversion, because from such and like things springs
> envy, contentiousness, and wars of words. The masters will stay up
> all night, working on solving questions of this type that it would be
> much better to despise than to solve.[55]

The overall thrust of the accusations is familiar, but it is intriguing to note
the extent to which method alone can prove as controversial as doctrine. In
1290 a scandalized Benedetto Gaetani (the future Pope Boniface VIII)
weighed in on academic affairs during the Council of Paris to voice his criticism of both method and doctrine: "You Parisian masters have succeeded in
making the doctrine of your field look foolish, and you continue to do so as
you disturb the whole world. You should dispute about useful questions, for
nowadays you take up all manner of frivolous tales (*fabulosa et frivola*)."[56] An
eventful decade as pope (r. 1294–1303), marked by his feud with the king of
France, prevented Boniface from playing an active part in the day-to-day
affairs of the University of Paris, but, in 1317, Pope John XXII renewed the
call for reform. Arguing that a veritable obsession with disputation was prop-
agating a litigious and bellicose corps of academics who immersed themselves
in idle curiosities and useless questions rather than edifying and instructive
doctrine, the pope concluded that the very foundation of their discipline
was being dissolved.[57] The mounting assault by outside critics of university
disputations (popes included) did little to stop what had quickly become one
of the most popular and inspiring activities of academic life.

The *disputatio de quolibet* inaugurated a new era of academic learning by
allowing the audience to question masters and topics, introducing the dramatic component of public performance, and inspiring fictive scenarios of
debate, such as the one between Albert the Great and the devil. As central as
the *disputatio* was to the learned and elite circles of the university milieu,
there is no reason to assume that it was uniquely restricted to them. To
claim the establishment of a culture of disputation requires asking a broader
question: can the scholastic method cultivated in the schools of Paris be
found in other elements of contemporary culture? The ceremonial and performative dimensions of quodlibetical disputations invite comparison with
one of the most innovative developments in medieval music: counterpoint.

The flowering of contrapuntal polyphony offers an especially intriguing cultural manifestation of scholastic disputation because it emanates not only from the same time and place (late twelfth-century Paris) but also from the same circle of scholars and teachers.

## Polyphony, Motets, and the Performance of Disputation

Music was at the center of liturgy, ceremony, and educational life throughout the Middle Ages, so it is all the more inexplicable that historians of scholasticism have not done more to integrate properly the musical innovations associated with late twelfth-century and early thirteenth-century Paris into the larger culture as a whole.[58] To be sure, polyphonic singing long predated the rise of scholastic learning in Paris. Its true origins, if there is such a thing, are undocumented and unrecoverable. The first medieval text to describe the simultaneous vertical combinations of pitches in performance, *organum* as it is more properly known, is a "musical handbook" (*Musica enchiriadis*) that is presumed to date from the end of the ninth century. Several techniques are described in this treatise, but in the simplest version the given chant (*vox principalis*) is placed above the added voice (*vox organalis*), which moves in strict parallels with the chant at the interval of a fourth, a fifth, or an octave. The first steps toward independent part writing were thus quite small, and it remained for later theorists and practitioners to build on new concepts of consonance (*consonantia*) and part writing that did eventually allow true independence in vocal counterpoint.[59] Important developments in the progression of *organum* occurred in Aquitaine in the early decades of the twelfth century, which boasted an important tradition of monastic exegesis, and then in Paris during the second half of the twelfth century. The importance of Parisian scholastic circles in the development of polyphony can hardly be overstated. As the eminent musicologist Richard Taruskin has succinctly put it, "the burgeoning of polyphonic composition followed the exact same trajectory [as scholastic education] . . . it reached its first great, transfiguring culmination in the cathedral schools of Paris, and in a new form it radiated from the cosmopolitan center throughout Western Christendom, receiving a special ancillary cultivation in the universities."[60] The theoretical and practical implications of performing polyphony require some elaboration from the vantage point of scholasticism.

In cultural terms, polyphony is one of a group of tactics deployed to enhance the delivery of liturgical song, the very song being an enhanced reading of a ritual text, and thus it is an enhancement of the ritual act itself. Polyphony served to bring to the fore the *harmonia*—the *consonantia* implicit in the song—and thus to highlight the text the song embellished. Since most liturgical polyphony from the twelfth century onward entailed responsorial chants either directly or indirectly, it threw into relief the relationship of the Mass (the gradual, the alleluia, etc.) with the Scripture on which the chant commented, hence emphasizing the overall *harmonia* inherent in the body of Scripture itself. Music theorists of the later Middle Ages frequently commented on the syncretism of polyphonic sonority. Arnulf of St. Ghislain, for example, writing around 1400, makes several references to how performers communicate musical understanding to listeners. "Who will not marvel to see with what expertise in performance some musical relationship, dissonant at first hearing, sweetens by means of their skillful performance and is brought back to the pleasantness of consonance."[61] While we do not know precisely when the Notre Dame tradition began, documentary evidence confirms the performance of polyphony in two, three, and four voices at the cathedral during the late 1190s.[62] The first theoretical treatises that synthesized the tradition and refined its musical notation appeared in the thirteenth century. This theory both regularized and shaped the tradition in Paris while facilitating the wider dissemination of the repertory throughout Europe. From a scholastic perspective, contemporary developments in the practice of polyphony both reflected and responded to the broader intellectual and cultural environment of its creators. This environment was conditioned by a deep meditation on the liberal arts that was cultivated in the schools and universities and that was now being applied to a range of cultural forms. Harmony, in simple terms, is counterpoint slowed down; counterpoint, like *disputatio*, is a cultural expression of dialectic and rhetoric. Broadly speaking, the hermeneutic principles that Abelard applied to theology and that Gratian applied to law, polyphony applied to music.

Closely affiliated with the early history of the University of Paris is another polyphonic musical innovation that is even more explicitly a dialogue of voices: the motet. Simply defined as a piece of music in several parts with words (from the Old French, *mot*), it first appeared in connection with Parisian scholastic circles, in particular, with the career of Philip the Chancellor of Notre Dame, head of the University of Paris from 1218 until his death in 1236.[63] Very early on, the capacity of the motet to carry arguments pro and contra, to engage in dialectic and irony, began to be exploited systematically and used in increasingly sophisticated ways, so that by the end of the thirteenth century the motet (like the quodlibet) deployed these tactics in virtuoso fashion.[64] Recently described as the least-studied major figure of thirteenth-century thought, Philip the Chancellor exemplifies the cultural fabric that braided music, poetry, and university administration.[65] He was especially well known for his contributions to the new genre of *conductus* music, a type of sacred but nonliturgical vocal composition for one or more voices. His poem *Beata viscera* ("O Blessed womb") praises the miracle of the Virgin Birth and was set to music by one of the most celebrated composers of Parisian polyphony, Perotin.[66] It takes as its point of (verbal) departure the Communion chant, sung at Mass on major Marian feasts at Notre Dame and elsewhere. It can be taken as a commentary on that chant, and perhaps on the significance of Communion within these feasts (the Assumption, the Nativity, etc.). It could have been used within the service, either to replace the original chant or as a sequence following the Alleluia (in some manuscripts, it is called "prosa"). Most of the text, however, is a comparison of those who have accepted the Virgin Birth and those who have not—the joys awaiting the one group and the fate awaiting the other. (Significantly, this is one the chief points of contentions in Jewish-Christian disputations.) Philip is also credited with two well-known debates that are found in several manuscripts with their melodies: *Disputatio membrorum* is a debate between various parts of the body, and the even better known *Quisquis cordis et oculi* is an *altercatio* between heart and eye.[67]

Close examination of other elements of his monophonic *conductus* repertoire reveals a composer who was highly attentive to vocabulary, logic, and the preaching power of the word.[68] In a newly published edition of Philip's motets, Thomas B. Payne has observed that the correspondence of at least three attributable multitexted polyphonic works operates explicitly as a debate, thus presenting the listener with a situation analogous to a scholastic disputation, particularly since the subject matter is the praise and criticism of the clergy.[69] According to Payne, the motets "adopt opposite stances in each of the upper voices, with the motetus dispensing an opinion on one side of the disputation, and the triplum taking the other. In each of these cases the disagreement between the texts is borne out ingeniously by their musical settings as double motets: each position is disclaimed simultaneously with the other, resulting in a verbal discord that, ironically, is offset by the harmonious musical setting that combines them."[70] The most fascinating example of this is Philip's motet *Ypocrite pseudopontifices*. The condemnatory language of the text and the particular types of misconduct enumerated almost certainly refer to Philip's conflict with William of Auvergne, the bishop of Paris (r. 1228–49) and a noted scholastic philosopher in his own right who regularly engaged in academic disputations or what he called the *quaestio sorbonica*.[71] As Payne has noted, the opening lines of the text that decry alleged "hypocritical bogus bishops" relate quite clearly to the suspect manner in which William initially acquired the See of Paris. William's actions during the Paris bishop elections of 1227–28 thwarted the traditional prerogative of the cathedral chapter of Notre Dame to elect its own bishop and prevented the installation of Philip's higher-ranking cousin to the post. Despite Philip's championing of the chapter's actions, William's eventual investiture by the pope was the first result in a series of conflicts that set the two men at odds.

Other disagreements between bishop and chancellor followed. A particular disagreement may be found in the allusions to avarice in lines 12–13 of *Ypocrite*, where false prelates "scrutinize every single purse and hiding place before their eyes."[72] This expression might well pertain to William's efforts to divest the cathedral clergy of the income it derived from multiple benefices. This conflict especially heightened the animosity between bishop and chancellor, resulting in a debate over the plurality of benefices held at Paris in 1235. At this gathering, Philip, supported by only one other colleague, prevented William from realizing his attempted reform. Once again, Philip's motet incorporates the social backdrop of this encounter into the rhythmic and musical patterns of the poem: "Just as the two poems in the motetus and triplum contend, each taking sides in a disputation on the morality and corruption of the clergy, so do all the voices spar rhythmically."[73] Not only are there simultaneous utterances on both sides of the debate, but, in some of Philip's *conductus* prosulas, there is the additional offering of a judgment by a third party, thus imitating the final determination that concludes a scholastic disputation.

The correlation between music and scholastic debate is traceable in other poems by Philip the Chancellor. The "false brothers" who are the specific targets of the motet *In omni fratre tuo* are doubtless the members of the Dominican Order. Philip's relations with this new preaching community were generally congenial, but, during his final days, he appears to have aroused their enmity. In a report contained in his *Bonum universale de apibus* (On the Universal Good of the Bees), written around 1250, the Dominican chronicler Thomas of Cantimpré relates that two weeks before the chancellor's death,

Philip and a certain Dominican preacher named Henry of Cologne sparred in a series of sermons that took issue with the conduct of the Dominicans. While not strictly speaking a debate of the question-and-answer type, the public sermons were clearly polemical and certainly disputational. According to Thomas, Henry's rebuttal to Philip's initial homily "most brilliantly and exhaustively rejected everything he had said with reference to divine Scripture."[74] If Thomas is to be believed, and here he may be exaggerating, the humiliation that Philip suffered at Henry's hands so discomposed him that he suffered a heart attack and died soon after. These and other instances in the social relations that undergird Philip's literary output reinforce the fluidity that existed between scholars and musicians. More than any other figure of the school of Notre Dame, Philip the Chancellor powerfully illustrates the penetration of scholastic ideas into multiple cultural spheres. It is no minor coincidence that his innovations in song, poetry, and polemic coincided with a remarkable output in debate poems (in vernacular languages as well as Latin) during the thirteenth century.[75] The Middle English poem *The Owl and the Nightingale*, examined in chapter 4 for its absorption of Aristotelian logic, belongs clearly to this repertory of debate literature, as does the late thirteenth-century Occitan encyclopedia, the *Breviari d'amor*, expertly treated by Helen Solterer.[76]

A final musical analogue for the praxis and performance of disputation in the thirteenth century is the *jeu-parti*, a vernacular genre of sung debate in  which two or more singers argued for and against a given question. The almost invariable subject of these debates is love, which is treated with varying degrees of witty dialectic, intellectual absurdity, and playful irreverence. Typically, a named poet poses a *question d'amour* to another named poet, who replies in the following stanza, and so on until the debate either concludes or ends in a standstill. Thus, Pierre de Corbie asked Guillaume le Vinier and Adam de Givenci, "which is better, a great joy lost, or a great hope never realized?"[77] In another opening gambit by Thibaut de Champagne, king of Navarre, to his fellow trouvère Baudoyn, a dilemma frames the debate: "If your lady has at long last agreed to see you and you wish to please her, which should you do first—kiss her mouth or her feet?"[78] Partly influenced by earlier examples of Latin and vernacular debate poetry (including the troubadour *tenso* of the twelfth century), this important genre developed and flowered over the course of the thirteenth century owing to an expanding and educated class of professional songwriters and performers and an elusive, but clearly receptive, urban audience. The performance and preservation of these debate songs are especially associated with the Franco-Flemish town of Arras, a bustling commercial town where the Old French dialect of Picard was spoken. The cultivation of the *jeu-parti* of northern France, thus, offers a prime example for locating the dissemination of scholastic learning into wider, cultural spheres.

In Arras, the city's minstrels were among the very first musicians to form their own confraternity, the Carité de Jongleurs et de Bourgeois d'Arras (Brotherhood of Minstrels and Townspeople of Arras). Nominally a lay religious guild in existence since the twelfth century, with ordinances written down in the mid-thirteenth century, it became a leading sponsor of musical-poetic pursuits. Through this act of incorporation, which parallels the institutionalization of universities described above, the trouvères (poets) and jongleurs (professional entertainers) of Arras claimed unprecedented cultural prestige and autonomy.[79] The confraternity included three of the most important trouvères of the thirteenth century: Moniot d'Arras (d. 1239), Jehan Bretel (d. 1272), and Adam de la Halle (d. 1307). Some two hundred *jeux-partis* in vernacular lyrics survive from Arras in song collections called *chansonniers*. Jehan Bretel was the genre's greatest practitioner, a wealthy burgher of the town. Nearly half the surviving lyrics are attributed to him. Scholars of medieval French poetry have noted before the resonance between the *jeu-parti* and the scholastic method fostered in urban universities. Historians of universities, on the other hand, have paid comparatively little attention to the scholastic influences in vernacular poetry and music.[80] Most recently, Jennifer Saltzstein has studied the *Chansonnier d'Arras*, one of the largest surviving collections of *jeux-partis* from Arras, and shown that the genre of poems was produced by trouvères who were also clerics, "many of whom seem to have been equally at home in the vernacular world of courtly love song and the scholarly environment associated with the universities and cathedral schools."[81] It is not the place here to analyze the rich corpus of texts associated with music and theater in Arras, but a few general observations relative to scholastic learning are in order.

Debate in one form or another was a staple of courtly and clerical entertainment even before the thirteenth century. In Latin literature, there are debates between Wine and Water and Winter and Summer, as well as many love dialogues, including *De Ganymede et Helena* and, most popular of all, the Knight versus the Clerk, a debate about who is the better lover. In Occitania, there were the vernacular *partimen* and *tenso* associated with the music of the troubadours.[82] Above and beyond these other forms of debate poetry, the *jeu-parti* belongs to the culture of disputation through its explicit engagement with the principles of dialectic and scholastic commentary, its public performance circumstances, and its educated (and even clerical), yet nonnoble, practitioners. Indeed, the *jeu-parti* of Arras is distinguished from its Occitanian counterparts partially because it is not written for an aristocratic and courtly class, nor was it dependent on noble patrons for financial sustenance. These "jousts-in-song," as Taruskin calls them, were performed and judged before a branch of the confraternity (often mistakenly labeled a "Puy") that held regular competitions at which songs were "crowned."[83] Jehan Bretel won these contests so often that he was elected "Prince" or presiding judge, thus putting him out of contention, a sort of formal assertion of artistic meritocracy. His role as a learned arbiter was, therefore, not unlike the university *magister* (Simon of Tournai, for instance) who presided over a classroom disputation. At least one manuscript from the period actually indicates with little cartoon crowns the *chansons couronées* that were so honored by the minstrels. A number of the *chansonniers* provide accompanying miniatures that suggest the spontaneity of live debate. The figures represented could be characters described in the song or clerics engaging in the performance of the debate itself. Thus, the opening miniature of the *Chansonnier d'Arras* depicts two clerics standing opposite one another, robed and tonsured, holding out long index fingers as though each is addressing his speech to the other (Figure 7). The debate posture and finger pointing align precisely with an iconography of debate current in the thirteenth century that is often associated with scholastic texts and masters. Carol Symes has argued vigorously for a public sphere of performance and debate in the urban milieu of Arras.[84] The *jeu-parti* would appear to occupy a pride of place in this sphere, significant especially because it straddled the world of clerics and entertainers, learned and lay audiences.

The clearest connection between the *jeu-parti* and scholastic disputation is the form itself. Georges Lavis has characterized the form as a game of refutation, opposition, and concession.[85] If it is indeed best understood as a game, as the name itself implies, we might push further the specifically scholastic learning that informs these playful debates.[86] According to Saltzstein, the opening question of the debate operates as a vernacular parody of the academic *sententia*.[87] An initial idea is proposed and the arguments pro and contra follow suit, just as in an ordinary disputation. Furthermore, the arguments advanced by the cleric-trouvères use vernacular analogues to the biblical and classical texts employed in academic disputations. The use of

Figure 7. Two clerics, robed and tonsured, engage in oral debate. The figures undoubtedly represent Giles le Vinier and Maistre Symon, who are featured in the accompanying text and music of the *jeu-parti*. *Le Chansonnier d'Arras*, thirteenth century. Arras, Bibliothèque Municipale, MS 657, fol. 145. Used by permission.

proverbs, for example, functions as a vernacular equivalent to the Latin scriptural and classical *auctoritates* that are deployed in disputations and scholastic commentaries. It is not uncommon for trouvères to use rhetorical figures such as analogies and metaphors to illustrate their arguments and even to provide allegorical interpretations of the authorities they quote. As Saltzstein suggests, "the *jeux-partis* could have functioned as a vernacular version of the academic sentences, which students learned and memorized while they prepared to argue in their own disputation; a new generation of trouvères could have similarly honed their craft through study of the manuscripts like the *Chansonnier d'Arras*."[88] In short, the songwriters of Arras invoked the academic techniques of quotation, citation, and gloss to create authorial genealogies that elevated the status of vernacular song. And while Arras could not boast a university, it did possess a cathedral school, Notre-Dame d'Arras, and the Abbey of Saint-Vaast, both distinguished centers of learning in the thirteenth century that provided financial and real estate sponsorship of the young confraternity.[89] Based on the enrollment capacity of the two institutions, Roger Berger calculated that roughly one in four men living in the city of Arras was educated in the liberal arts, a remarkably high number for a commercial town devoid of a major university.[90] Christopher Page notes that late thirteenth-century canon law specified that clerics who became jongleurs would lose their ecclesiastical privileges if they stayed with the trade for more than a year, implying that "jongleurie" was a popular occupation for unemployed clerics.[91]

What Arras exhibits, then, is an organization of composers and performers who made dialectic central to their vernacular song, were familiar with the world of clerical and university discourse, and used the sponsorship of the confraternity to offer a vernacular adaption (or parody) of contemporary scholastic procedures employed in the universities, cathedral schools, and monasteries. As the main site for the musical-literary activity among the French shifted from court and cathedral to town and square, the *jeu-parti* elegantly mirrored the general trajectory in scholastic learning and polyphonic composition, a trajectory that, as Taruskin put it, radiated from the cosmopolitan center of Paris throughout Western Christendom. In observing the rise of polyphony and medieval song as it migrated from private setting to urban public, the *jeu-parti* can also be said to mirror a broader evolution in medieval society that is characterized by the outward expansion of learning. Since clerics were among the trouvères and because members of the new mendicant orders were the targets of Philip the Chancellor's contrapuntal motets, it will be crucial to investigate next the use of *disputatio* among the friars, especially the Dominicans.

## Dominicans and Disputation

The practice of disputation can be said to have entered the public sphere when it transcended the academic circles where it first developed and reached audiences who were not trained in the methods of schools and universities.

Debate poems and polyphonic music offer suggestive instances of extra-university manifestations of scholastic disputation. An even more deliberate example of the practice of disputation in the thirteenth century is the church's public confrontations with heretics and non-Christians. The dialogic and disputational encounter between Christians and Jews is the focus of the following chapter. The Dominican appropriation of disputation as a constituent element of their preaching agenda occupies the remaining discussion of the present one.[92]

In the fall of 1215, Pope Innocent III called to Rome an unprecedented number of ecclesiastical officials from across Europe for a gathering now known as the Fourth Lateran Council.[93] The importance of this council has long been recognized. One eyewitness of the event describes seeing "a crowd of people like sand on the shores of the sea gathering from all parts of the world at the church of St. Peter and Paul."[94] The issues pronounced upon were mostly disciplinary in their nature, and they included condemnations against heretics and others who resisted the orders of the church, a mandate that auricular confession be done annually by all Christians, a directive that Jews wear clothing to distinguish them from non-Jews, preparations for a new crusade to the Holy Land, and the formation of an inquisitorial process for investigating those suspected of holding false doctrine.[95] Lateran IV was indeed one of the most far-reaching programs of reform that the church had ever seen.[96] The ordinances recognizing the corporation of Paris masters in the summer of 1215 by Pope Innocent's legate Robert of Courson were related to the gathering tide in Rome. That same year, inspired by the threat of heresy, Domingo de Guzmán and six of his followers formed a new order in Toulouse with the written approval of the local bishop and began preaching to heretics in southern France.[97] Dominic (as he is more usually known) and the bishop of Toulouse subsequently went to Rome to seek approval from Innocent, which they were eventually granted in 1217 by Innocent's successor, Honorius III.

The story of Dominic and the events that took him to the south of France to play his part in the battle against the alleged Cathar heresy are fairly well known.[98] In the years prior to Dominic's preaching activities in and around Toulouse, other groups had endeavored to preach in apostolic poverty, among them the Waldensians in Lyons, the Umiliati in Lombardy, and the Poor Catholics scattered in the lands between.[99] Such preachers were laymen who therefore had aroused considerable suspicion from priests and prelates who saw lay activities as an abrogation of their authority. The commission given to Dominic and his companions represented a new experiment in which the church hierarchy would for the first time employ its own clerics—ordained religious—as mendicant preachers.[100] The Dominican Order was officially recognized in 1217 as the *Ordo praedicatorum* (Order of Preachers), and it adopted the rule of St. Augustine. Preaching was not only a duty of the Dominicans: it constituted the very livelihood of the order, since members were expected to live off whatever was given to them in return for their good preaching.

From the earliest days of the order, disputation played an important role in training young mendicants and preparing them for face-to-face confrontation with heretics.[101] This is not surprising given that disputation played an important part in Dominic's earliest encounters with heretics and shaped his initial philosophy with regard to the missionary goals of the order.[102] According to the early Dominican chronicler Jordan of Saxony (master general of the order between 1222 and 1237), Dominic believed strongly that one needed "to match steel with steel" to win people back to the faith.[103] He describes Dominic and his brethren arriving in town squares throughout the south of France for frequent public disputations presided over by approved judges, in towns such a Pamiers, Lavaur, Montréal, and Fanjeaux. These were not random confrontations but prearranged spectacles for everyone to observe: "On established days these [disputations] were attended by rulers and magistrates and their wives, as well as by all the common people who wanted to attend a disputation of the faith."[104] Not unlike the university disputation days (*dies disputationes*) and the well-attended quodlibetical disputations, Dominic's public debates were organized affairs, performed at a set time and place.

According to Jordan's account, public disputations play a central role in the early years of Dominic's activities—sometimes by showing the superiority of Dominic's reasoning over that of his opponents, at other times by giving occasion to a miracle. At Montréal in 1207, for instance, Jordan describes a "solemn disputation" (the words recall the university terminology) that lasted for several days. The event featured Dominic, the ill-fated papal legate Peter of Castelnau (whose murder a year later would launch the Albigensian Crusade), and various named heretics belonging to the alleged Cathar sect. The debate must have been particularly intense, since the jury was unable to reach a verdict after the tireless presentation of both sides. Jordan explains that the subsequent invasion by the crusader armies sent by Innocent III apparently prevented the affair from ever reaching a final settlement and also destroyed many of the documents that had been presented to the judges. Yet according

to the first-hand testimony of one Lord Bernard of Villeneuve, as many as
one hundred and fifty heretics were converted on account of Dominic's participation in the disputation. At another "famous disputation" also held at
Montréal, many faithful Christians and many unbelievers gathered to hear
the two positions square off against one another.[105] Many defenders of orthodoxy had brought books containing arguments and authorities in support of
the faith. Dominic's book was judged the best. His work and the books
produced by the heretics were then given to the judges who would pronounce
on which of the two sides was most convincing. Once again, the jury found
itself unable to come to a decision, but this time it resolved to submit the
written evidence to a trial by fire: the book that did not burn would be
considered as containing the true faith. Astonishingly, Dominic's book leapt
out of the fire for all to see, not once but several times, a scene famously
depicted in Pedro Berruguete's "St. Dominic and the Albigenses" (c. 1495).
Spectacle and miracle, one is lead to believe, combined to make Dominic's
disputation a powerful performance experience to relate.

   Elsewhere in Jordan's *Libellus*, we hear of Diego, the bishop of Osma
(Dominic's mentor and companion), engaging in debate with the Waldensians at Pamiers. Not only did many Waldensians present subsequently convert to Catholicism but even the appointed judge of the disputation, "an
important man in the village who had favored the Waldensians," renounced
his heresy and offered himself and his possessions to the bishop. That Dominic and his entourage should repeatedly emerge victorious in his confrontations is hardly surprising given that these early accounts of Dominican
activities were written with panegyric intent. What is important to note is
the emphasis placed on the rhetoric of performance. The early Dominicans
were spreading the truth of the Catholic faith by virtue of their profound
knowledge of Christian authorities *and* their ability to defeat heretical opponents in open debates for everyone to observe. Here, too, the scenario is
dramatic, combative, and public. So how, precisely, did disputation become
formalized in the Dominican educational procedures, and what relation does
it hold to the larger culture of disputation in the thirteenth century?

   The first order of business following the official recognition of the *Ordo
praedicatorum* was the establishment of formal constitutions for the governance of the new order and a reorganization of the "preaching brothers"
(*fratres praedicatores*) into an international society. In 1220, under Dominic's
leadership, representatives from the dozen or so houses that had been established in France, Spain, and Italy met in chapter in Bologna for the purpose

of establishing a constitutional foundation. The chapter divided its work into three main parts, one concerning the government of the order, one concerning study, and one concerning preaching.[106] From its beginnings, the Dominican Order stressed the importance of study and learning to produce effective preachers. Because the essential purpose of preaching to the public was so different from the other orders that stressed the cloistered and contemplative life, the Dominicans had to develop a routine of study and training considerably different from earlier models. It was most fitting, then, that the Dominican cloister should look to a typically scholastic method of organization. The chapter of 1220 stipulated that no convent could be set up without a teacher (*doctor*), thus making every convent also a school.[107] Each convent was required to appoint a second brother to assist the teacher by tutoring the students and monitoring their progress.[108] This teaching assistant, or "master of students," was to organize academic exercises such as disputations and was to observe how each young brother performed in these drills. It was his responsibility, for example, to decide which students would benefit most from being given a private cell. Students of particular promise (*fratres studentes*) could in a private cell not only enjoy the tranquility of sleeping apart from their common brothers (*fratres communes*) in the dormitory, but they could also use the solace for greater focus, to read, write, pray, and to stay up by the candlelight.[109] The reference to disputations in the original constitution says nothing of the actual content or procedures or the disputation beyond the presence of an *opponens* and *respondens*, but it does state that they are to be followed by sessions of *dubitationes* or *quaestiones* at a later time. In this, they likewise resemble the distinct sessions of the university. The overall importance of these exercises is further apparent in the constitution's emphasis that students should be made to attend these exercises and that they be made to behave during them.[110] The stress on education and the intellectual formation of young brothers evident in the first constitution of 1220 reflects Dominic's avowed commitment to education while also living the *vita apostolica*. Dominic seems to have believed that study was of such critical importance to the friar's work that certain traditional elements of monastic life should even be subordinated to it.[111] Dominic's early disputations, after all, convinced him of the need to train preachers of the highest intellectual sort and arm them with the tools of rhetoric and logic necessary for successful preaching and disputations. Or as the Dominican schoolman Hugh of St. Cher (c. 1200–63) so memorably visualized it, "first the bow is bent in study, then the arrow is released in preaching."[112] The sharper the education a brother receives in training, the more penetrating the encounter with public opponents.

By the second half of the thirteenth century, Dominican education had thoroughly embraced the scholastic practices of *lectio*, *repetitio*, and *disputatio*. As we know it, the formal course of a Dominican convent school consisted in two daily lectures, one on the Bible, one on the *Sentences* of Peter Lombard, a daily repetition over both of these, a weekly disputation, and a weekly *repetitio generalis* in which everything covered in the week's coursework was reviewed.[113] From their earliest days, the Dominicans expended considerable energy working to ensure the high quality of the debates that took place in their priory schools, perhaps all the more so since these disputations, like the lectures, were open to the public. In 1246, for example, the general chapter proposed an amendment to the constitutions that would require lectors to obtain a special license (*licencia*) from their provincial prior and chapter before mounting disputations.[114] Whether the idea of a *licentia disputandi* owes its formulation to the parallel *licentia docendi* of the university is difficult to establish, especially since the proposal did not receive the further review necessary for it to become Dominican law until sometime later (it is first attested to in the constitutions of 1274). On the other hand, as Michèle Mulchahey has pointed out, the proposal illustrates "that public debate was a common feature of conventual education—and perhaps that some reports of the quality of local disputations were none too good."[115] Much as in the scholastic regimens of the universities, maintaining a high standard with regard to teaching and disputation was a constant concern of the order.

The special importance of disputation within the order's educational training was further underscored in 1259 when the general chapter called a committee of five university masters, among them Thomas Aquinas, Albert the Great, and Peter of Tarentaise (later Pope Innocent V), and asked them to report back to the chapter with recommendations on how best to advance the order's academic program. Among their recommendations, the committee reminded Dominican lectors of their special obligations with regard to disputing. Lectors currently not on active duty (*lectores vacantes*) were told to attend classes in their schools with everyone else and, above all, to observe the disputations, keeping their eyes and ears open to current issues. Those lectors who were active would be monitored in visitations both for how much material they covered annually in their lectures and how often they disputed and determined over the course of the year.[116] Ultimately what resulted from this *ratio studiorum*, or new program of studies, was the formalization of *studia generalia* within the Dominican establishment, schools not so much intended to offer the equivalency of the university arts degree (natural philosophy, for example, was not part of their mandate), but rather devoted to providing through lectures and disputation the logical reasoning necessary to become effective preachers on par with the highest university standards.[117]

Humbert of Romans, master general from 1254 to 1263, offers insightful comments regarding the activities of these disputations. A prolific commentator on the early constitutions of the order, Humbert did most of his writing after retiring from his position as master general. His special concern with the education of young Dominicans inspired him to compose in the mid-1260s his *Instructiones de officiis ordinis*, a treatise on the duties of the master of novices. Outside the *schola*, the teacher should be available on an informal basis to answer questions; he should generally set an example of holiness by virtue, humility, patience, and sobriety; and, in accordance with every order's emphasis on brotherhood, he should be called "brother" and not "master," "doctor," or "lector" (as might be expected in a university setting).[118] But in the school, the lector has two formal duties: to lecture upon the set texts and, when the needs of his students dictate, to hold disputations, because "sometimes it is profitable to dispute."[119] According to Humbert of Romans, it was the master of students who took the decision to organize disputations when he felt they would benefit the students; it was also his duty to prevent disputations from being held if the community had neither students capable of opposing and responding nor a lector competent to make the determination.[120] Thus, unlike the heavily regulated schedule of university disputations, there was within the Dominican schools no fixed schedule for disputations, so they occurred on the initiation of the master as and when the situation required. Once scheduled, the master of students and the lector convened for deciding on the topic of the disputation. The lector had the responsibility of choosing material that would be useful and understandable for the debate, "especially if the disputation is among less-experienced brothers."[121] It was the job of the master of students to confirm for the lector that the subject he proposed was adequately covered in the holdings of the convent's library. The students would then be expected to prepare for the forthcoming disputation by consulting the appropriate works. The master of students also had responsibilities concerning the participants in the disputation: he was charged with selecting one of the brothers to act as respondent during the disputation and ensuring that there were at least a few students ready to oppose, even if he had to coach them beforehand over any material they would not be expected to know already.[122]

Dominican disputations were not safely guarded exercises for the private education of the brothers. In his guide to Dominican education, Humbert of Romans also confirms that the conventual disputations were open to the public and that any visitors who wished to take part in the debate were allowed to do so freely. In such circumstances, the friars were under strict orders not to interrupt their guests or to shame them for their ideas if they appeared poorly conceived or ill expressed.[123] Even among themselves, the brothers needed the master of student's permission before they spoke either for or against the proposition on the floor. The importance of these efficient and open séances is further confirmed by the acts of the general chapter and the acts of the province of Lombardy. In 1278, Dominican lectors were urged to keep up the pace when the general chapter reminded them that, as Humbert said, to lecture and dispute were their primary obligations.[124] In that same year, the province of Lombardy asked its unassigned lectors and bachelors to take an active part in the local disputations held at the Dominican schools.[125] Like the quodlibetical disputations in Paris, these debates appear to have attracted the attention of interested locals.

With a reputation for debate extending beyond the order's schools, potential transgressions must have occurred. Just as in the schools of Paris, the free-ranging *disputatio de quolibet* achieved popularity within some ranks of the Dominican Order while simultaneously arousing the suspicion of others who saw the intellectual freedom of questioning as useless and even dangerous. Doubtless it was the condemnations of Paris in the late 1270s and the controversies surrounding the order's activities in Oxford that led to a meeting of the general chapter in 1280 expressly to state that, in the future, the only lectors who would be allowed to schedule quodlibets were those who were also masters of theology, teachers in possession of the university degree and experience.[126] The restrictions placed on exactly who was allowed to dispute was accompanied by a stern warning (*monemus*) to both lectors and masters of students that they should dispute theological and moral questions rather than philosophical, speculative ones (*questionibus theologiciis et moralibus pocius quam philosophicis et curiosis*).[127] The concern over the direction that quodlibetical disputations were taking was not entirely new. Already in 1274, the general chapter admonished lectors who had been granted the *licentia disputandi* for wasting their valuable time debating vain or useless questions.[128] The purpose of these warnings, it would seem, was to remind Dominican lectors that they had the responsibility to focus on the matters of faith and morals that would most benefit their students in their ministry and to eschew those topics that deviated from the prescribed course of studies. As the scholastic curriculum increasingly absorbed the works of Aristotle over the course of the thirteenth century and veered increasingly in the direction of philosophy and metaphysics, one can easily picture a similar development taking place in the Dominican schools, a tendency that would not sit well in the order's Scripture-based program of education. "The problem with the *disputatio de quodlibet* for the Dominican teacher," Mulchahey notes, "was that by definition it implied a free-ranging exploration of timely issues, it implied questions raised by any present at the exercise, rather than the more circumscribed treatment of a theological topic which could be choreographed for a standard disputed question."[129] While it could be a valuable exercise under the right circumstances, the quodlibetal disputation among Dominican lectors, no less than among university masters, promised to draw the disputant into areas he might not have chosen to go. Its unpredictability, as well as the introduction of new ideas (the speculative questions frowned upon by the general chapter), brought about greater restrictions on the disputations and warnings to the lectors who conducted them. In brief, what is only mentioned in passing in the order's primitive constitutions (though apparently already taken for granted) becomes, in a matter of a few decades, a staple of Dominican education, one that soon elicits pronouncements on the duties, responsibilities, and pitfalls associated with its pedagogical utility. As with its rise in the twelfth-century schools and its codification in the early university statutes, disputation has once again succeeded in pushing the boundaries of speculative thought and permeating the cultural practices of the order. Were it not for the concern and reaction that disputation provoked on the part of Dominican authorities, we would know much less.

The precise relation between university disputations and Dominican conventual disputations during the formative years of the two institutions remains difficult to pin down, but it is evident that, by the third quarter of the thirteenth century, the practice of disputation had become a central feature in the two institutions that held primacy over educational training in medieval Europe. It follows that the institutionalization of the *disputatio* in the university curriculum, as well as in the Dominican convent, provides the essential context for understanding the Dominican master who most influentially bridged these two worlds: Thomas Aquinas.

## Thomas Aquinas and Disputation

*Doctor Universalis* and scholastic *Magister* par excellence, Thomas Aquinas was very willing to sacrifice brevity for totality. His voluminous theological writings were intended to pronounce on every conceivable topic of his day and have resulted in an equally vast amount of secondary literature explaining and interpreting his thought.[130] Thomas's involvement with the institutionalization of pedagogy commands our attention, for it is precisely in the area of scholastic disputation that he epitomizes the confluence of Dominican education and university practices. His career path has been often told and can be summarized briefly. In 1239, at the age of fifteen, Aquinas went to Naples to study the liberal arts. There, in 1244, he joined the Dominican Order. He pursued his studies in theology at Paris and then at the Dominican school in Cologne where he studied with Albert the Great. To complete his theological training, Aquinas followed Albert to the University of Paris (1252–56). During these years, the theological faculty harbored an air of hostility toward the mendicants, as the secular masters began to fear that their autonomous guild would come to be dominated by members of these religious orders. Throughout the academic year 1255–56, William of Saint-Amour, one of the most radically antimendicant of the secular masters, preached vitriolic sermons against the new Franciscan and Dominican friars and prepared the first version of a diatribe on the dangers of the new orders aimed at proving that mendicants were the ministers of the antichrist and heralds of the apocalypse.[131] William held public disputations against the mendicant's right to exist and, along with his colleagues Chrétien of Beauvais and Odo of Douai, succeeded in arousing physical violence among not only the secular students of the university but a section of the laity as well.[132] Only through papal intervention was their resistance brought to an end.[133] Aquinas's early years at Paris were, thus, inhospitable times marked by his having to be on the defensive against secular masters who preached and disputed against the presence of the new orders at the university. Given these circumstances, it is perhaps not altogether coincidental that Aquinas and other university-trained Dominicans should excel precisely in the field of intellectual argumentation.[134] Their expertise reflects the social and intellectual challenges they faced in Paris, as well as their primary role as preachers against heresy.

In the spring of 1256, amid the controversy between secular masters and mendicants, Thomas obtained his *licentia docendi* and made his inception in theology. The inception was a solemn ceremony that took place over two days, whereby a new master was inaugurated into a faculty of the university and began his duties of lecturing and determining disputed questions. As a *Magister de sacra pagina* over the next three years (1256–59), Thomas lectured on various books of the Bible and conducted both private disputations (*disputata privata*) within the school and public disputations (*disputata publica* or *ordinaria*) a number of times throughout the academic year.[135] Many of these *quaestiones disputatae* were written down (and, therefore, reedited for public consumption) and circulated under the title of the disputed subject, such as *De veritate*, which, in its modern edition, contains 29 questions of 253 articles.[136] Some of these questions were disputed during his two regencies in Paris (1256–59 and 1268–72), others, such as *De anima* and *De spiritualibus creaturis*, while teaching at the Dominican convents in Italy (1265–68).[137] During his years in Italy, Aquinas was directly involved in the formation of several Dominican *studia*. Their programs of study included vigorous training in disputations, undoubtedly modeled both on the Paris university system and on the *studia* he had come to know in Cologne and Paris. At the *studium* of Santa Sabina in Rome, which opened in 1265 under his auspices, Thomas wasted no time in appointing a bachelor or senior student to respond in disputations, and there may have been a lector to assist him in reading the Bible. "It was not enough to hear the great books of western thought expounded by a master," James Weisheipl notes, "it was essential that the great ideas be examined critically in the disputation."[138] This feature of Thomas's intellectual program runs through all his works and, as we will see, had direct consequences for his cultural surroundings.

In addition to the disputations conducted within the university faculty in Paris and the Dominican *studia*, Thomas also conducted public university quodlibetical disputations, a nascent practice that was still unique to the Paris community at that time. These, too, would be reedited for publication and intended for the studies of advanced students. Because they reflect the essential arguments and final solutions (or determinations) of the master, the *quaestiones disputatae* and the quodlibetical questions are generally devoid of any commentary about the nature of disputation itself. But in article XVIII of his fourth quodlibet, Aquinas presents a rare glimpse into the practice itself when he takes on the question whether theological determinations should be made by authority or by reason (*Utrum determinationes theologicae debeant fieri auctoritate, vel ratione*). The question of reason versus authority essentially takes the theological controversy aroused by twelfth-century masters and transposes it onto the formalized academic scene where disputation is now the locus, and no longer the target, of such debate. There are two forms of the ordinary *disputatio*, Aquinas explains: one that exists to remove doubt, and the other, the *disputatio magistralis in scholis*, that serves not so much to eliminate error as to guide the listeners toward an understanding of the truth that the master has in mind. In the first case, one must employ arguments based on authorities accepted by the adversary; in the second, one must employ arguments (*rationibus*) that delve into the roots of truth and make one understand the why and how, for if only authorities (*auctoritatibus*) are used, the listener will learn the truth without truly grasping a knowledge or understanding of that truth and, thus, depart with an empty mind (*sed vacuus abscedet*).[139] In short, the syllogistic discourse of natural reason forces the student's mind to adopt the "requisite mental postures" to grasp the truth fully.[140] It could certainly be argued that a degree of artifice underscores this explanation. Aquinas is assuming that a master has choices as to what form the magisterial determination will take and that such a choice must be based on recognizing that alternative methods exist for guiding the mind toward truth, in accordance with the character and experience of the student or audience. The disputation represents a pedagogically effective method of procedure that achieves its aims better than any other predetermined form of argumentation. In some respects, this represents an extension of Anselm's principles of monastic conversation described in Chapter 2. Like Anselm, and others, Aquinas sees the role of disputation as a rhetorical tool toward unlocking that greater understanding—a stimulus for the mind. The didactic dialogue that had been Anselm's literary form of choice has fully and officially mutated into the formal disputation conducted by university masters.

The most ambitious undertaking of Aquinas—perhaps of any medieval author—was his *Summa theologiae*, the massive multivolume work that, as its title suggests, was intended to lay out in totality the fundamentals of the Christian faith. The contents of the *Summa* have been explored many times before. While it is not my intention to reduce this or any other theological work solely to its social context, the structure and literary form of the *Summa* must also be recognized as responding to the practice of university disputations no less than the collected disputed questions already mentioned.[141] The *Summa* was a work aimed for beginners, and, for this reason, its literary form is as instructive as the explanations it contains. A question is put forth, followed by an argument, a counterargument (*sed contra*), and a resolution, just as in the classroom debates. Aquinas's prefatory comment regarding his authorial intention merit attention:

> Students in this science have not seldom been hampered by what they found written by other authors, partly on account of the multiplicity of useless questions, articles, and arguments; partly also

because the things they need to know are not taught according to the order of learning (*ordinem disciplinae*), but according as the plan of the book might require or the occasion of disputing (*occasio disputandi*) might offer; partly, too, because frequent repetition brought weariness and confusion to the minds of listening students. Anxious, therefore, to overcome these and other obstacles, we will try, confident of divine help, to present those things pertaining to sacred doctrine briefly and clearly insofar as the matter will permit.[142]

Thomas is offering a new presentation of theology because, in his mind, (1) current works of theology are unsuitable for beginners; (2) present works are too verbose and detailed; (3) they are all unsystematic and are too repetitious because they are unsystematic.[143] Consequently, Thomas has conceived of a work that will address these deficiencies, and his method will be to replace the random sequencing and questions of the earlier works with an ordered format that reflects the systematic, logical procedure of contemporary university classroom disputation. Among many other things, the *Summa* is a testament to the profound influence of dialectical pedagogy in the oral culture of the university—a *summa* not just of theology but also of the institutionalized form of debate, commentary, and exegesis that had become central to the day-to-day practices of scholastic culture.[144] These observations are not new, but they must be integrated within the broader scholastic culture of disputation that existed within and outside the university. Elsewhere in his exegesis, Aquinas insists that both Job and the apostle Paul employed the "disputative method" (*modus disputativus*), by which he meant that the dialectical give-and-take of an argument provided a more persuasive hermeneutic tool than mere contemplation or commentary.[145] This point is well illustrated by a twelfth-century enamel that shows Paul disputing with Jews and Gentiles (Figure 8). Aquinas is articulating in words what has gradually been absorbed into the broader culture as a whole, for, before the late twelfth century, such an image of Paul was not common. Throughout his work, Aquinas consistently upheld the value of properly controlled disputation, suggesting (as Abelard did) that Scripture has itself sanctioned its value and that contemporary circumstances require it. How natural, then, that disputation should play a special role in his treatment of Jews, whose ancient books formed the very wellspring of Christian exegesis.

In the *Summa Theologiae*, Thomas Aquinas outlined arguments for and against public disputations with Jews as part of a broader discussion on disbelief in general (*de infidelitate in communi*). On the one hand, all matters of

Figure 8. Paul disputing with Jews (bearded in the foreground) and Gentiles. One of the figures in front has an inscription, *revincebat Iudaeos*, in reference to the passage from the Latin Vulgate (Acts 18:28): "For he vigorously refuted the Jews in public debate." An inscription with the words *disputabat cum Graecis* is issuing from Paul's left hand. Enamel plate, c. 1170. Victoria and Albert Museum, London. Erich Lessing / Art Resource NY.

faith have been settled through church councils, so it would be a grave sin to presume to engage in public debates on matters of faith (*graviter peccat . . . fidei publice disputare praesumat*).[146] Both Paul and the law of church councils warned against opening up to public debate matters that were judged as settled. Since a disputation is conducted through argument (*disputatio argumentis aliquibus agitur*) and an argument is intended to settle a matter of doubt through reasoning, consequently, one should not debate with unbelievers in public. On the other hand, citing Acts 9:22, Aquinas reasons that Paul gained much more in strength by confounding the Jews and disputing with gentiles and Greeks (see again Figure 8). As an academic principle, Aquinas believed that it was praiseworthy to debate for theological practice (*exercitium*) or to refute error. He therefore affirms the virtue of public disputation for those who are learned and wise but draws a distinction among the simple-minded folk (*simplices*). Among those who are harassed by infidels, whether Jews, heretics, or heathens, Aquinas resolutely states that public debate about faith is necessary (*necessarium est publice disputare de fide*), pro-vided it be conducted by those who are equal and fitted to the task. For those who are not under such duress, however, there is no advantage in hearing the criticisms of disbelievers: to debate in public is dangerous (*periculosum*), and it is best avoided.

Aquinas's recommendations on disputing with Jews are, of course, part of a broader ecclesiastical concern with the proper control over Jewish-Christian relations and should not be divorced from that context. Before looking at that context more holistically, let us first step back for a moment and assess the implications of scholastic disputation as a major cultural force in the age of the universities.

## Toward a Scholastic Theory of Disputation

The importance of disputation as an essential ingredient in the university culture can hardly be overstated. It played a determining role in the oral methods of teaching and learning, it impacted the literary form (*forma tract-andi*) of a range of scholastic texts, and it crossed the threshold of popular culture when it became absorbed into contemporary musical, poetical, and polemical genres. Visual depictions of debate were rare before the twelfth century, but they are commonplace in the thirteenth. With its institutional importance so clearly documented and its cultural dissemination so far-reaching, an obvious question has to be whether schoolmen themselves pos-sessed a coherent theory regarding the practical and performative functions of their disputations. Most *Quaestiones disputata* texts are edited versions of the arguments advanced during a disputation and do not comment on any broader epistemological purpose. Independent treatises on the art of dialogue and the art of disputation would become common in the fifteenth and six-teenth centuries but not before. Still, the elevation of the *disputatio* as a formal procedure within the highest institutions of learning presupposes a shared commitment to dialectical reasoning that harkens back to the monas-tic pedagogy of Anselm and his circle. Because disputation was a method rather than a goal, a practical understanding of its rhetorical and demonstra-tive functions would not require a genre unto itself, such as the *ars dictaminis* or the *ars praedicandi*. A range of insights on the practical purposes of debate has been gleaned from prologues to dialogues, scholastic *quaestiones*, and accounts of disputations within and outside universities. A. J. Minnis has located a medieval theory of authorship in the prologues to scholastic glosses and commentaries of the *ad autcores* genre.[147] May we also speak of a scholastic theory of disputation? A full exploration of this issue would require a study in itself, but a few preliminary suggestions may be advanced by way of this chapter's conclusion.

Thomas Aquinas stated that disputation held a dual purpose: to eliminate error and to guide students toward a greater understanding of the truth. Dominicans more generally were early supporters of the art of disputation precisely because of its practical advantages in the service of preaching. To follow the analogy of Hugh of St. Cher, it constituted the arrow in their preaching quiver. Siger of Brabant, a contemporary of Aquinas, articulated a similar philosophy, stating that the goal of teaching is to find truth, and finding truth presupposes the ability to solve any objection or doubt against the proposition accepted as true. If one does not know how to solve objections that may arise in a question or disputation, then one is not in possession of the truth since, in that case, the procedure for finding truth has not been assimilated. Consequently, it will not be possible to know whether or when one has arrived at the truth.[148] Around 1300, Henry of Brussels also raised the very problem of epistemology, stating that, through a lecture in the form of a (fictitious) disputation read aloud, procedures for finding the truth are presented, and, through the act of disputation, one learns to find truth by actually evaluating and solving arguments.[149] If these statements appear to suggest that dialectic is a negotiable system of rhetorical constructs, as the satirists of scholastic practices perennially implied, then they also underscore a general belief that the truth was "out there" and could be accessed dialectically. As such, scholastic disputation in the hands of its practitioners played for serious truth stakes. They raised consciousness not simply about the issues in dispute—that happened self-evidently—but also about the dialectical process itself and then, by association, about the truth stakes of dialectical thinking. This was the position broached by Abelard, articulated by Aquinas, and upheld by the Dominican John Capreolus (1380–1444), who lectured on the *Sentences* at Paris and was obliged to stage fictitious disputations in his commentaries to defend against a new generation of theologians, such as Peter Aureolus, Gregory of Rimini, Henry of Ghent, and Durandus of St. Pourçain, all of whom had arrived at fundamentally different conclusions regarding the status and aims of theology. "In many ways," Mishtooni Bose notes, "the disputation by Capreolus anticipated the contours of much ensuing debate in the fifteenth and early sixteenth centuries concerning the legitimacy of disputative theology, not least in the different and often contrasting uses to which patristic literature was put by the participants."[150] As a method of pursuing this dialectical quest for truth, disputation functioned as both a literary form and a cultural practice. One way to appreciate this statement is to picture scholastic disputation archaeologically. What we have are the various shards of a broken pot. That it was a culturally significant pot is clear because its shards have been scattered not only across various fields but also across different temporal strata. In other words, this pot was long in the making and long in its functionality, and we must look horizontally as well as vertically to reconstruct its remains. Very succinctly, our narrative looks like this: disputation was (re)introduced through the dialogical pedagogy of Anselm and his circle, practiced by the scholastics of the twelfth century who made recourse to patristic authority, and institutionalized by the university  schoolmen in the thirteenth century who systematized it and carried it over to other areas of cultural activity such as music and polemic, where its practical benefits were assumed rather than explained, performed rather than meditated upon. To better grasp this polemical and performative dimension of disputation, we turn finally to a topic of medieval culture deeply embedded in the medieval dialogic imagination, one that has never been far from the surface of the preceding chapters: the Jewish-Christian debate.

CHAPTER 6

# Drama and Publicity
# in Jewish-Christian Disputations

The evolution of disputation as a cultural practice has been examined from its origins in antiquity to its institutionalization and cultural expression in theology, poetry, and music during the thirteenth century and later. Disputation was a natural vehicle for polemical delivery, championed by controversialists in the twelfth century and by Dominicans in the thirteenth, who welded scholastic argumentation to their obligations as itinerant preachers. Of all the manifestations of polemical disputation encountered thus far, one genre stands out from the others because of its centrality to medieval Christian thought and culture: the Jewish-Christian debate. There is nothing remarkable about this claim. From earliest times, Christian authors positioned their teachings and their identity in contradistinction to Judaism, which according to medieval theologians remained stationary and obsolete, a living witness to the validity of Christian law.[1] The presence and frequent vilification of Jews and Judaism is an unmistakable theme in the writings of medieval authors. From works with an avowed anti-Jewish title, such as Peter the Venerable's *Adversus Iudaeorum inveteratam duritiem* (Against the Inveterate Obstinacy of the Jews, c. 1144–47) or Raymond Martí's *Pugio fidei adversus Mauros et Iudaeos* (Dagger of the Faith Against the Muslims and the Jews, c. 1278) to the poetry and legends of medieval literature that casually but deliberately include the figure of a disbelieving or murderous Jew, such as Geoffrey Chaucer's Pardoner's and Prioress's Tales, the Jews of medieval society furnished Christian authors with a constant subject for comment and polemic.[2] From both a theological and a literary perspective, and undoubtedly a psychological one as well, Jews constituted the dialogical "other" par excellence, a construct embedded in the very fabric of medieval Christian identity.[3]

The theme of Jewish-Christian dialogues has already surfaced in our discussion of Anselm and his circle in Chapter 2. We are now in a better position to examine this literature in light of the overall evolution of scholastic disputation between the twelfth and the thirteenth centuries, the very centuries when disputation became institutionalized in medieval learning and culture. To be clear, I am here less concerned with the theological genesis and historical causes for the long and complicated narrative of medieval Christian-Jewish relations—expertly handled in recent years by scholars such as Jeremy Cohen, Gilbert Dahan, Robert Chazan, Anna Sapir Abulafia, David Berger, and others—than with understanding the role of disputation in this encounter.[4] What follows is an attempt to ask new questions of an old problem, and to fold methodological and contextual considerations from earlier chapters into this one: How did the literary form of the dialogue function in the anti-Jewish literature of the High Middle Ages? How did the scholastic culture of disputation serve to relocate the Jewish-Christian debate into a wider, more public sphere of dramatized public debates?

## Historical Backdrop

The importance of the twelfth century as a moment of transition in the deteriorating image of the Jews is now generally acknowledged.[5] The number of *Adversus Iudaeos* works (many of them in dialogue form) that constitute volume two (eleventh–thirteenth centuries) of Heinz Schreckenberg's magisterial three-volume inventory is a quantitative demonstration of the continued concern with Jews and Judaism during the High Middle Ages.[6] Jaroslav Pelikan has suggested that the twelfth century produced more Christian anti-Jewish treatises than all the previous centuries combined.[7] Several causes have been adduced for this shift, many of them having to do with an evolving Christian understanding of what Judaism and the Jewish people represented to Christian identity, what Jeremy Cohen has dubbed the problem of the "hermeneutical Jew."[8] The emphasis on reason (*ratio*) within Christian argumentation, the perceived irrationality of Jewish disbelief in Jesus as the Messiah, the accusation of Jewish literalness in their interpretation of the Bible, and the gradual awareness of—and attack on—the existence of postbiblical Jewish literature such as the Talmud were among the chief intellectual motives driving the increasingly aggressive attitude of Christian theologians. Other developments, rarely considered alongside these intellectual trends, are equally important to evaluate. The rise of liturgical drama over the course of the twelfth century provided a new (and still insufficiently explored) venue for staging debates between Christianity and Judaism. The Anglo-Norman *Ordo representaciones Ade* (Mystery of Adam) play of the late twelfth century, for instance, has the distinction of being the first of the religious dramas in France to be enacted outside the precincts of the church and the first to employ the vernacular exclusively in its dialogue.[9] It is perhaps also the first drama in which any serious attempt was made to delineate character, with stage directions supplied in Latin. In the final act of the play, the prophets, patriarchs, and pagans come forward in turn to bear witness to the coming of the Christ. Known henceforth as the *Ordo prophetarum* (Order of the Prophets), this central form of liturgical drama offers a dramatic rendering of the popular fifth-century sermon "Vos inquam invenio" written "contra Iudaeos, paganos et arianos" to demonstrate that proof for Christian mysteries can be found in Old Testament and even pagan texts, and it is taken up in many different cycles over the succeeding centuries.[10] It appears in three of the four surviving English Corpus Christi cycles between the Old Testament pageants and the series of Nativity plays.[11] The dramatization of Jewish-Christian debates is but one powerful example of how an intellectual discourse can give rise to its performance. A similar drama is vividly evoked in a sculpture of the prophets Jonah and Hosea on the north side of the choir screen at Bamberg Cathedral (Figure 9). The workshop that produced these sculptures, as well as other lifelike figures such as the Bamberg Rider and the figures of Ecclesia and Synagoga, is believed to have come from Reims around 1225, thus again suggesting a northern French origin for the radiant diffusion of scholastic practices.[12] We shall return to this essential paradigm of the performance and representation of debate in the context of public disputations below.

On a more popular level, the spread of the blood libel and accusations of ritual murder also contributed to the increasingly negative image of Jews and Judaism during the course of the twelfth century and were responsible for several instances of mob violence, such as the incidents in Norwich in 1144 at the time of the Second Crusade and in Blois in 1171.[13] The lead-up to all the major crusading expeditions of the late eleventh and twelfth centuries resulted in outbreaks of anti-Jewish violence.[14] Developments in statehood beginning in the twelfth century also had direct consequences on the Jewish

Figure 9. The Old Testament prophets Jonah and Hosea in dispute. This iconography has more in common with contemporary images of scholastic disputation, scenes from liturgical drama, and representations of Jewish-Christian debates than with traditional depictions of the prophets. Carved reliefs from the choir screen of Bamberg cathedral (c. 1230). Uwe Gaasch / Foto Marburg / Art Resource NY.

communities of Western Europe. As the Capetian monarchy in France moved to consolidate its power and authority, Jews living within the royal territory found themselves victims of numerous expulsions: first in France in 1182 (but recalled several years later), again in France in 1306 (and again permitted to return), and more permanently from England in 1290 and Spain in 1492, to cite the more familiar instances.[15] R. I. Moore generated much discussion by going so far as to argue that the Christian antipathy toward Jews and other minority groups during the eleventh and twelfth centuries formed a basic ingredient in the emergence of a coherent but persecuting European society.[16] This somewhat essentialist view of the medieval origins of modern hatred has been attacked and countered by many scholars but never fully overturned. The problem of the decline in Jewish-Christian relations during the High Middle Ages, and especially of the role played by Jewish converts to Christianity, remains a topic of vigorous scholarly research.[17] Certainly not all the reasons for the decline in the Christian regard for Jews and Judaism during this transitional period have been entirely deciphered. The revival of dialectic, the institutionalization of learning, and the cultivation of disputation as an academic practice must also be integrated into the evolution of the Christian engagement with Jews and Judaism. Observing the Jewish-Christian encounter from the vantage point of our general paradigm of literary dialogue to scholastic disputation will offer both a new angle on medieval anti-Judaism and a more holistic appreciation of the medieval culture of disputation. The situating of Jewish-Christian relations within this broader scholastic context will further illustrate how one particular mechanism for the transmission of knowledge—*disputatio*—transitions from private to public spheres.

## Monastic Writers and Jewish-Christian Dialogue

Anselm of Bec is as central to the evolution of the Jewish-Christian debate as he is to the history of medieval theology, even though he did not explicitly polemicize against Jews. This is not as paradoxical as it might seem given that the two areas of medieval thought were so tightly intertwined. The source of his influence in the realm of the Jewish-Christian debate lies in his emphasis on verbal disputation (as evidenced in his debates with his students at Bec) and his novel ideas about the role of reason in proving the validity of Christianity. As we have seen in Chapter 2, Anselm inherited his interest in dialectic from his teacher Lanfranc, and as he rose to prominence at Bec and then at Canterbury, his ideas about the rational inquiry of God's existence and his literary style of recording his teachings in dialogue form proved to be an immense influence on subsequent monastic authors who *did* polemicize against Jews. To be sure, the literary genre of the dialogue between Christian and Jew, or church and synagogue, had been widely used in Late Antiquity and throughout the early Middle Ages. Nevertheless, the pedagogical debates that lie behind Anselm's didactic dialogues and the lively and perhaps even actual debates that form the basis of Gilbert Crispin's disputations do mark a turning point in the history of the genre. They reflect not only the effects of the renewed interest in dialectic and the increasing attempts by Christian authors to apply these logical techniques to the Jewish-Christian debate but also the increasing encounters between Jews and Christians, a phenomenon attested to later on in the twelfth century by the Parisian monks at St. Victor who sought instruction in Hebrew and Old Testament exegesis from local Jews.[18] Rapidly, the Anselmian emphasis on proving arguments *sola ratione* rather than *sola scriptura* proved to be a major influence on Christian thinkers, and, no doubt because of the desire to demonstrate actively the power of rational arguments over their opponents, writers turned increasingly to a genre that best provided such a demonstrative and dramatic scenario. Over the next several generations, many other monastic and nonmonastic authors would take up the dialogue form and the Anselmian reliance on reason in addressing the Jewish-Christian controversy directly.

The influence of Anselm's teachings in the Jewish-Christian debate are most immediately borne out in the writings of Gilbert Crispin, Odo of Tournai, Pseudo-William of Champeaux, and Pseudo-Anselm, each of whom used principles drawn from Anselmian reasoning in composing their own *Adversus Iudaeos* dialogues purporting to be encounters between a Christian protagonist and a Jewish (or gentile) opponent. Crispin's *Disputatio Iudei et Christiani* was among the most widely disseminated of such works, perhaps because of the unusual space allotted to the Jew and the relative civility of their discussion, thus lending the work an air of authenticity. His *Disputatio Christiani cum Gentili* was, in many respects, a continuation of the earlier disputation on account of the topics discussed, but, because the opponent in this debate is described as a gentile (here to be understood as synonymous with a pagan), there is, unlike the disputation with the Jew, little likelihood that it was based on a real debate, since there is virtually no evidence of paganism in twelfth-century England. Yet, of the two disputations, this one is most

dramatically and intellectually innovative. The introduction to the disputation describes Gilbert being led by the hand of a friend to a meeting of
philosophers in London so that he might hear "assertions of the true faith."[19]
The gentile describes himself and the men of his company as experts of reason
who devote themselves to a rational investigation of the truth. It has been
suggested that this should probably be interpreted allegorically, signifying
that it was Anselm who urged his former student to try his hand at rational
argument.[20] What ensues is a discussion in which both participants initially
agree to argue from the basis of reason (*ratio*), a theme that will prove common to many of the anti-Jewish dialogues of the next century. As the discussion unfolds, the gentile admits to believing in one God. For this reason, he
may perhaps best be described as a rational Jew asking what the Jew had
asked in the *Disputatio Iudei et Christiani*, but this time in a rational setting.[21]
In fact, Gilbert proves less than successful in keeping to rational arguments,
for, as he did in the first disputation, he repeatedly turns to the authority of
the Bible to prove his case.

The exact arguments that Gilbert uses and his method of exegesis have
been analyzed before. Scholars agree that this second disputation has no basis
in fact but is more of a construct, a "figment of Crispin's imagination."[22] The
fictitiousness of the work aside, what needs emphasis is that it *was* written as
a disputation and that Crispin *did* try to present the encounter as if it really
happened. The implicit virtue of the unusual setting that animate both the
*Disputatio Iudei et Christiani* and the *Disputatio Christiani cum Gentili* is
perhaps best revealed by a scribal error in another dialogue, *De altaris sacramento*, preserved in a manuscript that contains most of Gilbert's works (British Library, Additional 8166). This work lacks the dramatic scenery of either
of the interreligious disputations and is simply framed as a question-and-
answer dialogue between *interrogatio* and *responsio* on the issue of the Eucharist. Shortly into the conversation, the scribe actually replaces the original
rubrics with *Iudeus* and *Christianus*, and this continues until the end of the
dialogue. This significance of the scribal slip is that it suggests how closely all
types of questions about the Christian faith were associated with Jews.[23] It
underscores how easy it was for a scribe (and one must assume other readers
as well) to forget who the unspecified interlocutors were and then lapse into
recalling the more vivid, more specific, characters that animate the religious
disputation.

These general observations regarding Gilbert Crispin and his works
apply equally to the other authors of interreligious disputations directly
influenced by Anselm.[24] Pseudo-Anselm, we have also noted earlier, framed

his *Disputatio inter Gentilem et Christianum* between a Christian and an unspecified "gentile" who does not acknowledge the authority of the Bible but who clearly stands for a "rational" skeptic of Christianity (and specifically the doctrine of the Incarnation), but one who is eventually led to convert.[25] The anonymity of Pseudo-Anselm forbids us from saying more on the issue of Jewish-Christian contact than that he was clearly influenced by his reading of Anselm (or perhaps his studies with him). More can be said, however, about the secular master-turned-monk Odo of Tournai, who also falls squarely within this ambit of thought. Odo was born in Orléans around 1060 during the reign of King Philip I of France.[26] While still in his twenties, he went to the cathedral school of Notre Dame of Tournai, in Normandy, where he had a flourishing career as a secular master (*magister*) before experiencing, like many others at this time, a religious conversion to the monastic way of life. He became a canon of St. Augustine, then the first abbot of the restored monastery of St. Martin of Tournai, renowned for its excellent library and scriptorium, and finally a bishop of the town of Cambrai (just south of Tournai), a position he held from 1105 until his death in 1113.[27] Odo was, thus, an important member of the Norman religious and intellectual scene at the same time that Anselm was teaching at Bec, the turn of the twelfth century. In fact, similarities of understanding on the question of original sin in Odo's treatise and Anselm's *Cur Deus homo* have led scholars to wonder in which direction the influence between Anselm and Odo ran.[28] In any case, it was early in his episcopate (perhaps 1105 or 1106) that he composed his own brief Jewish-Christian disputation, the *Disputatio contra Judaeum Leonem nomine de adventu Christi filii Dei* (Disputation with the Jew, Leo, Concerning the Advent of Christ, the Son of God).[29] The prologue of the work reports that Odo was on his way to attend a church council when a certain Jew named Leo approached Odo and inquired about the Messiah and the Incarnation. The chance encounter provides the justification for the literary form: "Because on one day I went to the council of Poitiers I was pressed into a discussion with a certain Jew of Senlis—quite fittingly, on this very matter (with the help of God)—so it seemed appropriate to me to pursue this question in the form of a dialogue, where the Jew had asked and I had responded."[30] The debate continues along already familiar lines. Odo uses the first part of his disputation to argue the Anselmian case for the necessity of the Incarnation, while Leo admits he cannot think of any rational arguments that could refute those of Odo, but nor is he willing to accept Christianity. On the contrary, he proceeds to deride the Virgin Birth as being not only irrational but also unpalatable. (This acceptance and rejection of the

Virgin Birth are central themes, we recall, in the motet *Beata viscera* by Philip the Chancellor.) In the end, Leo states adamantly that he does not accept Christianity because "I dare not entrust the truth of our heritage to your words."[31] Odo concludes his work by dedicating the work to a certain brother Acard, saying that he has presented these reasoned arguments regarding the Advent of Christ because certain Catholics had sided with the views of the Jew.[32] Odo's disputation, then, begins and ends with statements suggesting that a real encounter compelled him to compose the work. It is tempting to speculate further about the historicity of this encounter, but, for the moment, we must simply note that Odo follows his monastic predecessors in relying on rational argumentation, in stressing the necessity of the Incarnation, in using the dialogue genre, and, like Anselm, Crispin, and Pseudo-Anselm, on insisting that he is providing a literary rendition of an actual conversation.

## Twelfth-Century Anti-Jewish Dialogues: A Bird's Eye View

The remarkable proliferation of anti-Jewish dialogues during the early rise of scholasticism is no minor coincidence. Rekindled by the pedagogical and theological influence of Anselm and his circle, the genre provided an appealing and versatile tool with which to take up the time-honored themes of the Jewish-Christian debate. An overview of some of the most significant works will illustrate how twelfth-century currents in dialectic and rhetoric shaped this polemic into a new art and thus solidified the connection between the hermeneutics of the Jewish-Christian debate and the wider culture of disputation.

The anti-Jewish dialogue genre is given a new dimension, as well as some important substantive additions, by Peter Alfonsi, an Iberian Jew who converted to Christianity in the Aragonese town of Huesca in 1106 before emigrating first to England and then to France. He appears to have returned to his homeland before his death, for his signature witnesses a bill of sale by which a French knight who had served under Alfonso I obtained an estate in Saragossa that had previously belonged to a Muslim.[33] Raised in a Jewish community in southern Iberia, Peter was well acquainted with the traditions of Muslim Spain, which included an Arabic education in letters, science, and philosophy, in addition to his familial grounding in Jewish traditions.[34] His widely influential *Disciplina clericalis* (often translated as The Scholar's

Guide) is a collection of moralistic tales from the Arabic as well as Christian and Jewish traditions that influenced many later writers, including Chaucer.[35] The heroes of many of these fables are philosophers who help those in need, offer advice to kings, and prepare themselves for death through asceticism.[36] Peter's literary gift as a moralizing storyteller is equally on display in his influential, and much commented upon, *Dialogi contra Iudaeos*, composed around 1110. Seventy-nine medieval manuscripts of this work survive, making it a veritable bestseller by medieval standards.[37] Like many of the other work of the anti-Jewish genre, the *Dialogi* offer a series of conversations (twelve in total, hence the plural in the title) between a Christian and a Jew, but here the Jew is the author's former self, Moses, conversing with his converted identity, Peter. The work is in this sense psychologically reflective, as it seeks to bring the beliefs and identity of his past into confrontation with his present as they discuss a wide range of topics from Mosaic law and the coming of the Messiah to science and astronomy. But whereas Anselm's *Cur Deus homo* and Guibert of Nogent's contemporary *Tractatus de incarnatione contra Iudaeos* (c. 1111) aimed their arguments primarily at Christians and whereas the Jews depicted in the disputations of Gilbert Crispin and Odo of Cambrai did not accept Christianity, Peter's *Dialogi* retrace the process whereby rational argument did, in fact, effect conversion, in this case, the conversion of the author himself.[38] His authorial intentions are particularly insightful. In the prologue that precedes the dialogues proper, Alfonsi states his reasons for giving the dialogues their literary form:

> I have arranged the entire book as a dialogue, so that the reader's mind may more quickly achieve an understanding (*ut lectoris animus promptior fiat ad intelligendum*). To defend the arguments of the Christians, I have used the name that I now have as a Christian, whereas in the arguments of the adversary refuting them, I have used the name Moses, which I had before baptism. I have divided the book into twelve headings, so that the reader may find whatever he desires in them more quickly.[39]

The imaginary framework of having the author dispute his former self is novel, but the stated premise for selecting the literary form of the dialogue we have seen before. The phrasing in the prologue bears a striking resemblance both to Anselm, who, we recall, wrote *Cur Deus homo* in the form of a dialogue to benefit "slower minds," and to Gilbert Crispin, who, in his

*Disputatio Iudei et Christiani*, made a very similar claim. Another substantive similarity with Anselm's circle is Peter's reliance on reason alone (*sola ratione*) for upholding Christian beliefs against the objections raised by Moses, which is in line with the Anselmian focus on rationality and dialectic, and with twelfth-century developments more generally.[40] One does not generally associate Peter Alfonsi with the circle of Anselm and Gilbert Crispin, and there is no solid evidence that Alfonsi was personally acquainted with either of the two men.[41] It is worth speculating further on these intriguingly similarities.

The prefatory comments and the division of the *Dialogi* into twelve convenient headings suggest that the work was designed and intended for use as a handbook in disputative argumentation, and not just a personal reflection or a justification of the author's choices in life. Scholastic authors often gave great attention to the ordering and organization of their works. Beyond the obvious goals shared by early twelfth-century dialogues in subordinating an outdated Judaism to the enduring validity of Christianity, what is especially worth noting are the similar statements that explain the didactic function of the literary form and the subsequent cultivation of a dramatic scenario in which the reader can more easily visualize the characters in dispute (Figure 10). Alfonsi should perhaps, therefore, be included in what G. R. Evans has described as an Anselmian "community of thought" at the turn of the twelfth century.[42] Not only were Anselm, Gilbert, and Alfonsi rational polemicists who concerned themselves with various elements of the hermeneutic Jew, but they also each exploited the drama of dispute in a literary dialogue that was implicitly or explicitly didactic. In his *Epistola ad peripateticos*, Alfonsi praises the current study of the art of dialectic. He identifies it as the first among the arts (*prima omnium artem*), precisely because of its value to other fields: "The art of dialectic, I say, is sublime and valid; it is not useful in and of itself, but it is useful and necessary to the arts. . . . through dialectic right is discerned from wrong, and true from false."[43] The *Dialogi* might therefore be seen as enacting this principle within the service of polemic.

Alfonsi's most singular contribution to the Jewish-Christian debate was that he provided the first full-scale assault on the Talmud.[44] His influence is indisputable. It was the most widely circulated anti-Jewish work of the later Middle Ages, used by many later medieval polemicists including Peter the Venerable; Peter of Cornwall (discussed below); Vincent of Beauvais, who included a long extract from the dialogue in his popular encyclopedia, the *Speculum historiale*; and Raymond Martí, who mined the work for his monumental *Pugio fidei*. Another Jewish convert to Christianity, Abner of Burgos

Figure 10. Peter Alfonsi in dispute with his former self, Moses (left). Note the Jewish hat worn by Moses, the staging of the debate framed by pillars in the background, and the singular strength of Peter's reasoning embodied by his one finger versus Moses' many. Image from a thirteenth-century Belgian copy of the *Dialogi contra Iudaeos*.

(1270–1347), later made use of the text in his *Mostrador de Justicia* (Teacher of Righteousness), also a dialogue in ten chapters. Irven Resnick has suggested that Alfonsi's work was employed by the convert Pablo Christiani at the public disputation at Barcelona in 1263 and later by Jerome de Santa Fe (another Jewish convert) during his involvement in the disputation at Tortosa (1413–14).[45] The spectacular success of this anti-Jewish dialogue brings us back to what distinguishes certain anti-Jewish tracts from others: Alfonsi's *Dialogi*, like Gilbert Crispin's *Disputatio Iudei et Christiani*, must have earned its success at least partially because of its ability to captivate and stimulate its readership, dramatizing tangible personas ("authentic" Jews) for an audience already familiar with the theological stakes of the Jewish-Christian debate.

Peter Abelard's *Collationes* has already been discussed in chapter 3 as part of his broader engagements with the theory and practice of scholastic disputation. It can now be situated within the context of the anti-Jewish dialogues of its period. Despite the alluring framework of three characters approaching Abelard in a dream vision, the work did not enjoy the same success as the dialogues of Alfonsi and Gilbert Crispin. Its manuscript survival was minimal, as was the case, it should be added, with most of Abelard's works. But it must also be noted that the *Collationes* is not strictly speaking a work of the anti-Jewish genre; nor does it end with the conversion that is common in so many of these anti-Jewish dialogues.[46] This is not to say that the work does not contain insightful comments about Abelard's conception of Jews and Judaism—scholars have rightfully called attention to Abelard's debasing assumptions about Judaism inherent in the discussions—but the work is not primarily concerned with the topic of the Jewish-Christian debate. Rather, the *Collationes* is explicitly concerned with the ethical question of how to achieve the highest good. The dialogue with the Jew serves as a first round encounter for the Philosopher before he moves on toward locating that good in a conversation with the Christian. What is interesting from the perspective of Jewish-Christian disputations is that Abelard again gives an ingenious and original twist to an established literary genre, and he does so by upholding the value of intellectual debate rather than by rejecting Jewish claims and texts outright. The speeches by all three characters are lengthy, the arguments presented on both sides of the issues resonate with legitimacy (if not an occasional modicum of compassion), and the procedure for intellectual advancement—what we might call the scholastic method in the service of moral philosophy and the Jewish-Christian debate—rests on the stated merits of a thoroughly rational and open-ended discussion, with a clear favoritism for the neutral Philosopher. He is described as following no law, having more practice in reasoning, and in possession of a fuller philosophical armor. Everything we need to know about Abelard's intellectual program is clearly stated in the preface to the work, where he humbly agrees to serve as the judge of the discussions:

> Then I replied: "Rather than one of the wise, you have decided on
> a foolish person as your judge; but I do not reject the honor you
> have been so kind as to pay me. For being used myself, as you are,
> to the empty disputes of this world, it will not be hard for me to
> listen to what I usually enjoy. But you, Philosopher, who profess no
> law and yield only to reasoning, should not consider it anything
> great if you appear to be the strongest in this contest, since you have
> two swords for the fight, but the others battle against you with only
> one. You are able to use both written authority and reasoning against
> them, but they cannot base any objections to your position on a
> written law, since you follow no law; also the fact that you, being
> more accustomed to reasoning, have a fuller philosophical armory,
> means that it is harder for them to tackle you by reasoning. Yet,
> since you have made a binding and equable agreement to do this,
> and I see that you are each trusting in your own powers, I certainly
> shall not let my embarrassment at my unsuitability as a judge stand
> in the way of your venture, especially since I believe that I will learn
> something from it. For, as one of our writers [Augustine] once
> noted, no teaching is so false, that there is not truth mixed in with
> it; and, in my view, no debate is so frivolous that it does not teach
> us something (*nullam adeo frivolam esse disputationem arbitror, ut
> non aliquod habeat documentum*).[47]

As a tireless proponent of argumentative reasoning, Abelard insists on the value of arguing both sides of the issue before proceeding toward a verdict, something that we have noted is never given. The dialogue with the Jew thus concludes in much the same way that it began, with Abelard as judge withholding his pronouncement until he has had the opportunity to listen to the words of the Christian, "so that being made wiser by hearing them, I would judge more finely."[48] We are being compelled to learn not from the conclusion of the debate, but from the debate itself. In more fashionable words, the journey is the destination.

Abelard makes one other curious appearance in the context of the Jewish-Christian debate. Gerald of Wales in his *Itenerarium Kambriae* (Journey Through Wales; c. 1191) recalls a story he had heard in Paris of Peter Abelard disputing with a Jew in the presence of King Philip I of France on the question why it appears that lightning never seems to land on synagogues.[49] The anecdote is an odd insertion in Gerald's travel account, which was based on a voyage he had undertaken in 1188 with Archbishop Baldwin of Canterbury. The essential point of the story seems to be that Abelard's reputation as a debater earned him an audience with the king himself and that his method of approach was to first allow the Jew a chance to explain his side, only to reply more convincingly with quotations from Ovid and Horace. As apocryphal or distorted as Gerald's anecdote may be, the passing reference to Abelard reinforces the mental connection that was established in the twelfth century between Jews and Christians in dispute and that Abelard was the disputer par excellence. The idea that such a debate took place in the presence of the king of France has no basis in fact and would seem to respond more directly to contemporary ecclesiastical regulations about debates between Jews and Christians. More about these below.

It was probably sometime in the 1150s or 1160s that the poet and learned courtier Walter of Châtillon composed his own dialogue relating to the Jewish-Christian debate, his *Tractatus sive Dialogus contra Iudaeos*. Walter was a native of Flanders, and, like many of the other writers encountered thus far, he seems to have spent time as a student in Paris, Reims, and even Bologna before serving as a notary and administrator for William of Champagne (whose uncle Theobald V of Blois was responsible for the thirty-two Jews burnt in 1171 on the charge of murdering a Christian). His *Tractatus*, however, appears to have been an early work, as he situates himself in Châtillon-sur-Marne, where he was head of the school, claiming to have conferred with Jews in the town as he wrote it. A curious novelty in Walter's dialogue is his claim that he initiated the contact with Jews. "Having nothing to do one Sunday," Walter writes, "I went according to my habit to the home of a certain Hebrew, so as to hear something extraordinary."[50] Eschewing the more obvious literary scenario of constructing a debate with one of the town Jews, Walter instead frames the dialogue between himself and another Christian, Baldwin of Valencienne, a canon of the nearby Premonstratensian abbey of Braine.[51] Baldwin's role in the dialogue is not to offer objections, as might be the case with a Jewish interlocutor, or to serve as a faithful student in search of answers to a vexed question, as is the case with Moses interrogating

Peter in Alfonsi's *Dialogi*. Instead, Baldwin serves the rhetorical function of providing a sounding board for Walter's comments while at the same time informing the reader that he, too, has "disputed with a Jew whose coreligionists had named their advocate."[52] While it may well be the case that Baldwin did have contact with Jews, his statements seem most likely included for their rhetorical effect. Elsewhere, for instance, Baldwin makes the rather unlikely claim that he had discussed with a Muslim whether Jesus was the Son of God.[53] Rather than speculate further over how "realistic" these claims are, we will instead note the use of public debate as a point of departure in a Christian treatise attacking Jews. Unlike other dialogues that handled the theological divide between Jews and Christians using two opposing characters, Walter's *Tractatus* introduces a second learned Christian discussant who confirms Walter's points.

The second half of the twelfth century saw a continued Christian interest in Jews and Judaism. Curiously, there were fewer dialogues or works that purported to be the record of disputations between Jews and Christians. In fact, there were fewer overtly anti-Jewish polemics as a whole during the second half of the twelfth century, although this must surely not be understood as sign of improving relations. The seizing of Jewish property and the temporary expulsion of Jews from the royal territories of France in 1182 by edict of the king of France might explain the comparative decline in anti-Jewish polemical writings during the period when scholastic disputation and dialogue writing were otherwise on the rise. Continuity of the anti-Jewish dialogue in the late twelfth century can instead be found in England. Chief among these works are the *Dialogus contra Iudaeos* (1180–84) by Bishop Bartholomew of Exeter; the brief and little-known *Arma contra Iudeos*, an anonymous dialogue that was probably composed in England during the final years of the twelfth century; and the disputation of Peter of Cornwall.[54]

Bartholomew of Exeter offers a minor but instructive example of the diffusion of scholastic disputation within the Jewish-Christian debate. A native of Normandy, he clerked for Theobald of Bec, archbishop of Canterbury, in the illustrious company of John of Salisbury (with whom he corresponded and remained good friends) and Thomas Becket (with whom he lost favor) before being elected bishop of Exeter in 1155. He was involved in a number of ecclesiastical disputes in England and on the continent, and, at some point in his career, he taught law in Paris. Addressed to Baldwin, bishop of Worcester and later archbishop of Canterbury, the *Dialogus* follows an older, monastic convention of presenting an anonymous teacher (*Magister*) in conversation with a questioning student (*Discipulus*). It is original in emphasizing and refining the long-perceived difference between Christian allegorical interpretations of Scripture and Jewish literal interpretation. The teacher states,

> The chief cause of disagreement between ourselves and the Jews seems to me to be this: they take the Old Testament literally, wherever they can find a literal sense . . . we interpret not only the words of Scripture, but the things done, and the deeds themselves, in a mystical sense, yet in such a way that the freedom of allegory may in no wise nullify, either history in the events, or proper understanding of the words, of Scripture.[55]

Far from the "rather dull theological treatise" that one biographer has called it, Bartholomew's dialogue notably reflects the very issues that were at the forefront of the Victorine exegetes in Paris.[56] Although Bartholomew is too late to be connected to the immediate school of Anselm, his use of dialogue in the context of the Jewish-Christian debate follows similar patterns to the other monastic writers from Normandy. Moreover, Bartholomew appears to have been the first polemicist in England to quote directly from Alfonsi's *Dialogi*.[57] Even if the dialogue adds little to the content of the Jewish-Christian debate per se, Bartholomew belongs to a second generation of twelfth-century polemicists who brought models of scholastic exegetical discourse from Paris and the continent to England.

The English contribution to the Jewish-Christian debate is best showcased by Peter of Cornwall, the prior of a small London monastery who, around 1208, composed a lengthy *Liber disputationum contra Symonem Iudeorum de confutatione Iudeorem* (Disputation against Symon the Jew on the refutation of the Jews).[58] He dedicated the work to Stephen Langton, the former Paris master who was recently appointed archbishop of Canterbury amid great resistance from England's King John. The "disputation" is framed as a dialogue between the author and Symon, a Jew who has converted to Christianity and become a canon of Holy Trinity, Aldgate, alongside Peter. In this way, the work echoes the example of Herman the Jew and his entrance into the Premonstratensian abbey of Cappenberg, only here Symon's conversion to Christianity in the final chapter follows sequentially and directly from the alleged disputation. In the prologue, we learn that the work was originally divided into two parts; the first, which is not known to survive, contained a collection of passages chiefly from the Old Testament, which refer to Christ, the true Messiah, and to his church. The contents of this lost portion most probably reproduced many of the familiar examples already known from earlier collections of *testimonia* aimed at demonstrating Christian truth.[59] The second part of the work contains the disputation proper and is itself divided into three books in which Peter levels many of the more common medieval accusations against Jews and Judaism, including that Jesus is the Messiah and has fulfilled Jewish law, that the Jews interpret the Old Testament too literally, and that certain Jewish rites and ceremonies were rightly abolished after the advent of Christ. If the content of most of this disputation (and the lost portion of the work that preceded it) revisits well-worn themes in the Jewish-Christian debate, the prologue offers several intriguing peculiarities. First, Peter announces that he has disputed with Symon at greater length than any other Christian has against any other Jew, an intriguing claim given the amount of interest in the Hebrew Bible by twelfth-century exegetes of the school of St. Victor in Paris.[60] Second, although Peter displays no knowledge of the interchange of ideas between Christians and Jews that had taken place in his lifetime (for instance, the biblical exegesis of Andrew of St. Victor), he does appear to be well acquainted with the earlier works of the Jewish-Christian debate that were in circulation in England. Like Bartholomew of Exeter before him, who came from the neighboring county of Devon, he quotes Alfonsi's *Dialogi*, and like Gilbert Crispin, who was active in London, he draws attention to the civility in which the disputation was allegedly carried out:

> It is necessary to understand that when we met together for the first time to discuss matters, this Jew and I agreed to debate with each other without quarreling or shouting (*non contentiose nec clamose*), without any desire for victory, but peaceably and in complete tranquility, neither one of us cutting the other off short and, should one of us bring up a problematic theme, the other quietly hearing him out until his argument was complete.[61]

Peter makes the mutual respect between Symon and himself a fundamental principle of their encounter. Symon, after all, is first described as "a Jew instructed in his religion and our literature," and one is led to believe by the end that the politeness of their exchange and the evenhandedness of their debate have as much to do with his eventual conversion as the arguments

Peter puts forward. In the conclusion of the work, Symon offers his abundant thanks (*gratias . . . immensas*) to Peter and to God for having been led through the invincible arguments of disputation to the salvation of the Christian faith.[62]

The disputations of Bartholomew of Exeter and Peter of Cornwall, both still unpublished, provide important instances of the continued cultivation of key themes of the Jewish-Christian debate by monastic writers in England. They echo the style and substance of their Norman and northern French counterparts from earlier in the century and remind us that by the end of the twelfth century the theological goal of demonstrating and dramatizing the subordination of Judaism to Christianity was inextricably bound up in literary form of the dialogue.

## From Literary Genre to the Public Sphere

The early thirteenth century saw a return of the Jewish communities to Capetian France (Jews were readmitted in 1198), the formal emergence of the University of Paris, the rapid expansion of the Dominican Order, and new directions in the Jewish-Christian debate, including the first vernacular dialogues between Christians and Jews and several celebrated public disputations, such as the Talmud disputation in Paris in 1240 and the Barcelona disputation of 1263. While it may seem logical that Jewish-Christian encounters would be given a new thrust by the formalization of disputation in these new institutions, there is, in fact, a paradox: throughout the thirteenth century, the church was perpetually concerned to regulate the interactions between Christians and Jews. The imposition of the notorious "Jewish Badge" at Lateran IV in 1215 is the most obvious example of an attempt to maintain social segregation between Christian and Jewish communities, but many other edicts of church councils and missives of the popes are more specific, for they seek to forbid religious disputations of the sort that are described in the dialogues of the twelfth century. Thus, in an addendum to the synodical rules issued around 1200 by Odo of Sully, the archbishop of Paris (1197–1208), it is stated that "laymen shall, under pain of excommunication, be forbidden ever to dare to dispute (*presumant disputare*) with Jews about the articles of the Christian faith."[63] The Council of Treves in March 1227 repeated the injunction that "ignorant clergymen shall not dispute with Jews in the presence of laity."[64] Rising to yet higher levels of authority, Pope

Gregory IX in March 1233 wrote to the archbishops, bishops, and other prelates of the church in Germany to prohibit them "most stringently" from at any time daring to dispute about their faith or their rites, "lest under pretext of such disputation (*sub pretextu disputationis*) the simple-minded slide into a snare of error, which God forbid."[65]And at the Council of Tarragona in 1233, a territory under the jurisdiction of James I of Aragon, it was also strictly forbidden that "any lay person [should] dispute about the Catholic faith whether publicly or privately (*publice vel privatim de fide catholica disputare*). Whoever shall be found acting contrary to our prohibition shall be excommunicated by his own bishops, and, unless he purges himself, shall be suspected of heresy."[66] This last prohibition about disputing either publicly *or* privately, a formulation repeated by Pope Alexander IV (r. 1254–61), signals a major evolution in the extent of the church's concern.[67] The presumption is that debates *are* taking place and that officials are none too pleased with their outcomes. In the 1190s, Peter of Blois warned in his own anti-Jewish tract that, "as a result of illicit and careless debates, a virulent crop of heresies runs wild."[68] These developments return us to the Dominicans, who manipulated the dramatic setting of public disputations to combat heresy and Jews.

Ecclesiastical decrees explicitly limiting both open and private exchanges between Christians and Jews during the first sixty years of the thirteenth century represent one aspect of the papal monarchy's consolidation of power. The circumstances that led to the Paris disputation in 1240 represent another: the church's sanctioning of properly controlled public disputations. Just as the Dominican Order's preaching activities demonstrates the importance of disputation as a weapon for combating heretics and nonbelievers, so too does the Paris disputation, or "Talmud Trial" as it is often called, demonstrate the church's attempt to manipulate disputation on an unprecedented scale. The events and texts associated with the Talmud Trial have been extensively treated before. Rather than review the full historiography of this episode, we shall instead focus on the manner in which this disputation combines the scholastic, polemic, and "public" elements associated with the thirteenth-century culture of disputation.

The immediate causes for the events of 1240–42 were a series of condemnatory bulls issued by Pope Gregory IX in 1239 ordering rulers and prelates of Europe to impound the Talmud and other Jewish writings on the first Sabbath during Lent in 1240 and to submit the books to ecclesiastical authorities.[69] Gregory's call represented a delayed reaction to a plea he had received in 1236 from an evidently embittered Jewish apostate named Nicholas Donin, who presented the pope with thirty-five accusations against the Talmud and its Jewish exponents.[70] There is little that can be said with certainty about Donin's Jewish background or, for that matter, his motives. Some scholars have suggested that he may have had Karaite leanings.[71] At least a dozen of the thirty-five articles condemned the Talmud for its perceived absurd homilies and anti-Christian comments, much along the same lines as Peter Alfonsi and Peter the Venerable had done a century earlier. Donin goes further, however, adducing additional charges against the Talmud's nonscriptural basis and making more specific and substantial use of Jewish texts.[72] It is not unreasonable to suppose that Nicholas was familiar with those earlier polemical works or, at any rate, with the arguments contained therein, although this remains unproven. Other elements in the cultural history of medieval Jewry may also have been in play. In a provocative reassessment of the medieval transmission of the Talmud, Talya Fishman has suggested that its preeminence in Jewish life and learning was not solidified until the eleventh and twelfth centuries and that the cultural shift embodied in the transition from oral law to written text may have contributed to a certain level of Jewish discontent and, indirectly, to the Christian attack on the Talmud.[73] These are important considerations to bear in mind when examining the wider cultural canvas on which the Talmud becomes the object of attack. Whereas Alfonsi and Peter the Venerable's works remained textual and scripted (in Alfonsi's case, an imaginary and autobiographical disputation), Donin's accusations were transformed into a staged and public event when King Louis IX responded to Gregory IX's bulls—the only recipient of the pope's call to do so—by confiscating rabbinic texts and summoning leading French rabbis to his court to defend the Talmud against Donin's charge.

Donin's decision to take his plaint directly to the pope may belie a greater determinacy on his part than his *converso* predecessors. Perhaps he was additionally aware of the growing body of Jewish anti-Christian literature that had developed in the intervening century.[74] Donin's move also reflects the new authority of the papacy, whose authority was exponentially greater than it had been in the early decades of the twelfth century. The same may be said of the French monarchy, which had grown measurably since the reign of Philip II. Thus, it is less the critique of Judaism and its texts that is new in 1240 (although Donin certainly added to it) or even the role of a Jewish convert in launching the attack; rather, it is the institutional establishment that was markedly more competent in handling (or presuming that it could control) a show trial with the most knowledgeable Jews of the day. The fact that King Louis IX was the only monarch to respond to the pope's request is another indication of how important the institutional context is for understanding the Paris disputation: King Louis IX of France was the only monarch who had the political stability and requisite means to organize such an event. Most important of all, Paris in the mid-thirteenth century had become the epicenter of a culture of debate and disputation, one that King Louis himself actively promoted. A helpful illustration of the king's interest in disputation is Joinville's *Life of Saint Louis* (completed in 1309), where a story is told of "a great debate" between clerics and Jews at the monastery in Cluny.[75] The abbot reprimands the knight for reacting with violence, while the knight, in turn, chides the abbot for organizing such a debate in the first place. The moral of the story, the king explains to his biographer in language that echoes contemporary church councils, is "that no man, unless he is a skilled theologian, should debate with Jews." This concern over who should debate with Jews helps explain the more famous comment that follows, namely, that the proper manner for a layman to debate with a Jew is to plunge a sword into his belly as far as it will go.[76] Professionally trained schoolmen should dispute; laymen should not. In another passage in the panegyric, Louis presides at supper over a debate between Joinville and Master Robert de Sorbon (Louis's chaplain and the founder of the Collège de Sorbonne) on the respective merits of laymen and friars, pronouncing his judgment (or, in scholastic terms, determination) following the discussion.[77] Dialogue and dispute animate many stories found in Joinville's biography. In life and in legend, King Louis IX was a patron of the schools and a champion of organized, scholastic disputation.

A precise chronology of the events that took place in Paris in 1240 is desirable, but unfortunately hampered by the limited and occasionally contradictory information contained in the Christian and (multiple) Hebrew accounts.[78] Some scholars have posited that the disputation was only an inquisitorial proceeding and involved no actual debate per se. Chen Merchavia's careful analysis of Latin manuscript 16558 in the Bibliothèque Nationale de Paris, the so-called standard version, has established that the proceedings in Paris 1240 were divided into two stages: the disputation between Donin and the French rabbis, principally Yehiel ben Joseph, and the more formal ecclesiastical inquiry into the content of the texts that eventually led to the burning of the Talmud sometime between June 1241 and 1243.[79] The Talmud Trial of 1240 thus bears witness to the confluence of two major, and related, developments in the rhetoric and performance of polemic: the formal public disputation as an organized event demonstrating truth and the inquisitorial trial as a method for legally proving that truth and convicting the guilty parties.[80] The principal Christian clerics who served as witnesses during the inquest were Archbishop Walter de Cornut of Sens, Bishop of Paris William of Auvergne, Geoffrey of Belleville (chaplain to King Louis IX), Adam of Chambly, and Eudes of Châteauroux (chancellor of the University of Paris, later a papal legate). Although the meeting took place on the king's direct orders, Louis IX did not personally preside over the disputation. That task was left to his mother, Queen Blanche of Castile, who in later years would govern the entire realm when her son departed on the first of his two unsuccessful crusades (1248–52).[81]

In addition to Yehiel ben Joseph, three other rabbis are known to have taken some part in the trial: Judah ben David of Melun, Samuel ben Solomon of Château Thierry, and Moses of Coucy, whose *Sefer Mitzvot Gadol* (Great Book of Commandments) is one of the earliest codifications of Jewish law and has itself been shown to contain an oblique rebuttal of Donin's attacks.[82] The authorities responsible for organizing the disputation were well aware of the rabbis' reputation for learning. The Christian account of the disputation is explicit in stating that the authorities "summoned the teachers of the Jews who were regarded among themselves as experts," and that the first to be brought in was Yehiel ben Joseph, "the most expert in their eyes, and a very famous person throughout Jewry."[83] Excepting Gerald of Wales's somewhat dubious account of Abelard's debate with a Jew in the presence of King Philip I, the disputation of 1240 marks the first recorded instance of a Jewish-Christian disputation in the presence of royalty, the first instance of a Jewish-Christian disputation that was presided over by a university official, and the first known instance of university officials pursuing the characteristically academic *disputatio* in a nonacademic context. The deliberate mention of Yehiel's high standing within the Jewish community, while undoubtedly true, is also a trope that we have already encountered in the dialogues of Gilbert Crispin, Walter of Châtillon, and Peter of Cornwall, thus suggesting a certain degree of continuity with earlier conventions.

The substance of the inquest has been discussed many times before and need not be analyzed in any great detail here.[84] In essence, Nicholas Donin's original accusations about the alleged blasphemies contained in the Talmud were submitted to Yehiel ben Joseph, who was then forced to respond.[85] According to the Christian account of the disputation, the discussion began with Donin's announcement that he intended to question Yehiel about the

Talmud, which he states is four hundred years old, and ends with the so-called confession of Yehiel ben Joseph and Judah ben David, admitting that the Talmud passages were correctly quoted but resolutely denying that they contained any blasphemies against Christ or Christians.[86] As a result of the proceeding, the books of the Talmud were found guilty as charged, and some twenty to twenty-four wagonloads of manuscripts—perhaps ten to twelve thousand volumes, according to Jeremy Cohen—were burned in the Place de Grève in June 1241 or later.[87] Here, it is again worth pausing to consider local iconography. A roundel from the contemporary Oxford-Paris-London version of the *Bible moralisée* shows a personification of Ecclesia presiding over a disputation between Jews and clerics. The close dating of the manuscript (c. 1240) to the disputation in Paris raises the very real possibility that the regnant queen equally represents Blanche of Castile herself, not least because she may have commissioned the bible for the instruction of her son Louis IX who was still early in his reign (Figure 11). A roundel on an earlier folio of the same manuscript shows a similar disputation between Jews and Christians, this time presided over by a king. Unfortunately there is little contextual information within the manuscript to work with. The accompanying text is a verse from Psalm 14, and the roundel above it shows Jesus preaching to the Jews. However, the fact that images of Jewish-Christian disputations in the presence of crowned royalty were included in this version of the *Bible moralisée* and *not* in the slightly earlier and more famous versions now in Vienna, makes the identification of the royal figures in these disputation all the more intriguing.[88] Indeed, it opens the possibility that the designer(s) of the manuscript may have been intending in some way to either reflect or even influence royal policy. Moreover, it has been argued that the St. Stephen Portal of Notre Dame Cathedral (c. 1258) itself presents a retelling of anti-Judaism inflected by King Louis's sponsorship of the disputation of 1240.[89] While this is slightly more conjectural, the suggestion is hardly far-fetched when one considers that the same ecclesiastical authorities who attended the disputation in 1240 would have commissioned the tympanum for the new cathedral and at approximately the same time. Establishing a direct connection between local events and local iconography is rarely simple or straightforward, but visual representations are assuredly not divorced from their broader intellectual and cultural surroundings. It is thus essential that ideas, events, and iconography be treated syncretically and not, as they so often are, as distinct categories. This is especially the case here because it is the culture of disputation we are tracing and not merely one manifestation of the debate.

Figure 11. Left: Jews disputing with bishops at the feet of enthroned Ecclesia, who personifies the church and the Virgin Mary and possibly also Queen Blanche of Castile. The figure on the left points to a Torah scroll, while the crowned female figure looks approvingly in the direction of the bishops. Right: A king presides over another Jewish-Christian disputation. The fact that this was produced in a Bible intended for moral instruction, and possibly designed by Queen Blanche herself for the instruction of her son Louis IX, makes the identification of these figures of royalty particularly intriguing. Miniatures in the *Bible moralisée*, Paris, c. 1240. Bibliothèque Nationale de France, MS Lat. 11560, fols 87v and 5v.

The burning of the Talmud that resulted from the disputation and trial in 1240 proved to be the first in a series of large-scale attacks on rabbinic Judaism emanating from the papal court and carried out by the orders of the French monarchy and the Dominican friars in connection with the University of Paris. In May 1244, Pope Innocent IV renewed Gregory's original injunctions and asked Louis IX to burn any copies of the Talmud that could be found to have survived the first burning. When the Jews this time appealed the sentence to Rome, complaining that they could not practice their religion without the Talmud, the pope commissioned a legatine tribunal to reopen the inquiry. The person chosen to head that inquiry was again Eudes of Châteauroux (now cardinal-bishop of Tusculum), who submitted the Talmud and the other books to the scholars and clerics of the University of Paris. In May 1248, they issued a document upholding the verdict, this time with a list of forty-one illustrious signatories from the academic and clerical communities of Paris.[90] The coordination among university and ecclesiastical officials is worth underscoring. No other Jewish-Christian disputation or intellectual encounter of any sort in the preceding millennium had achieved such publicity. In 1254, Louis IX again renewed the order to burn any copies of the Talmud that could be found. Louis's two successors, Philip III and Philip IV, followed suit during their own regimes and issued decrees to the French royal bureaucracy ordering complete cooperation with the inquisitors. Finally, when in 1315 Louis X readmitted the Jews and their books into France, he specifically excepted the Talmud.

Scholars of medieval Jewish-Christian relations have long known about the events of 1240. Jeremy Cohen has argued that Dominican involvement then as well as in later attacks on the Talmud constituted a new thrust in the Christian confrontation with Judaism, one that went beyond the earlier theological basis of a limited tolerance by attacking Judaism on the grounds of heresy.[91] Yet as much as Dominican involvement in these and subsequent events mark a new shift in the Christian engagement with Jews and Judaism, the events of 1240 also demonstrate an important continuity with, or extension of, the broader culture of disputation, and it is that connection that I here wish to emphasize. For while the king's role in convoking the event and the setting for the disputation at the royal court are novelties for the period, the presence of Eudes of Châtoureaux, the chancellor of the University of Paris, is highly suggestive that the disputation was conceived along academic principles and, in any case, under academic scrutiny and approval. The two-part disputation and trial, followed by the official verdict, evokes the now-established pattern of the university disputation and final determination. Moreover, the dating of the Talmud trial is contemporary with the first appearance of the *disputatio de quolibet*, and, while the topic of the disputation at the royal court is no surprise to the participants, the manner in which it has come down to us as the record of a public battle of arguments presents unmistakable similarities to the Rue du Fouarre's "agonistic" environment and the scholastic culture of disputation more generally. After all, both the Christian and the Hebrew accounts emphasize not just the encounter, but the live "debate" (the questioning and answering) that took place among the participants, and both sides (Christian and Jewish) followed it up with efforts to publicize their version of events.[92] The efforts of one figure in particular stand out: Thibaut of Sézanne.

Thibaut was among the signatories of the document issued in May 1248 by the University of Paris, and he also helped compile translations of numerous passages of the rabbinical literature for the Latin dossier of the encounter (BnF 16558). Like Donin, Thibaut was a Jewish convert who became a Dominican friar in Paris. Almost nothing else of his life is known. There are two works credited to him that point to the practice of disputation in the Christian encounter with Jews during and after 1240. The first of these is a list of "Excerpts" from the Talmud intended to illustrate the error of the Jews. Although these excerpts are usually attributed solely to Thibaut, they may well have included the hands of other converts.[93] These errors are listed under rubrics that address the topic of the error and are presented in such a way that they are clearly intended for future consultation. The penultimate of these errors is titled "the disputation of the Jews against the Christians" (*Disputatio Iudeorum contra Christianos*).[94] This rubric would seem an odd insertion within the larger compilation, not least because it purports to be a disputation by Jews *against* a Christian, rather than the typical reverse. In other words, it is more than merely formulaic. Furthermore, there are good reasons to believe that this disputation revisits the disputation between Donin and the Jewish scholars in 1240. The discussion reviews the familiar disagreements over Mosaic law, faithfully presenting the arguments that a Jew might raise. The text is continuously animated in the present tense ("Iudei dixerunt," "Christianus dixit"), suggesting that multiple Jews were answering a single Christian. The debate culminates in a speech by the Christian who declaratively invokes the names and statements of various Hebrew prophets, including Hosea.[95] The repeated admonitions to listen (*audite*) and behold (*ecce*) what the prophets are saying bear striking similarity to the sculptures on the Bamberg cathedral choir screen (see Figure 9), which likewise evokes the live experience of debate. In the conclusion to the disputation, the Jews publicly acknowledge their error and convert: "And, since the Jews could not speak against this, they rose up, and were confounded, bewildered, and apprehensive; they were silenced . . . thus, many of them, after faithfully relinquishing their error were baptized and believing in Christ."[96] Speculative as it may be, there is much in this brief disputation to suggest that it is a manipulation of the encounter that took place in 1240 and a valuable artifact of a larger culture of disputation. It reissues arguments that were addressed in the encounter in 1240, it describes "the Jews" and "a Christian" in the act of debate, it evokes imagery familiar to Christians in contemporary iconography, and it is composed by a Dominican friar who was probably in attendance in 1240 and who signed the document condemning the Talmud in 1248. The purpose of manipulating the encounter would be not just to give a partisan side of the story, but more specifically to offer guidance on how to conduct future such disputations. The second work by Thibaut, his *Pharetra fidei contra Iudeos* (Quiver of Faith Against the Jews), confirms that these are his overall intentions. The prologue provides nothing short of a handbook for engaging Jews in disputation:

> In disputing with the Jews, it is necessary to observe a three-part precaution. First, do your best to refute their errors in numerous discussions, as much because it is easier to refute the articles of their faith than to rely upon proving those of our own, as because the seeds of virtue and truth serve no purpose if the thorns and weeds of falsehood are not first rooted out. Second, do not touch upon those points of contention which seem to come between us, at least until the Jew brings them up himself. Then, resolve them, as you will have found resolutions to them. Third, when you debate in the presence of many Jews, make them all keep quiet, except the single one who will respond, until that time when, the first one being defeated, another responds. In this way you will avoid being over-whelmed by their clamor, and when one of them speaks the others will not try to find ways out or cause distractions.[97]

A better description of how to conduct a disputation could hardly be had.

At about the same time that Rabbi Yehiel and several of his coreligionists were disputing the contents of the Talmud in Paris, discussions of another sort seem to have been taking place in southern France in the region of Narbonne. Evidence for these disputations derives principally from a single Hebrew copy of Meir ben Simeon's *Milhemeth Mitzvah* (Obligatory War), which records a series of debates between himself and Christian opponents in the presence of "many great and important people."[98] Robert Chazan and others have examined the content and importance of this polemical work for understanding the Jewish counterarguments to thirteenth-century Christian missionizing in detail.[99] Restating the argumentative contents of this work is not necessary. What might be stressed is the similarity between the dialogue form chosen by Meir ben Simeon and the culture of disputation that was spreading throughout the thirteenth century. The Christians who dispute with Meir include ordinary priests, archbishops (including Archbishop Guy Fulcoldi, who was later elected Pope Clement IV), and an anonymous Dominican who is referred to derisively as a male prostitute (*ha-Kadhesh ha-Doresh*).[100] This Dominican may possibly have been Paul Christiani, the Jewish convert who served as the principal Christian debater in the Barcelona disputation of 1263, which we will come to below. As compared to the sixteen folios of one of the Hebrew versions of the Paris disputation or the nineteen that make up the Jewish account of the 1263 Barcelona disputation, the *Mil-hemeth Mitzvah* includes two hundred and fifty closely written folios, of which only some forty have been edited or translated. The subject matter treated in these various disputations touch on a wide variety of topics relating to thirteenth-century Jewish life and Jewish-Christian intellectual relations: refutations of Christological interpretations of Old Testament texts known in Jewish source material of the time, critical observations on the historical records of the Gospels, a few lengthy translations of the New Testament passages into Hebrew, popular philosophical reflections, references to current affairs, an exceedingly long draft of a letter to Louis IX sharply criticizing the king's legislation against Jewish usury, and much more. As Siegfried Stein observed, it is "by far the longest Hebrew work of the 13th century which covers [the] most controversial aspects of its time on an inter-confessional, and—to a quantitatively lesser extent—on an inter-Jewish plane."[101] In short, public disputations between Jews and Christians were no longer restricted to a literary genre nor confined to scholastic centers such as Paris but were becoming increasingly common features of Jewish-Christian intellectual relations. The polemical output by both Christians and Jews testifies to the escalation of tensions in interfaith contacts, and the culture of disputation (both a literary form and a practice) provided essential weaponry in that escalation.[102] The performance of public disputations as witnessed and recorded by both Jews and Christians brings us to a final such example in the publicity of the Jewish-Christian debate: the Barcelona disputation of 1263.

## Dialogue and Disputation in Spain

The culture of disputation and the Dominican involvement in the promotion of prearranged public debates converged in spectacular fashion in the summer of 1263 in the Aragonese capital of Barcelona. On several (perhaps four) separate occasions, spread over the course of about one week in July, the Provençal Jew turned Dominican friar Paul Christiani and the venerable rabbi Moses ben Nachman of Girona (also known as Nachmanides or Ramban) met before King James I of Aragon and numerous others to debate key theological issues in the Jewish-Christian controversy. It is undoubtedly one of the best-known encounters in the medieval history of Jewish-Christian relations, and, unlike at Paris (where Queen Blanche stood in for the absent king), here the king played an active part as host and adjudicator of the disputation. No book burnings followed this encounter, and Nachmanides was allowed to leave in peace and in dignity, possibly even with a monetary token of good-will from the king.[103] A century of historiographical discussion about the reliability of the surviving Christian and Hebrew accounts, about the broader Christian missionizing impulse that does (or does not) undergird the event, and about the vexed question of who actually won the contest has helped secure this particular disputation as one of the most hotly debated topics in the medieval Jewish-Christian encounter.[104] A traditional interpretation has been to see this disputation as reflecting a broader conversionary campaign among Dominicans, one that targeted Jews, and then eventually Muslims as well, in a broader ecclesiastical ambition that R. I. Burns alluringly termed the "thirteenth-century dream of conversion."[105] Criticizing this "maximal-ist" view, Robin Vose has recently argued for a much less actively aggressive interpretation of the events of 1263, positing that a somewhat exaggerated emphasis on Hebrew (and Arabic) study among Dominicans has skewed the picture and that the disputation represents "more of a discrete and passing series of historical events than a manifestation of long-term Dominican poli-cies and practices in the region."[106] While I believe that there are dangers in both overplaying and minimizing the conversionary goals of this encounter, it is, predictably, the disputational and specifically public element of this encounter that I here wish to examine.

Regulations concerning Jewish-Christian disputations were as much a feature in Iberian lands as they were in northern Europe.[107] Thus was it stipulated at the Council of Tarragona in 1233, during the early years of James I of Aragon's long reign (1218–76), that laypersons were forbidden to dispute about the Catholic faith both publicly and privately (*publice vel privatim de fide catholica disputare*), a phrasing that echoes earlier councils north of the Pyrenees.[108] There is also a generous body of polemical literature that was generated by both Christians and Jews in Spain. Writing in Aragon in the early twelfth century, Peter Alfonsi attacked the Talmud with reason and logical argumentation in his widely circulated *Dialogi*. A copy of the work appears to have been included in the holdings of the medieval library at St. Catherine's (Santa Caterina) in Barcelona, along with an early medieval *Altercatio sinagoge et ecclesie* and copies of Raymond Martí's anti-Jewish works.[109] We shall return to the location of the Dominican convent of St. Catherine's. In the 1140s, the Sephardic Jew Yehuda Halevi wrote in Judeo-Arabic what is arguably the first Jewish literary account of an interreligious disputation. His *Kuzari* recounts a series of conversations at the court of a pagan Khazar king, in which representatives of Judaism, Christianity, Islam, and philosophy make their bid before a king who is in search of a new religion for his people. (The structural resemblance to Abelard's *Collationes* is striking, as is the proximity in the dates of their compositions, although there is no evidence to suggest that either author was aware of the other.) The Khazar king's eventual conversion to Judaism, along with that of his flock, is the only known instance of a mass conversion to Judaism. Long believed to be a literary invention by a creative poet who wrote moving verses about his longing to live in *Eretz Israel* and who eventually fled Andalusia for the Holy Land, the story has been discovered to have at least some basis in fact.[110] While the work would unlikely have been known to Christians, it was certainly known to the Jews of Iberia and southern France, including potentially to those few who converted from Judaism to Christianity, for it was translated into Hebrew by the scholar Judah ibn Tibbon in 1167.[111] Halevi's *Kuzari*, therefore, shows an early Jewish awareness and adaption of the dialogue genre for apologetic purposes, even if, like its Christian *Adversus Iudaeos* counterparts, it was primarily intended for internal consumption.

An even more relevant precedent to Barcelona is the career and polemical writings of Archbishop Rodrigo Jiménez de Rada, whose involvement in territorial conquest and Jewish-Christian relations might well be compared to that of James of Aragon later in the thirteenth century. Rodrigo was archbishop of Toledo from 1209 to 1247. H was a leading ecclesiastical figure in Spain and abroad and a chief organizer of the military efforts that culminated in the joint Christian victory over the Almohads at Las Navas de Tolosa in 1212.[112] In addition to his ecclesiastical and administrative duties, he was also a prolific author, most notably of *De rebus Hispanie*, a charged account of the crusading nature of the Reconquest written toward the end of his long career. Among his other works is an anti-Jewish dialogue titled *Dialogus libri uita*, which seems to have been written very shortly after the battle in 1212. In a study of Rodrigo's interactions with the Jews and Muslims of Castile, Lucy Pick has stressed the connection between the polemic of the *Dialogus* and the Jewish community of Toledo, as well as the connection to the performance of Christianity in the well-known *Auto de los Reyes Magos*, a short Castilian play depicting the Three Kings story.[113] While some of her conclusions remain speculative, these suggestions are worth considering in light of contemporary developments in the performance of disputation.

Rodrigo's *Dialogus*, like his episcopacy more generally, is characterized by an acute awareness of contemporary issues within both Christian and

Jewish intellectual circles. Like so many of its predecessors in the *Adversus Iudaeos* genre, it is framed as a dialogue between the author and an unnamed Jew and covers familiar themes of the Jewish-Christian debate (the Incarnation, the Trinity, the Messiah).[114] Yet it is more than a mere rehearsal of the well-worn Christian charge that Jews do not understand the full meaning of Scripture. Rodrigo asserts that Jews have deliberately obstructed others from understanding Scripture's true meaning by constructing fables (that is, post-biblical works) to explain difficult prophecies. Rodrigo's detailed engagement with the various levels of interpretation of Scripture notably reflects contemporary Christian and Jewish discussions of the Bible that were thriving at that time.[115] From his earlier sojourn in Paris, he may have learned about (or from) the school of canons at St. Victor, exegetes of the Bible who were actively engaged in deciphering the multiple senses of Scripture. From the Jewish community of Toledo, or Jewish converts from it, he may have learned about the Talmud and the Midrash and their medieval Jewish commentary tradition, to which he obliquely refers in the course of the debate. Many of the passages that Rodrigo cites when discussing the literal sense of Scripture come from sources that were unknown to earlier Christian authors, including Peter Alfonsi and Peter the Venerable. The textual redaction of ancient Talmudic traditions that occurred over the course of the twelfth century was provoking reactions in medieval Jewish communities in Ashkenaz, and it might well have done so among Sephardic Jews. Some Jews, for instance, noted that books had replaced teachers, while others protested the elevation of Talmud-centered erudition and casuistic virtuosity into standards of religious excellence, at the expense of spiritual refinement.[116] In refracting and critiquing Jewish understandings of the Talmud, Rodrigo's dialogue may well reflect contemporary currents of thought in multiple communities. He also commissioned a new translation of the Qur'an from Mark of Toledo immediately before the campaign of Las Navas, further suggesting that the archbishop was eager to have at his disposal texts and ideas not available to prior polemicists.[117]

It is difficult to know where or from whom Rodrigo may have gained access to the Jewish texts that would become the focus of his polemic. Pick hypothesizes that "Rodrigo gained his familiarity with rabbinic traditions through oral contact with the Jews, either privately and informally or possibly in the context of formal, public disputation."[118] This element of public disputation merits reflection, particularly in light of the increasing prominence of disputation in interfaith relations in Iberia and beyond. Rodrigo was archbishop at precisely the time that university and Dominican disputations were gaining currency north of the Pyrenees. His travels to Paris and his extensive dealings in trans-European ecclesiastical affairs would undoubtedly have made him aware of scholastic methods and of the increasing volume of polemical discourse. Pick goes on to identify the preeminent rabbi of Toledo, Meir ben Todros Abulafia (Ramah) as a potential candidate for Rodrigo's interlocutor, chiefly on the basis of the rabbi's involvement in internal Jewish debates about the teachings of Maimonides. Perhaps Ramah was Rodrigo's sparring partner in some formal (or informal) context, but it is also clear that Rodrigo's literary output overlaps with a broader evolution in the transition from private to public disputations during the very years of his episcopacy.

Among the most imaginative suggestions regarding Rodrigo's literary output is the idea that he may have dictated the Castilian play *Auto de los Reyes Magos*, a work traditionally ascribed to the late twelfth century.[119] The verdict is still out on the likelihood of his authorship, but the argument for connecting polemic with performance is again relevant. As we have already seen in chapter 5, performances of various sorts were flourishing in the early thirteenth century. Recent scholarship has given increasing attention to the performative nature of religion at this time and the self-definition within Christian identity that accompanied medieval polemic. The declarative second person "you!" that recurs in Rodrigo's *Dialogus* might be taken as evidence of the debate's real-life origins, but more likely it was added to convey a sense of drama and to urge the educated reader into action. The work is, after all, explicitly didactic: so that Christians "might learn that the sacraments and articles of the faith were not recently invented."[120] Rodrigo's debate, like much of the Jewish-Christian discourse, seems at least as destined for internal consumption as it was for cross-border polemic. With these considerations in mind, we can now return to the larger significance of Barcelona 1263, both as an instance of disputation and as an instance in the public performance of truth.

## Urban and Performative Dimmensions of the Barcelona Disputation

Friar Paul Christiani was the latest in a long line of Jewish converts who contributed to the Christian attack on Judaism, and the Talmud in particular. Most medieval converts from Judaism appear to have been relatively young males, and this would seem to be the case with Christiani.[121] Born Saul in the Jewish community of Montpellier, Paul had studied Jewish literature under the direction of Rabbis Eliezer ben Emmanuel of Tarascon and Jacob ben Elijah Lattes of Venice before converting to Christianity around 1229, evidently a consequence of the Dominican master Raymond of Penyaforte's preaching and missionizing in Provence.[122] Following his mentor's lead, Paul devoted the rest of his life to proselytizing among the Jewish communities of southern France, northern Spain, and eventually northern France as well. In the view of at least one modern scholar, Paul had already debated the distinguished rabbi Meir ben Simeon of Narbonne several years before the disputation at Barcelona, and 1263 may not have been his first meeting with Nachmanides either.[123] The precise extent of Paul's travels and the number of debates he took part in are unknown, but Nachmanides in his Hebrew account refers to Christiani's reputation as a roving disputant: "I heard that he [Frai Pul] previously went about Provence and many other places saying such things [about the Talmud's teaching on the Messiah] to the Jews."[124] There is ample evidence that Christiani continued to work against the Jewish communities after the disputation. In 1269, he interceded with King Louis IX of France and obtained from him the enforcement of the canonical edict requiring Jews to wear badges.

At best guess, the disputation of Barcelona was conducted between Friday, July 20, and Friday, July 27, 1263. As with the Paris disputation, both Latin and Hebrew accounts of the sessions survive, allowing for some relatively sophisticated judgments to be made concerning how the events unfolded and what, in fact, was said. The Latin account is a brief summary drawn up by the Dominicans and confirmed by James I shortly after the debate. It survives in two very similar versions, one from Barcelona and the other from Girona.[125] The Hebrew account (*Vikuah* in Hebrew) is a longer and considerably more detailed account written by Nachmanides himself, ostensibly written at the behest of the bishop of Girona.[126] While there are some substantial differences between these two accounts of the disputation, including, most especially, who emerged victorious, both the Latin and the Hebrew accounts broadly agree that the four sessions corresponded to the following four propositions: (1) that the Messiah whom the Jews have been awaiting has come, (2) that the same Messiah, as had been prophesized, should be both divine and human, (3) that he, in fact, suffered and died for the salvation of the human race, and (4) that the legal cercmonial provisions outlined in the Old Testament terminated and were supposed to terminate after the arrival of the said Messiah.[127] Significantly, both accounts also agree on a diverse attendance and the public nature of the gathering. The Latin account describes the "many barons, prelates, religious [friars] and knights" who assembled at the palace of King James to hear the disputation.[128] It further states that Rabbi Moses was accompanied by "many other Jews, who were seen and believed to be the most skilled of all the Jews," presumably other Talmud scholars who accompanied the rabbi, although this is also a ubiquitous phrase in Christian-Jewish disputational literature. Nachmanides's Hebrew version of the encounter corroborates this report, noting the initial palace setting and the presence of distinguished figures such as the bishop, princes, knights, friars and royal judges. The Hebrew account also mentions "many from the [Jewish] community" who came forward during the final session and urged Nachmanides to withdraw from the debate, stating as well that many knights from the king's household and a Franciscan scholar named Pere of Girona likewise urged Nachmanides to desist from disputing the tenets of their faith.

A notable feature of Nachmanides's version of events is that he tells us a good deal more about the audience and its participation, including, most notably, the involvement of the king. According to the *Vikuah*, James of Aragon not only presides over the debate, but he often interjects, asks questions, and generally moves the discussion along when an impasse is reached or a new topic is introduced. The Hebrew account also stresses the presence of the clerical and urban populace. Unlike the Christian account, the Hebrew version describes the four sessions taking place in two distinct locations. Both accounts agree that the first session was held on Friday in the presence of the king and his councilors in the palace in Barcelona. According to Nachmanides, the second was held "on the following Monday" at an unnamed cloister in the city: "On that day the king went to the cloisters in the city and gathered there all of the people of the city, gentiles and Jews. And the bishop [of Barcelona] and all the priests (*ve-khol ha-galahim*), Franciscan scholars, and preachers. [Fray Pul] arose to speak."[129]

The rabbi's failure to identify the cloister leaves the exact location of this second gathering open to speculation, and many commentators have ignored the passage altogether, but judging from Nachmanides's comments the change of venue seems to have been decided precisely to accommodate a larger crowd, thus opening the debate up to an even broader audience. The Hebrew *ha-galahim* refers specifically to the tonsure, and, while it is traditionally translated as "priests," it could also refer to "monks." The word "preachers" in the second sentence does not modify Franciscans, as some translations of this passage would suggest. The preachers in question are almost surely the Dominicans (*ha-doreshim*). The topic of this session, perhaps the most central of the entire debate, is why the Jews do not believe that the Messiah has come and why Christians believe that he has and that he is divine. In the *Vikuah*, the meeting in the cloister is the longest of the four sessions, occupying fifteen pages in Chavel's modern English translation. So, what cloister might this have been and who was the audience? On the basis of archival and archaeological sources in Barcelona, I believe there is good reason to place the location of this second session in the Dominican convent of St. Catherine's (the present Mercat de Santa Caterina), and that Dominican friars, ecclesiastical officials, and local councilmen were the intended public.

The spread of the Dominican Order in Catalonia was early and rapid. When Domingo de Guzmán asked the Vatican for official recognition of his order in 1216, the first preachers of his band of companions numbered only sixteen, but seven of them were from Iberia. Three of these Iberians, along with four others, were sent to Paris in 1217 to found a convent close to the university there. Miguel de Fabra, who was a member of the group, was the first Dominican to hold a chair at the University of Paris. Fabra later founded houses in Catalonia and Aragon and became confessor of James I of Aragon, accompanying the king on his conquests to Valencia and Majorca. Fabra also organized the order's schools in Barcelona, bringing with him the scholastic methods that were cultivated in Paris. The convent of Saint Catherine's was first given its official authorization in April 1248 when Pope Innocent IV signed a bull for the construction of "a church and other buildings" (*ecclesiam et alia edificia*).[130] Later that year, the local bishop Pere de Centelles gave 2,000 *solidi* in financial support for the construction of a new church and convent (*sustentatione operis ecclesiae sancta caterina*). In 1252, James I bestowed further privileges on the convent when he granted that taxes collected at the city gate be given over to the convent, and in a charter dated September 13, 1262, James I granted the convent additional funds arriving from "Tunisia, Sicily, and elsewhere" so that the buildings could be completed without disturbance and without delay.[131] While construction continued until the end of the thirteenth century, the buildings were sufficiently advanced and spacious enough in 1261 to accommodate a meeting of the general chapter of the order. Archaeological excavations undertaken in the late 1990s before the creation of the current market have confirmed the existence of the largest cloister in thirteenth-century Barcelona, measuring

approximately twenty-eight meters by twenty five meters, centrally located
near the cathedral, the marketplace, and the city gate.[132] Although close to
the royal palace, it was technically just outside the city walls, making the
space even more accessible to "all the people of the city" (*kol anshei ha-'ir*)
mentioned in the Hebrew account. Not only was the Dominican convent
of St. Catherine's geographically and institutionally well placed for the staging of a disputation, but it was the very convent where Raymond of Panya-
forte, third master general of the Dominican Order and Paul Christiani's
personal mentor, spent some thirty-five years organizing his polemical and
missionizing campaigns against Jews and Muslims. Moreover, at the second
disputation in Paris c. 1269, where Paul Christiani may well be one and the
same with "Paul the convert from Spain" who lead that charge against the
Jews, the surviving Hebrew account specifies that, at one point, a vast gathering took place in the "house of the Jacobins," the Dominican convent in
the rue St. Jacques.[133] The figure of twenty thousand in attendance—
probably best understood as simply "a great number"—reinforces the point:
in 1269, the Dominican convent was the location for an especially large
gathering, and the grandness of the crowd impressed the anonymous Jewish
author, just as the size of the crowd in 1263 elicited a similar comment from
Nachmanides.[134]

No documents from the Dominican Order have yet turned up to confirm the presence of a portion of the Barcelona disputation at the convent of
St. Catherine's. Very few from the thirteenth century survived the fire of 1835
that destroyed the convent. Still, all the circumstantial evidence points in that
direction: the size and prestige of the cloister, the central location in town
yet away from the Jewish quarter, the royal patronage of James I, and the
Dominican involvement in the art of disputation, both in Barcelona and in
general. In addition, the newly formed municipal government, the Consell
de Cent (Council of One Hundred), is known to have met in St. Catherine's
in the late thirteenth century until it was granted a more official space elsewhere, although exactly when the council began meeting in the convent
remains unclear. What is known is that James I first established the basic
institution of a municipal government in 1249, and, after several modifica-
tions, it achieved its more permanent structure of a council of one hundred
no later than 1265. St. Catherine's Convent, it would seem, was as public a
space for official gatherings as any other at the time of the disputation in
1263, and there is no reason to discount the likelihood that members of the
incipient municipal government would have been in attendance at the

debate. Indeed, these may be the unnamed royal judges mentioned in the Latin account.

Let us return to the narrative of the *Vikuah*. According to Nachmanides, the third session returned to the royal palace on a Thursday but was held near the palace entrance. The Hebrew phrase *be-tsinʿah* (meaning restrained and in more private quarters) clearly contrasts with the ostentation of the second session and suggests as well that there were fewer attendees at this gathering.[135] Finally, "on the next day [Friday]," a row of seats was set up in the royal palace to accommodate "the bishop and many of his ministers, and Giles De'Sergon, and Pere Barga, and many knights, and all those who are shunned from the city and [including] the poor of the nation."[136] At this point, Nachmanides mentions the presence of many Jews urging him to withdraw from the debate, noting as well that the "people of the city said to the Jews that I should not continue."[137] The phrasing here is somewhat ambiguous. Nachmanides could either be saying that rumors of the debate had aroused the attention (and displeasure) of those townsfolk who were not in attendance and who, therefore, complained to the local Jews or that those common people of the city who were in attendance complained to the Jews who were also in attendance. In either case, Nachmanides emphatically states that there was a good deal of discomfort among both Jews and Christians, and that people of all social classes were in attendance at this final session. Were the townsfolk and poor of the nation (*ve-khol mi-goreshei*) invited to hear the final verdict (that is, determination) of the king? The alleged public of this final gathering is once again striking, even if there is little to confirm or contradict the statement. What is clear is that the disputation continued only because that was the king's wish. This time, says Nachmanides, "I would ask the questions and Frai Pul would answer me, since he had asked me and I answered for three days." Insisting that the rabbi continue to answer Paul's questions, the king agrees to allow the debate to continue. Finally, if Nachmanides's version it to be trusted—and here there are good reasons for being skeptical—the king at the conclusion of the debate praised the rabbi for his eloquence and allowed him to depart in peace, granting him 300 *solidi* in admiration for his efforts.

A striking feature of the Barcelona disputation is not just the royal grandeur of the gathering but how deliberately *public* it became when the disputation changed venues. The range of spectators referred to in the Hebrew account—courtiers, ecclesiastical officials, friars, Christian townsfolk, and Jews—suggests that the disputation was conceived for as broad an audience as possible. The Latin account does not mention the session in the cloister, but even the Christian summary version of events suggests that the disputation was above all an <u>exercise in publicity</u>:

> Since he [Nachmanides] could not reply and had been defeated many times in public (*pluries publice confusus*), and both Jews and Christians were treating him with scorn, he said obstinately in front of everyone that he would not reply at all, because the Jews had told him not to, and some Christians namely Brother P. de Janua and some respectable citizens had sent to him to advise him not to reply at all. This lie was publicly refuted (*fuit publice redargutus*) by the said Brother P. and the respectable citizens. From this it was plain that he was trying to escape from the Disputation by lies.[138]

Scholars have long debated who the true victor of this encounter actually was, since the two accounts offer such markedly different conclusions. But that is far from the most interesting, or meaningful, point of comparison. In the Latin account, the implication is that the friar and the townsfolk wanted the debate to continue and that it was Nachmanides who deceptively tried to back out. Both accounts, in other words, make recourse to the wishes of the audience and spectators as a prime motivation for the continuity of the debate. Since both sides in one way or another emphasized the special debating skills of their protagonist and both accounts noted the vast public that witnessed the event, it is also reasonable to suggest that both Christians and Jews shared a cultural understanding of what this encounter represented to their adversaries and to their own: namely, a public performance of their faith and identity. This point can be amplified by briefly returning to the issue of literary form.

The mid-thirteenth century saw the development of a significant body of literature written in the Catalan vernacular, including works written for James I. "Prominent themes in the representative works of the tradition," writes Nina Caputo, "include an interest in preserving events of the moment and recording individual accomplishments in <u>dramatic narrative form</u>."[139] Similar patterns of form may be equally true of the Jewish side. In a broad survey of Jewish polemical literature and identity from this period, Robert Chazan has observed that "the literary genre most regularly utilized by our Jewish polemicists is the dialogue. This is hardly surprising, since in a more general way dialogue was the genre of choice of medieval polemical literature altogether. What the dialogue format offered was an opportunity to present claim and counter-claim in an easy and appealing format."[140] This is certainly the case with the *Vikuah*, where Nachmanides appears throughout in two separate voices: first as the narrator and commentator, who speaks in the definite past tense ("I said," "he replied," etc.); and second as subject, whose speech is constantly animated in the present tense.[141] Among both Christian and Jewish polemicists, the use of dialogue seems especially though by no means exclusively helpful when arguing from a position of weakness—effective when trying to convey something of the arguments that should have or could have been advanced. The Latin account of the Barcelona disputation dispenses with the dialogue format of earlier anti-Jewish works because it is composed as a triumphant verdict of a concluded debate. The Hebrew account exploits the drama of dialogue to lend legitimacy to the public defense of the Talmud that Nachmanides was called upon to provide. In sum, while the two accounts suggest contradictory outcomes, the cultural assumptions undergirding the memorialization of the debate are similar.

Since no official decree was issued and no books burned, an obvious question remains: what did King James and the Dominicans hope the disputation would achieve? In an intriguing attempt to answer this question, Martin Cohen suggested that the king was using the rising power of the Dominicans to counteract the pressure against him from the high nobility with whom, at the time, he was almost at the point of civil war.[142] A carefully staged triumph by the Dominicans in a disputation against the Jews would help in this political aim, since it would increase the prestige of the Dominicans and make them more powerful allies for the king. This geopolitical approach to the question has often been accepted, but it assumes a level of missionizing and political involvement among the Dominicans that recent scholarship has shown to be considerably at odds with the local evidence.[143] If the Barcelona disputation is instead viewed in the longue durée of Jewish-Christian disputations and the two contrasting accounts are employed with judicious caution, as most scholars now seem prepared to do, a different sort of conclusion might be advanced. The distinctly public and open setting for the debate (open in its location within the city and open in allowing each side to voice its arguments) and the range of auditors on hand to observe the week-long encounter instead suggest that this disputation was organized and geared toward a predominantly Christian public as an educative performance of theological truth. Additional interpretive conclusions follow if we entertain the convent of St. Catherine's as a likely location for the so-called second session. A portion of the disputation was conducted in the Dominican convent in order to provide a prearranged display of the art of disputation that brothers could learn from and assimilate before going out into the field to preach and to dispute. In this sense, the events of 1263 might perhaps best be characterized as a public enactment of the practical and educative merits of interfaith disputation that was refined over the course of the thirteenth century and articulated by Aquinas a few years later in his *Summa theologiae* (c. 1270–74). The "public" nature of the encounter is implicit in both the Latin and Hebrew accounts by virtue of the fact that the disputation was conducted, and indeed performed, before a broad audience of friars, royal and religious officials, Christians and Jews, townsfolk, and perhaps even civil magistrates who also served the pubic interest. The possible hope for resulting conversions is not excluded from this scenario, but nor was it the immediate purpose of the disputation.

The Jewish-Christian debate and scholastic education converged in spectacular fashion at several moments in the thirteenth century when the appropriate ingredients were mixed: royal patronage, academic methods, Jewish converts, Dominican disputants, an audience and space recognized by both sides as out in the public, and a common tradition of pedagogical dialogue that provides models for dramatizing debate. The Paris and Barcelona disputations underscore the broad impact of scholastic learning, thus helping propel the Jewish-Christian controversy from elite theological circles in the twelfth century into a cultural practice in the thirteenth.

## Vernacular Literary Disputations

Another important cultural manifestation of the Jewish-Christian debate in the thirteenth century is the appearance of vernacular works that offer fictional corollaries to the public disputations and *Adversus Iudaeos* dialogues that preceded them. While the substantive contribution of these works are few, the very emergence of a vernacular tradition of Jews and Christians in dispute may be seen as responding to an expanding public imbued with an increasing awareness of the contents of theological controversy, a phenomenon that literary historian Nicholas Watson has in a different context described as "vernacular theology."[144] These vernacular debates depend on an earlier Latin tradition of dialogue while simultaneously drawing from new developments in liturgical drama and vernacular literature. The twelfth-century Anglo-Norman *Ordo representaciones Ade* provides a vernacular debut of sorts for this genre. While analysis of literary texts is often confined to the history of vernacular language and literature, these texts are in every respect a part of the rhetoric and dialectic of the anti-Jewish polemic and of the medieval culture of disputation more generally.[145] The main works of this body of literature may, therefore, profitably be situated within the larger matrix that spawned them.

The Middle French *Desputoison de la Sinagogue et de Sainte Yglise* (Disputation Between Synagogue and Holy Church) is an early thirteenth-century vernacular application of polemical and allegorical themes drawn from the Jewish-Christian debate.[146] Composed of thirty-six quatrains written in rhymed alexandrines, the work is brief and devoid of any significant theological issues in comparison to its Latin equivalents. What the work lacks in substance, it makes up for in dramatic creativity. The debate makes use of the familiar dream framework, reproducing a nocturnal vision that the author Clopin says he had the night before, a dream more beautiful than any mortal man could dream (*hom mortex ne porroit plus biau songe songier*). Nothing else is known about Clopin, although the most recent editor of this work, Arié Serper, believes the author may have been a thirteenth-century minstrel whose primary interest was in amusing the crowd.[147] The entertainment value of the work should certainly not be ignored. Debate poetry and satire, as we have seen, manipulated scholastic disputation for comedic effect; it is only a small step to absorb the Jewish-Christian debate within the category of entertainment. Yet the subject matter is also one of the most vexed questions in theological controversy. In the dream, Clopin sees two ladies undertake a dispute (*deus dames ont contençon emprise*), one being the Synagogue the other being the Holy Church. We are provided vivid detail about the personifications. A ruby-red Holy Church is described as holding in one hand a chalice, a lance, and a banner with a red cross and three nails, and in the other a crown of thorns. Synagogue, on the other hand, is dark; she carries a broken lance, and at her feet lies the broken tables of Moses. The allegorical representations of Judaism and Christianity are so formulaic for their time that they simply must be read in the context of a broader artistic culture of disputation. The descriptions correspond almost exactly to the statues that adorned the newly completed Gothic cathedrals that occupy the urban public spaces in Latin Christendom. It is as if the sculptures of Ecclesia and Synagoga from the south façade of Strasbourg Cathedral descended from their elevated mounts and began to debate openly in front of the public (Figure 12).[148] Such sculptures, it is worth emphasizing, also emanated from the broader thirteenth-century concern over the position of Jews in Christian society, projecting a general theological message of the ascendancy of the church and an ideal of Jewish submission in a correctly ordered Christian realm.[149] Clopin's disputation animates these ideals while simultaneously exaggerating the formalism of a serious debate. Thus, for instance, the text of the *Desputoison* is characterized less by a reasoned discussion over the tenets of the two faiths and more by a constant exchange of abusive insults. Synagogue begins the debate, calling on Holy Church to listen to her words and to obey her, saying that she is the product of Synagogue's school (*tu issis de m'escole*). "Shut up, you old fool," Holy Church shouts back, as she then launches into an exegesis of the Old Testament, reminding Synagogue of Isaiah's prophecy that from the tree of Jesse there will be born a virgin and from that virgin a flower will blossom. Nearly every monologue opens with an insult. At the end of the debate, Holy Church accuses Synagogue of harming Jews and scattering them through her false words, causing Jews everywhere to search for things that do not exist, perhaps an oblique reference to the alleged falsities of the Talmud that occupied much of contemporary thinking about Jews. The work is clearly grounded in an expectation of familiarity with personifications of Judaism and Christianity. As such, the work is highly suggestive about the vernacular absorption of a key theological theme, even if it makes little contribution to the theological substance of the Jewish-Christian debate. In the final stanza, Clopin awakens from his dream and wishes his audience a long life.

The Jewish-Christian debate provides the backdrop for another Middle French dialogue, the anonymous *Desputoison du juyf et du crestien* (Disputation Between a Jew and a Christian), which, unfortunately, cannot be more securely dated than from about the middle of the thirteenth century.[150] Less insulting than Clopin's visionary debate poem, this disputation is written in rhymed alexandrines and features a Christian and a Jew debating in rational terms some of the traditional topics of the Jewish-Christian controversy, including the Incarnation and the mystery of the Trinity. The novelty of carrying on a discussion in French serves as a springboard for the theological altercation. The Christian opens the discussion by reciting a liturgical hymn in Latin but is interrupted by the confusion of the Jew who interjects, saying in a state of confusion, "I don't understand, you speak mysteriously. Speak to me in French and explain your words."[151] The Christian responds with

Figure 12. Ecclesia and Synagoga, c. 1230. These statues at Strasbourg Cathedral contrast the vision and strength of the Church (left) with the blindness and broken powers of the Synagogue (right). Similar personifications of Church and Synagogue can be found in other cathedrals of the thirteenth century, and they are directly alluded to in the thirteenth-century *Desputoison de la Sinagogue et de Sainte Yglise*. Foto Marbourg / Art Resource NY.

chastisement, saying that it is not just a game to understand something so obscure. For all the dramatic cleverness of this opening gambit, it also recalls the familiar twelfth-century accusation that Jews do not understand because they either lack reason or proper motivation. Only here the Jew insists that he does want to understand: "What you said in Latin, give me a gloss of it in French" (*Ce que diz en latin, en françois le me glose*). The anonymous author is clearly playing with the issue of language that mediates the exchange, a form of code switching scholars call diglossia, before even turning to the theological substance of the debate.[152]

As the disputation unfolds, the Jew shows himself to be an intelligent and reasoned debater. There are few instances of verbal invectives in this debate, and the Jew's speeches occupy 205 of the 432 lines, making for a remarkably even discussion, in quantity if not always in content. The Jew states repeatedly that Christian doctrines such as the Virgin Birth are plainly contrary to reason.[153] The Christian responds that they are not and, in very Anselmian fashion, argues the rationality and necessity of the God-Man.[154] The author of this debate would seem well acquainted with contemporary Jewish and Christian argumentation and takes pleasure in allowing the contrapuntal debate to follow its course. Still unconvinced, the Jew explains that the notion of God becoming a man is contrary to Scripture as well as reason. He presses for better answers: "Is my argument no good? Do you think I am lying? . . . answer me with reason. . . . give me proof." The patient Christian is happy to do so (*par mon chief, volentiers!*), and, after further proof texts are listed, the Jew is at last dutifully convinced: "Now I know the truth / For nothing can contradict such authority / We are deceived by our foolish belief / . . . The Messiah has come; I wish to be baptized."[155] The Christian rejoices that he has successfully brought a Jew to belief, and the dramatic encounter comes to a close. What is ingenious about this debate is that it mimics the argumentation of Jewish-Christian disputations and follows the scholastic method of analysis, with objections being raised only to be defeated, all self-consciously in the vernacular, before ultimately arriving at a conversion that would have been expected from the beginning by any reader (or listener) of the debate.

Two English poems from the thirteenth century provide final instances of vernacular debates between Christians and Jews: the *Disputisoun Bitwene Childe Jesu and Maistres of the Lawe of Jewes* and the *Disputisoun Bytwene a Cristenmon and a Jew*.[156] Both debates are preserved in the famous fourteenth-century Vernon manuscript, the largest surviving Middle English literary manuscript, although an earlier date for the composition of each of these works is likely. Central to both these poems is the fundamental significance of the Trinity. A second important concern in *Jesus and the Masters* (an alternate name for the first dialogue) is the reconciling of the Virgin Birth as recorded in the New Testament with the messianic prophecies of the Old Testament, particularly those found in Isaiah, a familiar topic in the Jewish-Christian debate. The peculiarity of *Jesus and the Masters* is that it does not involve two adults in a sparing contest over the interpretation of Scripture, but the twelve-year-old Christ confounding the learned doctors in the temple, likewise a popular scene in late medieval iconography. In this way, the disputation belongs to the medieval tradition of biblical narrative poems in which specific episodes from Scripture are imaginatively recounted. Here the biblical source is the eleven verses of the Gospel of Luke (2:41–51), the only portion of the canonical gospels to describe episodes from the boyhood of Christ.

The *Disputisoun Bytwene a Cristenmon and a Jew* follows a more traditional formula: a Christian and a Jew meet in the glimmering city of Paris (*In the toun of Parys / that is a citee of prys*) and undertake a debate. The Jew is described as holding firmly to his beliefs, a just Jew (*Jeuz riht*). Like the Christian, he is a follower of righteous law.[157] The Christian is an English cleric, identified later in the poem as Walter of Berwick. We are told that he became an important church official in Rome, but about him nothing more is known. At the outset of the debate, it is said that neither participant could best the other in argument, a somewhat unusual scenario for the genre given the contemporary proclivity for demonstrating the victory of rational Christian arguments over Jewish disbelief, but one that adequately sets up the dramatic encounter. Paris is lauded as the place where clerics study (*thei weore clerkes of Diuinite / crafti men in heore degree*) and where the man of greatest worth must become a master of divinity (*the man that most is of prys / Maister moste be*).[158] The location, characters, and battle of wits are set for what should be a classic scholastic encounter between a learned Christian and a disbelieving Jew. In fact, the poem unfolds as an extended *exemplum* that is merely couched in the familiar format of a Jewish-Christian debate. The narrative elements of the poem are drawn largely from romance literature and from folklore, reflecting themes commonly encountered in the Celtic tradition, including the subterranean passage into the Other World, a magic fairy castle, the danger posed for a mortal by a sumptuous fairy feast, and an unexpected and instantaneous return to the earthly reality.[159] The final conversion of the Jew results more from the power of the Christian's "magic" (that is, the power of the Eucharist) than from the power of his arguments. As with many other Latin or vernacular dialogues, what this Middle English disputation does offer is a retelling of traditional themes but with some interesting variations. The author of this debate poem is clearly drawing on several traditions at once. The first portion of the debate reinforces the reputation of Paris as the radiant center of theological disputation, the middle narrative blurs the distinction between folklore and theological controversy, and the conversionary ending returns the debate back to where any clerical or lay reader would expect the disputation to conclude: with the conversion of the Jew.

## Conclusions

The Jewish-Christian debate struck at the heart of medieval Europe's culture of disputation. The reasons for its centrality are relatively easy to explain. A shared biblical heritage and the enduring (urban) presence of Jewish communities provided fertile ground for Christian scholars to engage dialogically with Jews and Judaism. As scholastic learning developed and formalized, it naturally impacted the methods and strategies of this engagement. No attempt has been made here to analyze all the facets of the Jewish-Christian debate or to look much beyond the thirteenth century when the genre evolved and diversified even further. Important later examples of Jewish-Christian disputation include the account given by the Genoese merchant Inghetto Contardo of a dispute in Majorca in 1286 and the lengthy disputation at Tortosa (in Catalonia) in 1413–14, presided over by the pope. The well-studied Ramon Llull (c. 1235–1315) was explicitly concerned with articulating an art of debate in his voluminous polemical works,[160] and a wealth of information regarding Jewish responses to such disputations can equally be gleaned from the Hebrew literature of the period, recently and ably studied by Ram Ben-Shalom.[161] The Frankfurt passion plays of the later Middle Ages elevated these "dramatized disputations" to new levels of public instruction and performance and drew their inspiration from ancient polemic (including the pseudo-Augustinian *De altercatione ecclesiae et synagoga*), medieval liturgical drama such as the *Ordo prophetarum*, and vernacular debates representing Jews as hostile to Christians and ignorant of their own traditions.[162] Other examples still could be cited. Neither the quantity nor even the quality of these disputes forms the basis of this conclusion. Rather, it is the role of the Jewish-Christian debate in the larger culture of disputation that merits comment.

Several related themes emerge from the examination of Jews and Christians in dispute during the scholastic period. The first is the continuity of an ancient form. A major reason for examining the history of the dialogue over many centuries has been to recognize better the recurrence of familiar themes, including the very narrative framework of the literary form. Scholasticism neither introduced dialectic into the Jewish-Christian debate nor created any permanent rupture with preexistent discourse. It did, however, infuse new currents of thought concerning the virtues and boundaries of interreligious debates by assimilating and reproducing the scholastic methods of proof and demonstration. The scholastic culture of the schools and universities trained new participants (schoolmen, Dominicans, and poets), introduced new spaces (classrooms and universities), and appropriated old ones (courts, convents, urban squares) for staging these debates or imaginatively depicting them in poems, illuminated manuscripts, and cathedral facades. The convergence of scholastic reasoning and the thirteenth-century public helped shift the Jewish-Christian debate from a subset of theological hermeneutics to a practice and a motif, embedding it in the wider culture more generally. In time, the advent of print culture provided yet a new medium for the dissemination of images of Jewish-Christian disputations. A fifteenth-century woodcut of Jews and Christians in dispute, one of many published among the earliest incunabula, captures well the visual and indeed mental overlap between scholastic disputation and the Jewish-Christian debate (Figure 13).

A second theme is the pedagogical function of disputation, likewise traceable to the new scholastic environment fostered by schools and universities. Just as scholastic disputation evolved for the educative purpose of accessing the deeper recesses of theology's hidden truths, so too does the anti-Jewish polemic evolve within a similar set of exegetical concerns. The *Adversus Iudaeos* genre was, of course, polemical in origin, but what is equally striking is the level of internal Christian pedagogy exhibited by many of the literary and public disputations of the twelfth and thirteenth centuries. A stated goal in the prologues to many of the anti-Jewish dialogues of the twelfth century is to educate the reader by presenting the arguments in an appealing format. The disputations of the thirteenth century staged these debates in public with the deliberate aim of demonstrating and dramatizing (to both Jews and Christians) the validity of Christian claims. As the genre

Figure 13. Christians and Jews in dispute. The gestures and finger-pointing recall the scholastic method of point and counterpoint. Note that the postures and crowd suggest a public and even performative dimension of Jewish-Christian disputations. Hundreds of such images were designed and disseminated in the late fifteenth century with the help of print. Woodcut by Johann von Armssheim, *Der Seelen Wurzgarten* (Ulm: Konrad Dinckmut, 1483), 144.

joined forces with vernacular poetry, a once-theological dialogue with Jews restricted to professional clerics became bonded conceptually to a wider audience who read, consumed, and manipulated the anti-Jewish dialogue form for their own, even entertainment, purposes. This wider, cultural practice was one in which all consumers of public disputations and debate poems were invited to participate, whose theological and pedagogical values they would come intellectually to recognize and through that recognition securely ingest.

A final theme that emerges from the study of the Jewish-Christian debate is therefore the perfomative nature of public disputation. The royal patronage and ecclesiastical oversight of the disputations in Paris and Barcelona are exceptional events, to be sure, yet they are also paradigmatic of disputation's passage from exegesis into performance art amid a growing class of professional debaters and invited onlookers. The drama of dispute, always latent in the dialogue genre, becomes public spectacle when the scholastic art of disputation is placed in the service of an ancient polemic and performed in front of a receptive audience. An increasingly abundant variety of iconographic depictions and vernacular works attest to the establishment of Jewish-Christian disputations as a normative cultural practice in the public sphere.

# Conclusions: The Medieval
# Culture of Disputation

The goal of this book has been to trace the origins and influence of scholastic disputation as a normative cultural practice in medieval Europe. Owing to important changes in the cultural and institutional landscape of Europe, the focus of attention has been on developments that extend from the late eleventh century until the end of the thirteenth century. Before returning to the evidence, it will be instructive to look forward to the afterlife of medieval disputation, when modern characterizations of scholasticism take shape. If recovering the medieval culture of disputation is our goal, it is important to know how it first became covered up.

Beginning as early as the fifteenth century, the utility of scholastic disputation was deliberately minimized or condemned. This phenomenon extends to the modern interpreters of authors who trivialize the premodern era in a dialectical one-upmanship that C. Stephan Jaeger has appropriately called the problem of the "diminutive Middle Ages."[1] The disconnect between medieval and "modernity" is especially aggravated in the case of scholastic disputation perhaps precisely because it embodies a core feature of the medieval worldview, and it was from just that world that many authors of the fifteenth and sixteenth centuries (and their modern interpreters) thought they were escaping. True, many writers of the Middle Ages criticized or satirized the logic of the schools and universities, but it was the humanists of the Italian Renaissance who first associated scholasticism with a distinctly medieval and backward-looking outlook, a view that, mutatis mutandis, has persisted ever since. Broadly, there are three "diminishments" of scholastic disputation that can be discerned in the early modern period: assimilation, rejection, and condemnation.

The humanist Torquato Tasso (d. 1595) lived at the tail end of a generation of university-trained theorists who were inspired by new translations of Aristotle's *Poetics* and Plato's dialogues.[2] His *Discorso dell'arte del dialogo*

(Discourse on the Art of Dialogue, 1585), one of several such treatises written in the sixteenth century, reflects both an explicit indebtedness to classical forms and an implicit engagement with scholastic argumentation. In his *Discourse*, he described the dialogue as being of two kinds: "One deals with choosing and avoiding; the other is speculative and takes for the subjects of its debates matters that touch on truth and knowledge. In both, one imitates not only the disputation (*la disputa*) but also the characters of those who are disputing, and in both one employs a style that is sometimes highly ornamental and sometimes very pure, as befits the subject."[3] Scholars have often seized upon Tasso's art of dialogue and those of other Italian humanists to point to a distinctly new literary and philosophic ideal that originated in the quattrocento revival of the classics. But if the Renaissance dialogue and contemporary theories of them are studied purely in relation to antiquity, "a literary genre emerging out of the Renaissance reinvention of the mood of the classical discourses of Plato," then it ignores an important intellectual inheritance that Tasso and other university-trained humanists knew well and assumed.[4] Classical authors were indeed crucial to shaping the Renaissance literary and philosophical ideals, but could Tasso's interest in the art of dialogue have existed without the medieval fascination with Aristotelian dialectic, the scholastic conventions of university disputation, and the medieval tradition of polemical dialogue?

For René Descartes, it was the exaggerated use of university-based techniques that inspired him to write *Meditationes de prima philosophia* (1647), and to return to the inner dialogue he believed was more conducive to inquiry. Scholastic debate, he reasoned, reduced the literary production of authors by inciting them to cultivate the art of discussion and to privilege argumentation over in-depth explication. Inspired by his reading of canonical and scholastic authors, Descartes offered the following explanation of his method:

> That is why I wrote "Meditations" rather than "Disputations," as the philosophers have done, or "Theorems and Problems" as the geometers would have done. In so doing I wanted to make it clear that I would have nothing to do with anyone who was not willing to join me in meditating and giving the subject attentive consideration."[5]

The originality of Descartes's philosophical enterprise is indisputable, but in privileging one medieval genre (*meditatio*) over another (*disputatio*) it must be emphasized that he too was in some sense working within the categories of the medieval scholastic tradition. Anselm, as we have seen, practiced and perfected both genres, and there was scarcely more relevant a precedent for Descartes than Anselm.

The early modern dismissal of scholastic disputation took many forms, depending on time and place. A long list of such examples would be pedantic. One further instance shall suffice. John Locke, in his *Essay Concerning Human Understanding* (1690), provides the archetypal image passed down in the English-speaking world:

> For, notwithstanding these learned disputants, these all-knowing doctors, it was to the unscholastic statesman that the governments of the world owed their peace, defence, and liberties. . . . Nevertheless, this artificial ignorance, and learned gibberish, prevailed mightily in these last ages, by the interest and artifice of those who found no easier way to that pitch of authority and dominion they have attained, than by amusing the men of business, and ignorant, with hard words, or employing the ingenious and idle in intricate disputes about unintelligible terms, and holding them perpetually entangled in that endless labyrinth.[6]

As a product of London's Westminster School and the University of Oxford, Locke seriously underestimated his own indebtedness to scholastic learning. Locke was concerned with many of the problems, topics, and notions that had occupied the attention of science and philosophy in the previous centuries. In reacting to the content of his curriculum, he ignored the essential method of argumentation that allowed every challenge to the scholastic curriculum from Luther to Leibnitz to take place. More important, he assumed that the form and content of scholastic learning did not, and could not, affect the world beyond the academic arena. Over time, the notion of breaking free from the constraints of idle medieval debates has only been reinforced by modern scholars who insist on rupture with the scholastic past when continuity, change, and reform might equally be stressed.[7] With these "diminutive" perceptions of scholastic learning in mind, let us now return to the medieval evidence.

The history of the dialogue genre has its origins in antiquity, when public disputation and literary accounts of disputations, both real and invented, were established features of intellectual life. Following the rise of monasticism and Augustine's opening the doors to an inner dialogue, the genre shifted toward expressing a meditative, contemplative spirituality, occasionally treating other topics such as the allegorical debate between church and synagogue, at other times embodying an essentially didactic purpose, as witnessed by the steady persistence of teacher-student colloquies. Public disputation, meanwhile, ceased to be a structured part of everyday life, although this is not to say that oral debates did not take place at courts and councils. The proliferation of dialogue writing that began toward the end of the eleventh century and that came of age in the twelfth century, where Latin dialogues were eventually joined by the appearance of vernacular dialogues and debate poems, must be considered as part and parcel of the broader cultural and intellectual renewal wherein a more active and practical engagement with authoritative texts was sought. The educational and institutional changes that emerged during this long twelfth century provided the necessary context for understanding the didactic dialogue's mutation into a vehicle of polemical delivery. Thus, the perennial problem of trying to resolve whether the alleged disputations recorded in dialogues actually occurred, or, if they did, to what extent they are accurately reflected in the dialogues, has been eschewed in favor of the more relevant fact that the genre flourished and became polemical weaponry at the same time as the formalization of scholastic procedures of debate.

From a sustained and interdisciplinary investigation of the scholastic method, a cultural logic of medieval disputation emerges. In five discernable stages, disputation evolved from a pedagogical ideal in a monastic setting to become one of the defining features of medieval intellectual life, with formative and performative cultural manifestations at multiple levels of society.

First, Anselm and his circle pioneered a more dynamic and persuasive approach to articulating the tenets of faith, one that relied heavily on the dual power of reason and dialogue. More than any single other individual in the eleventh century, it was Anselm who successfully demonstrated to many of his students and contemporaries the dual power of reason and dialectic in expounding the tenets of Christianity, arguing for their rationality and demonstrating that a deeper understanding of faith could be taught through the ruminative practice of questions and answers. Authors such as Gilbert Crispin, Honorius Augustodunensis, Pseudo-Anselm, and Odo of Cambrai were among the early twelfth-century scholars who followed Anselm's lead in placing great emphasis on the role of reason and in choosing the dialogue form as the literary genre most suited to their philosophical and theological purposes. While Anselm was not alone in teaching through dialogue, and much of his pedagogical approach must have been inherited rather than invented, he provided the charismatic impulse that launched a new wave of speculative inquiry in Normandy, France, and England.

Second, the rise of new schools in Italy and northern France and the passage of dialogical writing and learning to these circles allowed disputation to be absorbed into a new scholastic milieu. The transference of dialogical learning out of the monasteries and into the tutorials of private masters and cathedral schools allowed the new interest in dialectic to develop slowly into systematic disputation. Several important figures from the early twelfth century such as Rupert of Deutz, Bernard of Clairvaux, and William of St. Thierry frowned upon this new interest in dialectic and the disputatious methods of studying scripture. Nevertheless, those very critics who deplored the new practice of disputation were themselves attracted to the polemical dialogue, composing literary disputations to demonstrate the superiority of their positions. The combative, feudal vocabulary with which authors of different social milieus described the new trends in disputation is an illustrative reminder not only of how pervasive and influential disputation had become but also of its penetrating potential for polemic.

Third, the recovery of Aristotle's New Logic in the middle decades of the twelfth century helped to catalyze this new and controversial use of disputation by providing models of dialectic argumentation. Adam of Balsham was one of the first authors to consider the value of Aristotle's logic in relation to the art of discourse (*ars disserendi*), something that he believed, quite correctly, was in its earliest developmental stages. John of Salisbury presented in his *Metalogicon* the clearest picture of how Aristotelian logic had become both fashionable and misused within the study of the *trivium*. John's mitigated endorsement of scholastic disputation lies in his explaining the value of Aristotelian logic on the one hand, while chiding the useless verbosity of contemporary masters who devalue its worth on the other. The dialectical exchange of the *Dialogus Ratii et Everardi* by Everard of Ypres discloses an awareness of Book VIII of Aristotle's *Topics*, as does in more parodic fashion the anthropomorphic debates featured in the thirteenth-century *Owl and the Nightingale*. The anonymous author of this Middle English debate is clearly well versed in contemporary academic instruction, even if the precise nature of his scholastic background is frustratingly elusive. The *Owl and the Nightingale* represents the earliest of many vernacular dialogues that feature animals engaged in a fictional disputation (the *Parliament of Fowls* being a later example), soon joined by a range of other debate poems that make playful art out of the dialectical process of opposing positions. Collectively, these works may be described as scholastic learning's ripple effects on the literary imagination.

Fourth, the integration of disputation as a fixture within the teaching program of the university and the Dominican Order established systematic and formal procedures in the art of debate. In a word, disputation became institutionalized. Although founded for different purposes, the university curriculum of Paris and the Dominican schools were coterminous institutions, each owing their formal institutional beginnings to the pontificate of Innocent III. Both institutions sent their graduates off into the world, taking their methods of scholastic argumentation with them. The *quaestiones disputatae* of the schools of theology, law, and medicine were soon joined by the *disputatio de quolibet*, a curricular-centered public disputation in which university masters demonstrated their knowledge and argumentative skills without restriction of subject. These curricular debates gave rise to an entire genre of quodlibetical literature that preserved in edited form the questions and arguments that arose from such debates. Thomas Aquinas's *Summa theologiae*, to take the most exemplary product of the thirteenth-century university, preserves the essential structure of the classroom debate, presenting arguments pro and contra before resolving the contradictions with a final determination and responding categorically to the opposing objections. Aquinas's involvement in the Dominican Order and his detailed comments on the value and dangers of Jewish-Christian disputations highlight the multiple and interweaving braids that form the third, fourth, and fifth elements of the medieval culture of disputation. While room must also be allowed for disputation among other mendicant orders, the Dominicans were especially engaged with disputation because of their special missionary purpose of convincing heretics and unbelievers of the errors of their beliefs.

Fifth, and most essential, disputation penetrated a public sphere when it became applied—indeed performed—before and among audiences not trained in the lecture halls of the medieval university or the teaching convents of the Dominican Order. Three such examples of the performance of disputation, I have argued, are the principles of counterpoint and polyphony evident in the school of Notre Dame, the motets that likewise grow out of Parisian scholastic circles, and the debate poems of the northern French trouvères. An even more poignant example of the cultural application of disputation is the Christian encounter with Jews, the Christian dialogical "other" par excellence. Although the *Adversus Iudaeos* genre extends as far back as the early centuries of Christianity, it witnessed a remarkable proliferation during scholasticism's most formative period. This included many dialogues purporting to be based on actual encounters between Christians and Jews and instruction manuals for future debates. Disputations between Christians and Jews achieved even greater public dimensions in the thirteenth century, as royal patronage and Dominican involvement in the incidents at Paris in 1240 and Barcelona in 1263 illustrate. Papal attempts to place restrictions on debates between unqualified priests and Jews and the leading role played by Dominican missionaries in organizing public debates indicate the complexity of the church's encounter with Jews and Judaism, a paradox that, in some sense, mirrors the perpetual paradox of Europe's Jewish communities: tolerated on the one hand, yet debased and increasingly resented on the other. The scholastic culture of disputation did not in any way resolve this paradox, but it did provide new rhetorical tools that disseminated the arguments of the discourse to a broader audience. The vernacular dialogues between Jews and Christians and the iconographic motif of Christians disputing with Jews reflect this broader evolution of scholastic disputation.

The medieval culture of disputation thus unfolds as an exercise in interdisciplinary reconstruction. It is the conclusion of this book that an idea and a literary form originally limited to small intellectual circles in the late eleventh century evolved though multiple stages to become a cultural practice within the larger public sphere in the thirteenth, perceptible within and beyond the university context. Taking place on the frontier between learned and popular culture, between public and private spheres, between tragedy and comedy, and between polemic and performance, the rise of disputation represents a cultural mutation in medieval society that can be fully understood only with a broad and cross-disciplinary approach to cultural history, one that adequately accounts for the evolution of ideas into practices, across both time and place. The acknowledged centrality of disputation in the late Middle Ages and well into the early modern period, where dialogues and disputations abound, suggests that there are more areas to be explored and more connections to be found. This book makes no claim to have given a complete study of medieval disputation. Rather, it is hoped that the categories of analysis offered and the range of evidence employed will stimulate future investigations into scholasticism's deep impact on medieval and postmedieval culture.

# NOTES

## INTRODUCTION

1. In his influential study *The Dialogic Imagination*, literary theorist Mikhail Bakhtin saw an important linguistic and semiotic shift in the rise of the "dialogical" novel of the eighteenth and nineteenth centuries, which he contrasted with the ancient epic. For recent reflections on the opposition between medieval and modern, see Symes, "When We Talk About Modernity."

2. Murphy, *Rhetoric in the Middle Ages*, 102 n. 47. I am grateful to the author for bringing this passage to my attention.

3. Constable, *The Reformation of the Twelfth Century*, 130.

4. On the problems of medieval authorship in the scholastic period, see Boureau, "Peut-on parler d'auteurs scolastiques?" who would rather avoid the term altoegther. A highly informed discussion of how twelfth-century "schools" were labeled centuries later by historians trying to sort out the diversity of medieval thinkers is given by Courtenay, "Schools and Schools of Thought in the Twelfth Century." For general theoretical considerations regarding texts and authorship, see the penetrating study by Spiegel, "History, Historicism, and the Social Logic of the Text in the Middle Ages."

5. As just one example of the plurality of definitions offered, see Burke, *Varieties of Cultural History*. For an attempt at a cultural history of medieval France, see Sot, Boudet, and Guerreau-Jalabert, *Histoire culturelle de la France*, where disputation is mentioned in passing (e.g., 127, 145, 176) but not discussed at any length.

6. See Burke, "Strengths and Weaknesses of the History of Mentalities," in Burke, *Varieties of Cultural History*, 162–82, here 163. The textbook of sorts for the history-of-mentalities approach Martin, *Mentalités médiévales, XIe–XVeXV^e siècle*. For critique and analysis of the French approach, see Chartier, "Intellectual History or Sociocultural History?" More recently, see Poirrier, *Les enjeux de l'histoire culturelle*.

7. Panofsky's now-famous insight was slightly anticipated in a review article by Lucien Febvre, "Histoire des idées, histoire des sociétés: Une question de climat": "We must not underestimate the role of ideas in history. . . . We must show that a Gothic cathedral, the marketplace of Ypres and one of those great cathedrals of ideas such as those Etienne Gilson describes to us in his book are daughters of a single epoch, sisters reared in the same household" (161).

8. George Makdisi, "The Scholastic Method in Medieval Education." Most scholars have not been convinced by the argument for an Islamic root to the Western legal tradition, but see more recently John A. Makdisi, "The Islamic Origins of the Common Law." A fascinating though tendentious account of the recursive argument method in medieval central Asia is by Christopher I. Beckwith, *Warriors of the Cloister: The Central Asian Origins of Science in the Medieval World*, who reorients Makdisi's thesis by placing its origins even farther East, but also systematically ignores the ancient

and early medieval western European tradition of debate and argumentation. It seems to me that so long as scholars continue to argue over who arrived at the scientific method first, and there are plenty of equally tendentious counter-claims to Beckwith's book, we will not actually appreciate how and why that method flourished in the places and ways that it did.

9. Above all, one thinks of the influential studies by Jacques Le Goff, *The Birth of Purgatory*; *The Medieval Imagination*; and *Intellectuals in the Middle Ages*. For a discussion of Le Goff's methodology, see Gurevich, "Popular and Scholarly Medieval Cultural Traditions." Caroline Walker Bynum might also be said to move in the cultural-historical direction, and she has on several occasions emphasized the need to go beyond what she calls "old-style intellectual history." See Bynum, *The Resurrection of the Body*, xvi, and *Wonderful Blood*, xv–xviii. A sociological approach to medieval thought is D'Avray, *Medieval Religious Rationalities*.

10. On the semantic difficulties involved in discussing the concepts of "private" and "public" in the Middle Ages, see von Moos, *"Öffentlich" und "privat" im Mittelalter*; and McSheffrey, "Place, Space, and Situation."

11. For example, Boucheron and Offenstadt, eds., *L'espace public au Moyen Âge*, with a short essay on university *disputatio* by Bénédicte Sère, 251–62. For another attempt at locating a public sphere in the thirteenth century, see the remarkable study by Symes, *A Common Stage*. A more radical application of Habermas's concept is Melve, *Inventing the Public Sphere*, who advances the curious argument that a public sphere existed in the predominantly textual context of the eleventh-century controversy over investiture but that it then did not reappear until after the Middle Ages. In addition to the critique by medievalists, a number of early modernists are also challenging the Habermasian concept of the representational public sphere, particularly as it relates to theater and public opinion. Two excellent contributions in this area are Rospocher, ed., *Beyond the Public Sphere: Opinions, Publics, Spaces in Early Modern Europe*, and Bloemendal, Eversmann, and Streitman, eds., *Drama, Performance, and Debate: Theatre and Public Opinion in the Early Modern Period*.

12. Habermas, *The Structural Transformation of the Public Sphere*, esp. 5–12.

13. A particularly fine example that has influenced my own thinking on the topic and likewise deals with the wider cultural dimension of medieval learning is Hobbins, *Authorship and Publicity Before Print*. On law, see Smail, *The Consumption of Justice*; and Mostert and Barnwell, eds., *Medieval Legal Process*.

## CHAPTER 1. THE SOCRATIC INHERITANCE

1. The roles of reason and debate are currently being rethought from the perspective of the cognitive sciences. See the positions for and against this theory in *Behavioral and Brain Sciences* 34, 2 (April 2011): 57–111. For a précis of this theory, see P. Cohen, "Reason Seen More as Weapon."

2. The concept of deep history has most notably explored by Daniel Lord Smail, *On Deep History and the Brain*, which should be read in connection with the collaborative essays in Shryock and Smail, eds., *Deep History*. It should be noted that the "neurohistory" that Smail and others propose is considerably different from more traditional models of evolutionary psychology. An excellent overview of the return of "deep history" or "big history" in connection with the modern practice of intellectual history is offered by David Armitage, "What's the Big Idea?"

3. For literary and historical analysis of the dialogue genre in the ancient Near East, see Reinink and Vanstiphout, eds., *Dispute Poems and Dialogues in the Ancient and Mediaeval Near East*. Discussion in this chapter is necessarily limited to the major influences on the Western tradition, although this is not to deny the obvious existence of dialogical texts in other ancient cultures.

4. Diogenes Laertius, *Lives of the Ancient Philosophers*, III.48.

5. See Kahn, *Plato and the Socratic Dialogue*, 1–35. In this chapter and in general, Greek works have been translated into English while Latin and vernacular works have been left in their original.

6. The question of form is an old one, but it has received considerable attention from scholars in recent years. See, for example, Long, "Plato's Dialogues and a Common Rationale for Dialogue Form"; McCabe, "Plato's Ways of Writing"; and Rowe, *Plato and the Art of Philosophical Writing*, esp. 7–37. A useful study of Plato's engagement with rhetoric and poetry in the articulation of his own philosophical enterprise is Nightingale, *Genres in Dialogue*. The foundational study of the ancient dialogue is Hirzel, *Der Dialog*, esp. 68–271 for his discussion of the ancient model.

7. These and many other issues are explored in Montuori, ed., *The Socratic Problem*.

8. Although some scholars have questioned the authenticity of this letter, the majority accept it unreservedly. Here I follow Kahn, *Plato*, 48 n. 22; and Sayre, *Plato's Literary Garden*, xi–xxiii.

9. Quoted in Sayre, *Plato's Literary Garden*, xiii. The full English translation of the text of the epistle is contained in *Plato's Epistles*, ed. and trans. Glenn Murrow, 215–50. For historical commentary on the epistle, see Murrow, ibid., and Edelstein, *Plato's Seventh Letter*.

10. Sayre, *Plato's Literary Garden*, iv.

11. Ibid.

12. Diogenes Laertius, *Lives*, III.50.

13. Guthrie, *History of Greek Philosophy*, 4:58–59.

14. Many aspects of the medieval interpretation of Aristotle's *Rhetorica* are taken up in the essays in Dahan and Rosier-Catach, eds., *La rhétoriqe d'Aristote*. A useful summary of the transmission of Aristotle's corpus in the Middle Ages is Dod, "Aristoteles latinus." See also Murphy, *Rhetoric in the Middle Ages*.

15. Aristotle may have been less interested than Plato in the issue of literary form, but he was no less attuned to the relation between the spoken and written word. In *Poetics* (47b) he describes the Socratic dialogue in terms of *mimesis* (imitation): "The art which uses language unaccompanied, either in prose or in verse (either combining verse-forms with each other or using a single kind of verse), remains without a name to the present day. We have no general term referring to the mimes of Sophron and Xenarchus and Socratic dialogues, nor to any imitation that one might produce using iambic trimeters, elegiac couplets or any other such verse form" (4).

16. Schofield, "Ciceronian Dialogue." The indispensable study of Ciceronian dialogue is Ruch, *Le Préambule dans les oeuvres philosophiques de Cicéron*. But now see Gorman, *The Socratic Method in the Dialogues of Cicero*, who argues that Cicero's interest in Socratic dialectic stems mainly from its capacity to detach one from the views one originally held. See also Hirzel, *Der Dialog*, 433–565; and, for an early modern context, Wilson, *Incomplete Fictions*, chap. 2.

17. Cicero, *De officiis*, 1:132.

18. Cicero, *De oratore*, III.80.

19. Cicero, *Tusculan Disputations*, II.9.

20. See Schofield, "Ciceronian Dialogue," 68–69.

21. Wilson, *Incomplete Fictions*, 36.

22. Schofield, "Ciceronian Dialogue," 70.

23. Cicero's dialogues, in particular, circulated widely because the early church declared him a "virtuous pagan," and consequently many of his works were deemed worthy of preservation. Indeed, more works survived in the Middle Ages by Cicero than by any other Latin author. See Rolfe, *Cicero and His Influence*; and Paratore, "Cicerone attraverso i secoli," 237–44, for indications of their medieval manuscript tradition. Cicero's moral philosophy proved especially influential in the

twelfth century. This has been especially well traced by Delhaye, "La place de l'éthique parmi les disciplines scientifiques au XIIe siècle"; "L'enseignement de la philosophie morale au XIIe siècle"; and "Une adaptation du 'De officiis' au XIIe siècle: Le 'Moralium dogma philosophorum'." For the special place given to the *Rhetorica ad Herennium* in the twelfth century, see Ward, *Ciceronian Rhetoric.*

24. The most thorough examination of this form of dialogue remains Daly, *Alercatio Hadriani Augusti et Epicteti Philosophi and the Question-and-Answer Dialogue.*

25. Ibid., 12.

26. Ibid., 20.

27. W. Suchier, *L'Enfant Sage*, 253.

28. The *Dialogus* has long been Tacitus's most neglected work. While perhaps his most original as well, it should be read along with the *Agricola* as an expression of Tacitus's disillusion with the careers open to a Roman in public life. For an extended treatment of this work, see Rutledge, "The Literary, Cultural, and Historical Background of Tacitus' *Dialogus de oratoribus.*"

29. For extended discussions of dialogue in postbiblical Jewish writings, namely the Talmud, see the essays by Seth Schwartz and Daniel Boyarin in Goldhill, ed., *End of Dialogue in Antiquity.*

30. See, very generally, Bruns, "Midrash and Allegory."

31. Ibid., 630.

32. Much work remains to be done on the commentary tradition of Job in the Middle Ages. All scholars in the field of the study of the Bible in the Middle Ages owe a great deal to the work of Beryl Smalley and Henri de Lubac. More recently, see Dahan, *L'exegèse chrétienne de la Bible en Occident médiévale, XII–XIV siècle.* Bridging the medieval and reformation interest in the story of Job is Schreiner, *Where Shall Wisdom Be Found?*

33. An early and detailed and still valuable study of the genre is Williams, *Adversus Judaeos.* Extremely useful and more up to date is Krauss and Horbury, *The Jewish-Christian Controversy from the Earliest Times to 1789*, vol. 1, *History.* Also essential is Schreckenberg, *Die christlichen Adversus-Judaeos-Texte und ihr literarisches und historisches Umfeld (1.–11. Jh.).*

34. Pelikan, *The Emergence of the Catholic Tradition (100–600)*, 15.

35. For a recent assessment of the work and its relevance to nascent Christianity, see Boyarin, *Border Lines*, chap 2.

36. Eusebius, *Ecclesiastical History*, IV.xviii.6.

37. Pelikan, *Emergence of the Catholic Tradition*, 15.

38. Williams, *Adversus Judaeos*, 42.

39. Pelikan, *Emergence of the Catholic Tradition*, 15.

40. These works are discussed in turn in Williams, *Adversus Judaeos.* A detailed analysis of Origen's relation to Jews and Judaism is De Lange, *Origen and the Jews.*

41. Lim, *Public Disputation, Power, and Social Order in Late Antiquity.*

42. See Krauss and Horbury, *The Jewish-Christian Controversy*, 43–51.

43. A bibliography of this disputation can be found in ibid., 44 n. 1.

44. The text of this disputation is contained in Migne, ed., *Patrologiae cursus completus: Series Graeca* 86, 621–784. See also Krauss and Horbury, *The Jewish-Christian Controversy*, 48–49; as well as Schreckenberg, *1–11 Jh*, 397–99, 632.

45. Lim, *Public Disputation*, chap. 3.

46. Ibid., 106.

47. The very same technique deployed against Manichean belief John used to combat Islam, composing the *Dialogue Between a Saracen and a Christian*, in which a Muslim puts questions to a Christian on such matters as the nature of Christ, creation, and free will.

48. Lim, *Public Disputation*, 109–48.

49. In broad terms, these are the themes of parts 3 and 4 of *The End of Dialogue in Antiquity*, ed. Simon Goldhill.

50. See Lim, *Public Disputation*, 219.

51. Ibid., 220.

52. An English translation of this text can be found in *Vitas sanctorum patrum emeritensium*, translated by Garvin, 199–219. For a more recent critical edition of the text, see the 1992 edition, ed. Sánchez.

53. Most recently, see the essays by Gillian Clark and Richard Miles in *The End of Dialogue in Antiquity*. For the biographical details of Augustine's life, I rely primarily on Brown, *Augustine of Hippo*.

54. Proponents for the historicity of the dialogues include Alfaric, *L'évolution intellectuelle de S. Augustin*; Heil, "Augustine's Attack on Skepticism: The 'Contra Academicos'"; Madec, "L'historicité des Dialogues de Cassiciacum"; and Doignon, "État des questions relatives aux premiers dialogues de saint Augustin." Those who hold that the dialogues are substantially the work of Augustine include O'Meara, in his introduction to *Against the Academics*, and Morrison, *Conversion and Text*.

55. Chadwick, *Augustine*, 32.

56. Augustine, *Soliloquies and Immortality of the Soul*, 2.14, 89.

57. A penetrating analysis of this development is given by Stock, *Augustine the Reader*.

58. *Soliloquies*, 2.14, 89.

59. Lerer, *Boethius and Dialogue*, 51.

60. Courcelle, *Les Confessions de S. Augustin dans la tradition littéraire* is both a magisterial study of the influence of the *Confessions* in European literature and an indispensable introduction to the resources of scholarship mobilized around this single text.

61. Saenger, *Space Between Words*.

62. Boethius, *Comentarii in Librum Aristotelis Perihermeneias*, 79–80.

63. Courcelle, *La Consolation de philosophie dans la tradition littéraire* is a masterful study of Boethius, his incorporation of classical knowledge, and interpretation of his major work through the centuries.

64. The plot recalls the story of Job and the dialogue that ensues with his friends over the very same question.

65. Lerer, *Boethius and Dialogue*, 69.

66. Ibid., 77.

67. The manuscript tradition of the *Consolation of Philosophy* is extraordinarily rich. For its reception during the Middle Ages, see Hoenen and Nauta, eds., *Boethius in the Middle Ages*.

68. A good introduction to the social background of the work is Peterson, *The Dialogues of Gregory the Great in Their Late Antique Cultural Background*.

69. Gregory the Great, *Dialogues*, 39:3.

70. Scholarship on the Carolingian Renaissance is plentiful. On the theme of continuity and originality, see McKitterick, ed., *Carolingian Culture*; and Bullough, *Carolingian Renewal*.

71. Especially significant was the Carolingian emphasis on the written word, a field most notably explored in McKitterick, *The Carolingians and the Written Word*; Bischoff, *Manuscripts and*

*Libraries in the Age of Charlemagne*, as well as the essays by Janet Nelson and Rosamond McKitterick in *The Uses of Literacy in Early Medieval Europe*, ed. McKitterick.

72. Dated, but still profitable for its discussion of education, is Wallach, *Alcuin and Charlemagne*. See above for more recent bibliography.

73. The text is in *PL* 101:949–75.

74. The *interrogationes et responsiones*, as it is known in its Latin title, was formerly ascribed to Alcuin. See Marenbon, *From the Circle of Alcuin to the School of Auxerre*, 154–57.

75. A related musical treatise of the ninth century that also testifies to Carolingian practicality is the *Musica enchiriadis*, also of unknown authorship. Both are translated with an introduction and commentary by Erickson, *Musica Enchiriadis and Scolica Enchiriadis*.

76. See the detailed introduction by Erickson, especially xxiv and xvii.

77. The literature on John Scotus, particularly his philosophy, is vast. See very generally Moran, *The Philosophy of John Scottus Eriugena*; and Rudnick, *Das System des Johannes Scottus Eriugena*. A recent overview of his life and thought is Carabine, *John Scottus Eriugena*. See also the collected articles in Van Riel, Steel, and McEvoy, eds., *Iohannes Scottus Eriugena*. The Latin text of the *Periphyseon*, also known as *De divisione naturae*, is in *PL* 122: 411–1022. For an English rendering, see *Eriugena: Periphyseon (The Division of Nature)*, trans. Sheldon-Williams, rev. O'Meara.

78. A detailed commentary on the literary tradition of the dialogues is supplied by Menner, ed., *The Poetical Dialogues of Solomon and Saturn*, 1–70.

79. Here I follow Menner is his distinction between Poem I and Poem II.

80. Menner, *Poetical Dialogues*, 6.

81. On the medieval amalgam of Saturn and Marcolf, see ibid., 26–35; and now the learned study of this work by Ziolkowski, *Solomon and Marcolf*, esp. 1–50.

82. A translation of the *Enchiridion musices* appears in *Strunk's Source Readings in Music History*, 199–210. Berno's *Dialogus* is contained in *PL* 142: 1087–98. Editions of the Latin colloquies on grammar can be found in Stevenson, ed., *Early Scholastic Colloquies* and Gwara, ed., *Latin Colloquies from Pre-Conquest Britain*.

83. See Kuchenbuch, "Ordnungsverhalten im grundherrlichen Schriftgut vom 9. zum 12. Jahrhundert"; Marenbon, *Early Medieval Philosophy (480–1150)*, chap. 8.

84. For an overview of the political and theological questions raised in the Formosan controversy, see Pop, *La Défense du pape Formose*. A recent summary of the events surrounding the trial of Formosus can be found in Logan, *A History of the Church in the Middle Ages*, 97–100. The texts of Auxilius are printed in *PL* 129:1073–1102 and 1101–12.

85. The works of both Auxilius and Eugenius are long overdue for a fresh assessment. For a comparative evaluation of their treatment of the papacy, see Dümmler, *Auxilius und Vulgarius*, who describes Eugenius's works at 39–46 and provides an edition of his other Formosan treatise, his letters, and poetry at 107–56.

86. Leonardi, "Intellectual Life," 207.

87. A critical edition of the text is *Ratherii Veronensis Praeloquiorum libri IV*, ed. Reid, CCCM 46A 219–65. It more frequently appears under the Latin title *Excerptum ex dialogo confessionali*.

88. See Blumenkranz, "Altercatio Aecclesie contra Synagogam."

89. He later made amends by dedicating to the pope many flattering verses.

90. A very detailed chronology of Damian's life is given in Luchesi, "Per una Vita di San Pier Damiani," 1:13–180; 2:13–160. A prolific author, Damian has been the focus of sustained scholarly attention. Most recently see Ranft, *The Theology of Work*; see also Freund, *Studien zur literarischen*

*Wirksamkeit des Petrus Damiani,* who situates Damian's writings amid other eleventh-century polemicists.

91. John of Lodi's *Vita B. Petri Damiani* is found in *PL* 144: 114–46.

92. A critical edition of all Peter's letters exists in *Die Briefe des Petrus Damiani.* English translation from Peter Damian, *Letters 1–30,* 38.

93. Cf. Abulafia, "An Eleventh-Century Exchange of Letters Between a Christian and a Jew."

94. On the role of reason in the Jewish-Christian debate and its consequences for the rise of anti-Judaism, see Abulafia, *Christians and Jews in the Twelfth-Century Renaissance.* On the importance of reason in medieval thought and society more generally, see Murray, *Reason and Society in the Middle Ages*; Fichtenau, *Heretics and Scholars in the High Middle Ages, 1000–1200,* part III; and Grant, *God and Reason in the Middle Ages.*

95. Peter Damian, *Letters 1–30,* 66.

96. See Balboni, "San Pier Damiano, Maestro e Discepolo in Pomposa." On Peter Damian's access to books at the library of Fonte Avellana, see Blum, chap. 2.

97. Oakley, *Omnipotence, Covenant, and Order,* 41–45. A detailed study of this work is given in Resnick, *Divine Power and Possibility in St. Peter Damian's De Divina Omnipotentia.*

98. See *Die Briefe des Petrus Damiani,* 2:531–72.

99. Formerly treated as a separate work, the *Disceptatio synodalis* is now recognized as belonging to Letter 89. A critical edition of the Latin text can be found in ibid., 2:541–72. An English translation can be found in Peter Damian, *Letters 61–90,* 336–69.

100. Ibid., 368.

101. Peter cautions his fellow monks against the dialecticians of the day in *De divina omnipotentia* and in Letter 21. On Damian's attitude toward rhetoric and dialectic, see Gonsette, *Pierre Damien et la culture profane.*

## CHAPTER 2. ANSELM, DIALOGUE, AND THE RISE OF SCHOLASTIC DISPUTATION

1. Grabmann, *Die Geschichte der scholastischen Methode,* 1:7. See also the remarks of Southern, "St Anselm of Canterbury: His Mission of Reconciliation," 24.

2. Two leading examples of this recent attention to monastic learning in the age of Anselm are Gasper and Logan, eds., *Saint Anselm of Canterbury and His Legacy*; and Vaughn and Rubenstein, eds., *Teaching and Learning in Northern Europe, 1000–1200,* with further bibliographic orientation in the excellent introduction by Vaughn and Rubenstein. An excellent recent study of Anselm's thought that came to my attention after completion of this book is Sweeney, *Anselm of Canterbury and the Desire for the Word*; chapter 7, in particular, arrives at conclusions very similar to the argument of this chapter. The locus classicus for a sweeping historical assessment of Anselm remains Southern, *Saint Anselm,* the author's second biography of Anselm, although a number of elements of Southern's portrayal have been modified by subsequent scholarship (cited below); in this essay, I endeavor to continue that modification, but in a different direction. Gasper, *Anselm of Canterbury and His Theological Inheritance,* considers the relatively unexplored realm of Anselm's use of patristic authorities (other than Augustine). A diverse appraisal of Anselm's significance for the modern world is offered in Viola and van Fleteren, eds., *Saint Anselm,* which presents papers at a 1990 conference on Anselm. Still very useful because of the range of historical themes touched upon are the proceedings from the 1982 Anselm conference at Bec: Foreville, ed., *Les mutations socioculturelles au tournant des XIe–XIIe siècles,* although it is perplexing that so little attention has since been paid to the sociocultural atmosphere of monastic learning. For fresh introductions to Anselm's philosophy see Visser and Williams,

*Anselm*; and Davies and Leftow, eds., *The Cambridge Companion to Anselm*, both of which focus almost exclusively on Anselm's philosophy.

3. Radding and Clark, *Medieval Architecture, Medieval Learning*. This work resurrects and develops the famous argument proposed by Panofsky, *Gothic Architecture and Scholasticism*. See also Radding, *A World Made by Men*. Not to be ignored in the context of how medieval architecture encodes a shift in the way medieval thinkers perceived their relationship with their world is the eminently accessible book by Ball, *Universe of Stone*. An even bolder case for bringing neuroscience and human biology into the realm of history (and vice versa) has been made by another medievalist: Smail, *On Deep History and the Brain*.

4. Vaughn, "'Among These Authors Are the Men of Bec': Historical Writing Among the Monks of Bec," at 3. The overall history of Bec is much in need of a fresh assessment; the foundational study remains Porée's two-volume 1901 study, *Histoire de l'abbeye du Bec*.

5. In these areas the scholarship of Sally Vaughn is preeminent. On the study of history at Bec, see Vaughn, "Among These Authors." For the suggestion that law was also taught at Bec, by both Lanfranc and Anselm, see eadem, "The Concept of Law at the Abbey of Bec, 1034–1136: How Law and Legal Concepts Were Described, Taught and Practiced at Bec in the Time of Lanfranc and Anselm," as well as eadem, "Anselm of Bec: The Pattern of His Teaching"; and Watkins, "Lanfranc at Caen: Teaching by Example." On the administrative careers of the students at Bec, see again Vaughn, "Anselm, Lanfranc, and the School of Bec: Searching for the Students of Bec." In an extension of her earlier work on Anselm and his correspondence with women, Vaughn has most recently approached Anselm as having developed theological theories that were foundational to the development of the twelfth-century concept of courtly love: Vaughn, "Saint Anselm and His Students Writing About Love: A Theological Foundation for the Rise of Romantic Love in Europe."

6. Sharpe, "Anselm as Author: Publishing in the Late Eleventh Century." Also relevant is the edition and translation of three important texts from the early twelfth century that deal with the position of Bec in relation to episcopal and ducal authorities: Constable, ed., *Three Treatises from Bec on the Nature of Monastic Life*.

7. The classics in this field remain Ghellinck, *Le mouvement théologique du XIIe siècle*; and Chenu, *La théologie au douzième siècle*. For a treatment of dialectic in the writings of four of the authors discussed in this paper, see Holopainen, *Dialectic and Theology in the Eleventh Century*.

8. The notion of "philosophy" itself during this period is also being rethought from the perspective of the history of education. See Jaeger, "Philosophy, ca. 950–ca. 1050."

9. On Lanfranc's career, see most recently Cowdrey, *Lanfranc*. Still indispensable is Gibson, *Lanfranc of Bec*. The diversity of Lanfranc's contributions is explored in D'Onofrio, ed., *Lanfranco di Pavia e l'Europa del secolo XI*. Much of what we know about Lanfranc's early life comes from the *Vita Lanfranci* published in *PL* 150: 29–58, trans. in Vaughn, *The Abbey of Bec and the Anglo-Norman State, 1034–1136*, 87–111.

10. See Radding, *A World Made by Men*, esp. 156–86; and discussions in Cowdrey, *Lanfranc*, 5–8; and Gibson, *Lanfranc of Bec*, 4–15. More recently, Winroth has argued that the origins of legal education are to be sought in the twelfth century and not in the eleventh: "The Teaching of Law in the Twelfth Century."

11. Jaeger, *The Envy of Angels*, 4–9 and passim.

12. Barlow, *The English Church, 1000–1066*, 12–13, 20–22.

13. Cited in Cowdrey, *Lanfranc*, 9.

14. See especially Gibson, *Lanfranc of Bec*, chaps. 2–3. On Lanfranc's educational and administrative influence in neighboring Caen, see Watkins, "Lanfranc at Caen."

15. Gilbert Crispin, *Vita Herluini*, in *The Works of Gilbert Crispin, Abbot of Westminster*, 197.

16. Pope Nicholas II was consecrated in January 1059 and began almost at once to lay down lines of political and ecclesiastical development that altered the general development of papal government. He was working toward a new procedure for papal elections that would diminish, if not virtually eliminate, imperial participation in papal elections. The letter is reproduced in Southern, *Saint Anselm*, 32–33, translated at 20–21. See also Cowdrey, *Lanfranc*, esp. 41–45.

17. Orderic Vitalis, *The Ecclesiastical History of Orderic Vitalis*, ed. and trans. Marjorie Chibnall, 2:251. All translations of this text are from Chibnall.

18. A considerable body of literature exists on this now-famous dispute, in part because it led to the doctrine of transubstantiation. Especially important is Montclos, *Lanfranc et Bérenger*. See also Holopainen, *Dialectic and Theology*, chaps. 3–4; and Macdonald, *Berengar and the Reform of Sacramental Doctrine*. A useful summary of the debate is given in the recent study by M. Radding and Newton, *Theology, Rhetoric, and Politics in the Eucharistic Controversy*, chap. 1.

19. In his *De corpore et sanguine Domini*, c. 831–33 (in *PL* 120: 1255–1350), Paschasius Radbertus insisted that the body of Christ as received in the sacrament was identical both with the earthly body that the incarnate Christ took from Mary and with the body now in heaven that is eternally glorified. Some ten years later, another monk from the same abbey of Corbie, Ratramnus, replied in a similarly titled work (*PL* 121: 125–70) to specific questions put to him by Emperor Charles the Bald. Ratramnus maintained that the bread and wine of the Eucharist, after consecration, did not become the body and blood of Christ in an actual or material sense, as Radbertus had taught, but only in a spiritual sense. Other works dealing with the Carolingian controversy include Chazelle, *The Crucified God in the Carolingian Era*; and Jones, *Christ's Eucharistic Presence*. Ganz, *Corbie in the Carolingian Renaissance*, provides a useful overview of the monastery during the period but does not go into the controversy. For further discussion of the controversy itself, see Fahey, *The Eucharistic Teaching of Ratramn of Corbie*.

20. Theoduin's letter to Henry I of France is printed in *PL* 146: 1439–42.

21. The Latin text is printed in R. B. C. Huygens, "Textes latins du XIe au XIIIe siècle," 456, with discussion by Huygens and Jean de Montclos at 451–59. See also Gibson, *Lanfranc of Bec*, 66.

22. The last synod condemning Berengar and his teachings took place in Rome in 1078–79 during the pontificate of Gregory VII. A treatise written against Berenger by Alberic of Monte Cassino resulted from this synod. Once thought lost, it has been identified and translated by Radding and Newton, *Theology, Rhetoric, and Politics*, 123–70.

23. *Ecclesiastical History*, 2:252–53.

24. Holopainen, *Dialectic and Theology*, chap. 3, challenges the notion that Lanfranc was systematic or responsible in his application of dialectic to theology. Nevertheless, in his commentary on the Epistles of St. Paul, Lanfranc is even more explicit in his identification of dialectic and philosophy as a rational method and related inquiry. See his *Commentarius in Epistolas Pauli, PL* 150, esp. 323–24.

25. Southern, *Saint Anselm*, 48. See also d'Onofrio, "*Respondeant pro me*: La dialectique anselmienne et les dialecticiens du haut moyen âge." On the medieval reception of Aristotle's Old Logic, see Marenbon, "Glosses and Commentaries on the *Categories* and *De interpretatione* before Abelard," as well as Chapter 4 of this book.

26. *PL* 150: 407–42.

27. The work has been dated as early as 1061 and as late as 1068. The various proposals are summarized by Holopainen, *Dialectic and Theology*, 45 n. 6. An important discussion connecting this famous Eucharistic debate to the devotion to Christ in his humanity is Fulton, *From Judgment to Passion*, 121–41.

28. Cowdrey, *Lanfranc*, 64. A note in some German manuscripts says that he was prompted by his pupil Theodoric of Paderborn at Bec or Caen. See also Montclos, *Lanfranc et Bérenger*, 196.

29. *PL* 150: 407.

30. Hildebert of Lavardin, a contemporary of Berengar if not his pupil, first used the term *transubstantiation*. See his *Sermones* 93, *PL* 176: 776. On the early development of the theory of transubstantiation, see Jorissen, *Die Entfaltung der Transsubstantionslehre bis zum Beginn der Hochscholastik*; and, for its later development, Rubin, *Corpus Christi*.

31. See Somerville, "The Case Against Berengar of Tours: A New Text," who discusses Guitmund's text and the wider context of his writing.

32. *PL* 149: 1427–94. The work was written sometime between 1073 (when Gregory was elected pope) and 1078 (when the synod in Rome was convened again to debate Berengar's position).

33. The text of the commentary on the Pauline Epistles is printed in *PL* 150: 105–406. A recent and detailed study of Lanfranc's commentary and its manuscript tradition is Collins, *Teacher in Faith and Virtue*.

34. Collins, *Teacher*, 92–93. Similar conclusions are also reached by d'Onofrio, *Vera philosophia*, chap. 4, esp. 223–26.

35. Collins, *Teacher*, 203–4.

36. Sigebert of Gembloux, *De scriptoribus ecclesiasticis*, *PL* 160: 582–83.

37. Contra Margaret Gibson, who argues that the school of Bec lasted only a few years after its foundation by Lanfranc, Sally Vaughn has done the most to argue for its continuity and reputation, while admitting that the nature of this school remains a puzzle. (See the works cited above in nn. 5 and 9.) Stimulating interdisciplinary perspectives on this general development in medieval Europe are offered in Fenster and Smail, eds., *Fama*.

38. *Ecclesiastical History*, 2: 295.

39. Anselm's intellectual debt to his teacher Lanfranc was very great indeed. His devotion to Lanfranc is vividly described, perhaps with some exaggeration, in Eadmer's *Vita Anselmi*. See also the meticulous reconstruction of the student-teacher relation done by Southern, *Saint Anselm*, chaps. 2–3. Southern's subsequent comment that Anselm, on first meeting Lanfranc at age twenty-six, was "a fairly mature drop out, who had so far failed in everything he had undertaken" is perhaps a bit harsh, but it underscores the extent to which Lanfranc could and would shape Anselm's career; see Southern, "The Relationship Between Anselm's Thought and His Life at Bec and Canterbury," at 12.

40. Southern, *Saint Anselm*, 52.

41. Ibid. Riché, "La vie scolaire et la vie pédagogique au Bec au temps de Lanfranc et de Saint Anselme."

42. Anselm, *Monologion*, in *S. Anselmi opera omnia*, 1:7. All translations of Anselm are my own unless otherwise stated.

43. The novelty of Anselm's reliance on reason as an aid to faith has been much commented on by historians, theologians, and philosophers alike. For a fresh assessment, see Adams, "Anselm on Reason and Faith."

44. Anselm of Canterbury, *Epistola* 77, in *S. Anselmi opera omnia*, 3:199–200.

45. See Cowdrey, *Lanfranc*, 208–13, for a discussion of the epistolary correspondence between Anselm and Lanfranc regarding the *Monologion*.

46. Gasper, *Anselm of Canterbury*, especially emphasizes Anselm's debt to other patristic sources.

47. On this initiative, see most recently Evans, "Anselm's Life, Works, and Immediate Influence," 10–11. Cf. the first biography of Anselm by Southern, *Saint Anselm and His Biographer*, 30–31.

48. *Ecclesiastical History*, 2:295. See also Eadmer, *The Life of St Anselm, Archbishop of Canterbury*, henceforth cited as *Vita Anselmi*, who says at 39–40 that Anselm's reputation spread across Normandy, France, and Flanders and that "from every nation there rose up and came to him many noblemen, learned clerks, and active knights offering themselves and their goods to the service of God in the monastery." It is also the case that more monks professed under Anselm than under Lanfranc, as the profession list clearly demonstrates. See Porée, *Histoire de l'abbaye du Bec*, 1:629–31.

49. See the perceptive remarks by Campbell, "The Systematic Character of Anselm's Thought," 553–54: "What I find striking about Anselm's arguments, whether in the more philosophical works or in the more theological, is the way they always proceed within the context of *what someone says*. . . . In the dialogue form adopted in many of the later works all of the statements are, of course, owned by one or other of the participants. . . . Anselm is not indulging in idle speculation or intellectual games; he will only consider propositions which are 'owned' by one speaker. . . . Even in the *Monologion*, where the protagonist is most shadowy, and which Anselm tells us was written in the manner of one arguing with himself, it is clear that the questions raised are designed to clarify what is inherent in the domain of discourse within which Anselm was speaking." See also Southern, "The Relationship," 11–12: "Anselm's approach to theology is through the discussions, mounting experiences, and the final triumphs of thought and experience in friendship."

50. The foundational study of the dialogue genre is Hirzel, *Der Dialog*, which, however, offers minimal consideration of the medieval dialogue. A more satisfactory look at medieval dialogues, but again from the vantage point of philosophy and with consideration of individual philosophers (or works) rather than emerging trends, is Jacobi, ed., *Gespräche lesen*. Recent considerations on the decline of the dialogue genre following Augustine are to be found in Goldhill, ed., *The End of Dialogue in Antiquity*. A very valuable repertory and study of medieval Latin dialogues is de Hartmann, *Lateinische Dialoge, 1200–1400*. On the earlier end, an elegant investigation of early medieval monastic dialogue is offered by Fontaine, "Le genre littéraire du dialogue monastique dans l'Occident latin des Ve et VIe siècles." See also the general remarks by Sweeney, "Anselm und der Dialog: Distanz und Versöhnung"; and the theoretical discussion of the dialogue genre by Peter von Moos, "Gespräche, Dialogform und Dialog nach älterer Theorie."

51. This total counts only works that are overtly cast as dialogues between two characters. As I argue in this chapter, the early meditations and the *Monologion* in particular could also be included within the spirit of dialogue as they are essentially internal conversations.

52. The authoritative commentary on this early work is Henry, *Commentary on De grammatico*.

53. Marenbon, *Early Medieval Philosophy (480–1150)*, 102.

54. Anselm, *De grammatico*, in *Operia omnia*, 1:146.

55. Ibid., 168.

56. Southern, *Saint Anselm*, 65.

57. Eadmer, *Vita Anselmi*, 1.19, 28. Of some relevance to the overall thrust of this paper is Alain Galonnier's important discussion of how *De grammatico* anticipates later logical *sophismata* treatises. See "Sur quelques aspects annonciateurs de la littérature sophismatique dans le *De grammatico*," 210, where Galonnier notes, "Nous touchons peut-être ici à la difficulté majeure du dialogue sur *grammaticus*, et probablement à ce qui détourne souvent de lui l'intérêt que manquent d'attacher à ses pages la plupart des historiens de la logique médiévale: le fond s'y dilue dans la forme."

58. The best overall discussion of these treatises is to be found in Pouchet, *La rectitudo chez Saint Anselme*.

59. Anselm, *De veritate*, in *Opera omnia*, 1:177.

60. Anselm, *Praefatio*, in *Opera omnia*, 1:173–74. It should be pointed out that most translations of this preface elide the word "disputationis" from the sentence, simply rendering the phrase

"in similar form" or "in similar style." While Anselm is clearly using the word *disputatio* in a more benign sense than the word would come to have later in the twelfth century, its repeated use in his texts should not go unnoticed.

61. See Eadmer, *Vita Anselmi*, esp. 1.26–28, 44–48. On the dating of these works see Sharpe, "Anselm as Author," 15–23. See also Southern, *Anselm and His Biographer*, 66.

62. His exile notwithstanding, Anselm's competence and experience in the world of politics should not be underestimated. On this very able aspect of Anselm, see especially Vaughn, *Anselm of Bec and Robert of Meulan*, esp. chaps. 7–8.

63. An essential guide to this important work is Gilbert, Kohlenberger, and Salmann, eds., *Cur Deus homo*, whose forty-seven contributory essays attest to the work's enduring scholarly interest.

64. Southern, *Saint Anselm*, 203.

65. Anselm, *Cur Deus homo*, in *Opera omnia*, 2:47–48.

66. For an argument in favor of Anselm's anti-Jewish position, see Dahan, "Saint Anselme, les juifs, le judaïsme." Opposite this interpretation is Abulafia, "St. Anselm and Those Outside the Church," who argues against either Jews or Muslims being the target of Anselm's polemic. See also the detailed discussion in Cohen, *Living Letters of the Law*, 167–79, who takes a more moderate position and posits a "contrived, hermeneutically crafted Jew in Anselm's thought," here at 178.

67. Southern, *Saint Anselm*, 203.

68. Boso's early life is described in the *Vita venerabilis Bosonis*, PL 150: 725–26. See also Southern, *Saint Anselm*, 202 n. 7.

69. See Southern, *Saint Anselm*, 202–5.

70. For Lanfranc, this is the method of teaching stressed by Watkins, "Lanfranc at Caen."

71. Eadmer, *Vita Anselmi* 1.19, 29–30. Both works belong to the years between 1076 and 1078.

72. The resulting dispute with Gaunilo was the second such debate to occur in Anselm's career. In his later years as abbot of Bec, around 1089, Anselm became involved in a dispute with Roscelin of Compiègne (an eventual teacher of Abelard), who charged him with heresy. The dispute resulted, after several attempts, in Anselm's treatise *De Incarnatione Verbi*.

73. The theology and logic of the debate, with which I am only incidentally concerned here, are closely analyzed by Hopkins, "Anselm's Debate with Gaunilo." See also Evans, *Anselm and Talking About God*, chap. 3.

74. Anselm, *Opera omnia*, 2:130.

75. Ibid., p. 137.

76. For these figures, I rely on Evans, ed., *A Concordance to the Works of St. Anselm*, s.v. disputabo-disputet.

77. Southern, *Saint Anselm*, 119.

78. Eadmer, *Vita Anselmi*, 31, 55–56.

79. Southern, *Saint Anselm*, 119, and again in chap. 18.

80. *Ecclesiastical History*, 2:296–97. Note here that the words Orderic chooses at the end of the quotation ("et ex collocutione eorum etiam qui uidentur inter eos illiterati et uocantur rustici") seem to imply that even peasants ("rustici") who were not monks had been taught at Bec, again suggesting that Anselm's teaching appealed to students of diverse ranks.

81. The arduous task of distinguishing the genuine Anselmian works from the spurious ones was begun in 1923 by Dom André Wilmart. His articles from 1923 to 1932 laid the foundations on which all later scholars have built.

82. A critical edition of this text on the basis of five manuscripts has been made by Southern and Schmitt, eds., *Memorials of St. Anselm*, 354–60.

83. For manuscript material on the literary history of this allegory, see Becker, "The Literary Treatment of the Pseudo-Anselmian Dialogue *De custodia interioris hominis* in England and France."

84. The authenticity of this work has long been doubted. It is listed as Pseudo-Anselm in *PL* 159: 272–90. The argument for its Franciscan attribution is made by Neff, "The *Dialogus Beatae Mariae et Anselmi de Passione Domini*: Toward an Attribution."

85. The disputation exists in at least ten manuscripts of which the earliest dates to the second half of the twelfth century and was likely produced at the Benedictine abbey of Maria Laach near Koblenz. For the manuscripts see B. Blumenkranz, ed., *Gisleberti Crispini Disputatio Iudei et Christiani, Stromata Patristica et Mediaevalia* 3 (Utrecht, 1956), 7.

86. A thirteenth-century manuscript of the text from the British Library is transcribed by Mews, "St Anselm and Roscelin: Some New Texts and Their Implications," at 86–98.

87. Abulafia, "Christians Disputing Disbelief: St Anselm, Gilbert Crispin and Pseudo-Anselm," at 143.

88. Ibid., 145.

89. In fact, in the London manuscript transcribed by Constant Mews, the gentile becomes *Fidelis* and *Discipulus fidelis* as well as simply *Discipulus*. See Mews, "St. Anselm and Roscelin," 96.

90. Citing the text in Mews, "St. Anselm and Roscelin," 95: "*Christianus*. Deo gratias quod iam non loquimur infideli et contradicenti, sed ei qui etsi ualuerimus exprimere quod credimus a fide tamen Christi nullo umquam modo separabitur; sed aderit dominus qui linguas infantium facit desertas, ut aperiat nobis quod querimus, dum inuicem patienter interrogando et beniuole respondendo auctoritatem sanctarum scripturarum, quasi patronum adducem sequimur."

91. Ibid., 96: "*Fidelis*: Rogo pater, ne me iam quasi alienum habeas, sed sicut pater filium, magister discipulum me familiarius salutem meam doceas."

92. For example, the Gentile in Pseudo-Anselm's *disputatio* is of no clear religious or nonreligious persuasion when he begins his dialogue with the Christian. His conversion to Christianity and the lessons he learns, however, are very clear.

93. A useful treatment of Anselm's impact on other authors of the late eleventh and early twelfth centuries is Evans, *Anselm and a New Generation*, although the question of the dialogue form is not considered at any length. An important complement to that study is also by Evans, *Old Arts and New Theology*.

94. Discussion of Anselm's students here is necessarily selective, but an honorable mention should be given to Ralph, prior of Rochester and abbot of Battle (fl. 1107–24), who composed theological dialogues and meditations in a style that is clearly derived from Anselm. Indeed, he owed his circulation throughout the Middle Ages to the mistaken attribution of his writings to Anselm. The longest and most important of his dialogues were a sequence of discussions between Nesciens and Sciens and between Inquirens and Respondens. In a manner similar to Gilbert Crispin's dialogue between a Christian and a pagan, the discussion between Nesciens and Sciens starts with a skeptic who refuses to believe anything for which he has not the evidence of his eyes. The discussion gradually leads him to accept the evidence of his other senses and then, finally, to posit the existence of an invisible intelligence as a source of knowledge (a First Cause). For Ralph's career and writings, see Searle, ed. and trans., *The Chronicle of Battle Abbey*, 116–32; and Southern, *Saint Anselm*, 372–76. A further dialogue, "De peccatore qui desperat," in an early twelfth-century manuscript from Rochester appears to have been prepared under Ralph's direction, if not written by Ralph himself. See Warner and Gilson, *Catalogue of Western Manuscripts in the Old Royal and King's Collections*, 2:22; and Cottier, "Le recueil apocryphe des *Orationes sive meditationes* de Saint Anselme," 285–86. For valuable discussions of other students and other aspects of Anselm's teaching, see the contributions by Vaughn,

Brasington, Rubenstein, North, and Ott in Vaughn and Rubinstein, eds., *Teaching and Learning*. Additional students from Bec who went on to administrative careers are given in Vaughn, "Anselm, Lanfranc, and the School of Bec."

95. The *Disputatio Iudei et Christiani* has been edited several times. All references here are to the edition by Abulafia in Abulafia and Evans, eds., *Works of Gilbert Crispin*, 1–53.

96. Ibid., xxvii.

97. Further nuance to Gilbert Crispin's discussion of images in the context of the Jewish-Christian debate can be found in Schmitt, *The Conversion of Herman the Jew*, 124–38.

98. Abulafia in *Works of Gilbert Crispin*, xxvii–xxx. An attempt to reconstruct that conversation is presented in Abulafia, "The *Ars disputandi* of Gilbert Crispin, Abbot of Westminster."

99. *Disputatio Iudei et Christiani*, in *Works of Gilbert Crispin*, 9: "Paternitati et prudentie tue discutiendum mitto libellum, quem nuper scripsi, pagine commendans que Iudeus quidam olim mecum disputans contra fidem nostram de lege sua proferebat et que ego ad obiecta illius pro fide nostra respondebam. Nescio unde ortus, sed apud Maguntiam litteris educatus, legis et litterarum etiam nostrarum bene sciens erat, et exercitatum in scripturis atque disputationibus contra nos ingenium habebat. Plurimum mihi familiaris sepe ad me ueniebat, tum negotii sui causa, tum me uidendi gratia, quoniam in aliquibus illi multum necessarius eram; et quotiens conueniebamus, mox de Scripturis ac de fide nostra sermonem amico animo habebamus. Quadam ergo die, solito maius mihi et illi Deus ocium concessit, et mox, unde solebamus, inter nos questionari cepimus. Et quoniam, que opponebat, conuenienter satis et consequenter opponebat, et ea, que opposuerat, non minus conuenienter prosequendo explicabat, nostra uero responsio uicino satis pede ad proposita illius respondebat, et Scripturarum eque testimonio nitens eidem ipsi concessu facilis esse uidebatur et approbanda, rogauerunt, qui aderant, ut memorie darem hanc nostrum disceptatiunculam, fortasse aliquibus profuturam."

100. Exchanges between Jews and Christians can be found earlier in the eleventh century but are of a more primitive and formulaic sort. See Abulafia, "An Eleventh-Century Exchange of Letters Between a Christian and a Jew."

101. Robinson, *Gilbert Crispin, Abbot of Westminster*, 11–12. Gilbert still awaits a more recent and more comprehensive evaluation of his life and writings.

102. Southern, "St. Anselm and Gilbert Crispin, Abbot of Westminster."

103. *Disputatio Christiani cum Gentili*, in *Works of Gilbert Crispin*, 61–87.

104. Note the interesting resemblance between this setting and Orderic Vitalis's description of the intellectual milieu at Bec quoted above.

105. See the discussion of Gilbert Crispin in Cohen, *Living Letters*, 180–85.

106. *Works of Gilbert Crispin*, 65: "Cede paulisper fidei, nam cedendo fidei, uenies ad cognitionem tante rei." Also cited in Cohen, *Living Letters*, 184 n. 45.

107. For the Jewish element in Gilbert's gentile, see Abulafia, "Christians Disputing Disbelief," 137. On the (rather unlikely) possibility of the disputant being a Muslim, see Gauss, "Anselm von Canterbury," 296.

108. *Works of Gilbert Crispin*, xxxv.

109. Ibid., xxxvi.

110. See Evans, "Gilbert Crispin on the Eucharist: A Monastic Postscript to Lanfranc and Berengar." Gilbert's discussion of the validity of simoniacal consecration serves as a prelude of sorts to his later and longer treatise *De simoniacis*.

111. A detailed statement about Honorius's career is given in Flint, *Honorius Augustodunensis of Regensburg*, esp. 16–23.

112. Ibid., 32–33.

113. Jeremy Cohen has recently called attention to Honorius's contribution to the medieval Christian idea of the Jew in his commentary on the Song of Songs. See Cohen, "*Synagoga conversa*: Honorius Augustodunensis, the Song of Songs, and Christianity's 'Eschatalogical Jew'." Notwithstanding some obvious parallels, Cohen also points out (326) that Honorius's commentary does not betray the influence of Anselm's *Cur Deus homo* or of the anti-Jewish polemics of Anselm's disciples Gilbert Crispin, Odo of Cambrai, and Guibert of Nogent.

114. Flint, *Honorius*, 1.

115. *PL* 172: 232–34; quoted and translated in Flint, *Honorius*, 3.

116. *Clavis physicae, Elucidarium, Libellus octo quaestionum de angelis et homine, Inevitabile sive De praedestinatione et libero arbitrio dialogus*, and *Scala Coeli major*. A handlist of surviving Latin manuscripts for these works can be found in Flint, *Honorius*, 65–88.

117. *De vita vere apostolica dialogorum libri V, Cognitio vitae, De anima et de Deo, De esu volatilium*, and *De musica*.

118. An edition of the text accompanied by a thorough examination of its manuscript tradition was done by Lefèvre in *L'Elucidarium et les lucidaires*.

119. In at least two manuscripts, it is incorrectly attributed to Lanfranc. See Gibson, *Lanfranc of Bec*, 242.

120. Flint, *Honorius*, 35.

121. Honorius Augustodunensis, *L'Elucidarium*, 359: "Saepius rogatus a condiscipulis quasdam quaestiunculas enodare, importunitati illorum non fuit facultas negando obviare, praesertim metuens illo elogio multari si creditum talentum mallem in terra silendo occultari."

122. In his exegetical writings, Honorius thus also contributed to the early scholastic *accessus ad auctores*. See Minnis, *Medieval Theory of Authorship*, chap. 2; and Matter, *The Voice of My Beloved*, 60–64.

123. Honorius Augustodunensis, *Clavis physicae*, 3: "Cuius stilum ideo verti in dialogum quia summis philosophis, Socrati scilicet et Platoni ac Tullio nec non nostro Augustino et Boetio, visum est id genus docendi quam maximam vim optinere introducendi."

124. See the learned discussion of bodily resurrection in both the *Clavis physicae* and the *Elucidarium* in Bynum, *The Resurrection of the Body in Western Christianity, 200–1336*, 137–55.

125. *Cognitio vitae, PL* 40: 1005–32.

126. Letter 4, in *S. Anselmi opera omnia*, 3:104; Eadmer, *Vita Anselmi* 1.11 and 1.22, 20–21 and 37–38.

127. Bedos-Rezak, "The Social Implications of the Art of Chivalry: The Sigillographic Evidence (France, 1050–1250)," reprinted with new pagination in her *Form and Order in Medieval France*; and eadem, "Medieval Identity: A Sign and a Concept."

128. Hugh of St. Victor, *De institutione novitiorum* 7, *PL* 176: 932–33. See also Bynum, *Jesus as Mother*, 97–98; and Vaughn, *St. Anselm and the Handmaidens of God*, 32, and chap. 2 where she suggests that Anselm's educational ideas originated with the model of his mother.

129. *Cognitio vitae, PL* 40: 1024–25.

130. Here again one must rely on the work of Flint, *Honorius*, 2–3, 8–14, 16, 28–34, 42, 52–53, 73–75, and 78–79.

131. Honorius Augustodunensis, *Sigillum Sanctae Mariae, PL* 172: 495–518. For an English translation of this work, see *The Seal of Blessed Mary*.

132. Fulton, *From Judgment to Passion*, 248–49.

133. Ibid., 251. Fulton, accepting a theory proposed by Valerie Flint, suggests (286–88) that the work was intended to gain the favor of the very pious Queen Matilda of England (1080–1118) and

that it was Matilda who was responsible for arranging Honorius's appointment to a canonry in Regensburg, thereby launching his career. Moreover, Fulton argues, Matilda may have been inspired by Honorius's *Sigillum* to create her own, literal, seal—"the earliest extant of any English queen" (288). I find both arguments tantalizing and plausible.

134. Ibid., 274–75.

135. *Sigillum Sanctae Mariae, PL* 172: 515–16.

136. Ibid., col. 516, and quoted in Fulton, *From Judgment to Passion*, 280.

137. Fulton, *From Judgment to Passion*, 284. Fulton goes on to suggest that Honorius might actually have been party to such conversations and that, as a student of Anselm at Canterbury, he could not help knowing about them.

138. The connection between Anselm and Abelard has been explored before, most notably by David Luscombe, but almost always centers on the issue of the relation between reason and faith and their particular positions on theological questions such as atonement. The specific use of dialogue and disputation has largely escaped comment. See Luscombe, "St. Anselm and Abelard"; and "St. Anselm and Abelard: A Restatement." See also Clanchy, "Abelard's Mockery of St. Anselm." But see also the remarks by Lutz Geldsetzer, "'Sic et non' sive 'sic aut non': La méthode des questions chez Abélard et la stratégie de la recherche"; and those by Mews, "Peter Abelard and the Enigma of Dialogue."

CHAPTER 3. SCHOLASTIC PRACTICES OF THE TWELFTH-CENTURY RENAISSANCE

1. *Metalogicon*, 116. Translation modified from *The Metalogicon of John of Salisbury*, 167. This famous aphorism is also quoted by Alexander Neckam (1157–1217) in his *De naturis rerum*, and Isaac Newton (1642–1727) paraphrased the quote in a letter to Robert Hook. See Klibansky, "Standing on the Shoulders of Giants." In more modern times, this phrase has supplied the title to American sociologist Robert Merton's influential *On The Shoulders of Giants*.

2. Over the years, historians have somewhat blithely assumed that it was Haskins who first introduced the concept of the twelfth-century renaissance to medieval scholarship. His contribution was, in fact, a little more modest, though still influential. For a historiographical corrective, see Novikoff, "The Renaissance of the Twelfth Century Before Haskins." For an evaluation on the field of twelfth-century studies by a doyenne in the field, see Colish, "Haskins's Renaissance Seventy Years Later: Beyond Anti-Burckhardtianism." See also Melve, "'The Revolt of The Medievalists': New Directions in Recent Research on the Twelfth-Century Renaissance."

3. The literature on the intellectual trends of the twelfth century is vast and growing. An excellent survey of the period with a focus on the religious aspects is Constable, *The Reformation of the Twelfth Century*, who briefly discusses dialogues and debates at 128–35. See also the essays in Constable and Benson, eds., *Renaissance and Renewal in the Twelfth Century*, for many individual aspects of these changes; as well as the valuable essays in Dronke, ed., *A History of Western Philosophy in the Twelfth Century*. More recently, see Noble and Van Engen, eds., *European Transformations*.

4. The role theology in the twelfth century is perhaps nowhere better documented and explained than in the in the volume of essays by Chenu, *La théologie au douzième siècle*, partially translated by Taylor and Little as *Nature, Man, and Society in the Twelfth Century*.

5. For a useful review of this literature, see Van Engen, "The Twelfth Century: Reading, Reason, and Revolt in a World of Custom." The most productive critique of the concept of a twelfth-century renaissance, though to my mind not entirely convincing, is Jaeger, "Pessimism in the Twelfth-Century 'Renaissance'."

6. The most detailed description of all the major schools and scholars in France during this formative period remains Lesne, *Les écoles, de la fin du VIIIe a la fin du XIIe*.

7. The most famous, and most debated, of these "schools" was Chartres. For a recent revisiting of the topic by a leading scholar in the field, see Jeauneau, *Rethinking the School of Chartres*.

8. See John of Salisbury, *Metalogicon*, I.17, I.24.

9. Jaeger, *The Envy of Angels*, 63–73.

10. For a summary of the evidence, see Burnett, "The Coherence of the Arabic-Latin Translation Program in Toledo in the Twelfth Century," vii.

11. Evans, *Old Arts and New Theology*, 13.

12. For a more detailed analysis of Figure 3, see Griffiths, *The Garden of Delights*, 148–51.

13. Ward's bibliography in this field is prolific. Particularly relevant essays here are his "Quintilian and the Rhetorical Revolution of the Middle Ages" and "From Marginal Gloss to *Catena* Commentary: The Eleventh-Century Origins of a Rhetorical Teaching Tradition in the Medieval West"; also Ward and Fredborg, "Rhetoric in the Time of William of Champeaux."

14. For a current "state of the field," see Marenbon, "Logic at the Turn of the Twelfth Century: A Synthesis."

15. Cf. ibid., 181: "The material is still too sparsely published, too little read, too poorly understood for any proper synthesis to be possible."

16. These figures are my own. For a later period than the one covered in this chapter, a very helpful compendium of such dialogues has been assembled by De Hartmann, *Lateinische Dialoge 1200–1400*, with a brief discussion of the relation between dialogue and *disputatio* at 48–50.

17. The classic study of the scholastic method is Grabmann, *Die Geschichte der scholastischen Methode*, who adopts the broadest possible scope and examines authors from Late Antiquity until the beginning of the thirteenth century. Important themes related to scholastic thought are discussed in the various essays in Kretzmann, Kenny, and Pinborg, eds., *The Cambridge History of Later Medieval Philosophy* (hereafter *CHLMP*).

18. For a recent study of twelfth-century prosimetrum (a text that includes both verse and prose), see Balint, *Ordering Chaos*.

19. The third of the late medieval rhetorical genres was the *ars praedicandi* (art of preaching), which was less important in the twelfth century but very widespread beginning in the thirteenth. For an overview of all three genres, see Murphy, *Rhetoric in the Middle Ages*. On the importance in letter writing during the eleventh and twelfth centuries, see Van Engen, "Letter, Schools, and Written Culture in the Eleventh and Twelfth Centuries," as well as Constable, *Letters and Letter Collections*.

20. Cotts, *The Clerical Dilemma*.

21. For a concise statement on the importance of commentaries during this period, see the introduction in Minnis, Scott, and Wallace, eds., *Medieval Literary Theory and Criticism, c. 1100–1375*. See also Marenbon, "Glosses and Commentaries on the *Categories* and *De interpretatione* before Abelard."

22. For the twelfth-century Parisian context of such glosses, see De Hamel, *Glossed Books of the Bible and the Origins of the Paris Book Trade*.

23. Both the gloss and the *quaestio* are discussed in Smalley, *The Study of the Bible in the Middle Ages*, 46–82.

24. See the classic work on literacy in England during this period: Clanchy, *From Memory to Written Record*. On literacy in the twelfth century, see Stock, *The Implications of Literacy*, esp. chap. 3. On history writing in the twelfth century, see Smalley, *Historians of the Middle Ages*; Davis et al., eds., *The Writing of History in the Middle Ages*; and, with greater theoretical considerations, the essays in Spiegel, *The Past as Text*.

25. This is not to deny the influence of Platonist concepts during the period, especially regarding nature and the ordering of the world, which exerted a strong influence on a range of prose and poetry writers. Cf. Wetherbee, *Platonism and Poetry in the Twelfth Century*, as well influential earlier studies by M.-D. Chenu, Henri de Lubac, and Marie-Thérèse d'Alverny.

26. There is as yet no study that treats systematically the totality of the evidence for disputation in the twelfth century. This chapter and the one that follows are in part an attempt to help fill that gap. For general remarks, see Lawn, *The Rise and Decline of the Scholastic "Quaestio Disputata"*, chaps. 1–3. See also Delhaye, "L'organisation scholaire au XIIe siècle," and the concise overview of the origins of disputation by Kenny in *CHLMP*, 24–29.

27. The theme of dialogue as pedagogy is explored in Ronquist, "Learning and Teaching in Twelfth-Century Dialogues." For another analysis similar to my own, but focusing on other dialogues both before and after the twelfth century, see Breitenstein, "'Ins Gespräch gebracht': Der Dialog als Prinzip monastischer Unterweisung."

28. For an extended discussion of this work, see Whitbread, "Conrad of Hirsau as Literary Critic."

29. The Latin text is published in Conrad of Hirsau, *Accessus ad auctores; Bernard d'Utrecht; Conrad d'Hirsau*. Extracts translated in Minnis, Scott, and Wallace, eds., *Medieval Literary Theory and Criticism*, 39–64, here 39.

30. Ibid.

31. *Dialogus de Mundi contemptu vel amore attribué à Conrad d'Hirsau*, 41.

32. An edition and translation of these works along with a third, *De avibus tractatus* (also in dialogue form), has been made available in *Adelard of Bath, Conversations with his Nephew*. Adelard has been described as anticipating in important ways the Platonism of the school of Chartres in Wetherbee, *Platonism and Poetry in the Twelfth Century*, 20–22. For Adelard's contribution to the history of science, particularly his important translations from Arabic of Euclid's *Elements* and al-Khwarizmi's astronomical tables, see Burnett, ed., *Adelard of Bath*.

33. Burnett, ed., *Adelard of Bath*, 91, 73.

34. Scholars have hotly debated the personalities, teachings, and even existence of the so-called school of Chartres for well over a century. It was first introduced as such by Poole, *Illustrations of the History of Medieval Thought and Learning*, chap 4, and taken up on several occasions in the pioneering work of Southern, with a final modification of his position in *Scholastic Humanism and the Unification of Europe*, vol. 1, *Foundations*, 58–101. For a recent overview, see Jeauneau, *Rethinking the School of Chartres*.

35. Cf. Speer, "Ratione duce: Die naturphilosophischen Dialoge des Adelard von Bath und des Wilhelm von Conches."

36. Burnett, ed., *Adelard of Bath*, 3.

37. Ibid., 240–41: "ut quicunque his intentus hanc disputationem habeat, si negotium exercuerit, peritus esse posit."

38. See Arduini, *Rupert von Deutz (1079–1129) und der "status christianus" seiner Zeit*.

39. Cf. Van Engen, *Rupert of Deutz*, 200–215.

40. Rupert of Deutz, *Super quaedam capitula regulae divi benedicti abbatis*, PL 170, 482–83. See the eloquent reconstruction of this episode in Van Engen, *Rupert of Deutz*, 211–12. The same passage is quoted in Chenu, *Nature, Man, and Society*, 270.

41. Peter Abelard, *Historia Calamitatum*, 63–64. For a discussion of this passage, see Le Goff, "Quelle conscience l'université médiévale a-t-elle d'elle-même?" 16–19. On Abelard as autobiographer, see Vitz, "Abelard's *Historia Calamitatum* and Medieval Autobiography," in her *Medieval Narrative and Modern Narratology*, 11–37.

42. The historiographical debate over the "authenticity" of this account is fully reviewed in the recent study of Herman-Judah by Schmitt, *The Conversion of Herman the Jew*, chap. 1. Schmitt himself adopts a more nuanced position, suggesting that a real Jew named Herman may indeed lie behind the account but that the *Opusculum* as the text exists is the product of a community of Premonstratensians whose main ambition was to augment the new order's prestige by embellishing a foundation legend.

43. Herman-Judah, *Hermannus Quondam Judaeus: Opusculum de Conversione Sua*, 76. A slightly different translation from mine is given in Morrison, *Conversion and Text*, 81.

44. *PL* 170: 537–42.

45. Van Engen, *Rupert of Deutz*, 310.

46. Philip of Harvengt, *De institutione clericorum*, *PL* 203: 807.

47. A critical edition of the text edited by Rhabanus Haacke is printed in Arduini, *Ruperto di Deutz e la Controversia tra Christiani ed Ebrei nel Secolo XII.*

48. For an analytic comparison of Rupert and Herman regarding Jews and Judaism, see Abulafia, "The Ideology of Reform and Changing Ideas Concerning Jews in the Works of Rupert of Deutz and Hermannus Quondam Iudeus," reprinted in her *Christians and Jews in Dispute*, xv. See also the discussion in Schmitt, *The Conversion of Herman the Jew*, 130–44.

49. Arduini, *Ruperto di Deutz*, 184.

50. Over a century ago, Von Harnack, *History of Dogma*, 6:44, called Hugh "the most important theologian of the twelfth century." The long-standing need for a comprehensive study of Hugh's historical theology has been largely remedied in the recent study by Harkins, *Reading and the Work of Restoration.*

51. For some cross-disciplinary considerations of the meaning of this work, see Illich, *In the Vineyard of the Text*; and Harkins, *Reading and the Work*, chap. 2 and passim.

52. Hugh of St. Victor, *Hugonis de Sancto Victore Didascalicon, De Studio Legendi*, I.11.

53. Ibid., III.5, 56. Translation from *The Didascalicon of Hugh of St. Victor*, III.5, 90.

54. Wetherbee, *Platonism and Poetry in the Twelfth Century*, 49. See also the discussion of Smalley, *The Study of the Bible*, 85–106, who argued that Hugh revealed a new dimension of exegesis by his insistence on the grounding of the *lection divina*. Hugh's originality has been disputed by Henri de Lubac.

55. *Epitome Dindimi in Philosophiam*, in *Hugonis de Sancto Victore Opera Propaedeutica*, 203.

56. Hugh of Saint-Victor, *De vanitate mundi*, *PL* 176: 706. See the similar translation of the same passage in *Hugh of Saint-Victor: Selected Spiritual Writings*, 160.

57. *De vanitate mundi*, 710. This passage is quoted with a similar translation in Taylor, *The Medieval Mind*, II:137–38. Cf. also *Selected Spiritual Writings*, 168.

58. A recent edition of *De arrha animae* by Feiss and Sicard with an accompanying French translation can be found in *L'Oeuvre de Hugues de Saint-Victor* 1:211ff.

59. Goy lists 327 medieval manuscripts of this work in his exhaustive study *Die Überlieferung der Werke Hugos von St. Viktor*, 277ff.

60. Translation adapted from Hugh of St. Victor, *Soliloquy on the Earnest Money of the Soul*, 13. For an analysis of theology and interiority in Hugh's spiritual works, see Van't Spijker, *Fictions of the Inner Life*, chap. 3.

61. For analysis of the specific differences in the mystical way, see Gilson, *History of Christian Philosophy in the Middle Ages*, 154–71.

62. Peter Abelard, *Historia calamitatum*, 64: "Proinde diversas disputando perambulans provincias, ubicunque hujus artis vigere studium audieram, peripateticorum emulator factus sum," translation mine. For a slightly different rendition, see *The Letters of Abelard and Heloise*, 3.

63. The violent and feudal side of Abelard's writings is expertly exposed by Taylor, "A Second Ajax: Peter Abelard and the Violence of Dialectic."

64. On Abelard's followers (and detractors) in the twelfth century, see the classic study by Luscombe, *The School of Peter Abelard*, esp. chap 2. See also the informed comments of Clark, *Academic Charisma and the Origins of the Research University*, 74–76.

65. The starting points in this vast corpus of scholarship include Clanchy, *Abelard*; Marenbon, *The Philosophy of Peter Abelard*; Mews, *Abelard and Heloise*; Jolivet, *La théologie d'Abélard*; idem, *Arts du langage et théologie chez Abélard*; and the various essays in Brower and Guilfoy, eds., *The Cambridge Companion to Abelard*. A sparkling discussion of Abelard and his censors forms the backbone of an eloquent and animated study by Godman, *The Silent Masters*. A succinct and highly informed précis of an otherwise considerable corpus of Abelardian scholarship is provided in Ziolkowski, ed., *Letters of Peter Abelard*, xiii–lii.

66. For the latest installment of this authenticity debate, see Mews, "Discussing Love: The *Epistolae duorum amantium* and Abelard's *Sic et Non*."

67. Martin Grabmann called Anselm the "father of the Scholastics" but considered Abelard a key innovator in the scholastic approach of harmonizing reason and faith. See Grabmann, *Geschichte*, 1:258.

68. Cf. Kenny, *A New History of Western Philosophy*, vol. 2, *Medieval Philosophy*, 47: "In the heyday of medieval universities, a favourite teaching method was the disputation. . . . Abelard's *Sic et Non* is the ancestor of these medieval disputations."

69. Cf. Flanagan, *Doubt in an Age of Faith*. The underlying interpretive principles of the prologue are more satisfactorily explained by Rizek-Pfister, "Die hermeneutischen Prinzipien in Abaelards *Sic et non*."

70. *Peter Abelard: Collationes*, with further bibliographic orientation in the introduction by the editors. On the scope and ambivalence of the medieval dream, see Kruger, *Dreaming in the Middle Ages*, who curiously does not discuss Abelard; and Schmitt, *The Conversion of Herman the Jew*, chap. 3, who does.

71. *Collationes*, 6–7: "nullam adeo friuolam esse disputationem arbitror, ut non aliquod habeat documentum." Translations from this work are after Marenbon.

72. "Peter Abelard *Soliloquium*: A Critical Edition," at 885–94.

73. The resemblance to the *Collationes* concerns the importance given to philosophy. In the *Collationes*, the character of the Philosopher scores points against both the Jew and the Christian, and, in the *Soliloquium*, the character "Peter" says that pagan philosophers expounded the whole sum of faith in the Trinity more thoroughly than the prophets.

74. Martin Grabmann, for instance, only considered the *Sic et Non* as an example of the scholastic method. "Disputatio" is treated, but in a strictly theological context, by Jolivet, *Arts du langage*, 306–20.

75. *Historia Calamitatum*, 65: "Hinc factum est ut de me amplius ipse presumens ad castrum Corbolii, quod Parisiace urbi vicinus est, quamtotius scolas nostras transferrem, ut inde videlicit crebriores disputationis assultus nostra daret importunitas."

76. Ibid.

77. The most recent edition with commentary of the letter (no. XIV) is by Smits, *Peter Abelard. Letters IX–XIV*, 279–80. See 180–202 for a discussion of the authenticity and dating of the letter. Epistle 14, as it is known, is extant in one manuscript from the second half of the thirteenth century: Paris, BnF, MS lat. 2923. It has recently been given its first translation into English by Jan M. Ziolkowski, *Letters of Peter Abelard* (at 194–96), who follows Smits and Mews in offering 1120 as the most plausible date of the letter.

78. Clanchy, *Abelard*, 296.

79. The finding, transcribing, editing, and appraising of these twelfth-century logical commentaries owes a great deal to the work of Yukio Iwakuma, even if not all his attributions have been followed. For a recent revisiting of his earlier work, see Yukio Iwakuma, "*Vocales* Revisited."

80. The chronology of these writings is a matter of considerable scholarly dispute. To complicate matters, there are important portions missing, and the transmission of the texts (whether they are multilayered or not) is far from clear. Still, there is little reason to doubt that they preserve the substance of a master's lectures and discussions, even if they have reached us in a perhaps slightly edited fashion. See discussion by Marenbon, *The Philosophy of Peter Abelard*, 43–44.

81. The text, also known as the *Glossulae*, is edited in Geyer, ed., *Peter Abaelards philosophische Schriften*, 505–588, here at 505.

82. *Petrus Abaelardus: Dialectica*, 141.

83. Ibid., 469.

84. For the citations, see Marenbon, *The Philosophy of Peter Abelard*, 44 n. 32.

85. *Dialectica*, 232: "in illa altercatione de loco et argumentatione monstrauimus quam ad simplicem dialecticorum institutionem conscripsimus." See Martin, "A Note on the Attribution of the *Literal Glosses*," 608.

86. Gibbons, ed., *Beati Gosvini vita*, bk. 1.4, 12–13: "Tunc temporis magister Petrus Abailardus, multis sibi scholaribus aggregatis in claustro S. Genouefae schola publica utebatur: qui probatae quidem scientiae, sublimis eloquentiae, sed inauditarum erat inuentor et assertor nouitatum; et suas quaerens statuere sententias, erat aliarum probatarum improbatur. Vnde in odium uenerat eorum qui sanius sapiebant; et sicut manus eius contra omnes, sic omnium contra eum armabantur. Dicebat quod nullus antea praesumpserat, ut omnes illum mirarentur. Cum igitur inaduentionum eius absurditas in notitiam peruenisset eorum qui Parisius doctrinae causa morabantur, primo stupore, deinde zelo quodam ducti confutandae falsitatis, coeperunt inter se quaerere quis esset ex eis aduersus eum disputandi negotium subiturus; indignum esse dumtaxat apud tot sapientes huiusmodi naeniarum dictorem non habere contradictorem, taliter oblatrantem baculo non arceri ueritatis; plura adinuenturum, et liberius declamaturum, si infaustis coeptis redargutor defuisset."

87. Ibid.

88. The text in question is from a manuscript preserved in Munich, Bayerische Staatsbibliothek, Clm 14779, with significant portions transcribed by Iwakuma, "Pierre Abélard et Guillaume de Champeaux dans les premières années du XIIe siècle: une étude préliminaire." Cf. f. 53v–55v (here translated from the transcription by Iwakuma at 95): "THE ONE RATHER. I have said that in both one is more likely to occur, but nevertheless that one does not occur determinately, because it may be impeded by chance or by *utrumlibet*. Here he indicates that there is a division such as the following: there are *utrumlibets* which are equally likely to result in affirmation and negation, such as 'she will fuck,' 'she will not fuck,' others which are more likely to turn out one way rather than another, such as 'she will rub you down,' 'she will not rub you down,' which is more likely to turn out one way, that is to rub, because she is from Chartres. Likewise, chances are equally likely to turn out either way, such as 'Peter will close the door,' 'P. will not close the door': more likely to turn out one way, such as 'P. will fall into the toilet,' 'P. will not fall into the toilet,' which is more likely to turn out one way, that is to fall 'into the toilet' because he is small, though his patience is great."

89. Ibid., 15–17: "Cum uenisset igitur ad locum certaminis (1 Sm 17, 22), id est scholam eius introisset, reperit eum legentem, et scholaribus suis suas inculcantem nouitates. Statim autem ut loqui orsus est qui aduenerat, ille toruos in eum deflexit obtutus; et cum se sciret uirum ab adolescentia bellatorem (1 Sm 17, 33), illum autem uideret pubescere incipientem, despexit cum (1 Sm 17,

42) in corde suo, forte non multo minus quam Dauid sanctum spurius Philistaeus (1 Sm 17, 4; 17, 23). Erat enim albus quidem et decorus aspect (cf. 1 Sm 17, 42), sed exilis corpulentiae et staturae non sublimis. Cumque superbus ille ad respondendum cogeretur, et impugnans eum uehementer immineret: "Vide, inquit, ut sileas, et caue ne perturbes meae series lectionis." Ille qui non ad silendum uenerat, acriter insistebat, cum aduersarius e contra eum habens despectui, non attenderet ad sermons oris eius, indignum iudicans a doctore tanto tantillo iuueni responderi. Iudicabat secundum faciem, quae pro aetate sibi contemptibilis apparebat; sed cor perspicaciter intellegens non attendebat. Cum autem ei diceretur a scholasticis suis, qui iuuenculum satis nouerant, ut non ommitteret respondere, esse illum disputatorem acutum et multum ei scientiae suffragari, non esse indecens cum eiusmodi subire negotium disputandi, indecentissimum esse talem ulteris aspernari: "Dicat, inquit, si quid habet as dicendum." Ille, dicendi nacta facultate, es his unde mouebatur propositionem facit adeo competentem, ut nullatenus leuem et garrulam redoleret uerbositatem, sed audientiam omnium sua mercaretur grauitate. Assumente illo, et affirmante isto, et affirmationibus eius illo penitus non ualente refragari; cum diuertendi ei penitus suffragia clauderentur ab isto qui non ignorabat eius astutias, tandem conuictus est asseruisse se quod non esset consentaneum rationi."

90. An exhaustive bibliography of the scholarship pertaining to the struggle between Abelard and Bernard is given by Mews, "The Council of Sens (1141): Abelard, Bernard, and the Fear of Social Upheaval," 343, n. 2. But see also Zerbi, *"Philosophi" e "Logici"*.

91. Déchanet, "L'amitié d'Abélard et de Guillaume de Saint Thierry."

92. William mentions the *Sic et non* in one of his letters to Bernard. See Clanchy, *Peter Abelard*, 100–101.

93. *Disputatio adversus Petrum Abaelardum, PL* 180, cols. 249–250: "Ipse vero de omnibus amat putare, qui de omnibus vult disputare, de divinis aeque ac de saecularibus."

94. Some of Abelard's sentences do survive. See Mews, "The *Sententie* of Peter Abelard."

95. The authorship of this work has been contested. The attribution to Thomas of Morigny is made by Mews, "The Lists of Heresies Imputed to Peter Abelard."

96. The *Disputatio* is printed in *PL* 180: 283–328, but misattributed to William of St. Thierry whose own *Disputatio adversum Petrum Abaelardum* it follows. It has been edited by Häring, "Thomas von Morigny. *Disputatio catholicorum patrum adversus dogmata Petri Abaelardi*." It is also discussed by Mews, "The Council of Sens (1141)," 367–68 and passim.

97. Marenbon, *Philosophy of Peter Abelard*, 27, believes it "most probable that there had been covert dislike, if not open hostility, for some years." For the opposite view, see Little, "Relations Between St. Bernard and Abelard Before 1139." See also Godman, *Silent Masters*, passim.

98. The most detailed and convincing case for a dating of 1141 (not 1140 or 1139) for this council is made by Mews, "The Council of Sens (1141)."

99. A remarkable instance is in 1144 when Pope Celestine II left his copies of Abelard's *Theologia* and *Sic et Non* to his church of Città di Castello. Celestine's predecessor, Innocent II, had in the wake of the Council of Sens (1141) ordered Abelard's "erroneous book" burned wherever found, and Celestine was previously a senior cardinal in Rome. See Luscombe, *School of Peter Abelard*, 22 n. 1.

100. Here I disagree slightly with Mews, "The Council of Sens (1141)," who says, "Bernard was a powerful speaker who could easily outclass Abelard in public oratory" (371). Bernard was indeed an accomplished orator to the masses, but Abelard was the sharper debater, partly because of his classroom experience, and debate is what he hoped for. See also Verbaal, "Sens: une victoire d'écrivain: les deux visages du process d'Abelard," at 88.

101. This is counted as "Letter Fifteen" in his correspondence, preserved in a single manuscript, Heidelberg, Universitätsbibliothek, Codex Heidelbergensis 71, fol. 14v–15v and edited twice, most

recently by Raymond Klibansky, "Peter Abailard and Bernard of Clairvaux: A Letter by Abailard," at 6–7. It has recently been translated by Ziolkowski, ed., *Letters of Peter Abelard*, 108–10.

102. *PL* 182: 540.

103. *Sancti Bernardi Opera*, vol. 8, *Epistola* 189, 14.

104. It is common but erroneous to imagine Bernard as the experienced elder of the intellectual pair, for, in fact, the opposite was true.

105. *Illustrative Stories from the Sermones Vulgares of Jacques de Vitry*, 13.

106. *The Steps of Humility*, 118. See also Evans, *The Mind of Bernard of Clairvaux*, 86–97, who discusses this passage.

107. For an analysis of Bernard's nineteen charges against Abelard and the council itself, see Little, "Bernard and Abelard at the Council of Sens."

108. *Dialectica*, 470. See also Mews, "Peter Abelard on Dialectic, Rhetoric, and the Principles of Argument," at 43.

109. Ontology and philosophical semantics occupy the bulk of Abelard's *Dialectica*. For an overview of this aspect of Abelard's logic, see Martin, "Logic."

110. Edmé Smits dates the letter to around 1130, while Jolivet dates it to around 1132 (Jolivet, *Arts du langage*, 269–72). The lack of an explicit recipient and the fact that no copy survives from before its 1616 *editio princeps* make it very difficult to date with any certainty, but the authenticity of letter itself has not been challenged.

111. The Latin text cited here is from *Peter Abelard: Letters IX–XIV*, 271–77. For a more recent edition, see Jolivet, *Abélard, ou la philosophie dans le langage*, 150–56. Translation here is after Ziolkowski, *Letters of Peter Abelard*, 179–87, here 179.

112. These are favorite citations of Abelard, and he uses them in the three versions of his *Theologia* as well as in his *Collationes*.

113. It should be noted that sophistry, or the art of trickery and the appearance of argumentation, was a frequent complaint from the twelfth century onward. For a discussion of its popularity in late medieval England, see Copeland, "Sophistic, Spectrality, Iconoclasm."

114. The study and translation of Aristotelian texts in the twelfth century are best surveyed by Dod, "Aristoteles latinus," although a number of points relating to knowledge of Aristotle's Old Logic have been modified since. See especially Marenbon, "Medieval Latin Commentaries and Glosses on Aristotelian Logical Texts, Before c. 1150 A.D.," published with "Supplement to the Working Catalogue and Supplementary Bibliography," in his *Aristotelian Logic, Platonism, and the Context of Early Medieval Philosophy in the West*, 128–40.

115. *Letters IX–XIV*, 274; *Letters of Peter Abelard*, 183.

116. *Letters IX–XIV*, 274: "Non enim haereticorum uel quorumlibet infidelium infestationes refellere sufficimus, nisi disputationes eorum dissoluere possimus et eorum sophismata ueris refellere rationibus"; *Letters of Peter Abelard*, 183.

117. *Letters IX–XIV*, 274; *Letters of Peter Abelard*, 184.

118. Cf. Ebbesen, "Ancient Scholastic Logic as a Source of Medieval Scholastic Logic."

119. Abelard's ideas about Jews and Judaism have been the subject of scholarly interest for some time. Important investigations include Liebeschütz, "The Significance of Judaism in Abelard's *Dialogus*." Graboïs, "Un chapitre de tolérance intellectuelle dans la societé occidentale au XIIe siècle: le 'Dialogus' de Pierre Abélard et le 'Kuzari' d'Yehuda Halevi"; Abulafia, "*Intentio Recta an Erronea? Peter Abelard's views on Judaism and the Jews*"; Von Moos, "Les *Collationes* d'Abélard et la 'question juive' au XIIe siècle"; Cohen, *Living Letters of the Law*, 275–89; and Mews, "Abelard and Heloise on Jews and *Hebraica Veritas*."

120. *Letters IX–XIV*, 276; *Letters of Peter Abelard*, 186.

121. On the date of the *Collationes*, see the introduction by Marenbon and Orlandi, *Peter Abelard: Collationes*, xxvii–xxxii.

122. For a good summary of the genre with generous citations from the sources themselves, see Dahan, *The Christian Polemic Against the Jews in the Middle Ages*, esp. 53–69.

123. Cf. Cohen, *Living Letters of the Law*, who discusses this Augustinian precept at length in chap. 1.

124. *Collationes*, 96–97.

125. Ibid., 96–97, 98–99.

126. Ibid., 114–15. This work will be examined again in chapter 6.

127. But see Radding, *The Origins of Medieval Jurisprudence*, who argued, rather unconvincingly according to many of the book's reviewers, for an even earlier influence from Pavia.

128. Winroth, *The Making of Gratian's Decretum*, esp. chap. 6 for the implications of the second recension on the study of Roman law in Bologna.

129. Brundage, *The Medieval Origins of the Legal Profession*, 77.

130. Ibid., 77–78. For a reconstruction of the gradual recovery of Justinian's *Digest*, see Müller, "The Recovery of Justinian's Digest in the Middle Ages."

131. Stephan Kuttner employed the very phraseology of the twelfth-century theologians, with a nod to the development of Parisian polyphony as well, in the title of his now-famous book on the topic: *Harmony from Dissonance*. Twenty-six years later, George Donahue, Jr., lamented the meager advances that had been made in interpreting the legal texts that survive: *Why the History of Canon Law Is Not Written*.

132. As with scholastic university disputations, scholarship on the legal uses of disputation has focused heavily on the later periods. See, for example, Bellomo, ed., *Die Kunst der Disputation*.

133. Fournier and le Bras, *Histoire des collections canoniques en Occident depuis les fausses décrétales jusqu'au Décret de Gratian*, 2:55–114, summarizing work originally published between 1896 and 1898.

134. Building on the manuscript collations of Martin Brett, see Rolker, *Canon Law and the Letters of Ivo of Chartres*, with a discussion of Fournier's thesis at 41–49.

135. A translation of Ivo's preface can be found in Somerville and Brasington, *Prefaces to Canon Law Books in Latin Christianity*, 132–157.

136. Kuttner, *Harmony from Dissonance*, 12; idem, "The Revival of Jurisprudence," 310.

137. Peter Landau, "The Development of Law," at 125.

138. Kuttner, "The Revival of Jurisprudence," at 314.

139. See again Winroth, *The Making of Gratian's Decretum*.

140. As but one example, see Luscombe, *The School of Peter Abelard*, chap. 9.

141. See the pioneering article by Kantorowicz, "The Quaestiones of the Glossators," 52: "Even in French theology which was, of course, much more closely connected with Aristotle than with Italian jurisprudence, disputations did not become a feature of the curriculum until well after the middle of the twelfth century, and it must therefore have been jurisprudence which influenced theology, Bologna which influences Paris, not *vice versa*."

142. See the relevant conclusions reached by Wei, "Gratian and the School of Laon," 320: "Gratian must have learned the scholastic method for reconciling contradictory authorities from a contemporary theologian or contemporary theological work." Cf. Landau, "The Development of Law," 122, discussing Ivo of Chartres: "As regards procedural law, his attitudes toward the ordeal (*judicium Dei*) betray an incipient rationalisation, doubtless under the influence of early scholasticism."

143. Kuttner, "Revival of Jurisprudence," 310.

144. For a partial translation of the *Decretum*, see *Gratian: The Treatise on Laws (Decretum DD 1–20) with the Ordinary Gloss*. Translations of the prefaces written by several Decretists, those who commented on Gratian's *Decretum*, are provided in chapter 5 of Somerville and Brasington, *Prefaces*.

145. Kantorowicz, "The Questiones Disputatae of the Glossators"; and idem, *Studies in the Glossators of the Roman Law*.

146. The text is printed in *Oeuvres de Robert de Melun*.

147. For a discussion of evidence that Peter himself engaged in disputations, see Landgraf, "Notes de critique textuelle sur les *Sentences* de Pierre Lombard," esp. 96–98. See also Colish, *Peter Lombard*, vol. 1, chap. 4.

148. Kuttner, "The Revival of Jurisprudence," 316; See also Lawn, *The Rise and Decline of the Scholastic "Quaestio Disputata"*, 4.

149. Kantorowicz, "The Questiones Disputatae of the Glossators," 5.

150. The *Stemma Bulgaricum* is edited and discussed at length in Kantorowicz's 1939 article and further contextualized in his *Studies in the Glossators*, 81–85. Long believed to have preceded Gratian at Bologna, Winroth now places Bulgarus as a junior contemporary of Gratian, active between 1141 and 1159. See Winroth, *The Making of Gratian's Decretum*, 159–62.

151. The following summary draws from the description offered in Kantorowicz, *Studies in the Glossators*, 81. On the parallels between these two areas of medieval knowledge in the history of medieval rhetoric, see also Winterbottom, "Schoolroom and Courtroom."

152. The *Enodationes* is edited in Kantorowicz, *Studies in the Glossators*, 281–93, discussed at 122–44.

153. Printed in ibid., 130.

154. Anselm of Havelberg, *Antikemenon, contrapositorum sub dialogo conscriptum ad venerabilem papam Eugenium*, PL 188: 1139.

155. Lees, *Anselm of Havelberg*.

156. The title of this work is sometimes also given as *De unitate fidei* (cf. Migne in *PL* 188: 1141), but Anselm himself in the prologue refers to the work as "on the single form of believing (*de una forma credendi*) and the multiplicity of ways of life from the time of Abel to the last of the elect." On the importance of this distinction, see Lees, *Anselm of Havelberg*, 173.

157. Lees (*Anselm of Havelberg*, 166) has suggested that the entire *Antikemenon* be seen as having five parts: (1) a prologue addressed to Pope Eugenius, (2) the text of *De una forma credendi*, (3) a proem addressed to the brothers that functions as a conclusion to the history and as an introduction to the debates, (4) the first debate with Nicetas over the question of the *Filioque*, and (5) the second debate with Nicetas, which concerns sacramental ritual.

158. Ibid., 167–70.

159. *Antikeimenon*, PL 188: 1139: "multas super hujusmodi doctrina et ritu collationes et quaestiones, modo in privates, modo in publicis."

160. Ibid.

161. Ibid., 1142; See Lees, *Anselm of Havelberg*, 168.

162. The speech at the Council of Bari is described in Eadmer, *Life of St. Anselm*, 112–13.

163. On the availability of Anselm's works at Laon, see Southern, *St. Anselm and His Biographer*, 357–62.

164. Evans, "Anselm of Canterbury and Anselm of Havelberg," 174.

165. *Antikeimenon, proemium*, PL 188: 1162.

166. Among those who accept the authenticity of the recorded debates are Beumer, "Ein Religionsgespräch aus dem zwölften Jahrhundert"; Russel, "Anselm of Havelberg and the Union of the

Churches"; and Morrison, "Anselm of Havelberg: Play and the Dilemma of Historical Progress," who at 226 describes Anselm's account as being "composed by revising transcripts of public debates held in 1136." A persuasive case for not reading the account at face value is made by Lees, *Anselm of Havelberg*, esp. 231–33.

167. Sieben, *Die Konzilsidee des Lateinischen Mittelalters (847–1378)*, esp. 157–67.

168. Interestingly, the second debate of the *Antikeimenon* (*PL* 188: 1209–48) is described as taking place in Hagia Sophia.

169. *Antikeimenon*, *PL* 188: 1163.

170. Ibid.: "Patres reverendi, ego ad contentions non veni . . . sed veni ad inquirendum et cognoscendum de fide vestra atque mea, maxime quia vobis ita placuit."

171. Ibid.: "Placet quod dicis, et humilitas tua nobis placet; nam in colloquendo et humiliter conferendo citius elucescit vertitas, quam si superbe et ad vincendum avidi contendamus."

172. Ibid., 1187: "damus vel suscipimus huiuscemodi similitudines tanquam scenicas, non quidem quae ipsarum rerum puram veritatem exprimant, sed animum audientis ad maiorem ipsius rei cognitionem petrahant; et fit plerumque per informationem talis doctrinae cognitum, quod prius pro magna suae naturae altitudine fuit incognitum."

173. Anselm's debates with Nicetas were not his last ecumenical encounter. Frederick Barbarossa sent him as an ambassador to Constantinople in 1152, and, on the voyage there, he had talks with Basil of Archrida at Thessalonika. No literary work resulted from this encounter, as far as we know. See Evans, "Unity and Diversity: Anselm of Havelberg as Ecumenist," 42.

174. Zumthor, *La lettre et la voix*, 92.

175. A masterful reconstruction and analysis of Peter the Chanter and his circle is Baldwin, *Masters, Princes, and Merchants*. An excellent recent study of Peter's involvement in the rhetoric against heresy and for crusade is Bird, "Heresy, Crusade, and Reform in the Circle of Peter the Chanter, c.1187–c.1240," a dissertation currently being revised for publication.

176. The source of this story is Caesar of Heisterbach's *Dialogus miraculorum*, rich in anecdotes about Paris at the turn of the century, although it was not composed until 1219–23. See John W. Baldwin, "A Debate at Paris over Thomas Becket Between Master Roger and Master Peter the Chanter."

177. *Petri Cantoris Parisiensis Verbum adbreviatum*, I.1, 9. This often-quoted passage is translated in Baldwin, *Masters, Princes, and Merchants*, 1:90–91. A short version of the *Verbum* is printed in *PL* 205: 1–554. For a discussion about the differences between the short and long versions of the *Verbum*, see the introduction by Boutry in *Verbum abbreviatum*. See also the review of this edition by John W. Baldwin, "An Edition of the Long Version of Peter the Chanter's *Verbum abbreviatum*." The architectural analogy of foundation, walls, and roof was a common device often employed to describe the various senses of Scripture, used for examples by Hugh of St. Victor and Peter Comestor. See Smalley, *The Study of the Bible in the Middle Ages*, 87, 242.

178. For the Chanter's contribution to preaching, see Bériou, *L'avènement des maitres de la Parole*, 1:30–48; and Bird, "Heresy, Crusade, and Reform," for discussion of the Chanter's circle more generally.

179. Valente, *Phantasia contrarietas*.

180. Valente rightly observes that the Chanter and his generation mediated between the semantics of the age of Abelard and the teachings of the more sophisticated practitioners of logic and speculative grammar in the thirteenth century.

181. *Verbum adbreviatum*, 15–16: "Dictum est de modo iaciendi fundamentum lectionis. Procedendum est ad modum erigiendi parietem disputationis. In disputatione vero theological quedam

sunt questiones futiles et inutiles que scilicet nec de fide nec de moribus sunt et ille penitus a consistorio sacro eliminande. Quaedem sunt utiles et plane et ille pretermittende. Quedam utiles et scrupulose et iste cum modestia discutiende et sine altercatione." Cited as well in Baldwin, *Master, Princes and Merchants*, 2: 68 n. 64.

182. *Contra perfidiam Judaeorum, PL* 207: 825. See Cotts, *The Clerical Dilemma*, 237.

183. Peter the Chanter, *Summa de sacramentis et animae consiliis*.

184. See Leclercq, "La récréation et le colloque dans la tradition monastique."

185. Bouchard, *"Every Valley Shall Be Exalted"*. For a critique of this book and its treatment of the scholastic context, see Colish's review in *Catholic Historical Review* 89, 4 (2003): 756–58.

186. De Lubac, *The Four Senses of Scripture*, 52.


CHAPTER 4. ARISTOTLE AND THE LOGIC OF DEBATE

1. The role of the medieval Arabic translations of Aristotle's texts and their Arabic commentators is of great importance, but beyond the scope of this project. However, a very intriguing examination of the continuity of medieval Aristotelian logic in a corner of Europe that was familiar with both the medieval Latin and Arabic traditions has recently been assembled by Ljubovic, *The Works in Logic by Bosnian Authors in Arabic*; see esp. 122–29 for discussion of the theory of disputation in the writings of the seventeenth-century author Mustafa Ayyubi-zade, who wrote no fewer than 13 treatises on the subject, inspired by both Aristotle's logic and the medieval reception of that logic. Further work on the comparative reception of Aristotelian logic in medieval Christendom and the Muslim world is needed. Beckwith, *Warriors of the Cloisters*, is informative but tendentious. See above, 230 n. 8.

2. Cf. Luscombe, *The School of Peter Abelard*; Iwakuma, "Influence."

3. Tony Hunt, "Aristotle, Dialectic, and Courtly Literature," at 101. Hunt was not the first to recognize its significance. Cf. Grabmann, "Aristoteles im zwölften Jahrhundert."

4. See the chapters by Dod, "Aristoteles latinus," 45–79; and Lohr, "The Medieval Reception of Aristotle," 80–98, in *CHLMP*, with the classification for the kinds of evidence for the medieval reception of Aristotle described by Dod at 69. The pioneering studies on the subject were conducted by Martin Grabmann in the early decades of the twentieth century. Still immensely useful because of his discussion of unedited manuscripts is chapter 3, "Aristoteles im 12. Jahrhundert," in his *Mittelalterliches Geistesleben*, 3:64–127.

5. Especially significant in this area has been the work of scholars such as Laurenzio Minio-Paluello, Lambertus de Rijk, Sten Ebbesen, Eleanore Stump, Alain de Libera, and John Marenbon.

6. Gouguenheim, *Aristote au Mont Saint-Michel*, esp. 120–24. It should be noted that this work is less of a detailed study of those MSS than it is a polemical counterargument to the notion that medieval Christian Europe owes its familiarity with Greek knowledge to the world of Arab translators and commentators, a bias made abundantly clear in the introduction. These early medieval translations and the glosses on them continue to be an unmined source for twelfth-century studies, as is powerfully demonstrated by John Marenbon's survey and working catalogue of the commentaries and glosses of the Old Logic: "Medieval Latin Commentaries and Glosses on Aristotelian Logical Texts, Before c. 1150 A.D.," in *Glosses and Commentaries on Aristotelian Logical Texts*, with a "Supplement to the Working Catalogue and Supplementary Bibliography" published in idem, *Aristotelian Logic, Platonism, and the Context of Early Medieval Philosophy in the West*, 128–40.

7. References to the *Topics* in the discussion below follow the translation and line numbers by W. A. Pickard-Cambridge in *The Complete Works of Aristotle*, 167–277.

8. Stump, *Dialectic and Its Place in the Development of Medieval Logic*, 3–4.

9. Ibid., chap. 1.

10. Although Adam is praised by Alexander Neckham, a later member of the Petit-Pont school, the adjective *parvipontani* was also used as a term of abuse for a sophistical hairsplitter and it is possibly to this sense that his kinsman John of Salisbury alludes when he suggests that Adam has fallen victim to the "vice" of following Aristotle too closely, resulting in a confusing babel of names, verbs, and subtle intricacies (*Metalogicon* IV.3).

11. The source for Adam's presence against Gilbert of Poitiers in the consistory held by Pope Eugenius III at Paris in 1147 is Otto of Freising's *Deeds of Frederick of Barbarossa* (I.53).

12. Minio-Paluello, "The *Ars Disserendi* of Adam of Balsham," 117. The surviving texts of both recensions are printed in their entirety in Minio-Paluello, ed., *Twelfth-Century Logic*.

13. *Metalogicon*, II.10 and IV.3.

14. Minio-Paluello, "The *Ars Disserendi* of Adam of Balsham," 116–17.

15. Minio-Paluello, *Twelfth-Century Logic*, 4: "Nondum igitur disserendi usus, nam adhuc tunc initium, nondum disserendi ars, prius enim desseri opportuit quam de hoc ars fieret, prius enim de quo ars quam ipsa."

16. Jacobi, "Logic: The Later Twelfth Century," 238.

17. Jeauneau, "Jean de Salisbury et la lecture des philosophes," at 103.

18. See the discussion of Peter of Celle in Ferruolo, *Origins of the University*, 25–26 and 86–92.

19. *Letters of Peter of Celle*, no. 170, 656–59 (Haseldine's translation).

20. Cf. Keats-Rohan, "John of Salisbury and Education in Twelfth-Century Paris."

21. *Metalogicon*, II.1: "logica est ratio disserendi." Note that *disserendi* is the same word employed by Adam of Balsham.

22. Ibid., II.18; trans. McGarry, 117.

23. Walter of Châtillon, *Felix Erat Studium*, in *Moralisch-Satirische Gedichte Walters von Châtillon*, no. 11, 113–15.

24. *Metalogicon*, II.8.

25. Ibid.

26. Godman, *Silent Masters*, xii,; see also 123–43 and 150–90 for further discussion of John of Salisbury.

27. *Metalogicon*, III.10; trans. McGarry, 189.

28. *Metalogicon*, III.10; trans. McGarry, 190.

29. John, in the same chapter, defines dialectic as consisting "entirely in a discussion carried on between questioner and answerer" (*inter opponentem et respondentem*).

30. Cf. Luscombe, "John of Salisbury in Recent Scholarship," 26.

31. The only surviving manuscript of this work (Cambrai, *MS* 259) is of the early thirteenth century. The text of that manuscript was first published and annotated by Nikolaus M. Häring, "A Latin Dialogue on the Doctrine of Gilbert of Poitiers." Häring identified Everard as the author of this work in a subsequent study, "The Cictercian Everard of Ypres and His Appraisal of the Conflict Between St. Bernard and Gilbert of Poitiers." The *Dialogus* is dated by its reference to Pope Celestine III (r. 1191–98).

32. On Gilbert of Poitiers's place in the schools and thought of the twelfth century, see the essays in Jolivet and de Libera, eds., *Gilbert de Poitiers et ses contemporains*.

33. On Gilbert's use of the *quaestio* technique, see Marenbon, "Gilbert of Poitiers," esp. 333–36.

34. A detailed contemporary description of this trial is given by Otto of Freising, *The Deeds of Frederick of Barbarossa*, Book I, 95–105, who singles out disputation as a source of general mistrust toward Abelard.

35. It is unclear when and where Everard obtained his training in canon law, but, in his *Summula decretalium quaestionum* (1181), which also takes the form of a question-and-answer dialogue, Everard identifies himself by both these vocations: "Everardus natione Yprensis, professione monachus Claravallensis, sed liberalium studio atrium et disciplina scholari aliarum facultatum Parisiensis." See Kuttner, *Repertorium der Kanonistik*, 1:137 (MS Reims 689), cited in Häring, "The Cistercian Everard of Ypres," 143 n. 6.

36. Godfrey de Clara-Valle, *Epistola ad Albinum*, PL 185: 587–596. Cf. Häring, "A Latin Dialogue," 244.

37. *Dialogus*, 252. For reflections on Ratius as Everard's "*alter ego*" see Von Moos, "Le dialogue latin au Moyen Âge: L'exemple d'Evrard d'Ypres," 1002.

38. *Dialogus*, 246.

39. Ibid.: "Ego itaque abiens apud me dicebam: 'Dicam huic hospiti ea quae mente paulo antea volvebam. Dicam equidem, nam ispe conscius est eorum quae apud claustrales cujusvis ordinis et habitus aguntur. Dicam, non causa diffamandi aliquos sed in dubio me confirmandi'."

40. Häring, "The Cistercian Everard of Ypres," 156.

41. Lees, *Anselm of Havelberg*, 231. Von Moos, "Le dialogue latin," 1001, traces the origin of this tripartite division back to Sulpicius Severus and his use of an epistolary, dialogical, and historical defense of the memory of Martin of Tours, although the order of Sulpicius's defense is epistolary, historical, and dialogic.

42. Von Moos, "Le dialogue latin"; Cf. idem, "Literatur- und bildungsgeschichtliche Aspekte der Dialogform im lateinischen Mittelalter."

43. Ibid.

44. *Dialogus*, 268: "Nunc scio quod impatiens es ire. Haec consuetude doctorum: quando quaestionibus artantur, impotens solvere rationis responsione, solvunt, immo effugiunt, irae et indignationis ostensione. At contra qui peritus est in solutione, gaudet oblata sibi solvendi opportunitate, et hoc ideo quia in contradictione exercetur sapientia." Cf. von Moos, "Le dialogue latin," 1010.

45. *Dialogus*, 276–77: "At hoc est quod dixi: Quidam claustrales literati, sed in scholis minime exercitati, qualiter in libris orthodoxorum partum inveniunt, in libris suis transcribunt, sed qualiter intelligendum sit, nec sciunt nec inquirere a scientibus solliciti sunt quia, quod ipsi nesciunt qui sancti sunt, peccatores scire minime credunt."

46. Ibid., 249.

47. Ibid., 250.

48. Ibid., 255.

49. Von Moos, "Le dialogue latin," 1012.

50. *Dialogus*, 257.

51. Cf. von Moos, "Le dialogue latin," 1013.

52. Jaeger, "Pessimism in the Twelfth-Century 'Renaissance'." On the twelfth-century satirists, see the discussion in Ferruolo, *The Origins of the University*, chap. 3.

53. A critical edition by E. Guilhou of Vital of Blois's *Geta* is printed in *La "Comedie" Latine en France au Douzième Siècle*, 1:1–57 (with a French translation), and, more recently, by Bate, ed., *Three Latin Comedies*, 15–34.

54. Especially informative in the study of this comedy has been the work of Ferruccio Bertini, who has edited and translated a number of the twelfth-century Latin comedies, including the *Geta*. See especially his "La Commedia Latina del XII secolo" and "Il *Geta* de Vitale di Blois e la scuola di Abelardo," which offers a brief but poignant discussion of the parody of Boethian logic. A slightly

dated but still an important discussion of the comedic genre is Vinay, "La commedia latina del secolo XII."

55. *Geta*, 41.

56. Ibid.

57. Ibid., 53–54.

58. *In sublimi solio*, 306; cited in Ferruolo, *The Origins of the University*, 115.

59. *Hora nona sabbati*, 310–17.

60. See, for example, the comparison drawn between the twelfth century and the fifteenth by Caruso, "On the Shoulders of *Grammatica*: John of Salisbury's *Metalogicon* and Poliziano's *Lamia*."

61. Copeland and Sluiter, eds., *Medieval Grammar and Rhetoric*, 707.

62. The French text and English translation are from Paetow, *The Battle of the Seven Arts*. A facsimile of the two surviving MSS is also provided at the end.

63. There is also evidence that these lines have been either lost or corrupted. See Paetow, *The Battle of the Seven Arts*, 58.

64. "A Paris s'en vint, ce me sanble / Boivre les vins de son celier / Par le conseil au chancelier, / Ou ele avoit molt grant fiance / Quar c'ert li mieldres clers de France; / Mès d'un petit la tint a fole, / Que quant el despute en s'escole / El lesse la droite clergie / Et corne la philosophie. / Et li arcien n'ont mès cure / Lire fors livres de nature."

65. Meyer, "Henri d'Andeli et le Chancelier Philippe."

66. The text is printed in Schneyer, *Die Sittenkritik in den Predigten Philipps des Kanzlers*, 90–91; and translated by Rüegg, "Themes," in *A History of the University in Europe*, 15, who mistakenly associates the Chancellor with the earlier Paris master Philip de Grève.

67. The dating 1189–1216 was accepted by the poem's two most authoritative twentieth-century editors: J. W. H Atkins, ed., *The Owl and the Nightingale*, xxxviii; and Eric Gerald Stanley, ed., *The Owl and the Nightingale*, 19. A major reason for favoring the earlier date had been that the handwriting of one of the two surviving copies (London, British Library, Cotton Caligula A. ix) was considered to date from the early to mid-thirteenth century. A number of scholars now favor a later dating of perhaps c. 1284. See Laing, *Catalogue of Sources for a Linguistic Atlas of Early Medieval English*, 70; and accepted by Fletcher, "The Genesis of *The Owl and Nightingale*."

68. Fletcher, "The Genesis of *The Owl and Nightingale*," adduces possible evidence for the Dominican friar Robert Holcot having been the first known reader of the poem and upholds the centrality of Guildford to the poem's historical consciousness.

69. An excellent précis of the considerable historiography concerning the many unknowns of the poem is provided in the introduction by its most recent editor, Neil Cartlidge, ed., *The Owl and the Nightingale: Text and Translation*, xiii–liv.

70. Cf. Atkins, ed., *The Owl and the Nightingale*, xlvii–xlix; Reed, *Middle English Debate Poetry and the Aesthetics of Irresolution*, 255.

71. Atkins, ed., lxxxii.

72. On the rhetorical aspects of the poem, see especially Carson, "Rhetorical Structure in The Owl and the Nightingale"; Reale, "Rhetorical Strategies in *The Owl and the Nightingale*"; and Mehl, "*The Owl and the Nightingale*: Mündlichkeit und Schriftlichkeit im Streigespräch."

73. An excellent overview of the theories proposed is listed by Cartlidge in *The Owl and the Nightingale*, xvi n. 22, with and an excellent and up-to-date bibliography of editions and studies at 142–65. Line numbers in the text refer to this edition.

74. Coleman, "*The Owl and the Nightingale* and Papal Theories of Marriage," 546–60.

75. Cf. the remarks of Bennett in his *Middle English Literature*, 10: "'miraculous' is merely a loose synonym for 'mysterious,' 'unaccountable': a confession that we know nothing of the cultural conditions and little of the literary context out of which it grew."

76. See Murphy, "Rhetoric and Dialectic in *The Owl and the Nightingale*." Murphy accepted the earlier date (1189–1216) of composition, but his insights are no less valid if we accept the later date, c. 1284.

77. *The Owl and the Nightingale*, ed. Cartlidge, 2.

78. The legal dimension of the poem has long been asserted because of the presence of cited authorities and legal terminology. This connection was challenged by Witt, "The Owl and the Nightingale and English Law Court Procedure of the Twelfth and Thirteenth Centuries," who suggested that the poet, while certainly familiar with judicial procedures, did not attempt to model the poem carefully on such procedures. The case for law has again been made by Wendy A. Matlock, "Law and Violence in the Owl and the Nightingale," who argues that the poem constructs a juridical domain that exists outside official legal culture to endorse that official culture.

79. *Metalogicon*, III.10.

80. Aristotle, *The Complete Works*, 268.

81. Ibid., 278.

82. Ibid., 271.

83. Fletcher, "The Genesis of *The Owl and Nightingale*," 245–46.

84. Ibid., 254.

## CHAPTER 5. THE INSTITUTIONALIZATION OF DISPUTATION: UNIVERSITIES AND BEYOND

1. For stimulating recent reflections on the time-honored theme of connecting architecture and learning during the Gothic era, see Binski, "'Working by Words Alone': The Architect, Scholasticism, and Rhetoric in Thirteenth-Century France"; and Tachau, "What Has Gothic to Do with Scholasticism?"

2. For extensive coverage of the formation of the first universities, see De Ridder-Symoens, ed., *Universities in the Middle Ages*. For broad historical context, see also Pedersen, *The First Universities*. Ferruolo, "*Parisius-Paradisius*: The City, Schools, and the Origins of the University of Paris," covers the debates and intellectual background to the University of Paris. For England's earliest universities, see Cobban, *Medieval English Universities*.

3. Cf. Lawn, *The Rise and Decline of the Scholastic "Quaestio Disputata"*, 2.

4. The transformation of the dissertation from its medieval oral origins to its modern, predominantly textual form is nicely described by Chang, "From Oral Disputation to Written Text: The Transformation of the Dissertation in Early Modern Europe."

5. See Baldwin, *Masters, Princes, and Merchants*, 1:25–31; Smalley, *The Study of the Bible in the Middle Ages*, chap. 5. The only overview of Stephen's career remains Powicke, *Stephen Langton*.

6. From MS Mazarine 177, f. 92d, cited in Smalley, *The Study of the Bible*, 212 n. 1: "Hinc est quod quidam in nullo sensu hoc concedunt: Pater et Filius et Spiritus Sanctus sunt tres omnipotentes. Ad hoc etiam inducunt illam partem glose Ieronimi. Ex hoc habemus ex solis vocibus inordinate prolatis heresim posse incurri. Dicimus quod hoc intelligitur de vocibus prophane novitatis, nec est concedendum in lectionibus sunt tres omnipotentes, sed in disputatione potest concedi ut omnipotens teneatur adiective."

7. *Obligationes Parienses*, in de Rijk, "Some Thirteenth Century Tracts on the Game of Obligation," 26–27.

8. *Ars Disserendi*, in Minio-Paluello, ed., *Twelfth-Century Logic*, 4.

9. Warichez, *Étienne de Tournai et son temps, 1128–1203*, 17–22.

10. Seven manuscripts of Simon's *Disputationes* are preserved. The standard critical edition of these texts is *Les Disputationes de Simon de Tournai*, ed. Warichez. Notes below refer to the individual disputations and page numbers contained in this edition.

11. *Disputatio*, LIX.168.

12. *Disputatio*, LIII.154.

13. *Disputatio*, XXX.92.

14. Cited by Warichez, *Les Disputationes de Simon de Tournai*, xliii.

15. Cited in Liebman, *The Old French Psalter Commentary*, 76–77.

16. *CUP* 1:47.

17. *CUP*, 1:47–48.

18. *CUP*, 1:48.

19. Ibid.

20. On the mythology and historiography of Bologna's foundation, see Rüegg, "Themes," in *A History of the University in Europe*, 4–8.

21. Compared to Paris, Oxford, or Cambridge, the University of Bologna in its early decades had the distinction of being a more democratic system in which the students themselves had the power to make or break professors. Frederick Barbarossa's letter confirmed the students' rights to be judged either by their teachers or by the bishop of the city. If their adversaries attempted to bring a case before any other judge, it lapsed automatically. These corporations of students had extensive powers to influence the selection of teachers and the conditions under which they worked. Teachers lacked a corresponding guild organization. It was not until the 1250s that the city of Bologna and the Holy See acknowledged the distinct nature and the statutes of the university, but at the same time awarded teachers the fundamental authority of invigilating examinations and issuing a license to teach. For more on the nature of the medieval university Bologna, see Rashdall, *Universities* (vol. 1); and Bellomo, *Saggio sull'università nell'età del diritto comune*.

22. Cf. Ferruolo, "The Paris Statutes of 1215 Reconsidered," 1.

23. On the social context of the early history of the University of Paris, see Rashdall, *Universities* (vol. 1); Ferruolo, *The Origins of the University*; and Verger, "A propos de la naissance de l'université de Paris: Contexte social, enjeu politique, portée intellectuelle."

24. Cf. Post, "Parisian Masters as a Corporation, 1200–1246," 44–46.

25. *CUP*, 1:78–79.

26. Ferruolo, "The Paris Statutes of 1215 Reconsidered," 2.

27. *CUP*, 1:67–68.

28. Baldwin, *Master, Princes, and Merchants*, 1:24–26.

29. In fact, from the thirteenth century onward, popes had, in most instances, attended a university, and they increasingly surrounded themselves with learned cardinals with backgrounds similar to that of Robert of Courson. See Miethke, "Die Kirzche und die Universitäten im 13. Jahrhundert"; and Yonah, "Career Trends of Parisian Masters of Theology."

30. See Ferruolo, *The Origins of the University*; and idem, "*Parisius-Paradisius*."

31. An early and still very valuable guide to the basic patterns of learning is Thurot, *De l'organisation de l'enseignement dans l'université de Paris*. See also Weijers, *Terminologie des universités au XIIIe siècle*, esp. part 3. Fresh perspectives on the subject can be found in Van Engen, ed., *Learning Institutionalized*.

32. Weijers, *La "disputatio" à la faculté des arts de Paris (1200–1350 environ)*; and eadem, *La disputatio dans les facultés des arts au Moyen Âge*. For the development of the *disputatio* in the faculties of theology, medicine, and law, see Bazàn, Wippel, Fransen, and Jacquart, eds., *Les questions disputées et les questions quodlibétiques dans les facultés de théologie, de droit et de médecine* (hereafter *LQD*).

33. The basic structure and procedures of the university disputations are outlined by Bernardo C. Bazàn, "Les questions disputées, principalement dans le facultés de theologie," in *LQD*, 21–49. In the Italian universities and at Oxford and Cambridge, which were founded as early thirteenth-century offshoots of the University of Paris, the documentation concerning academic practices is plentiful only from about the middle of the thirteenth century. See Little and Pelster, *Oxford Theology and Theologians, c. A.D. 1282–1302*, 29–30.

34. This basic form of disputation is also variously called a *disputatio solemnis* or *disputatio publica*. They could also be called a *disputatio communis* or a *disputatio generalis*.

35. For a technical discussion of the art, see Angelelli, "The Technique of Disputation in the History of Logic."

36. There is some uncertainty as to exactly how long after the disputation the determination took place. Palémon Glorieux maintained that this took place on the first reading day after the disputation. See Glorieux, "L'enseignement au Moyen Âge: Techniques et méthodes en usage à la Faculté de Théologie de Paris au XIIIe siècle," at 126. Cf. Little and Pelster, *Oxford Theology*, 229, who are less certain about how soon the determination might be. Bazàn, "Les questions disputées," in *LQD*, 61–62, has nothing further to add to this problem.

37. See Bazàn, "Les questions disputées," 62.

38. For further discussion of the dating and iconography of this image, see Åkestam and Kihlman, "Lire, comprendre et mémoriser l'Éthique à Nicomaque: Le rapport texte-image dans ms. Stockholm, Kungl. Bibl., Va 3." I am grateful to Jan-Eric Ericson of the National Library of Sweden for bringing this article to my attention.

39. The most comprehensive treatment of this literature, even if only intended as a "first orientational study," remains the two-volume study by Glorieux, *La littérature quodlibétique de 1260 à 1320* (hereafter *LQ*).

40. The quodlibetical disputation (and its twentieth-century historiography) is explained in detail in the section by John Wippel, "Quodlibetical Questions, Chiefly in Theology Faculties," in *LQD*, 153–222.

41. *LQ*, 2.10.

42. Lawn, *The Rise and Decline of the Scholastic "Quaestio Disputata"*, 16.

43. These later forms of argumentation flourished especially in England. For context, see Courtney's important study *Schools and Scholars in Fourteenth-Century England*.

44. Cf. Yrjönsuuri, ed., *Medieval Formal Logic: Obligations, Insolubles, and Consequences*.

45. Enders, "The Theater of Scholastic Erudition," at 344. See also eadem, *Rhetoric and the Origins of Medieval Drama*, 89–96. On the general importance of audience participation, see Rey-Flaud, *Pour une dramaturgie du Moyen Âge*, 15–22.

46. On medieval drama, see Axton, *European Drama in the Early Middle Ages*; Hardison, *Christian Rite and Christian Drama in the Middle Ages*, who located the origins of drama in sacramental rituals of the Catholic church; and Enders, *Rhetoric and the Origins of Medieval Drama*, who examines the interplay between legal rhetoric and dramatic practice in a broad array of sources from antiquity to the Renaissance and cites the university quodlibet as participating in what she calls the "aestheticization of rhetoric" (164).

47. Symes, *A Common Stage*, esp. chap. 3. The role of theater and performance in the formation of public opinion has been especially significant in recent reassessments of Habermas's concept of the

representational public sphere in early modern Europe. A superb example of this is the volume by Bloemendal, Eversmann, and Streitman, eds., *Drama, Performance and Debate: Theatre and Public Opinion in the Early Modern Period*.

48. Cf. Glorieux, *Répertoire des maîtres en théologie de Paris au XIIIe siècle*.

49. The quotation is found in De la Marche, *La chaire française au moyen âge*, 452; trans. in Enders, *Rhetoric and the Origins of Medieval Drama*, 95.

50. Vincent of Beauvais, *De eruditione filiorum nobilium*, chaps. 20–22, 70–78.

51. See Murray, *Reason and Society in the Middle Ages*, 235.

52. Jean de Jandun, *Tractatus de laudibus Parisius*. Here citing the text in De Lincy and Tisserand, eds., *Paris et ses historiens aux XIVe et XVe siècles*, 40–41.

53. Walter Ong, *Fighting for Life*, 118–148. See also idem, *Rhetoric, Romance, and Technology*, 119–24. The relation between university disputations and the formation of medieval masculinity is explored in Karras, *From Boys to Men*, chap. 3.

54. Cited in Glorieux, *LQ*, 2.49, according to the *Chronicon imagines mundi* by James of Aqui.

55. Paris, Bibliothèque Nationale, MS. Lat. 14,799, fol. 206, as cited in Hauréau, *Notices et extraits de quelques manuscrits latins de la Bibliothèque Nationale*, 3:111; and also cited in Glorieux, *LQ*, 1.15–16.

56. The text is from an account "De privilegio Martini," in Finke, *Aus den Tagen Bonifaz VIII*, 1–8; and quoted by Gloriuex, *LQ*, 1:15. See also Enders, "The Theater of Scholastic Erudition," 351.

57. Gloriuex, *LQ*, 1.57: "postpositis vel neglectis canonicis, necesariis, utilibus et aedificativis doctrinis, curiosis, inutilibus et supervacuis philosophiae questionibus et subtilitatibus se immiscent, ex quibus ipsius studii disciplina dissolvitur." See also Ender, *Rhetoric and the Origins of Medieval Drama*, 97, who cites the same passage.

58. The cultural-historical dimensions of medieval music are a topic of current scholarly attention. See, for example, Kirkman, *The Cultural Life of the Early Polyphonic Mass: Medieval Context to Modern Revival*; and Cullin, ed., *La place de la musique dans la culture médiévale*. For an excellent overview of Paris in the history of medieval music, see Wright, *Music and Ceremony at Notre Dame of Paris, 500–1550*. See also the influential study by Page, *The Owl and the Nightingale*.

59. Gushee, "The Polyphonic Music of the Medieval Monastery, Cathedral and University," at 144.

60. Taruskin, *Music from the Earliest Notation to the Sixteenth Century*, 149. For a comprehensive study of the musical culture of Notre Dame within the context of the cathedral and the city, see Wright, *Music and Ceremony at Notre Dame of Paris*, chaps. 7–8. For the more embellished forms of Notre Dame polyphony (*tripla* and *quadrupla*), see Gross, *Chanter en polyphonie à Notre Dame de Paris aux 12e et 13e siècles*. See also Janet Knapp, "Polyphony at Notre Dame of Paris." On the university context for early polyphony, see Gushee, "The Polyphonic Music of the Medieval Monastery, Cathedral and University."

61. Page, "A Treatise on Musicians from c. 1400: The *Tractatulus de differentiis et gradibus cantorum* by Arnulf de St Ghislain," at 16, 20. See also Bent, "Grammar and Rhetoric in Late Medieval Polyphony." For an Eastern European analogy, consider the Lithuanian *Sutartines*, polyphonic songs typically sung by women that derives from the verb *sutarti* (to agree or to attune to another person) and is apparently late medieval in origin. Račiūnaitė-Vyčinienė, *Sutartinės*.

62. An up-to-date overview of what is known about the school and composers of Notre Dame by a leading authority in the field is Roesner, "Notre Dame Polyphony," chap. 30 in *The Cambridge History of Medieval Music*, forthcoming. I am grateful to the author for sharing this chapter in advance of publication and for guiding my thoughts on the scholastic context of medieval music.

63. See especially Payne, "Aurelianis *civitas:* Student Unrest in Medieval France and a Conductus by Philip the Chancellor"; and idem, "Philip the Chancellor and the Conductus Prosula: 'Motetish' Works from the School of Notre Dame." A wealth of additional material can be found in Payne's unpublished dissertation, "Poetry, Politics, and Polyphony: Philip the Chancellor's Contribution to the Music of the Notre Dame School."

64. For a comprehensive overview of the motet, see E. H. Sanders, "The Medieval Motet." For a more recent and succinct overview of the motet literature, especially in comparison with other musical forms of the thirteenth century, see Everist, "The Thirteenth Century," esp. 77–85.

65. Houser, ed. and trans., *The Cardinal Virtues*, 42 n. 87. For Philip's general influence on thirteenth-century thought, see Lottin, "L'influence littéraire du chancelier Philippe," 6:149–69.

66. The source for this information is the thirteenth-century musical treatise *De mensuris et discantu*, written by an unnamed Englishman and known to posterity as *Anonymous IV.* The story of the misnomer and of its contents is nicely summarized by Taruskin, *Music from the Earliest Notation to the Sixteenth Century*, 173–74. See also Gushee, "The Polyphonic Music of the Medieval Monastery, Cathedral and University," 157–63. There is some speculation that Perotin (Petrus) and Peter the Chanter may be the same person, although this cannot be proved.

67. Stevens, "Medieval Song," 418. For discussion of the manuscripts, see L21 and K52 in Anderson, "Notre-Dame and Related Conductus: A Catalogue Raisonné." See as well the overview of Philip the Chancellor's poetry by Dronke, "The Lyrical Compositions of Philip the Chancellor."

68. Rillon, "Convaincre et émouvoir: Les conduits monodiques de Philippe le Chancelier, un médium pour la predication?" For further connections between scholastic life and music, see Jacques Verger, "La musique et le son chez Vincent de Beauvais et les encyclopédistes du XIIIe siècle."

69. Ypocrite pseudopontifices / Velut stelle fimamenti / Et gaudebit; Anima iuge lacrima; and O quam necessarium / Venditores labiorum / Domino [or *Eius*]. See Philip the Chancellor, *Motets and Prosulas*, 161–67, 35–37, and 142–45.

70. Ibid., xix.

71. William of Auvergne, *Selected Spiritual Writings*, 57. The only book-length study of William's life and works is Valois, *Guillaume d'Auvergne, Éveque de Paris (1228–1249).* For a more recent overview, see Teske, "William of Auvergne," 1–18.

72. The text, translation, music, and editor's commentary on this motet can be found in Payne, ed., *Philip the Chancellor: Motets and Prosulas*, 161–67.

73. Ibid., xxv.

74. Thomas of Cantimpré, *Bonum universale de apibus*, 2.10.36: "singulis, quae contra Fratres dictus Cancellarius praedicaverat, retractis, ad unguem omnia luculentissime per divinae scripturae paginam improbavit."

75. For a discussion of Philip the Chancellor's debate poems in this larger context, see Bossy, "Medieval Debates of Body and Soul." On the use of dialectics among the troubadours, see Bolduc, "Troubadours in Debate: The *Breviari d'amor.*"

76. Solterer, *The Master and Minerva.*

77. Långfors, Jeanroy, and Bandin, eds., *Receuil général des jeux-partis français*, song CXXVII.

78. The original text and the translation can be found in Goldin, *Lyrics of the Troubadours and Trouvères*, 470–71.

79. The confraternity was self-consciously authenticated through written texts and an official seal, which featured a motto inscribed in both vernacular and Latin. In practice, the identities of the trouvère and jongleur are hard to distinguish. For the history of Arras during the thirteenth century, see especially Delmaire, *Le diocèse d'Arras*; and Symes, *A Common Stage.*

80. But see Baldwin, "The Image of the *Jongleur* in Northern France Around 1200."

81. Saltzstein, "Cleric-Trouvères and the *Jeux-Partis* of Medieval Arras," 149.

82. For general orientation, see Bec, *La lyrique française au moyen-âge (XIIe–XIIIe siècle)*.

83. Taruskin, *Music from the Earliest Notation to the Sixteenth Century*, 121. On the myth of "the Puy" as an independent locus for performance in Arras, see Symes, *A Common Stage*, 216–27.

84. Most recently, see Symes, "Out in the Open, in Arras: Sightlines, Soundscapes, and the Shaping of a Medieval Public Sphere."

85. Lavis, "Le jeu-parti français: Jeu de refutation, d'opposition et de concession."

86. One can make a case for courtly love as an elaborate literary and philosophical game, in which the potential for unfulfilled love becomes more significant than any genuine emotional state and the process of striving to attain the object becomes more important than the object itself.

87. Saltzstein, "Cleric-Trouvères and the *Jeux-Partis* of Medieval Arras," 151.

88. Ibid., 161.

89. See Symes, *A Common Stage*, chap. 2, esp. 96, 111–12.

90. Berger, *Littérature et societé arrageoise au XIIIe siècle*, 58–60, 110.

91. Page, *The Owl and the Nightingale*, 74; Cf. Saltzstein, "Cleric-Trouvères and the *Jeux-Partis* of Medieval Arras," 150.

92. Focus is maintained on the Dominicans because of their explicitly polemical endeavors, but this is not to suggest that disputation is absent from the other mendicant orders. For discussion of the Franciscan disputations, see Piron, "Franciscan *Quodlibeta* in Southern *Studia* and at Paris, 1280–1300."

93. For a recent biography, see Moore, *Pope Innocent III (1160/61–1216)*. See also Moore, ed., *Pope Innocent III and His World*.

94. The anonymous Latin account is published in Kuttner and Garcia y Garcia, "A New Eyewitness Account of the Fourth Lateran Council"; trans. Constantin Fasolt in *Readings in Western Civilization*, vol. 4, *Medieval Europe*, at 372.

95. The Latin text of the council with facing English translation is printed in *Decrees of the Ecumenical Councils*, 1:230–71.

96. Peters, *Inquisition*, 50. Cf. Foucault, *History of Sexuality*, vol. 1, *An Introduction*, 58, who stated that Lateran IV marked a central moment in establishing "confession as one of the main rituals we rely on for the production of truth."

97. The text of the letter of Bishop Foulques of Toulouse can be found in *Monumenta diplomatica S. Dominici*, no. 63, 56–58.

98. There is a voluminous literature about the life of St. Dominic and the early history of the Dominican Order. Especially useful and reliable is Vicaire, *Saint Dominic and His Times*.

99. For a full discussion of pre-Dominican preaching, see Ladner, "*L'ordo praedicatorum* avant l'ordre des prêcheurs."

100. A close precedent might be sought in the Cistercians Innocent III had asked to preach in southern France, but their commission was temporary and, as Dominic later pointed out, evangelical poverty was noticeably lacking from their original tactics.

101. Mulchahey, *"First the Bow Is Bent in Study"*, 167 (hereafter *Dominican Education*).

102. Cf. Ames, *Righteous Persecution*, 28.

103. Jordan of Saxony, *Libellus de principiis Ordinis Praedicatorum*, no. 22. Jordan's chronicle is one of the earliest and more reliable sources for the early history of the order.

104. Ibid., nos. 23–25.

105. Jordan mistakenly places the event at Fanjeaux.

106. The legislation produced by the chapter of 1220 has been reconstructed by M.-H. Vicaire, in Mandonnet and Vicaire, eds., *Saint Dominique*, II:273–92.

107. *Constitutiones antiquae*, II.23, 358; cf. Mandonnet and Vicaire, eds., *Saint Dominique*, II:289.

108. *Constitutiones antiquae*, II.28, 361; cf. Mandonnet and Vicaire, eds., *Saint Dominique*, II:290.

109. *Constitutiones antiquae*, II.29, 362; Mandonnet and Vicaire, eds., *Saint Dominique*, II:290.

110. *Constitutiones antiquae*, II.29, 362: "Et secundum quod magistro studencium videbitur, locus proprius statuatur, in quo post disputationem vel vesperas vel alio etiam tempore, si vacaverint, ad dubitationes vel quaestiones proponendas ipso presente conveniant. Et uno querente vel proponente alii taceant, ne loquentem impediant. Et si aliquis inhoneste vel confuse vel clamose vel proterve querens vel opponens vel respondens offenderit, statim ab illo qui tunc inter eos preest, corripiatur."

111. Mulchahey, *Dominican Education*, 38.

112. Cited in ibid., ix.

113. A detailed overview of these three practices is given in ibid., 130–78, here 134.

114. *Acta capitulorum generalis ordinis Praedicatorum*, I.35: "Item, hanc. In constitutione ubi dicitur. Nullus fiat publicus doctor. nisi ad minus theologiam per quoattuor annos audierit. addatur. nec disputet. nisi per licenciam prioris provincialis. et diffinitiorum capituli provincialis."

115. Mulchahey, *Dominican Education*, 168.

116. *Acta I* (Valenciennes, 1259), 99–100: "Item, quod lectores vacantes vadant ad scholas, et precipue ad disputationem. . . . Visitatores singulis annis diligenter inquirant de lectoribus quantum legerint in anno. et quociens disputaverint ac determinaverint."

117. See Mulchahey, *Dominican Education*, 222–36.

118. Humbert of Romans, *Instructiones de officiis ordinis*, in *Opera de vita regulari*, II, c. II.1, 254–55.

119. Ibid., 254: "Cum vero exigente intelligentia utilitate auditorum, interdum expedit disputare, eligenda est ab eo material utilis et intelligibilis, maxime si sit disputatio inter minus peritos."

120. Ibid., 260–61.

121. Ibid., 254.

122. Ibid., 261. See also Mulchahey, *Dominican Education*, 170–71.

123. Humbert of Romans, *Instructiones de officiis ordinis*, 261.

124. *Acta capitulorum Lombardiae* (Milan, 1278), in *Acta capitulorum provinciae Romanae (1243–1344)*, 196–97.

125. Ibid., 155.

126. *Acta I* (Oxford, 1280), 208–9.

127. Ibid., 209.

128. *Acta capitulorum provinciae Romanae* (Naples, 1274), 43.

129. Mulchahey, *Dominican Education*, 175.

130. Of the countless works written about Thomas, his thought, and his career, three merit special attention: Chenu, *Toward Understanding Saint Thomas*, which has influenced an entire generation of Thomist scholarship; Weisheipl, *Friar Thomas d'Aquino*, which remains the best single-volume biography; and, most recently, Torrell, *Saint Thomas Aquinas*, 2 vols., which offers a fully up-to-date assessment of all his known writings.

131. *Tractatus de periculis novissimorum temporum*. For an analysis of this work and the various versions, see Dufeil, *Guillaume de Saint-Amour et la polémique universitaire parisienne 1250–1259*, 212–27, 241–42, and 252–53. The treatise has recently been translated with an excellent introduction by G. Geltner, *William of Saint Amour: Tractatus de periculis novissimorum temporum*.

132. Humbert of Romans records the mob violence that broke out in the streets of Paris in April 1256.

133. The friars were only partially victorious in their struggle against secular masters. After the death of Pope Alexander IV in 1261, the university succeeded in placing certain restrictions that limited the friars' role within the university: they were admitted to the faculty of theology but not that of the arts, and secular students could incept for the doctorate only under secular doctors. By 1318, an oath of obedience to statutes of the university was once more imposed upon the friars.

134. Mention must also be made of the Franciscan contribution to this dispute. Bonaventure, for example, completed his *Quaestiones disputatae de perfectione evangelica* against William of St. Amour in 1253 and *Apologia pauperum* against Gerard of Abbeville in 1269. These disputed questions and the treatise developed a rationale for the friars' activities within the schools and a theology of religious life, especially their adoption of evangelical poverty. His *Soliloquium*, cast in the form of a dialogue, provided an extended form of spiritual advice, demonstrating that the older form of the spiritual or monastic dialogue could coexist with the more ardently polemical debate of the *quaestiones disputatae*. Bonaventure resigned his chair of theology in 1257 when he was elected as the seventh minister general in order to devote his time and energies to the welfare of the order. See Robson, *The Franciscans in the Middle Ages*, chap. 7.

135. On this period in Thomas's career, see Chenu, *Towards Understanding*, esp. 242–49; and Torrell, *Saint Thomas Aquinas*, I, chap. IV. Other masters, it should be noted, occasionally tried to shirk their duties of holding public disputations.

136. Thomas Aquinas, *Quaestiones Disputatae*, vol. 1. Pierre Mandonnet was convinced that the basic unit of the disputation was the article within a question and devised a scheme to accommodate each article to a day in the academic year. But such a scheme implies that Thomas held 253 disputations in his three years at Paris, two every week, leaving no time for the other masters to dispute or teach at all. Antoine Dondaine has clearly shown the anomaly of Mandonnet's theory and claimed that the basic unit of the disputation was the entire question, no matter how many articles each question had. See Dondaine, *Les secrétaires des saint Thomas*, 209–16. More recently still, Bernardo Bazán has argued that that the diverse series of disputed questions by Thomas do not belong to the genre of ordinary or public disputes but indeed to private disputes. See Bazán, "Les questions disputées," esp. 70–85. See also Torrell, *Saint Thomas Aquinas*, I, 59–69, who accepts Bazán's hypothesis, and 334–35, which lists all the editions and translations of *De veritate*.

137. The English Dominican Nicholas Trevet (c. 1257–c. 1334) categorized all the disputed questions into three parts, stating tersely, "He wrote the first part of the questions *De veritate* and the rest, which were disputed in Paris. Likewise the second part of the disputed questions *De potentia Dei* and the rest, which he disputed in Italy. Likewise the third part of the disputed questions, the beginning of which is *De virtutibus*, which he disputed when he taught in Paris for the second time." Cited in Weisheipl, *Friar Thomas d'Aquino*, 198. Of course, there is considerable uncertainty about what is included in "the rest." The most recent assessment of which questions belong to which period is the discussion in Torrell, *Saint Thomas Aquinas*, 1:201–7.

138. Weisheipl, *Friar Thomas d'Aquino*, 198.

139. Thomas Aquinas, *Quaestiones Quodlibetales*, IV, a. 18 (p. 155): "Disputatio autem ad duplicem finem potest ordinaria. Quaedam enim disputatio ordinatur ad removendum dubitationem an ita sit; et in tali disputatione theological maxime utendum est auctoritatibus, quas recipiunt illi cum quibus disputatur; puta, si cum Judaeis disputatur, oportet inducere auctoritates veteris Testamenti: si cum Manichaeis qui vetus testamentum respuunt; oportet uti solum auctoritatibus novi testamenti:

si autem cum schismaticis, qui recipiunt vetus et novum Testamentum, non autem doctrinam Sanctorum nostrorum, sicut sunt Graeci, oporet cum eis disputare ex auctoritatibus novi vel veteris Testamenti, et illorum doctorum quos ipsi recipiunt. Si autem nullam auctoritatem recipiunt, oportet ad eos convicendos, ad rationes naturals confugere. Quaedam vero disputatio est magistralis in scholis non removendum errorem, sed ad instruendum auditores ut inducantur ad intellectum veritatis quam intendit: et tunc oportet rationibus inniti investigantibus veritatis radicem, et facientibus scire quomodo sit verum quod dicitur: alioquin si nullis auctoritatibus magister quaestionem determinet, certificabitur quidem auditor quod ita est; sed nihil scientiae vel intellectus acquiret, sed vacuus abscedet."

140. Here I follow the discussion by Bose, "The Issue of Theological Style in Late Medieval Disputations," 7.

141. See Chenu, *Towards Understanding*, who devotes chapter 2 of his magisterial study to the literary forms of Thomas's works and states (79) that the forms and structures of language are "the permanent support of thought, so that by examining the forms in which the mind is dressed, one has a good chance of discovering its very inner workings." For a recent overview of the *Summa* and its literary context, see Torrell, *Aquinas's Summa*.

142. Thomas Aquinas, *Summa Theologiae*, vol. 1, prologus.

143. These challenges, of course, were not new; they pertained, for instance, to the *Sentences* of Peter Lombard.

144. See also the remarks of Chenu, *Toward Understanding*, 318: "In order to test what a *summa* stands for as the literary form characterizing a system of thought and a particular age, recall the other forms of philosophical and religious thinking that appeared in the course of history: the Socratic *Dialogues* of Plato, the *Confessions* of Augustine, the *Meditations* of Descartes, the *Pensées* of Pascal, the *Treatises* of the eighteenth and nineteenth centuries, the *Journals* of Maine de Biran and of Gabriel Marcel. Each genre requires its own procedures in carrying out research and setting forth intelligibility. Differences in expression are no more than the outcome of even deeper differences in mental outlook."

145. *S. Thomae Aquinatis opera omnia*, xiv, 1–2, 148; Cf. *S. Thomae Aquinatis opuscula omnia*, vi, 488.

146. *Summa Theologiae*, II.2, q. 10, art. 7

147. Minnis, *Medieval Theory of Authorship*, esp. 118–47.

148. *Les Questions super librum de causis de Siger de Brabant*, 35.

149. The text is cited in Grabmann, "Die Aristoteleskommentare des Heinrich von Brüssel und der Einfluss Alberts des Grossen auf die mittelalterliche Aristoteleserkärung," 82.

150. Bose, "The Issue of Theological Style in Late Medieval Disputations," 10.

CHAPTER 6. DRAMA AND PUBLICITY IN JEWISH-CHRISTIAN DISPUTATIONS

1. For a recent revisiting of Augustine's famous pronouncements concerning Jewish witness, see Cohen, "Augustine's Doctrine of Jewish Witness Revisited." Indispensable as well is Fredriksen, *Augustine and the Jews*.

2. On Jews and Judaism in the work of Peter the Venerable, see Iogna-Prat, *Order and Exclusion*; and Cohen, *Living Letters of the Law*, 245–70. A detailed study of Martí's polemic and others of the same period is Chazan, *Daggers of Faith*. See also Cohen, *The Friars and the Jews*, 129–69, who

first called general attention to the missionizing activities of thirteenth-century Dominicans such as Raymond Martí. On Chaucer's involvement with Jews and Judaism, see the essays in Delaney, ed., *Chaucer and the Jews*. But see also Besserman, "Chaucer, Spain, and the Prioress's Antisemitism," who argues that it is unlikely that Chaucer subscribed wholeheartedly to the demonizing views of Jews and further that the Jews of Spain may have provided the historical source for his tale.

3. Cf. Pelikan, *The Emergence of the Catholic Tradition (100–600)*, 15: "virtually every major Christian writer of the first five centuries either composed a treatise in opposition to Judaism or made this issue the dominant theme in a treatise devoted to some other subject." For stimulating explorations of the theme of anti-Judaism in the context of medieval Christian art and sculpture, see Merback, ed., *Beyond the Yellow Badge*. The importance of anti-Jewish sentiment in European history has not always been recognized. A landmark survey of historical writings that neglect the place and importance of Jews in medieval western Europe is in Langmuir, "Majority Historians and Post-Biblical Jews."

4. Cohen, *Living Letters*; Langmuir, *History, Religion, and Antisemitism*; idem, *Towards a Definition of Antisemitism*; Dahan, *Les intellectuels chrétiens et les juifs au Moyen Age*; Chazan, *Medieval Stereotypes and Modern Antisemitism*; idem, *Fashioning Jewish Identity in Medieval Western Christendom*; Abulafia, *Christians and Jews in the Twelfth-Century Renaissance*. Most recently, see Nirenberg, *Anti-Judaism: The Western Tradition*, esp. chaps. 3 and 5.

5. A leading advocate in arguing for a connection between the intellectual developments of the twelfth-century renaissance and the negative impact on the Jewish-Christian debate is Anna Sapir Abulafia (see note 4 above). The foundational brick in this line of inquiry was laid by Funkenstein, "Changes in the Patterns of Christian Anti-Jewish Polemic in the Twelfth Century [Hebrew]." An abbreviated and slightly reoriented version of the essay subsequently appeared in English as "Basic Types of Christian Anti-Jewish Polemics in the Later Middle Ages." More recently, these arguments can be found in Funkenstein, *Perceptions of Jewish History*, 172–219. Jeremy Cohen, who initially argued in *The Friars and the Jews* that the missionary activities of the thirteenth century was the critical moment of transition, has now accepted, without detriment to his earlier argument, that the twelfth century did indeed witness a major change in Jewish-Christian relations: Cohen, *Living Letters*, 147–66, esp. 156. For further discussions of the social as well as intellectual relations between Christians and Jews during the period, see Signer and Van Engen, eds., *Jews and Christians in Twelfth-Century Europe*. See also Ben-Shalom, "Medieval Jewry in Christendom," 165, who says more neutrally that "the twelfth and the thirteenth centuries were thus a turning point in the history of Jewish life in Western Europe."

6. Heinz Schreckenberg, *Die christlichen Adversus-Judaeos-Texte (11.–13. Jh)*. This second volume (729 pp.) is as long as volume one of the same series, covering the first ten centuries of Christianity.

7. Pelikan, *The Growth of Medieval Theology*, 246. See also Cohen, "Scholarship and Intolerance in the Medieval Academy: The Study and Evaluation of Judaism in European Christendom."

8. For greater clarification of this term, see Cohen, *Living Letters*, 2–3 n. 3. Cf. also the expression "theological Jew" as described by Dahan, *Les intellectuels chrétiens*, 585.

9. There is a vast bibliography concerning the *Ordo*. For relevant discussions, see Fassler, "Representations of Time in *Ordo representaciones Ade*"; Vaughn, "The Prophets of the Anglo-Norman 'Adam'"; and Justice, "The Authority of Ritual in the *Jeu d'Adam*."

10. For the text of the sermon and extensive commentary on the plays, see Young, "Ordo prophetarum."

11. Cf. Happe, ed., *English Mystery Plays*, 188–215.

12. The standard understanding is that there were two successive sculptural workshops at the cathedral of Bamberg. The first sculpted the figures at the Gnadenpforte (northeast portal) and the southern side of that eastern choir screen around 1220. Those figures are blocky and rather rigid. The second workshop (sometimes called the "younger" workshop) apparently came to Bamberg from Reims around 1225 and is responsible for the figures shown on the north side of the choir screen as well as other figures that are commonly celebrated for their lifelike and dynamic character. The standard study of the Bamberg cathedral is by Fiedler, *Der Meister im Bamberger Dom: Magister de vivis lapidibus. Urgestalt deutschen Bildhauertums.* For the Bamberg-Reims connection, see Sauerländer, "Reims und Bamberg: Zu Art und Umfang der Übernahmen." I am indebted to Dr. Nina Rowe of Fordham University for both these references. See also the excellent article by Mia Münster-Swendsen, "The Model of Scholastic Mastery in Northern Europe c. 970–1200," who makes similar observations about the Bamberg sculpture at 329.

13. Whether there is a meaningful distinction between "ritual murder" and "blood libel" is a matter of some dispute. I am myself inclined to believe that the traditional distinction has been overblown.

14. The massacres of Rhineland Jews at the hands of the crusading armies in spring 1096 are certainly the most famous of such incidents and the most commented on, but as Jonathan Riley-Smith has pointed out, all the major crusading expeditions were accompanied by anti-Jewish violence in Europe. See Riley-Smith, "Christian Violence and the Crusades."

15. On the expulsions in France and their larger context, see Jordan, *The French Monarchy and the Jews.* For the situation in England, see Mundill, *England's Jewish Solution.* There is much literature on the expulsion of the Sephardic communities from Spain, but absolutely indispensable now is Beinart, *The Expulsion of the Jews from Spain.*

16. R. I. Moore, "Antisemitism and the Birth of Europe." See also his provocative and very influential *The Formation of a Persecuting Society, 950–1250.* A judicious critique of Moore's thesis and others of a similar nature is outlined in Nirenberg, *Communities of Violence,* 3–7.

17. Most recently, see Szpiech, *Conversion and Narrative,* as well as Frassetto, ed., *Christian Attitudes Toward the Jews in the Middle Ages*; and, from a literary perspective, Bale, *The Jew in the Medieval Book.* Approaching many of the same texts I discuss in this chapter but with greater focus on body, gender, and sexuality is Kruger, *The Spectral Jew.* A less cynical (and deceptively positive) view of Jewish-Christian relations is Elukin, *Living Together, Living Apart.* Important perspectives from many leading scholars in the field are represented in Cluse, ed., *The Jews of Europe in the Middle Ages.*

18. See Moore, *Jews and Christians in the Life and Thought of Hugh of Saint Victor.* Also important in twelfth-century Hebrew scholarship was Herbert of Bosham, whose knowledge of Hebrew was remarkable for his day. Long known through the pioneering efforts of Smalley, *The Study of The Bible in the Middle Ages,* chap. 4, Herbert has at last been given a detailed study by Goodwin, *"Take Hold of the Robe of a Jew".*

19. *Disputatio cum Gentili,* section 1; *Works of Gilbert Crispin,* 61.

20. Abulafia, "Christians Disputing Disbelief," 137.

21. Ibid.

22. Ibid. See also Jacobi, "Gilbert Crispin: Zwischen Realität und Fiktion."

23. Abulafia, "Christians Disputing Disbelief," 141.

24. Cohen, *Living Letters,* 179–218, who considers these and other authors in regard to their "application of Anselman teaching," but does not really address the question of literary form. To repeat an important point, it is the fact that so many of these anti-Jewish works *were* written as dialogues during a period of renewed emphasis of dialectic that needs explaining.

25. See Chapter 2.

26. For biographical detail about Odo, I rely on Irven Resnick's remarks in *On Original Sin and A Disputation with the Jew, Leo, Concerning the Advent of Christ, the Son of God: Two Theological Treatises, Odo of Tournai*, 1–21 (hereafter *Two Treatises*).

27. On Odo's entry into monastic life during the early twelfth century, see Dereine, "Odo de Tournai et la crise du cénobitisme au XIe siècle."

28. Martin Grabmann (*Die Geschicte der Scholastischen Methode*, 2:156) describes Odo as a member of Anselm's school of thought, at least in his teaching of original sin. Maurice de Wulf, (*Histoire de la philosophie mediévale*, 1:172) posits the reverse as a possibility. See also *Two Treatises*, 26, where Irven Resnick cannot resolve the ambiguity.

29. *PL* 160: 1101–12; trans. in Resnick, *Two Treatises*, 85–97.

30. *PL* 160: 1101; Resnick, *Two Treatises*, 85.

31. *PL* 160: 1112; Resnick, *Two Treatises*, 97.

32. Ibid.

33. Biographical information provided by Tolan, *Petrus Alfonsi and His Medieval Readers*, chap. 1, must now be supplemented by the excellent overview of recent scholarship provided by Resnick in his introduction to *Petrus Alfonsi: Dialogue Against the Jews*, 3–36, at 22.

34. There is some speculation that Peter Alfonsi and Peter of Toledo, a Jewish convert translating Arabic materials in Toledo in the third and fourth decades of the twelfth century, may be one and the same. See Van Koningsveld, "Historische betrekkingen tussen moslims en christenen."

35. There are over 160 extant medieval manuscripts of the work. On the medieval reception of Alfonsi's *Disciplina clericalis*, see Tolan, *Petrus Alfonsi and His Medieval Readers*, chap. 4.

36. There is a great deal of scholarship on Alfonsi's writings, his *Disciplina clericalis* and his translations of Arabic astronomical works especially. For bibliographic orientation, see Reinhart and Santiago-Otero, "Pedro Alfonso. Obras y Bibliografía."

37. According to Bernard Guenée's scheme for evaluating the success of medieval works, six manuscripts indicate a small degree of success, fifteen a limited success, thirty a considerable success, and seventy a great success. See his *Histoire et culture historique dans l'occident médiévale*, 249–95.

38. Cohen, *Living Letters*, 202.

39. *PL* 157: 535; *Dialogue Against the Jews*, 41.

40. Cf. *PL* 157: 538. On Alfonsi's use of reason, his similarities and departures from Anselm, see Cohen, *Living Letters*, 201–18; and Novikoff, "Reason and Natural Law in the Disputational Writings of Peter Alfonsi, Peter Abelard, and Yehuda Halevi," 111.

41. But see Cohen, *Living Letters*, 201–18, who discusses Alfonsi's polemic as rounding out a consideration of the new rationalist in Christian anti-Jewish polemic and likewise states, at 202, "one cannot help but wonder as to the extent of contact, if any at all, Alfonsi may have had with the Anselmian circle while in northern Europe."

42. Evans, *Anselm and a New Generation*, 139–47.

43. Tolan, *Petrus Alfonsi and his Medieval Readers*, 165 (Latin) and 173 (English translation).

44. In the fifth dialogue, Alfonsi addresses the question of why he "chose the faith of the Christians rather than that of the Saracens" by refuting the beliefs of Islam and the Arab people in general, whom he depicts as greedy, lustful, and essentially pagan.

45. Resnick, Introduction, *Petrus Alfonsi*, 28–29.

46. See the editor's introduction in *Collationes*, xxiii.

47. *Collationes*, 4–7.

48. *Collationes*, 76–77.

49. *Itinerarium Kambriae*, 6:95–96; Gerald of Wales, *The Journey Through Wales and The Description of Wales*, 153.

50. *Tractatus sive Dialogus contra Iudaeos*, PL 209: 457.

51. *PL* 209: 425.

52. *PL* 209: 455.

53. Ibid.

54. Neither Bartholomew of Exeter's *Dialogus* nor the anonymous *Arma contra Iudeos* have been edited. The only known copy of Bartholomew's *Dialogus* is MS. Bodley 482 (S.C. 2046), portions of which are transcribed by Hunt, "The Disputation of Peter of Cornwall Against Symon the Jew," 147–48; and quoted by Smalley, *The Study of the Bible*, 170–71. The anonymous *Arma contra Iudeos* is the title given in the catalogue of the library of Rochester Priory (1202). A copy is in Oxford, Jesus College 11, ff. 70v–76r, where it is titled *Incipit disputatio contra incredulitatem Iudeorum excerpta ex libris prophetarum*.

55. Quoted by Smalley, *Study of the Bible*, 170–71.

56. Morey, *Bartholomew of Exeter, Bishop and Canonist*, 109.

57. Among his other citations are passages from St. Gregory, Bede, Augustine, Tertullian, Origen, and Josephus (109). See Morey, *Bartholomew of Exeter, Bishop and Canonist*, 109.

58. The only surviving manuscript of this work is MS Eton College 130, ff. 92r-224r.

59. The prologue has been edited by Hunt, "The Disputation of Peter of Cornwall Against Symon the Jew," 153–56.

60. This preamble partially serves to justify the length of the work.

61. Hunt, "The Disputation of Peter of Cornwall," 155.

62. Ibid.

63. Grayzel, ed., *The Church and the Jews in the XIIIth Century*, 1:300–301.

64. Ibid., 19 (March 1, 1227), 318–19.

65. Ibid., 69 (March 5, 1233), 200–201.

66. Ibid., 27 (February 1233), 324–25.

67. Ibid., 2:67 (ed. Stow). The promulgation has no date and no addressee.

68. *Contra perfidiam Judaeorum*, PL 207:825. See also Cotts, *The Clerical Dilemma*, 237.

69. Loeb, *La controverse sur le Talmud sous Saint Louis*, 21–54; Rembaum, "The Talmud and the Popes: Reflections on the Talmud Trials of the 1240's"; Chazan, "The Condemnation of the Talmud Reconsidered (1239–1248)"; Maccoby, *Judaism on Trial*, 19–38.

70. For considerations about Donin's background and motives, see Cohen, "The Mentality of the Medieval Jewish Apostate," esp. 35–41.

71. Maccoby, *Judaism on Trial*, 41, accepts Donin's Karaite background, as does Grayzel, ed., *Church and the Jews*, 1:339–40. See Cohen, *Friars and the Jews*, 60–61 n. 19, for the lengthy historiography on what scholars have said about Donin's Jewish background and how one should understand his prior excommunication from French Jewry in 1225 as a motive for later approaching Pope Gregory IX in 1236.

72. For a breakdown of the charges leveled against the Talmud by Donin, see Eisenberg, "Reading Medieval Religious Disputation: The 1240 'Debate' Between Rabbi Yeḥiel of Paris and Friar Nicholas Donin," chap. 6, esp. 168–79.

73. Fishman, *Becoming the People of the Talmud*, esp. 167–74.

74. On the anti-Christian writings produced by Jews during the thirteenth century, see especially Berger, *The Jewish-Christian Debate in the High Middle Ages*; and Lasker, *Jewish Philosophical Polemics Against Christianity in the Middle Ages*.

75. Jean de Joinville, *Vie de Saint Louis*, §§51–53. For a recent English translation, see Joinville, *Chronicles of the Crusades*, 155.

76. Ibid. See also the discussion of this passage by Chazan, *Medieval Jewry in Northern France*, 102–3.

77. Joinville, *Vie de Saint Louis*, §§31–32; *Chronicles of the Crusades*, 150.

78. Only one of the three surviving Hebrew accounts of the *Vikkuah* (Disputation) has been published, although the latest of these (Vat. ebr. 324, fourteenth century) is only fragmentary. A close comparison of the three versions is undertaken by Galinsky, "The Different Hebrew Versions of the 'Talmud Trial' of 1240 in Paris." Galinsky concludes that, while the Paris and the Moscow versions are closely related, the Moscow version (Moscow-Guenzburg 1390) is more likely the older and should, therefore, be considered as the standard version. A critical edition of the *Vikkuah* is a major desideratum in the field. But see Capelli, "Il processo di Parigi del 1240 contro il Talmud: Verso un'edizione critica del testo ebraico."

79. Merchavia, *The Church Versus Talmudic and Midrashic Literature, 500–1248*, 240ff., cited in Cohen, *Living Letters*, 323. The traditional dating of the burning of the books has been 1242 or 1244, but now revised to 1241–43, and very probably June 1241, by Rose, "When Was the Talmud Burnt at Paris?" I am grateful to Prof. Rose for bringing this article to my attention.

80. Recent scholars have tended to downplay the earlier tradition of viewing the Talmud Trial as primarily an inquisitorial hearing, pointing out that the formal procedures of medieval "inquisition" were still in its infancy. See Eisenberg, "Reading Medieval Religious Disputation," chap. 4.

81. For context, see Jordan, *The French Monarchy and the Jews*, who discusses the disputation at 137–39; and idem, *Louis IX and the Challenge of the Crusade*.

82. This is the conclusion reached by Jeffrey R. Woolf, "Maimonides Revised: The Case of the *Sefer Miswot Gadol*'; and idem, "Some Polemical Emphases in the *Sefer Miswot Gadol* of Rabbi Moses of Coucy."

83. Maccoby, *Judaism on Trial*, 164.

84. Important analyses are given in Dahan, ed., *Le brûlement du Talmud à Paris, 1242–1244*. See also Cohen, *Living Letters*, 317–25; and Eisenberg, "Reading Medieval Religious Disputation," particularly the appendices. All the relevant bibliography can be found in those two works.

85. There is some uncertainty about whether Yehiel ben Joseph responded to Nicholas Donin face to face or whether he had to answer to the judges instead.

86. On the accusations of blasphemy against the Virgin, see Jordan, "Marian Devotion and the Talmud Trial of 1240."

87. Cohen, *Friars and the Jews*, 63. Cohen's figures are slightly conjectural and have been disputed by others. See again Rose, "When Was the Talmud Burnt?"

88. For the dating of this manuscript of the *Bible Moralisée*, I follow John Lowden, *The Making of the Bibles Moralisées*, 1:4, who dates this manuscript to "around 1240 (say 1235 to 1245)." On the basis of the apparent allusion to the Paris disputation of 1240, I would incline toward a date of shortly after 1240. A detailed study of Jews in the earlier Vienna manuscript of the *Bible moralisée* is by Lipton, *Images of Intolerance*, whom I thank for generously responding to some of my inquires.

89. This argument was advanced by Morrow, "Disputation in Stone: Jews Imagined on the St. Stephen Portal of Paris Cathedral."

90. *CUP*, I:209–11. Cf. Grayzel, ed., *The Church and the Jews*, 1:279.

91. A generation of scholarly attention since the publication of *The Friars and the Jews* (1982) has nuanced the role of the twelfth century in charting an equally novel and ultimately dangerous path but has generally upheld Cohen's view on the importance of the thirteenth-century developments. Indeed, there is general scholarly consensus that the Dominicans during this period played a

formative role in the evolution of the medieval inquisition and that the Talmud Trial of 1240 constitutes an important marker in that evolution.

92. Thus, in a second disputation (*Vikkuah*) in Paris that took place some thirty years after the Talmud was first burned, the Jews actually seemed to recall the events of 1240 as a great victory over Donin. See Shatzmiller, *La deuxième controverse de Paris*, 45.

93. Cf. Dahan, "Les traductions latines de Thibaud de Sézanne," 101–3.

94. A copy of the "Excerpts" unequivocally attributed to Thibaut survives in a fourteenth-century codex at the Universitätsbibliothek Graz, MS 1530, fol. 57r–69v. The *Disputatio iudeorum contra christianos* (fol. 64v–68r) has been transcribed and translated by Sherwood, "Thibaut de Sezanne & the Disputation of the Jews Against the Christians," unpublished but accessed online September 30, 2012. I follow Sherwood's transcription and translation.

95. Ibid., 15: "listen to the prophet Hosea when he says, 'the sun and the moon will be darkened, the stars will extinguish their light, since the Lord will cry out from Zion, and heaven and earth will shake' [Matt 24; 29; Eccl 12: 2–3; Joel 2: 10–11]."

96. Ibid., 16–17: "Cum autem iudei contra hoc dicere non possent surrexerunt / et turbati sunt, confusi sunt veriti sunt. obmutuerrunt discesserunt dicen / tes adonay. adonay erramus. devi(n)cti summus quid faciemus / § Plurimi ergo eorum suum errorem derelinquentes fideliter. / in christum credentes baptizati sunt."

97. The *Pharetra* frequently accompanies the first collection of "Excerpts." It is included in the Graz manuscript and was also published several times in the late fifteenth century under the name Theobaldus de Saxonia (or Sexannia): by Peter Attendorn in 1493, Arnold von Köln in 1494, Heinrich Quentell in 1494, Conrad Kachelofen in 1495, and Melchiorem Lotter in 1499. I have not consulted the Graz MS, but several of the later published versions are accessible through Google Books. The texts are not all identical. Translation here is slightly modified from Dahan, *The Christian Polemic Against the Jews in the Middle Ages*, 85, who bases himself on Graz MS 1530.

98. MS Parma 2749 has never been published in its entirety. Translations of the opening section of the work are provided by Stein, "A Disputation on Moneylending Between Jews and Gentiles in Me'ir b. Simeons Milhemeth Miswah (Narbonne, 13th Cent.)"; other portions of the dialogue are translated in Chazan, *Daggers of Faith*.

99. Chazan, *Daggers of Faith*; and more recently, idem, *Fashioning Jewish Identity*, 105–14.

100. Cf. Chazan, "Archbishop Fuculdi and His Jews."

101. Stein, "A Disputation on Moneylending Between Jews and Gentiles," 47.

102. It might additionally be noted that the absorption of scholasticism in Jewish circles is a notable feature of late medieval Hebrew scholarship, suggesting that there is an element of Jewish acculturation of scholastic practices in addition to their involvement (and compulsion) in theological debates. For examples of the Jewish incorporation of Christian scholastic discourse, see Zonta, *Hebrew Scholasticism in the Fifteenth Century*.

103. Nachmanides, in his account of the disputation, tells us that he received a sum of 300 *solidi* from the king at the conclusion of the debate. The likelihood of this gift has been much commented upon, but a document in the Archives of the Crown of Aragon (ACA reg. 14, fol 70r.) dated February 25, 1265, records James's debt of that very amount to a Jewish magister of Girona named Bonastrug de Porta, who has often been identified as the same Nachmanides. Other interpretations of this payment have also been advanced. See most recently Vose, *Dominicans, Muslims, and Jews in the Medieval Crown of Aragon*, 145 n. 40.

104. The fullest treatment of this disputation is Chazan, *Barcelona and Beyond*. See also his *Daggers of Faith*.

105. Burns, "Christian-Islamic Confrontation in the West: The Thirteenth-Century Dream of Conversion"; and idem, "The Barcelona 'Disputation' of 1263: Conversion and Talmud in Jewish-Christian Relations."

106. Vose, *Dominicans, Muslims, and Jews*, 155.

107. Iconographic depictions of Jewish-Christian disputations also begin to cluster in the Iberian peninsula beginning in the late twelfth century. See Patton, *Art of Estrangement: Redefining Jews in Reconquest Spain*, 42–47.

108. Grayzel, ed., *The Church and the Jews*, 27 (February 1233), 324–25.

109. See Vose, *Dominicans, Muslims, and Jews*, 119 and also 116. It should be noted that the earliest extant catalogue from St. Catherine's dates to the eighteenth century. Fortunately, data from this inventory can be checked against other medieval documentation, and a number of medieval manuscripts do survive in good condition in the library of the University of Barcello.

110. Among other evidence, a letter survives between Hasdai ibn Shaprut (Jewish emissary at the court of the Cordoban caliphate in the ninth century) and the Khazar king. For a comprehensive study of the kingdom, see Brook, *The Jews of Khazaria*. On Halevi's poetry and life, see the excellent recent biographies by Halkin, *Yehuda Halevi*; and Scheindlin, *The Song of Distant Love*.

111. See Shear, *The Kuzari and the Shaping of Jewish Identity, 1167–1900*. The *Kuzari* first circulated under the Hebrew title, *The Book of Refutation and Proof in Behalf of the Despised Religion*.

112. On Rodrigo's role in the Reconquest, see O'Callaghan, *Reconquest and Crusade in Medieval Spain*, passim. The following discussion draws from my article, "From Dialogue to Disputation in the Age of Archbishop Rodrigo Jiménez de Rada."

113. Pick, *Conflict and Coexistence: Archbishop Rodrigo and the Muslims and Jews of Medieval Spain*, chap. 4–5.

114. Rodrigo Jiménez de Rada, *Dialogus libri uita*.

115. Pick, *Conflict and Coexistence*, 138–64.

116. See Fishman, *Becoming the People of the Talmud*, esp. chap. 5. Fishman further suggests, especially in chap. 3, that this process of "textualization" was informed by contemporary classroom practices and pedagogical ideals within Christian circles. The medieval culture of disputation would certainly seem, to me at least, a poignant affirmation of this paradigm of cross-cultural hybridity, even if there is much nuancing of the direction of the flow of influence that remains to be done.

117. The eventual impact of this translation was ultimately quite minimal. See Burman, "Las Navas de Tolosa and *Liber Alchorani*: Reflections on Iberian Christians and the Qur'an."

118. Pick, *Conflict and Coexistence*, 165.

119. Ibid., chap. 5.

120. *Dialogus*, prologue, ll. 30–31, 176. Pick, *Conflict and Coexistence*, 138.

121. On conversion among Jewish youths, see Jordan, "Adolescence and Conversion in the Middle Ages: A Research Agenda." The exact date of Christiani's birth is unknown, but 1200–1210 seems likely, given that he was still active in the late 1260s and died in Sicily around 1274.

122. On Paul Christiani's Jewish background, see Chazan, *Barcelona and Beyond*, esp. 24–27.

123. Rosenthal, "A Religious Disputation between a Jew called Menahem and the convert Pablo Christiani [Hebrew]," 62. See also Robert Chazan, "Confrontation in the Synagogue of Narbonne: A Christian Sermon and a Jewish Reply," esp. 445–47.

124. There are several translations of Nachmanides's *Vikuah*. Here I cite the most recent one (it is only a partial translation) offered by Nina Caputo, in Constable, ed., *Medieval Iberia*, 332. For a slightly different translation, see Maccoby, *Judaism on Trial*, 103.

125. The Latin text was first printed by Denifle, "Quellen zur Disputation Pablos Christiani mit Mose Nachmani zu Barcelona 1263"; and again by Yitzhak Baer, "On the Disputation of R.

Yehiel of Paris and R. Moses ben Nahman [in Hebrew]." It is translated in Maccoby, *Judaism on Trial*, 147–50.

126. An overview of the textual history of the Hebrew text is given in Maccoby, *Judaism on Trial*, 76–78. See as well Chazan, *Barcelona and Beyond*, passim.

127. See Chazan, *Barcelona and Beyond*, chap. 2.

128. Denifle, "Quellen," 231: "presentibus domino rege Aragonum et multis aliis baronibus, prelatis, religiosis et multibus in palacio domini Regis Barchinone." Cf. Maccoby, *Judaism on Trial*, 147.

129. This is the English translation given by Chavel in *Ramban: Writings and Discourses*, 2:668. For the Hebrew text of the *Vikuah*, I have consulted the edition by Nachmanides of Gerona, *Kitvei Rabbenu Moshe ben Nahman*, 1:302–20, here 308. I am grateful to Dr. David Freidenreich (Colby College) for his assistance with the Hebrew text of the *Vikuah*. For a slightly different translation, see Caputo's rendition in *Medieval Iberia*, 336.

130. Information on the origins of the convent of St. Catherine's are taken from Ortoll i Martín, "Algunas consideraciones sobre la iglesia de Santa Caterina de Barcelona," here and below at 49. The most thorough investigation of this important thirteenth-century convent remains the unpublished dissertation by Andres i Blanch, "El Convent de Santa Caterina de Barcelona. S. XIII," which I consulted at the University of Barcelona's History Faculty library.

131. The latter charter is preserved in the library of the University of Barcelona (MS. 241, fol. 379) and transcribed by Andres i Blanch, "El Convent de Santa Caterina," doc. 102.

132. Results of the excavations are on display in the Espai Santa Caterina, a division of the Museu d'Història de Barcelona (MUHBA), located in the rear of the current market. Published and unpublished reports of the excavations were consulted at the Servei d'Arqueologia i Centre de documentació Patrimonial del MUHBA in Barcelona. I am grateful to Carles Vela i Aulesa of the Consejo Superior de Investigaciones Científicas and to Phil Banks of the University of Barcelona for helping me locate information pertaining to Santa Caterina.

133. Shatzmiller, *La deuxième controverse*, 56 (for the Hebrew), 74 (French translation). I am grateful to Dr. Harvey Haimes of Ben Gurion University for pointing this out to me.

134. The late date of the surviving copy (fourteenth century) may also explain the inconsistencies in the dates given for the encounter. The years 1269, 1271, and 1273 are all given. See Shatzmiller, *La deuxième controverse*, 17–18.

135. Maccoby, *Judaism on Trial*, 130, translates the phrase as "held in private." Chavel renders the Hebrew phrase "without ostentation": *Ramban*, 2:683. Both achieve the intended meaning, although again we might stress the contrast with the publicity of the second and the fourth meetings.

136. Caputo trans. in *Medieval Iberia*, 337. Cf. Chavel, *Ramban*, 2:685.

137. Caputo trans. in *Medieval Iberia*, 338.

138. Denifle, "Quellen," 233–34: "Item cum non posset respondere et esset pluries publice confuses, et tam Iudei quam Christiani contra eum insultarent, dixit pertinacitor coram omnibus, quod nullo modo responderet, quia Iudei ei prohibuerant, et Christiani scilicet fr. P. de Janua et quidam probi homines civitatis ei miserant dicere consulendo quod nullo modo responderet. De quo mendacio per dictum fratrum P. et per probos hominess fuit publice redargutus. Unde patet, quod per mendacia a disputacione supterfugere nitebatur." Cf. Maccoby, *Judaism on Trial*, 150.

139. Nina Caputo, *Nachmanides in Medieval Catalonia*, 101.

140. Chazan, *Fashioning Jewish Identity*, 331–32.

141. Caputo, *Nachmanides in Medieval Catalonia*, 107.

142. Martin Cohen, "Reflections on the Text and Context of the Disputation of Barcelona." This is the one point Maccoby concedes in his lengthy critique of Cohen in *Judaism on Trial*, 73.

143. In addition to Vose, *Dominicans, Muslims and Jews*, see also the critique of modern scholarship on the disputation provided by Caputo, *Nachmanides in Medieval Catalonia*, 95–107.

144. Watson, "Censorship and Cultural Change in Late-Medieval England: Vernacular Theology, the Oxford Translation Debate, and Arundel's Constitutions of 1409."

145. Essential for the medieval literary dimensions of the representations of *Ecclesia* and *Synagoga* is Pflaum, "Der allegorische Streit zwischen Synagoge und Kirchse." The absence of a more recent and comprehensive study of the literary dimensions of Church versus Synagogue remains a serious desideratum.

146. There are two surviving manuscripts of this work: Bibliothèque Nationale MS. Français 837, and Bibliothèque municipale de Tours MS. 948. The text has been edited three times (but never translated). The most recent edition is that of Serper, "Le débat entre synagogue et église au XIIIe siècle."

147. Ibid., 314.

148. The contrasting images of Ecclesia and Synagoga are one of the most formulaic in medieval iconography. For sculptural as well as manuscript and painted representations of this theme, see Schreckenberg, *The Jews in Christian Art*, chap. 2 and passim. The most accomplished book-length study of this important motif now is Rowe, *The Jew, the Cathedral and the Medieval City*. On Jews in medieval art more generally, see Lipton, *Images of Intolerance*; and Strickland, *Saracens, Demons, and Jews*, chap. 3. An excellent comparison between anti-Jewish theology and iconography in the context of Chartres Cathedral is Harris, "The Performative Terms of Jewish Iconoclasm and Conversion in Two Saint Nicholas Windows at Chartres Cathedral."

149. Rowe, "Rethinking Ecclesia and Synagoga," at 279; and eadem, *The Jew, the Cathedral and the Medieval City*, passim.

150. The text of this debate is found in Bibliotèque Nationale, MS. Français 19152. It has been edited by Pflaum, "Poems of Religious Disputations in the Middle Ages [Hebrew]."

151. Ibid., 459: "Ne t'entent pas, por ce c'oscurement paroles. / Parole a moi François et espon tes paroles!"

152. See the detailed study of this subject by Fudeman, *Vernacular Voices*, esp. 1–25.

153. Pflaum, "Poems of Religious Disputations," 459: "ce est contre raison et est plus que merveille . . . quar testate raison a ici contraire . . . ge ne puis pas voeir, con raison s'i adonge . . . mais n'as pas raison traite."

154. Ibid., 460: "deus-hom pot ici, que hom seus ne pot faire / Ne sor ce que dieus fist, ne doit nus raison querre."

155. Ibid., 475.

156. Both dialogues appear in Conlee, ed., *Middle English Debate Poetry*, 168–77 and 179–91, respectively.

157. Ibid., 179.

158. Ibid., 179–80, ll. 9–10, 23–24.

159. Ibid., 178.

160. For Llull's apologetic use of dialogue, see especially Friedlein, *Der Dialog bei Ramon Llull*. See also Johnston, *The Evangelical Rhetoric of Ramon Llull*; and Lohr, "Ramon Llull and Thirteenth-Century Religious Dialogue." See as well the excellent recent studies by Ames, *Righteous Persecution*; and Vose, *Dominicans, Muslims, and Jews*.

161. Ben-Shalom, "Between Official and Private Dispute: The Case of Christian Spain and Provence in the Late Middle Ages."

162. The *Frankfurter Dirigierrolle* (1343) begins with a confrontation between Hebrew prophets and a group of contemporary fourteenth-century Jews, in which the figure of St. Augustine serves as

moderator. Jews are portrayed as not so much interested in theological engagement as insulting representatives of Christianity, including Jesus himself. The 1493 *Frankfurter Passionspiel* by Nuremberg dramatist Hans Folz differs considerably, presenting a theological disputation that encourages lay Christian involvement in religious dialogue. See Wenzel, *"Do worden die Judden alle geschant*; nuanced by Martin, "Dramatized Disputations: Late Medieval German Dramatizations of Jewish-Christian Religious Disputations, Church Policy, and Local Social Climates."

### CONCLUSIONS: THE MEDIEVAL CULTURE OF DISPUTATION

1. See the introduction by Jaeger, ed., *Magnificence and the Sublime in Medieval Aesthetics*, 1–16.

2. See Snyder, *Writing the Scene of Speaking*, esp. chaps. 4–5.

3. Quoted from *Tasso's Dialogues*, 40–41.

4. Tyler, "Ode to Dialog on the Occasion of the Un-for-seen," 293. Cf. Marsh, "Dialogue and Discussion in the Renaissance," 265: "The Humanist dialogue arose in Italy around 1400 . . . [and] reflects the new philosophical freedom and eclecticism which were fostered by the rise of mercantile communes and by the weakening of papal authority through schism." See also idem, *The Quattrocento Dialogue*. To underscore Tasso's engagement with the Middle Ages, it might additionally be noted that he was best known for the poem *La Gerusalemme liberata* (Jerusalem Delivered, 1580), in which he depicts a highly imaginative version of the combats between Christians and Muslims during the siege of Jerusalem at the end of the First Crusade.

5. Quoted from the "Réponses aux secondes objections" in *The Philosophical Writings of Descartes*, 2:112.

6. John Locke, *Essay Concerning Human Understanding* (1690), bk. III, chap. 10, para. 9.

7. This point was well made by Lynn Thorndike over eighty years ago: "The Survival of Mediaeval Intellectual Interests into Early Modern Times."

# BIBLIOGRAPHY

Note: Primary source authors before 1500 are listed by first name. If no name is known, the work is listed alphabetically.

## ABBREVIATIONS

CCSL     Corpus Christianorum, Series Latina. Turnhout: Brepols, 1966–.

CCCM     Corpus Christianorum, Continuatio Mediaevalis. Turnhout: Brepols, 1966-.

*CHLMP*     *The Cambridge History of Later Medieval Philosophy.* Ed. Norman Kretzman, Anthony Kenny, and Jan Pinborg. Cambridge: Cambridge University Press, 1982.

CSEL     Corpus Scriptorum Ecclesiasticorum Latinorum. Vienna: apud C. Geroldi filium etc., 1866-.

*CUP*     *Chartularium Universitatis Parisiensis.* Ed. H. Denifle and E. Chatelain. 4 vols. Paris: Delalain, 1889–97.

MGH     Monumenta Germaniae Historica. Hannover: Hahn, 1826-.

*PL*     *Patrologiae cursus completus. Series Latina.* Ed. Jacques-Paul Migne. 221 vols. Paris: apud Garnier Fratres, 1844–1864.

## MANUSCRIPTS CITED

Barcelona, Archives of the Crown of Aragon, reg. 14, fol. 70r
Barcelona, University of Barcelona, MS 241
Cambrai, MS 259
Eton, MS Eton College 130
Graz, Universitätsbibliothek Graz, MS 1530
Heidelberg, Universitätsbibliothek, Codex Heidelbergensis 71
London, British Library, Additional 8166
Moscow, Moscow-Guenzburg 1390
Oxford, Jesus College MS 11.
Oxford, MS Bodley 482 (S.C. 2046)
Paris, Bibliothèque Nationale de France, ms. français 837, 19152
Paris, Bibliothèque Nationale de France, ms. lat. 11560, 2923, 14799, and 16558
Parma, MS 2749
Rome, Biblioteca apostolica vaticana, ebr. 324
Tours, Bibliothèque municipale de Tours MS 948

PRINTED PRIMARY SOURCES

*Acta capitulorum generalis ordinis Praedicatorum.* Vol. 1: *Ab anno 1220 usque as annum 1303.* Ed. B. M. Reichert. Monumenta Ordinis Fratrum Praedicatorum Historica 3. Rome-Stuttgart: In domo generalitia, 1898.

*Acta capitulorum provinciae Romanae* (1243–1344). Ed. T. Käppeli and A. Dondaine. Monumenta Ordinis Fratrum Praedicatorum Historica 20. Rome: Institutum Historicum Fratrum Praedicatorum, 1941.

*Ad Innocentium Pontificium, in persona Franciae episcoporum (epistola 885).* PL 182: 540–544.

Adam of Balsham. *Ars Disserendi.* In *Twelfth-Century Logic: Texts and Studies,* vol. 1, *Adam Balsamiensis Parvipontani Ars Disserendi,* ed. L. Minio-Paluello. Rome: Edizioni di Storia e Letteratura, 1956.

Adelard of Bath. *Adelard of Bath, Conversations with His Nephew.* Ed and trans. Charles Burnett. Cambridge: Cambridge University Press, 1998.

Alcuin of York. *De dialectica.* PL 101: 949–75.

Anselm of Canterbury. *Memorials of St. Anselm.* Ed. R. W. Southern and F. S. Schmitt, O.S.B. Auctores Britannici Medii Aevi 1. Oxford: British Academiy and Oxford University Press, 1969.

———. *S. Anselmi opera omnia.* Ed. Franciscus Salesius Schmitt. 6 vols. Edinburgh: Thomas Nelson & Sons, 1940–61.

Anselm of Havelberg. *Dialogi. (Antikeimenon contrapositorum sub dialogo conscriptum, ad venerabilem papam Eugenium III).* PL 188: 1139–1248.

Augustine. *Against the Academics.* Trans. J. J. O'Meara. Ancient Christian Writers 12. Westminster, Md.: Newman, 1950.

———. *Soliloquies and Immortality of the Soul.* Trans. Gerard Watson. Warminster: Aris & Phillips, 1990.

Aristotle. *The Complete Works of Aristotle: The Revised Oxford Translation.* 2 vols. Ed. Jonathan Barnes. Princeton, N.J.: Princeton University Press, 1984.

———. *Poetics.* Trans. Malcolm Heath. London: Penguin, 1996.

Auxilius Presbyter. *Liber cuiusdem requirentis et respondentis.* PL 129: 1073–1102.

———. *Tractatus qui infensor et defensor dicitur.* PL 129: 1101–12.

Bernard of Clairvaux. *Sancti Bernardi Opera.* Ed. Jean Leclercq, C. H. Talbot, and Henri-Marie Rochais. 8 vols. Rome: Editiones Cistercienses, 1977.

———. *The Steps of Humility.* Trans. George Bosworth Burch. Cambridge, Mass.: Harvard University Press, 1940.

Berno of Reichenau. *Dialogus.* PL 142: 1087–98.

Blumenkranz, Bernhard. "Altercatio Aecclesie contra Synagogam: Texte inédit du Xe siècle." *Revue du Moyen Âge Latin* 10 (1954): 5–159.

Boethius. *Comentarii in Librum Aristotelis Perihermeneias.* Ed. C. Meiser. Leipzig: Teubner, 1880.

*Chartularium Universitatis Parisiensis.* Ed. H. Denifle and E. Chatelain. 4 vols. Paris: Delalain, 1889–97.

Cicero. *De officiis.* Ed and trans. Walter Miller. Loeb Classical Library. Cambridge, Mass.: Harvard University Press, 1913.

———. *De oratore.* Ed and trans. E. W. Sutton and H. Rackham. Loeb Classical Library. Cambridge, Mass.: Harvard University Press, 1948.

———. *Tusculan Disputations.* Ed and trans. J. E. King. Loeb Classical Library. Cambridge, Mass.: Harvard University Press, 2001.

Conrad of Hirsau. *Accessus ad auctores; Bernard d'Utrecht; Conrad d'Hirsau.* Ed. R. B. C. Huygens. Leiden: Brill, 1970.

———. *Dialogus de Mundi contemptu vel amore attribué à Conrad d'Hirsau.* Ed. R. Bultot. Louvain: Nauwelaerts, 1966.

*Decrees of the Ecumenical Councils.* Ed. and trans. Norman P. Tanner. London: Sheed and Ward, 1990.

Descartes, René. *The Philosophical Writings of Descartes.* Trans John Cottingham, Robert Stoothoff, and Dugald Murdoch. 2 vols. Cambridge: Cambridge University Press, 1984.

*Dialogus Beatae Mariae et Anselmi de Passione Domini. PL* 159: 272–90.

Diogenes Laertius. *Lives of the Ancient Philosophers.* Ed. and trans. R. D. Hicks. Cambridge, Mass.: Harvard University Press, 1959.

Dümmler, Ernst Ludwig, ed. *Auxilius und Vulgarius: Quellen und Forschungen zu Geschichte des Papsttums im Anfange des Zehnten Jahrhunderts.* Leipzig: S. Hirzel, 1866.

Eadmer. *The Life of St. Anselm.* Ed. and trans. R. W. Southern. Oxford Medieval Texts. Oxford: Oxford University Press, 1972.

———. *The Life of St Anselm, Archbishop of Canterbury.* Ed. and trans. Richard W. Southern. London: Thomas Nelson, 1962.

*Enchiridion musices.* In *Strunk's Source Readings in Music History.* Ed. Leo Treitler. Rev. ed. New York: Norton, 1998. 199–210.

Erickson, Raymond, ed. *Musica Enchiriadis and Scolica Enchiriadis.* New Haven, Conn.: Yale University Press, 1995.

Eugenius Vulgarius. *De causa Formosiana. PL* 129: 1101–12.

Eusebius. *Ecclesiastical History.* Ed and trans. Kirsopp Lake. Loeb Classical Library. Cambridge, Mass.: Harvard University Press, 1980.

Gerald of Wales. *Itinerarium Kambriae.* Ed. J. F. Dimock. Vol. 6 of *Giraldi Cambrensis Opera.* Rerum Britannicarum medii aevii scriptores. London, 1868. Reprint Millwood, N.Y.: Kraus, 1964–66.

———. *The Journey Through Wales and The Description of Wales.* Trans. Lewis Thorpe. New York: Penguin, 1978.

Gibbons, Richard, ed. *Beati Gosvini vita . . . Aquicinctensis monasterii abbatis septimi, a duobus diversis ejusdem coenobii monachis separatim exarata; e veteribus ms. nunc primum edita.* Douai, 1620.

Gilbert Crispin. *Gisleberti Crispini Disputatio Iudei et Christiani.* Ed. Bernhard Blumenkranz. Stromata Patristica et Mediaevalia 3. Utrecht: Ultraiecti/Antiverpiae, 1956.

———. *The Works of Gilbert Crispin, Abbot of Westminster.* Ed. Anna Sapir Abulafia and G. R. Evans. Auctores Britannici Medii Aevi 8. London: British Academy and Oxford University Press, 1986.

Godfrey de Clara-Valle. *Epistola ad Albinum cardinalem et episcopum Albanensem. PL* 185: 587–96

Gratian. *Gratian: The Treatise on Laws (Decretum DD 1–20) with the Ordinary Gloss.* Trans. Augustine Thompson, O.P., and Games Gordley. Washington, D.C.: Catholic University Press, 1993.

Gregory the Great. *Dialogues.* Trans. Odo John Zimmerman. New York: Fathers of the Church, 1959.

Guitmund of Aversa. *De corporis et sanguinis Christi veritate in Eucharistia. PL* 149: 1427–94.

Gwara, Scott, ed. *Latin Colloquies from Pre-Conquest Britain.* Toronto: Pontifical Institute of Medieval Studies, 1996.

Happe, Peter, ed. *English Mystery Plays: A Selection.* London: Penguin, 1975.

Hauréau, Barthélemy. *Notices et extraits de quelques manuscrits latins de la Bibliothèque Nationale.* 6 vols. Paris: Librairie C. Klincksiek, 1891–96.

Herman-Judah. *Hermannus Quondam Judaeus: Opusculum de Conversione Sua.* Ed. Gerlinde Niemeyer. MGH Quellen zu Geistesgechichte 4. Weimar: Böhlaus Nachfolger, 1963.

Hildebert of Lavardin. *Sermones.* PL 171: 339–964.

Honorius Augustodunensis. *Clavis physicae.* Ed. Paolo Lucentini. Temi e Testi 21. Rome: Storia e
Letteratura, 1974.

———. *Cognitio vitae.* PL 40: 1003–32.

———. *L'Elucidarium et les lucidaires: Contribution, par l'histoire d'un texte, à l'histoire des croyances
religieuses en France au moyen âge.* Ed. Yves Lefèvre. Bibliothèque des Écoles Françaises
d'Athènes et de Rome 180. Paris, de Boccard, 1954.

———. *The Seal of Blessed Mary.* Trans. Amelia Carr. Peregrina Translation Series 18. Toronto:
Peregrina, 1991.

———. *Sigillum Sanctae Mariae.* PL 172: 495–518.

*Hora nona sabbati.* In *Notices et Extraits des Manuscrits de la Bibliothèque Nationale,* ed. B. Hauréau.
Vol. 6. Paris, 1896. 310–17.

Hugh of St. Victor. *De institutione novitiorum.* PL 176: 925–52.

———. *De vanitate mundi.* PL 176: 703–40.

———. *The Didascalicon of Hugh of St. Victor.* Trans. Jerome Taylor. New York: Columbia University Press, 1961.

———. *Hugh of Saint-Victor: Selected Spiritual Writings.* London: Faber and Faber, 1962.

———. *Hugonis de Sancto Victore Didascalicon, De Studio Legendi: A Critical Text,* Ed. Charles
Henry Buttimer. Washington, D.C.: Catholic University Press, 1939.

———. *Hugonis de Sancto Victore Opera Propaedeutica.* Ed. Roger Baron. Notre Dame, Ind.: University of Notre Dame Press, 1966.

———. *L'oeuvre de Hugues de Saint-Victor.* Ed. H. B. Feiss and P. Sicard. Turnhout: Brepols, 1997.

———. *Soliloquy on the Earnest Money of the Soul.* Trans. Kevin Herbert. Milwaukee: Marquette
University Press, 1956.

Humbert of Romans. *Opera de vita regulari.* Ed. J. J. Berthier. Paris: Typis A. Befani, 1888.

*In sublimi solio.* In *Notices et extraits des manuscrits de la Bibliothèque Nationale.* Ed. B. Hauréau. Vol.
6. Paris, 1896. 306–08.

Jacques de Vitry. *Illustrative Stories from the Sermones Vulgares of Jacques de Vitry.* Ed. Thomas F.
Crane. London: Nutt, 1890.

Jean de Jandun. *Tractatus de laudibus Parisius.* Paris: Imprimerie Impériale, 1867.

Jean de Joinville. *Chronicles of the Crusades.* Trans. Caroline Smith. New York: Penguin, 2008.

———. *Vie de Saint Louis.* Ed. Jacques Monfrin. Paris: J. Vrin, 1995.

John of Lodi. *Vita B. Petri Damiani.* PL 144: 114–46.

John of Salisbury. *Metalogicon.* Ed. J. B. Hall. CCCM 98. Turnhout: Brepols, 1991.

———. *The Metalogicon of John of Salisbury: A Twelfth-Century Defense of the Verbal and Logical Arts
of the Trivium.* Trans. Daniel McGarry. Berkeley: University of California Press, 1962.

John Scotus Eriugena. *Eriugena: Periphyseon (The Division of Nature).* Trans. I. P. Sheldon-Williams,
rev. John J. O'Meara. Washington, D.C.: Dumbarton Oaks, 1987.

———. *Periphyseon (De divisione naturae).* PL 122: 411–1022.

Jordan of Saxony. *Libellus de principiis Ordinis Praedicatorum.* Ed. M.-H. Laurent. Monumenta
ordinis fratrum Praedicatorum historica 16. Monumenta Historica Sancti Patris Nostri Dominici 2. Rome: Institutum Historicum Fratrum Praedicatorum, 1935.

Lanfranc of Pavia. *Commentarius in Epistolas Pauli.* PL 150: 101–408.

———. *De corpore et sanguine Domini.* PL 150: 407–42.

Locke, John. *An Essay Concerning Human Understanding.* London, 1689.

Menner, Robert J., ed. *The Poetical Dialogues of Solomon and Saturn.* New Haven, Conn.: Yale University Press, 1973.

*Monumenta diplomatica S. Dominici.* Ed. Vladimir J. Koudelka, O.P., and Raymundo J. Loenertz, O.P. Monumenta ordinis fratrum Praedicatorum historica 25. Rome: Institutum Historicum Fratrum Praedicatorum, 1966.

Nachmanides of Gerona. *Ramban: Writings and Discourses.* Ed. and trans. Charles B. Chavel. 2 vols. New York: Shilo, 1978.

———. *Vikuah.* In *Kitvei Rabbenu Moshe ben Nahman.* Ed. Charles B. Chavel. Jerusalem: Mossad ha-Rav Kook, 1963. 1:302–20.

Odo of Tournai. *On Original Sin and A Disputation with the Jew, Leo, Concerning the Advent of Christ, the Son of God: Two Theological Treatises.* Ed. Irven M. Resnick. Philadelphia: University of Pennsylvania Press, 1994.

Orderic Vitalis. *The Ecclesiastical History of Orderic Vitalis.* Ed. and trans. Marjorie Chibnall. 6 vols. Oxford: Oxford University Press, 1968–80.

Otto of Freising. *The Deeds of Frederick of Barbarossa.* Trans. Charles C. Mierow. Toronto: University of Toronto Press, 1994.

*The Owl and the Nightingale.* Ed. J. W. H. Atkins. Cambridge: Cambridge University Press, 1922.

*The Owl and the Nightingale.* Ed. Eric Gerald Stanley. London: Thomas Nelson, 1960.

*The Owl and the Nightingale: Text and Translation.* Ed. Neil Cartlidge. Exeter: University of Exeter Press, 2001.

Paschasius Radbertus. *De corpore et sanguine Domini. PL* 120: 1255–1350.

Peter Abelard. *Historia Calamitatum.* Ed. J. Monfrin. Paris: J. Vrin, 1959.

———. *The Letters of Abelard and Heloise.* Trans. Betty Radice, rev. Michael Clanchy. New York: Penguin, 2003.

———. *Letters of Peter Abelard: Beyond the Personal.* Trans. Jan M. Ziolkowski. Washington, D.C.: Catholic University of America Press, 2008.

———. *Peter Abaelards philosophische Schriften.* Ed. B. Geyer. Beiträge zur Geschichte der Philosophie und Theologie des Mittelalters 21. Münster: Aschendorff, 1933.

———. *Peter Abelard: Collationes.* Ed. and trans. John Marenbon and Giovanni Orlandi. Oxford Medieval Texts. Oxford: Oxford University Press, 2001.

———. *Peter Abelard: Letters IX–XIV: An Edition with an Introduction.* Ed. Edmé Renno Smits. Groningen: Rijksuniversiteit, 1983.

———. "Peter Abelard *Soliloquium*: A Critical Edition." Ed. Charles Burnett. *Studi Medievali* 25 (1984): 857–94.

———. *Petrus Abaelardus: Dialectica.* 2nd ed. Ed. L. M. de Rijk. Assen: Van Gorcum, 1970.

Peter Damian. *Die Briefe des Petrus Damiani.* Ed. Kurt Reindel. 4 vols. Munich: MGH, 1983–93.

———. *Letters 1–30.* Trans. Owen J. Blum. Washington, D.C.: Catholic University of America Press, 1989.

———. *Letters 61–90.* Trans. Owen J. Blum. Washington, D.C.: Catholic University of America Press, 1992.

Peter of Blois. *Contra perfidiam Judaeorum. PL* 207: 825–70.

Peter of Celle. *The Letters of Peter of Celle.* Ed. and trans. Julian Haseldine. Oxford Medieval Texts. Oxford: Oxford University Press, 2001.

Peter the Chanter. *Petri Cantoris Parisiensis Verbum abbreviatum: Textus Conflatus.* Ed. Monique Boutry. CCCM 196. Turnhout: Brepols, 2004.

————. *Summa de sacramentis et animae consiliis.* Ed. Jean-Abert Dugauquier. Louvain: Nauwelaerts, 1954.

————. *Verbum adbreviatum. PL* 205: 1–554.

Peter Damian. *Die Briefe des Petrus Damiani.* Ed. Kurt Reindel. Munich: Monumenta Germaniae Historica, 1983–93. 4 vols.

————. *Letters 1–30.* Trans. Owen J. Blum. Washington, D.C.: Catholic University of America Press, 1989.

Petrus Alfonsi. *Dialogi contra Iudaeos. PL* 157: 527–672.

————. *Epistola ad peripateticos.* In John Victor Tolan, *Petrus Alfonsi and His Medieval Readers.* Gainesville: University Press of Florida, 1993. 164–72.

————. *Petrus Alfonsi: Dialogue Against the Jews.* Trans. Irven M. Resnick. Washington, D.C.: Catholic University of America Press, 2006.

Philip of Harvengt. *De institutione clericorum. PL* 203: 665–1206.

Philip the Chancellor. *Motets and Prosulas.* Ed. Thomas B. Payne. Middleton, Wis.: A-R Editions, 2011.

Plato. *Plato's Epistles.* Ed. and trans. Glenn Murrow. Indianapolis: Bobbs-Merrill, 1961.

Pseudo-Anselm. *De custodia interioris hominis.* In *Memorials of St. Anselm,* ed. R. W. Southern and F. S. Schmitt, O.S.B. Auctores Britannici Medii Aevi 1. London: British Academy and Oxford University Press, 1969. 354–60.

Ratherius of Verona. *Excerptum ex dialogo confessionali.* In *Ratherii Veronensis Praeloquiorum libri IV.* Ed. Peter R. L. Reid. CCCM 46A. Turnhout: Brepols, 1984. 219–265.

Ratramnus. *De corpore et sanguine Domini. PL* 121: 125–170.

*Readings in Western Civilization.* Vol. 4, *Medieval Europe.* Ed. Julius Kirschner and Karl F. Morrison. Chicago: University of Chicago Press, 1986.

Robert of Melun. *Oeuvres de Robert de Melun.* Ed. Raymond Martin. Louvain: Spicilegium Sacrum Lovaniense, 1932.

Rodrigo Jiménez de Rada. *Dialogus libri uita.* Ed. Juan Fernández Valverde and Juan Antonio Estévez Sola. CCCM 72C. Turnhout: Brepols, 1999.

Rupert of Deutz. *Altercatio monachi et clerici. PL* 170: 537–42.

————. *Super quaedam capitula regulae divi benedicti abbatis. PL* 170: 447–538.

Searle, Eleanor, ed. and trans. *The Chronicle of Battle Abbey.* Oxford: Oxford University Press, 1980.

Sigebert of Gembloux. *Liber de scriptoribus ecclesiasticis. PL* 160: 547–92.

Siger of Brabant. *Les Questions super librum de causis de Siger de Brabant.* Ed. A. Marlasca. Louvain: Publications Universitaires de Louvain, 1972.

Stephen of Tournai. *Les Disputationes de Simon de Tournai.* Ed. Joseph Warichez. Louvain: Spicilegium Sacrum Lovaniense, 1932.

Stevenson, W. H., ed. *Early Scholastic Colloquies.* Oxford: Clarendon, 1929.

Theoduin of Liege. *Ad Henricum regem contra Brunonem et Berengarium epistola. PL* 146: 1439–42.

Thomas Aquinas. *Quaestiones Disputatae.* Ed. Pierre Mandonnet. Paris: Lethielleux, 1925.

————. *Quaestiones Quodlibetales.* Ed. Pierre Mandonnet. Paris: Lethielleux, 1926.

————. *S. Thomae Aquinatis opera omnia.* Parma, 1852–72.

————. *S. Thomae Aquinatis opuscula omnia.* Ed. Pierre Mandonnet. Paris: Lethielleux, 1927.

————. *Summa Theologiae.* Blackfriars ed. New York: McGraw-Hill, 1964.

Thomas of Cantimpré. *Bonum universale de apibus.* Douai: Balthazar Beller, 1627.

Thomas of Morigny. *Disputatio catholicorum patrum Adversus dogmati Petri Abaelardi. PL* 180: 283–328.

Torquato Tasso. *Tasso's Dialogues*. Trans. Carnes Lord and Dain A. Trafton. Berkeley: University of California Pres, 1982.

Vincent of Beauvais. *De eruditione filiorum nobilium*. Ed. Arpad Steiner. Cambridge: Medieval Academy of America, 1938.

*Vita Lanfranci. PL* 150: 29–58.

*Vita venerabilis Bosonis. PL* 150: 723–34.

Vital of Blois. *Geta*. In *La "Comedie" latine en France au douzième siècle*, ed. G. Cohen. Paris: Belles-Lettres, 1931. 1: 1–57. And in *Three Latin Comedies*, ed. Keith Bate. Toronto: Pontifical Institute of Medieval Studies, 1976. 15–34.

*Vitas sanctorum patrum emeritensium*. Ed A. Maya Sánchez. CCSL 116. Turnhout: Brepols, 1992.

*Vitas sanctorum patrum emeritensium*. Trans. Joseph N. Garvin. Washington, D.C.: Catholic University of America Press, 1946.

Walter of Châtillon. *Moralisch-Satirische Gedichte Walters von Châtillon*. Ed. Karl Strecker. Heidelberg: C. Winter, 1929.

———. *Tractatus sive Dialogus contra Iudaeos. PL* 209: 423–58.

William of Auvergne. *Selected Spiritual Writings*. Ed. Roland J. Teske. Toronto: Pontifical Institute of Medieval Studies: 2011.

William of St. Amour. *William of Saint Amour: De periculis novissimorum temporum*. Ed. G. Geltner. Leuven: Peeters, 2008.

William of St. Thierry. *Disputatio adversus Petrum Abaelardum. PL* 180: 249–82.


SECONDARY SOURCES


Abulafia, Anna Sapir. "The *Ars disputandi* of Gilbert Crispin, Abbot of Westminster." In *Ad fontes: Opstellen aangeboden aan Prof. Dr. C. van de Kieft*, ed. C. M. Cappon et al. Amsterdam: Verloren, 1984. 139–52.

———. *Christians and Jews in Dispute*. Aldershot: Ashgate, 1998.

———. *Christians and Jews in the Twelfth-Century Renaissance*. London: Routledge, 1995.

———. "Christians Disputing Disbelief: St Anselm, Gilbert Crispin and Pseudo-Anselm." In *Religiongespräche im Mittelalter*, ed. Bernard Lewis and Friedrich Niewöhner. Wolfenbütteler Mittelalter-Studien 4. Wiesbaden: Harrassowitz, 1992. 131–48.

———. "An Eleventh-Century Exchange of Letters Between a Christian and a Jew." *Journal of Medieval History* 7 (1981): 153–74.

———. "The Ideology of Reform and Changing Ideas Concerning Jews in the Works of Rupert of Deutz and Hermannus Quondam Iudeus." *Jewish History* 7 (1993): 43–63.

———. "*Intentio Recta an Erronea?* Peter Abelard's Views on Judaism and the Jews." In *Medieval Studies in Honour of Avrom Saltman*. Ed. B. Albert et al. Ramat-Gan, Israel: Bar-Ilan University Press, 1995. 13–30.

———. "St. Anselm and Those Outside the Church." In *Faith and Identity: Christian Political Experience*, ed. David Loades and Katherine Walsh. Studies in Church History, 6. Oxford: Clarendon, 1990. 11–37.

Adams, Marilyn McCord. "Anselm on Reason and Faith." In *The Cambridge Companion to Anselm*, ed. Davies and Leftow. 32–60.

Åkestam, Mia and Erika Kihlman. "Lire, comprendre et mémoriser l'Éthique à Nicomaque: Le rapport texte-image dans ms. Stockholm, Kungl. Bibl., Va 3." In *Regards sur la France du Moyen*

*Âge*, ed. Olle Ferm and Per Förnegård. Stockholm: Centre d'Études Médiévales de Stockholm, 2009. 110–53.

Alfaric, P. *L'évolution intellectuelle de S. Augustin: Du manichéisme au néoplatonisme.* Paris: Nourry, 1918.

Ames, Christine Caldwell. *Righteous Persecution: Inquisition, Dominicans, and Christianity in the Middle Ages.* Philadelphia: University of Pennsylvania Press, 2009.

Anderson, Gordon A. "Notre-Dame and Related Conductus: A Catalogue Raisonné." *Miscellanea Musicologica: Adelaide Studies in Musicology* 6 (1972): 152–229.

Andres i Blanch, Maria Rosa. "El Convent de Santa Caterina de Barcelona. S. XIII." Tesi de llicenciatura: University of Barcelona, 1985.

Angelelli, Ignacio. "The Technique of Disputation in the History of Logic." *Journal of Philosophy* 67 (1970): 800–815.

Arduini, Maria Ludovica. *Rupert von Deutz (1079–1129) und der "status christianus" seiner Zeit: Symbolisch-prophetische Deutung der Geschichte.* Vienna: Böhlau, 1987.

———. *Ruperto di Deutz e la Controversia tra Christiani ed Ebrei nel Secolo XII.* Rome: Istituto Storico Italiano, 1979.

Armitage, David. "What's the Big Idea?" *Times Literary Supplement,* September 20, 2012.

Axton, Richard. *European Drama in the Early Middle Ages.* London: Hutchinson, 1974.

Baer, Yitzhak. "On the Disputation of R. Yehiel of Paris and R. Moses ben Nahman [In Hebrew]." *Tarbiz* 2 (1930–31): 172–87.

Bakhtin, Mikhail. *The Dialogic Imagination.* Trans. Caryl Emerson and Michael Holquist. Austin: University of Texas Press, 1981.

Balboni, Dante. "San Pier Damiano, Maestro e Discepolo in Pomposa." *Benedictina* 22 (1975): 73–89.

Baldwin, John W. "A Debate at Paris over Thomas Becket Between Master Roger and Master Peter the Chanter." *Collectanea Stephan Kuttner* I. *Studia Gratiana* 11 (1967): 119–32.

———. "An Edition of the Long Version of Peter the Chanter's *Verbum abbreviatum.*" *Journal of Ecclesiastical History* 57 (2006): 78–85.

———. "The Image of the *Jongleur* in Northern France Around 1200." *Speculum* 72, 3 (1997): 635–63.

———. *Masters, Princes, and Merchants: The Social Views of Peter the Chanter and His Circle.* 2 vols. Princeton, N.J.: Princeton University Press, 1970.

Bale, Anthony. *The Jew in the Medieval Book: English Antisemitisms 1350–1500.* Cambridge: Cambridge University Press, 2007.

Balint, Bridget K. *Ordering Chaos: The Self and the Cosmos in Twelfth-Century Latin Prosimetrum.* Leiden: Brill, 2009.

Ball, Philip. *Universe of Stone: A Biography of Chartres Cathedral.* New York: Harper, 2008.

Barlow, Frank. *The English Church, 1000–1066: A History of the Later Anglo-Saxon Church.* 2nd ed. London: Longman, 1979.

Bate, Keith, ed. *Three Latin Comedies.* Toronto: Pontifical Institute of Medieval Studies, 1976.

Bazàn, Bernardo C.. "Les questions disputées, principalement dans les facultés de théologie." In *LQD,* ed. Bazàn, Wippel, Fransen, and Jacquart. 21–149.

Bazàn, Bernardo C., John W. Wippel, Gérard Fransen, and Danielle Jacquart, eds. *Les Questions disputées et Les Questions Quodlibétiques dans les Facultés de Théologie, de Droit et de Médecine* [*LQD*]. Typologie des Sources du Moyen Âge Occidental. 44–45. Turnhout: Brepols, 1985.

Bec, Pierre. *La Lyrique française au moyen-âge (XIIe–XIIIe siècle).* 2 vols. Paris: Picard, 1977–78.

Becker, Wolfgang. "The Literary Treatment of the Pseudo-Anselmian Dialogue *De custodia interioris hominis* in England and France." *Classica et Mediaevalia* 35 (1984): 215–33.

Beckwith, Christopher I. *Warriors of the Cloister: The Central Asian Origins of Science in the Medieval World.* Princeton, N.J.: Princeton University Press, 2012.

Bedos-Rezak, Brigitte. *Form and Order in Medieval France: Studies in Social and Quantitative Sigillography.* Collected Studies Series 424. Aldershot: Ashgate, 1993.

———. "Medieval Identity: A Sign and a Concept." *American Historical Review* 105, 5 (2000): 1489–1533.

———. "The Social Implications of the Art of Chivalry: The Sigillographic Evidence (France, 1050–1250)." In *The Medieval Court in Europe*, ed. Edward R. Haymes. Houston German Studies 6. Munich: Fink, 1986. 142–75.

Beinart, Haim. *The Expulsion of the Jews from Spain.* Trans. Jeffrey M. Green. Oxford: Littman Library of Jewish Civilization, 2002.

Bellomo, Manlio, ed. *Die Kunst der Disputation: Probleme der Rechtsauslegung und Rechtsanwendung im 13. und 14. Jahrhundert.* Munich: Oldenbourg, 1997.

———. *Saggio sull'università nell'età del diritto comune.* Catania, Sicily: Gianotta, 1979.

Bennett, J. A. W. *Middle English Literature.* Ed. Douglas Gray. Oxford: Oxford University Press, 1986.

Bent, Margaret. "Grammar and Rhetoric in Late Medieval Polyphony: Modern Metaphor or Old Simile?" In *Rhetoric Beyond Words*, ed. Carruthers. 52–71.

Ben-Shalom, Ram. "Between Official and Private Dispute: The Case of Christian Spain and Provence in the Late Middle Ages." *American Jewish Studies Review* 27, 1 (2003): 23–72.

———. "Medieval Jewry in Christendom." In *The Oxford Handbook of Jewish Studies*, ed. Martin Goodman et al. Oxford: Oxford University Press, 2002. 153–92.

Berger, David. *The Jewish-Christian Debate in the High Middle Ages: A Critical Edition of the Nizzahon Vetus.* Philadelphia: Jewish Publication Society of America, 1979.

Berger, Roger. *Littérature et societé arrageoise au XIIIe siècle: Les chansons et dits artésiens.* Arras: Commission départementale des monuments historiques du Pas-de-Calais, 1981.

Bériou, Nicole. *L'avènement des maîtres de la Parole: La prédication à Paris au XIIIe siècle.* 2 vols. Paris: Études Augustiniennes, 1998.

Bertini, Ferruccio. "La Commedia Latina del XII secolo." In idem, *L'eredità classica nel medioevo: Il linguaggio comico; Atti del III Convengo di Studio.* Viterbo: Agnesotti, 1979. 63–80.

———. "Il *Geta* de Vitale di Blois e la scuola di Abelardo." *Sandalion* 2 (1979): 257–65.

Besserman, Lawrence. "Chaucer, Spain, and the Prioress's Antisemitism." *Viator* 35 (2004): 329–53.

Beumer, Johannes. "Ein Religionsgespräch aus dem zwölften Jahrhundert." *Zeitschrift für Katholische Theologie* 78 (1951): 465–82.

Binski, Paul. " 'Working by Words Alone': The Architect, Scholasticism, and Rhetoric in Thirteenth-Century France." In *Rhetoric Beyond Words*, ed. Carruthers. 14–51.

Bird, Jessalyn Lea. "Heresy, Crusade and Reform in the Circle of Peter the Chanter, c.1187-c.1240." Ph.D. dissertation, University of Oxford, 2001.

Bischoff, Bernhard. *Manuscripts and Libraries in the Age of Charlemagne.* Cambridge: Cambridge University Press, 1994.

Bloemendal, Jan, Peter G. F. Eversmann, and Elsa Streitman, eds. *Drama, Performance and Debate: Theatre and Public Opinion in the Early Modern Period.* Leiden: Brill, 2013.

Blum, Owen J. *St. Peter Damian: His Teaching on the Spiritual Life.* Washington, D.C.: Catholic University of America, 1947.

Bolduc, Michelle. "Troubadours in Debate: The *Breviari d'Amor.*" *Romance Quarterly* 57 (2010): 53–76.

Bose, Mishtooni. "The Issue of Theological Style in Late Medieval Disputations." In *Medieval Forms of Argument: Disputation and Debate*, ed. Georgina Donavin, Carol Poster, and Richard Utz. Eugene, Ore.: Wipf and Stock, 2002. 1–21.

Bossy, Michel-André. "Medieval Debates of Body and Soul." *Comparative Literature* 28, 2 (1976): 144–63.

Bouchard, Constance Brittain. *"Every Valley Shall Be Exalted": The Discourse of Opposites in Twelfth-Century Thought.* Ithaca, N.Y.: Cornell University Press, 2003.

Boucheron, Patrick and Nicolas Offenstadt, eds. *L'espace public au Moyen Âge: Débats autour de Jürgen Habermas.* Paris: PUF, 2011.

Boureau, Alain. "Peut-on parler d'auteurs scolastiques?" In *Auctor et auctoritas: Invention et conformisme dans l'écriture médiévale*, ed. M. Zimmermann. Paris: École Nationale des Chartes, 2001. 267–79.

Boyarin, Daniel. *Border Lines: The Partition of Judeo-Christianity.* Philadelphia: University of Pennsylvania Press, 2004.

Breitenstein, Mirko. " 'Ins Gespräch gebracht': Der Dialog als Prinzip monastischer Unterweisung." In *Understanding Monastic Practices of Oral Communication (Western Europe, Tenth–Thirteenth Centuries)*, ed. Steven Vanderputten. Turnhout: Brepols, 2011. 205–230.

Brook, Kevin Alan. *The Jews of Khazaria.* 2nd ed. Lanham, Md.: Rowman & Littlefield, 2009.

Brower, Jeffrey E. and Kevin Guilfoy, eds. *The Cambridge Companion to Abelard.* Cambridge: Cambridge University Press, 2004.

Brown, Peter. *Augustine of Hippo.* 2nd ed. London: Faber and Faber, 2000.

Brundage, James A. *The Medieval Origins of the Legal Profession: Canonists, Civilians, and Courts.* Chicago: University of Chicago Press, 2008.

Bruns, Gerald L. "Midrash and Allegory: The Beginning of Scriptural Interpretation." In *The Literary Guide to the Bible*, ed. Robert Alter and Frank Kermode. Cambridge Mass.: Belknap Press of Harvard University Press, 1987. 625–46.

Bullough, Donald. *Carolingian Renewal: Sources and Heritage.* New York: St. Martin's, 1991.

Burke, Peter. *Varieties of Cultural History.* Ithaca, N.Y.: Cornell University Press, 1997.

Burman, Thomas E. "Las Navas de Tolosa and *Liber Alchorani*: Reflections on Iberian Christians and the Qur'an." *Journal of Medieval Iberian Studies* 4 (2012): 89–93.

Burnett, Charles, ed. *Adelard of Bath: An English Scientist and Arabist of the Early Twelfth Century.* London: Warburg Institute, 1987.

———. "The Coherence of the Arabic-Latin Translation Program in Toledo in the Twelfth Century." In idem, *Arabic into Latin in the Middle Ages: The Translators and Their Intellectual and Social Context*, Variorum Collected Studies Series. Aldershot: Ashgate, 2009. 249–88.

Burns, R. I. "The Barcelona 'Disputation' of 1263: Conversion and Talmud in Jewish-Christian Relations." *Catholic Historical Review* 69 (1993): 488–95.

———. "Christian-Islamic Confrontation in the West: The Thirteenth-Century Dream of Conversion." *American Historical Review* 76, 5 (1971): 1386–1434.

Bynum, Caroline Walker. *Jesus as Mother: Studies in the Spirituality of the High Middle Ages.* Publications of the UCLA Center for Medieval and Renaissance Studies 16. Berkeley: University of California Press, 1982.

———. *The Resurrection of the Body in Western Christianity, 200–1336.* New York: Columbia University Press, 1995.

———. *Wonderful Blood: Theology and Practice in Late Medieval Northern Germany and Beyond.* Philadelphia: University of Pennsylvania Press, 2007.

Campbell, Richard. "The Systematic Character of Anselm's Thought." In *Les mutations socio-culturelles*, ed. Foreville. 549–60.

Capelli, Piero. "Il processo di Parigi del 1240 contro il Talmud: Verso un'edizione critica del testo ebraico." *Materia Giudaica* 6 (2001): 85–90.

Caputo, Nina. *Nachmanides in Medieval Catalonia: History, Community, and Messianism.* Notre Dame, Ind.: University of Notre Dame Pres, 2007.

Carabine, Deirdre. *John Scottus Eriugena.* Great Medieval Thinkers. Oxford: Oxford University Press, 2000.

Carruthers, Mary, ed. *Rhetoric Beyond Words: Delight and Persuasion in the Arts of the Middle Ages.* Cambridge: Cambridge University Press, 2010.

Carson, M. Angela, O.S.U. "Rhetorical Structure in *The Owl and the Nightingale*." *Speculum* 42, 1 (1967): 92–103.

Caruso, Francesco. "On the Shoulders of *Grammatica*: John of Salisbury's *Metalogicon* and Poliziano's *Lamia*." In *Angelo's Poliziano's Lamia: Text Translation, and Introductory Studies*, ed. Christopher S. Celenza. Leiden: Brill, 2010. 47–94.

Chadwick, Henry. *Augustine.* Oxford: Oxford University Press, 1986.

Chang, Ku-ming (Kevin). "From Oral Disputation to Written Text: the Transformation of the Dissertation in Early Modern Europe." *History of Universities* 19 (2004): 129–87.

Chartier, Roger. "Intellectual History or Sociocultural History? The French Trajectories." In *Modern European Intellectual History: Reappraisals and New Perspectives*, ed. Dominick LaCapra and Steven L. Kaplan, trans. Jane P. Kaplan. Ithaca, N.Y.: Cornell University Press, 1982: 13–46.

Chazan, Robert. "Archbishop Fuculdi and His Jews." *Revue des Études Juives* 132 (1973): 587–94.

———. *Barcelona and Beyond: The Disputation of 1263 and Its Aftermath.* Berkeley: University of California Press, 1992.

———. "The Condemnation of the Talmud Reconsidered (1239–1248)." *Proceedings of the American Academy for Jewish Research* 55 (1988): 11–30.

———. "Confrontation in the Synagogue of Narbonne: A Christian Sermon and a Jewish Reply." *Harvard Theological Review* 67 (1974): 437–57.

———. *Daggers of Faith: Thirteenth-Century Missionizing and Jewish Response.* Berkeley: University of California Press, 1989.

———. *Fashioning Jewish Identity in Medieval Western Christendom.* Cambridge: Cambridge University Press, 2004.

———. *Medieval Jewry in Northern France: A Political and Social History.* Baltimore: Johns Hopkins University Press, 1973.

———. *Medieval Stereotypes and Modern Antisemitism.* Berkeley: University of California Press, 1997.

Chazelle, Celia. *The Crucified God in the Carolingian Era: Theology and Art of Christ's Passion.* Cambridge: Cambridge University Press, 2001.

Chenu, Marie-Dominique. *La théologie au douzième siècle.* Paris: J. Vrin, 1957.

———. *Nature, Man, and Society in the Twelfth Century.* Trans. Jerome Taylor and Lester K. Little. Toronto: University of Toronto Press, 1997.

———. *Toward Understanding Saint Thomas.* Trans. A.-M. Landry and D. Hughes. Chicago: Regnery, 1964.

Clanchy, Michael T. *Abelard: A Medieval Life.* Oxford: Blackwell, 1997.

———. "Abelard's Mockery of St. Anselm." *Journal of Ecclesiastical History* 41 (1990): 1–23.

———. *From Memory to Written Record: England 1066–1307*. Cambridge, Mass.: Harvard University Press, 1979.

Clark, William. *Academic Charisma and the Origins of the Research University*. Chicago: University of Chicago Press, 2006.

Cluse, Christoph, ed. *The Jews of Europe in the Middle Ages: Proceedings of the International Symposium Held at Speyer, 20–25 October 2002*. Turnhout: Brepols, 2004.

Cobban, Alan. *Medieval English Universities: Oxford and Cambridge to c. 1500*. Berkeley: University of California Press, 1988.

Cohen, Jeremy. "Augustine's Doctrine of Jewish Witness Revisited." *Journal of Religion* 89 (2009): 564–78.

———. *The Friars and the Jews: The Evolution of Medieval Anti-Judaism*. Ithaca, N.Y.: Cornell University Press, 1982.

———. *Living Letters of the Law: Ideas of the Jew in Medieval Christianity*. Berkeley: University of California Press, 1999.

———. "The Mentality of the Medieval Jewish Apostate." In *Jewish Apostasy in the Modern World*, ed. Todd M. Endelman. New York: Holmes and Meier, 1987. 20–47.

———. "Scholarship and Intolerance in the Medieval Academy: The Study and Evaluation of Judaism in European Christendom." *American Historical Review* 91, 3 (1986): 592–613.

———. "*Synagoga conversa*: Honorius Augustodunensis, the Song of Songs, and Christianity's 'Eschatalogical Jew'." *Speculum* 79, 2 (2004): 309–40.

Cohen, Martin. "Reflections on the Text and Context of the Disputation of Barcelona." *Hebrew Union College Annual* 35 (1964): 157–92.

Cohen, Patricia. "Reason Seen More as Weapon Than Path to Truth." *New York Times*, June 14, 2011.

Coleman, Janet. "*The Owl and the Nightingale* and Papal Theories of Marriage." *Journal of Ecclesiastical History* 38 (1987): 517–67.

Colish, Marcia L. "Haskins's Renaissance Seventy Years Later: Beyond Anti-Burckhardtianism." *Haskins Society Journal* 11 (2003): 1–15.

———. *Peter Lombard*. 2 vols. Leiden: Brill, 1994.

———. *Studies in Scholasticism*. Variorum Collected Studies Series. Aldershot: Ashgate, 2006.

Collins, Ann. *Teacher in Faith and Virtue: Lanfranc of Bec's Commentary on Saint Paul*. Leiden: Brill, 2007.

Conlee, John W, ed. *Middle English Debate Poetry*. East Lansing, Mich.: Colleagues Press, 1991.

Constable, Giles. *Letters and Letter Collections*. Typologie des Sources du Moyen Âge Occidental, fasc. 17. Turnhout: Brepols, 1978.

———. *The Reformation of the Twelfth Century*. Cambridge: Cambridge University Press, 1996.

———, ed. *Three Treatises from Bec on the Nature of Monastic Life*. Trans. Bernard S. Smith. Medieval Academy Books 109. Toronto: University of Toronto Press, 2008.

Constable, Giles and Robert Benson, eds. *Renaissance and Renewal in the Twelfth Century*. Cambridge, Mass.: Harvard University Press, 1982.

Constable, Olivia Remie, ed. *Medieval Iberia: Readings from Christian, Muslim, and Jewish Sources*. 2nd ed. Philadelphia: University of Pennsylvania Press, 2012.

Copeland, Rita. "Sophistic, Spectrality, Iconoclasm." In *Images, Idolatry, and Iconoclasm in Late Medieval England*, ed. Jeremy Dimmick, James Simpson, and Nicolette Zeeman. Oxford: Oxford University Pres, 2002. 112–30.

Copeland, Rita and Ineke Sluiter, eds. *Medieval Grammar and Rhetoric: Language Arts and Literary Theory, AD 300–1475*. Oxford: Oxford University Press, 2009.

Cottier, J. F. "Le recueil apocryphe des *Orationes sive meditationes* de Saint Anselme: Sa formation et sa réception en Angleterre et en France au XIIe siècle." In *Anselm*, ed. Luscombe and Evans. 282–95.

Cotts, John D. *The Clerical Dilemma: Peter of Blois and Literate Culture in the Twelfth Century.* Washington, D.C.: Catholic University Press of America, 2009.

Courcelle, Pierre. *Les Confessions de S. Augustin dans la tradition littéraire: Antécédents et postérité.* Paris: Études Augustiniennes, 1963.

———. *La Consolation de Philosophie dans la tradition littéraire: Antécédents et posterité de Boèce.* Paris: Études Augustiniennes, 1967.

Courtenay, William J. *Schools and Scholars in Fourteenth-Century England.* Princeton, N.J.: Princeton University Press, 1987.

———. "Schools and Schools of Thought in the Twelfth Century." In *Mind Matters: Studies of Medieval and Early Modern Intellectual History in Honour of Marcia Colish*, ed. Cary J. Nederman, Nancy Van Deusen, and E. Ann Matter. Turnhout: Brepols, 2010. 13–45.

Cowdrey, H. E. J. *Lanfranc: Scholar, Monk, and Archbishop.* Oxford: Oxford University Press, 2003.

Cullin, Olivier, ed. *La place de la musique dans la culture médiévale.* Turnhout: Brepols, 2007.

Dahan, Gilbert, ed. *Le brûlement du Talmud à Paris 1242–1244.* Paris: Cerf, 1999.

———. *The Christian Polemic Against the Jews in the Middle Ages.* Trans. Jody Gladding. Notre Dame, Ind.: University of Notre Dame Press, 1998.

———. *L'exégèse chrétienne de la Bible en Occident médiévale, XII–XIV siècle.* Paris: Cerf, 1999.

———. *Les intellectuels chrétiens et les juifs au Moyen Âge.* Paris: Cerf, 1990.

———. "Les traductions latines de Thibaud de Sézanne." In *Le brûlement du Talmud*, ed. Dahan. 95–100.

———. "Saint Anselme, les juifs, le judaïsme." In *Les mutations socio-culturelles*, ed. Foreville. 521–36.

Dahan, Gilbert and Irène Rosier-Catach. *La rhétoriqie d'Aristote: Traditions et commentaires de l'antiquité au XVIIe siècle.* Paris: J. Vrin, 1998.

Daly, Lloyd William. *Alercatio Hadriani Augusti et Epicteti Philosophi and the Question-and-Answer Dialogue.* Urbana: University of Illinois Press, 1939.

Davies, Brian and Brian Leftow, eds. *The Cambridge Companion to Anselm.* Cambridge: Cambridge University Press, 2004.

Davis, R. H. C. et al., eds. *The Writing of History in the Middle Ages: Essays Presented to Richard William Southern.* Oxford: Clarendon, 1981.

D'Avray, D. L. *Medieval Religious Rationalities: A Weberian Analysis.* Cambridge: Cambridge University Press, 2010.

De Hamel, Christopher. *Glossed Books of the Bible and the Origins of the Paris Book Trade.* Woodbridge: Brewer, 1984.

De Hartmann, Carmen Cardelle. *Lateinische Dialoge, 1200–1400: Literaturhistorische Studie und Repertorium.* Mittellateinische Studien und Texte 37. Leiden: Brill, 2006.

De la Marche, Lecoy. *La chaire française au moyen âge.* Paris: Renouard, 1886.

De Lange, Nicholas R. M. *Origen and the Jews.* Cambridge: Cambridge University Press, 1976.

De Lincy, Antoine LeRoux and L. M. Tisserand, eds. *Paris et ses historiens aux XIVe et XVe siècles.* Paris: Imprimerie Impériale, 1867.

De Lubac, Henri. *Medieval Exegesis.* Vol. 1, *The Four Senses of Scripture.* Trans. Mark Sebanc. Edinburgh: Eerdmans, 1998.

De Montclos, Jean. *Lanfranc et Bérenger: La controverse eucharistique du XIe siècle.* Spicilegium Sacrum Lovaniense. Études et Documents 37. Leuven: Spicilegium Sacrum Lovaniense, Justus Lipsius-str, 1971.

De Ridder-Symoens, H., ed. *Universities in the Middle Ages*. Cambridge: Cambridge University Press, 1992.

De Rijk, L. M. "Some Thirteenth Century Tracts on the Game of Obligation." *Vivarium* 12 (1975): 94–123.

De Wulf, Maurice. *Histoire de la philosophie médiévale*. 6th ed. Louvain: Institut Superier de Philosophie, 1934.

Déchanet, Jean Marie. "L'amitié d'Abélard et de Guillaume de Saint Thierry." *Revue d'Histoire Ecclesiastique* 35 (1939): 761–74.

Delaney, Sheila, ed. *Chaucer and the Jews*. London: Routledge, 2002.

Delhaye, Philippe. "L'enseignement de la philosophie morale au XIIe siècle," *Medieval Studies* 11 (1949): 77–99.

———. "L'organisation scholaire au XIIe siècle." *Traditio* 5 (1947): 211–68.

———. "La place de l'éthique parmi les disciplines scientifiques au XIIe siècle." In *Miscellanea moralia in honorem eximii domini Arthur Janssen, universitatis catholicae in oppido lovaniensi professoris*, 2 vols. Louvain, 1948. 1: 29–44.

———. "Une adaptation du 'De officiis' au XIIe siècle: Le 'Moralium dogma philosophorum,'" *Recherches de théologie ancienne et médiévale* 16 (1949): 227–258. 17 (1950): 5–28.

Delmaire, Bernard. *Le diocèse d'Arras: De 1093 au milieu du XIVe siècle: Recherches sur la vie religieuse dans le nord de la France au moyen âge*. 2 vols. Arras: Conseil Général du Pas-de-Calais, 1994.

Denifle, Heinrich. "Quellen zur Disputation Pablos Christiani mit Mose Nachmani zu Barcelona 1263." *Historisches Jahrbuch der Goerres Gesellschaft* 8 (1887): 225–44.

Dereine, C. "Odo de Tournai et la crise du cénobitisme au XIe siècle." *Revue du Moyen Âge Latin* 4 (1948): 137–54.

Dod, Bernard G. "Aristoteles latinus." In *CHLMP*, ed. Kretzmann et al. 45–79.

Doignon, J. "Etat des questions relatives aux premiers Dialogues de saint Augustin." In *Internationales Symposium über den Stand der Augustinus-Forschung: Festschrift für Luc Verheijen*, ed. C. P. Mayer and K. H. Chelius. Würzburg: Augustinus-Verlag, 1989. 42–87.

Donahue, George, Jr. *Why the History of Canon Law Is Not Written*. Selden Lecture, July 3, 1984. London: Selden Society, 1986.

Dondaine, A. *Les secrétaires des saint Thomas*. Rome: Comm. Leonine, 1956.

d'Onofrio, Giulio. "*Respondeant pro me*: La dialectique anselmienne et les dialecticiens du haut moyen âge." In *Saint Anselm*, ed. Viola and Van Fleteren. 29–50.

———. *Vera philosophia: Studies in Late Antique, Early Medieval, and Renaissance Christian Thought*. Nutrix 1. Turnhout: Brepols, 2008.

———, ed. *Lanfranco di Pavia e l'Europa del secolo XI nel IX centenario della morte (1089–1989)*. Italia Sacra 51. Rome: Herder, 1993.

Dronke, Peter. "The Lyrical Compositions of Philip the Chancellor." *Studi Medievali* ser. 3, 28 (1987): 563–92.

———, ed. *A History of Western Philosophy in the Twelfth Century*. Cambridge: Cambridge University Press, 1988

Dufeil, Marie-Michel. *Guillaume de Saint-Amour et la polémique universitaire parisienne 1250–1259*. Paris: Picard, 1972.

Dümmler, Ernst Ludwig. *Auxilius und Vulgarius: Quellen und Forschungen zu Geschichte des Papsttums im Anfange des Zehnten Jahrhunderts*. Leipzig: S. Hirzel, 1866.

Ebbesen, Sten. "Ancient Scholastic Logic as a Source of Medieval Scholastic Logic." In *CHLMP*, ed. Kretzmann et al. 101–27.

Edelstein, Ludwig. *Plato's Seventh Letter*. Leiden: Brill, 1966.

Eisenberg, Saadia R. "Reading Medieval Religious Disputation: The 1240 'Debate' Between Rabbi Yehiel of Paris and Friar Nicholas Donin." Ph.D. dissertation. University of Michigan, 2008.

Elukin, Jonathan. *Living Together, Living Apart: Rethinking Jewish-Christian Relations in the Middle Ages*. Princeton, N.J.: Princeton University Press, 2007.

Enders, Jody. *Rhetoric and the Origins of Medieval Drama*. Ithaca, N.Y.: Cornell University Press, 1992.

―――. "The Theater of Scholastic Erudition." *Comparative Drama* 27, 3 (1992): 341–63.

Evans, G. R. *Anselm and a New Generation*. Oxford: Oxford University Press, 1980.

―――. *Anselm and Talking About God*. Oxford: Clarendon, 1978.

―――. "Anselm of Canterbury and Anselm of Havelberg: The Controversy with the Greeks." *Analecta Praemonstratensia* 53 (1977): 158–75.

―――. "Anselm's Life, Works, and Immediate Influence." In *The Cambridge Companion to Anselm*, ed. Davies and Leftow. 5–31.

―――, ed. *A Concordance to the Works of St. Anselm*. 4 vols. Millwood, N.Y.: Kraus, 1984.

―――. "Gilbert Crispin on the Eucharist: A Monastic Postscript to Lanfranc and Berengar." *Journal of Theological Studies* 31 (1980): 28–43.

―――. *The Mind of Bernard of Clairvaux*. Oxford: Clarendon, 1983.

―――. *Old Arts and New Theology: The Beginnings of Theology as an Academic Discipline*. Oxford: Clarendon, 1980.

―――. "Unity and Diversity: Anselm of Havelberg as Ecumenist." *Analecta Praemonstratensia* 67 (1991): 42–52.

Everist, Mark. "The Thirteenth Century." In *The Cambridge Companion to Medieval Music*, ed. Mark Everist. Cambridge: Cambridge University Press, 2011. 63–86.

Fahey, John F. *The Eucharistic Teaching of Ratramn of Corbie*. Pontificia Facultas Theologica Seminarii Sanctae Mariae ad Lacum, Dissertationes ad Lauream, 22. Mundelein, Ill.: Saint Mary of the Lake Seminary, 1951.

Fassler, Margot. "Representations of Time in *Ordo representaciones Ade*." In *Contexts: Style and Values in Medieval Art and Literature*, ed. Daniel Poirion and Nancy F. Regalado. Special Issue of *Yale French Studies*. New Haven, Conn.: Yale University Press, 1991. 97–113.

Febvre, Lucien. "Histoire des idées, histoire des sociétés: Une question de climat." *Annales: Économies, Sociétés, Civilisations* 2 (1946): 158–61.

Fenster, Thelma and Daniel Lord Smail, eds. *Fama: The Politics of Talk and Reputation in Medieval Europe*. Ithaca, N.Y.: Cornell University Press, 2003.

Ferruolo, Stephen. *The Origins of the University: The Schools of Paris and Their Critics*. Stanford, Calif.: Stanford University Press, 1985.

―――. "*Parisius-Paradisius*: The City, Schools, and the Origins of the University of Paris." In *The University and the City: From Medieval Origins to the Present*, ed. Thomas Bender. Oxford: Oxford University Press, 1988. 22–46.

―――. "The Paris Statutes of 1215 Reconsidered." *History of Universities* 5 (1985): 1–14.

Fichtenau, Heinrich. *Heretics and Scholars in the High Middle Ages, 1000–1200*. Trans. Denise Kaiser. University Park: Penn State University Press, 1998.

Fiedler, Hans. *Der Meister im Bamberger Dom: Magister de vivis lapidibus. Urgestalt deutschen Bildhauertums*. Kempten im Allgäu: Pröptser, 1965.

Finke, H. "De privilegio Martini." In idem, *Aus den Tagen Bonifaz VIII: Fund und Forshungen*. Munster: Druck und Verlag der Aschendorffschen Buchhandlung, 1902. III–VII.

Fishman, Talya. *Becoming the People of the Talmud: Oral Torah as Written Tradition in Medieval Jewish Cultures*. Philadelphia: University of Pennsylvania Press, 2011.

Flanagan, Sabina. *Doubt in an Age of Faith: Uncertainty in the Long Twelfth Century*. Turnhout: Brepols, 2008.

Fletcher, Alan J. "The Genesis of *The Owl and Nightingale*: A New Hypothesis." *Chaucer Review* 34 (1999): 1–17.

———. "Middle English Debate Literature." In *Readings in Medieval Texts: Interpreting Old and Middle English Literature*, ed. David F. Johnson and Elaine Treharne. Oxford: Oxford University Press, 2005. 241–56.

Flint, V. I. J. *Honorius Augustodunensis of Regensburg*. Authors of the Middle Ages 6. Aldershot: Ashgate, 1995.

Fontaine, Jacques. "Le genre littéraire du dialogue monastique dans l'Occident latin des Ve et VIe siècles." In *The Spirituality of Ancient Monasticism*, ed. Marek Starowieyski. Cracow-Tyniec: Wydawnictwo Benedyktynów, 1995. 227–50.

Foreville, Raymonde, ed. *Les mutations socioculturelles au tournant des XIe–XIIe siècles*. Paris: CNRS, 1984.

Foucault, Michel. *History of Sexuality*. Trans. Robert Hurley. 3 vols. New York: Vintage, 1980.

Fournier, Paul and Gabriel le Bras. *Histoire des collections canoniques en Occident depuis les fausses décrétales jusqu'au Décret de Gratian*. 2 vols. Paris: Sirey, 1931–32.

Frassetto, Michael, ed. *Christian Attitudes Toward the Jews in the Middle Ages: A Casebook*. London: Routledge, 2007.

Fredriksen, Paula. *Augustine and the Jews: A Christian Defense of Jews and Judaism*. New York: Doubleday, 2008.

Freund, Stephan. *Studien zur literarischen Wirksamkeit des Petrus Damiani*. MGH Studien und Texte 13. Hannover: Hahnsche, 1995.

Fried, Johannes, ed. *Dialektik und Rhetorik im Früheren und Hohen Mittelalter: Rezeption, Überlieferung und gesellschaftliche Wirkung antiker Gelehrsamkeit, vornehmlich im 9. und 12. Jh.* Schriften des Historischen Kollegs, Kolloquien 27. Munich: Oldenbourg, 1997.

Friedlein, Roger. *Der Dialog bei Ramon Llull: Literarische Gestaltung als apologetische Strategie*. Tübingen: Niemeyer, 2004.

Fudeman, Kirsten A. *Vernacular Voices: Language and Identity in Medieval French Jewish Communities*. Philadelphia: University of Pennsylvania Press, 2010.

Fulton, Rachel. *From Judgment to Passion: Devotion to Christ and the Virgin Mary, 800–1200*. New York: Columbia University Press, 2002.

Funkenstein, Amos. "Basic Types of Christian Anti-Jewish Polemics in the Later Middle Ages." *Viator* 2 (1971): 373–82.

———. "Changes in the Patterns of Christian Anti-Jewish Polemic in the Twelfth Century [Hebrew]." *Zion* n.s. 33 (1968): 125–44.

———. *Perceptions of Jewish History*. Berkeley: University of California Press, 1993.

Galinsky, Judah. "The Different Hebrew Versions of the 'Talmud Trial' of 1240 in Paris." In *New Perspectives on Jewish-Christian Relations*, ed. Elisheva Carlbach and Jacob J. Schacter. Leiden: Brill, 2011. 109–40.

Galonnier, Alain. "Sur quelques aspects annonciateurs de la littérature sophismatique dans le *De grammatico*." In *Anselm: Aosta, Bec and Canterbury*, ed. Luscombe and Evans. 209–28.

Ganz, David. *Corbie in the Carolingian Renaissance*. Beihefte der Francia 20. Sigmaringen: Thorbecke, 1990.

Gasper, Giles E. M. *Anselm of Canterbury and His Theological Inheritance.* Aldershot: Ashgate, 2004.

Gasper, Giles E. M. and Ian Logan, eds. *Saint Anselm of Canterbury and His Legacy.* Toronto: Pontifical Institute of Medieval Studies, 2012.

Gauss, Julia. "Anselm von Canterbury: Zur Begegnung und Auseinandersetzung der Religionen." *Saeculum* 17 (1966): 277–363.

Geldsetzer, Lutz. " 'Sic et non' sive 'sic aut non': La méthode des questions chez Abélard et la stratégie de la recherché." In *Pierre Abélard: Colloque international de Nantes*, ed. Jean Jolivet and Henri Habrias. Rennes: Presses Universitaires de Rennes, 2003. 407–15.

Ghellinck, J. de. *Le mouvement théologique du XIIe siècle.* 2nd ed. Museum Lessianum, Section historique, 10. Bruges: Editions de Tempel, 1948. Repr. Brussels: Culture et Civilisation, 1969.

Gibson, Margaret T. *Lanfranc of Bec.* Oxford: Clarendon, 1978.

Gilbert, Paul, Helmut Kohlenberger, and Elmar Salmann, eds. *Cur Deus homo: Atti del Congresso anselmiano internazionale; Roma, 21–23 maggio 1998.* Studia Anselmiana 128. Rome: Centro studi S. Anselmo, 1999.

Gilson, Etienne. *History of Christian Philosophy in the Middle Ages.* New York: Random House, 1955.

Glorieux, Palémon. "L'enseignement au Moyen Âge: Techniques et méthodes en usage à la Faculté de Theologie de Paris au XIIIe siècle." *Archives d'Histoire Doctrinale et Littérature du Moyen Âge* 43 (1968): 65–186.

———. *La littérature quodlibétique de 1260 à 1320.* Le Salchoir Kain, Belgium: Revue des Sciences Philosophiques et Théologiques, 1925–35.

———. *Répertoire des maîtres en théologie de Paris au XIIIe siècle.* 2 vols. Paris: J. Vrin, 1933–34.

Godman, Peter. *The Silent Masters: Latin Literature and Its Censors in the High Middle Ages.* Princeton, N.J.: Princeton University Press, 2000.

Goldhill, Simon, ed. *The End of Dialogue in Antiquity.* Cambridge: Cambridge University Press, 2008.

Goldin, Frederick. *Lyrics of the Troubadours and Trouvères: An Anthology and a History.* Gloucester, Mass.: Peter Smith, 1983.

Gonsette, Jean A. D. *Pierre Damien et la culture profane.* Louvain: Publications Universitaires de Louvain, 1956.

Goodwin, Deborah. *"Take Hold of the Robe of a Jew": Herbert of Bosham's Christian Hebraism.* Leiden: Brill, 2005.

Gorman, Robert. *The Socratic Method in the Dialogues of Cicero.* Stuttgart: Franz Steiner, 2005.

Gouguenheim, Sylvain. *Aristote au Mont Saint-Michel: Les racines greques de l'Europe chrétienne.* Paris: Seuil, 2007.

Goy, Rudolf. *Die Überlieferung der Werke Hugos von St. Viktor.* Stuttgart: Hiersemann, 1976.

Grabmann, Martin. "Aristoteles im zwölften Jahrhundert." *Medieval Studies* 12 (1950): 123–62.

———. *Die Aristoteleskommentare des Heinrich von Brüssel und der Einfluss Alberts des Grossen auf die mittelalterliche Aristoteleserkärung.* München: Verlag der Bayerischen Akademie der Wissenschaften, 1944.

———. *Die Geschichte der scholastischen Methode.* 2 vols. Freiburg: Herder, 1909–11.

———. *Mittelalterliches Geistesleben: Abhandlungen zur Geschichte der Scholastik und Mystik*, Vol. 3. Ed. Ludwig Lott. Munich: Max Hueberg, 1956.

Graboïs, Aryeh. "Un chapitre de tolérance intellectuelle dans la societé occidentale au XIIe siècle: le 'Dialogus' de Pierre Abélard et le 'Kuzari' d'Yehuda Halevi." In *Pierre Abélard—Pierre le Vénérable: Les courants philosophiques, littéraires et artistiques en Occident au milieu du XIIe siècle*, ed. René Louis and Jean Jolivet. Paris: CNRS, 1975. 641–52.

Grant, Edward. *God and Reason in the Middle Ages.* Cambridge: Cambridge University Press, 2001.

Grayzel, Solomon, ed. *The Church and the Jews in the XIIIth Century.* Vol. 1. Rev. ed. New York: Hermon Press, 1966. Vol. 2, ed. Kenneth Stow. Detroit: Wayne State University Press, 1989.

Griffiths, Fiona J. *The Garden of Delights: Reform and Renaissance for Women in the Twelfth Century.* Philadelphia: University of Pennsylvania Press, 2007.

Gross, Guillaume. *Chanter en polyphonie à Notre Dame de Paris aux 12e et 13e siècles.* Turnhout: Brepols, 2007.

Guenée, Bernard. *Histoire et culture historique dans l'occident médiévale.* Paris: Aubier Montaigne, 1980.

Guilhou, E. *La "Comedie" Latine en France au douzième siècle.* Paris: Belles-Lettres, 1931.

Gurevich, Aaron. "Popular and Scholarly Medieval Cultural Traditions: Notes in the Margins of Jacques Le Goff's Book." *Journal of Medieval History* 9 (1983): 71–90.

Gushee, Marion S. "The Polyphonic Music of the Medieval Monastery, Cathedral and University." In *Antiquity and the Middle Ages: From Ancient Greece to the 15th Century*, ed. James McKinnon. London: Macmillan, 1990. 143–69.

Guthrie, W. K. C. *A History of Greek Philosophy.* Cambridge: Cambridge University Press, 1975.

Habermas, Jürgen. *The Structural Transformation of the Public Sphere: An Inquiry into a Category of Bourgeois Society.* Trans. Thomas Burger. Cambridge, Mass.: Harvard University Press, 1989.

Halkin, Hillel. *Yehuda Halevi.* New York: Schocken, 2010.

Hardison, O. B., Jr. *Christian Rite and Christian Drama in the Middle Ages.* Baltimore: Johns Hopkins University Press, 1965.

Häring, Nikolaus M. "The Cictercian Everard of Ypres and His Appraisal of the Conflict Between St. Bernard and Gilbert of Poitiers." *Mediaeval Studies* 17 (1955): 143–72.

———. "A Latin Dialogue on the Doctrine of Gilbert of Poitiers." *Mediaeval Studies* 15 (1953): 243–89.

———. "Thomas von Morigny. *Disputatio catholicorum patrum adversus dogmata Petri Abaelardi.*" *Studi Medievali* 3rd ser. 22 (1981): 299–376.

Harkins, Franklin T. *Reading and the Work of Restoration: History and Scripture in the Theology of Hugh of St. Victor.* Toronto: Pontifical Institute of Medieval Studies, 2009.

Harris, Anne F. "The Performative Terms of Jewish Iconoclasm and Conversion in Two Saint Nicholas Windows at Chartres Cathedral" In *Beyond the Yellow Badge*, ed. Mitchell Merbeck. 119–43.

Heil, J. "Augustine's Attack on Skepticism: The 'Contra Academicos'." *History of Theology Review* 65 (1962): 99–116.

Henry, Desmond Paul. *Commentary on De grammatico: The Historical-Logical Dimensions of a Dialogue of St. Anselm's.* 2 vols. Dordrecht: Reidel, 1974.

Hirzel, Rudolf. *Der Dialog: Ein literarhistorischer Versuch.* 2 vols. Leipzig: Hirzel, 1895.

Hobbins, Daniel. *Authorship and Publicity Before Print: Jean Gerson and the Transformation of Late Medieval Learning.* Philadelphia: University of Pennsylvania Press, 2009.

Hoenen, Maarten J. F. M. and Lodi Nauta, eds. *Boethius in the Middle Ages: Latin and Vernacular Traditions of the Consolatio Philosophiae.* Leiden: Brill, 1997.

Holopainen, Toivo J. *Dialectic and Theology in the Eleventh Century.* Studien und Texte zur Geistesgeschichte des Mittelalaters 54. Leiden: Brill, 1996.

Hopkins, Jasper. "Anselm's Debate with Gaunilo." *Analecta Anselmiana* 5 (1976): 25–53.

Hourihane, Colum, ed. *Gothic Art and Thought in the Later Medieval Period: Essays in Honor of Willibald Sauerländer.* Index of Christian Art. University Park: Pennsylvania State University Press, 2011.

Houser, R. E., ed. and trans. *The Cardinal Virtues: Aquinas, Albert, and Philip the Chancellor.* Toronto: University of Toronto Press, 2004.

Hunt, Richard W. "The Disputation of Peter of Cornwall Against Symon the Jew." In *Studies in Medieval History Presented to Frederick Maurice Powicke,* ed. R. W. Hunt, W. A. Pantin, and R. W. Southern. Oxford: Clarendon, 1948. 143–56.

Hunt, Tony. "Aristotle, Dialectic, and Courtly Literature." *Viator* 10 (1979): 95–130.

Huygens, R. B. C. "Textes latins du XIe au XIIIe siècle." *Studi Medievali* 3rd ser. 8 (1967): 451–503.

Illich, Ivan. *In the Vineyard of the Text: A Commentary to Hugh's Didascalicon.* Chicago: University of Chicago Press, 1993.

Iogna-Prat, Dominique. *Order and Exclusion: Cluny and Christendom Face Heresy, Judaism, and Islam (1000–1150).* Trans. Graham R. Edwards. Ithaca, N.Y.: Cornell University Press, 2002.

Iwakuma, "Influence." In *The Cambridge Companion to Abelard,* ed. Brower and Guilfoy. 305–35.

———. "Pierre Abélard et Guillaume de Champeaux dans les premières années du XIIe siècle: une étude préliminaire." In *Langage, sciences, philosophie au XIIe siècle. Actes de la table ronde internationale des 25–26 mars 1998,* ed. Joël Biard. Paris: J. Vrin, 1999. 92–123.

———. "*Vocales* Revisited." In *The Word in Medieval Logic, Theology and Psychology,* ed. Tetsuro Shimizu and Charles Burnett. Turnhout: Brepols, 2009: 81–171.

Jacobi, Klaus, ed. *Gespräche lesen: Philosophische Dialoge im Mittelalter.* ScriptOralia 115. Tübingen: G. Narr, 1999.

———. "Gilbert Crispin—Zwischen Realität und Fiktion." In *Gespräche lesse,* ed. Jacobi. 125–38.

———. "Logic: The Later Twelfth Century." In *A History of Western Philosophy in the Twelfth Century,* ed. Dronke. 227–51.

Jaeger, C. Stephen. *The Envy of Angels: Cathedral Schools and Social Ideals in Medieval Europe, 950–1200.* Philadelphia: University of Pennsylvania Press, 1994.

———, ed. *Magnificence and the Sublime in Medieval Aesthetics: Art, Architecture, Literature, Music.* London: Palgrave Macmillan, 2010.

———. "Pessimism in the Twelfth-Century 'Renaissance'." *Speculum* 78, 4 (2003): 1151–83.

———. "Philosophy, ca. 950–ca. 1050." *Viator* 40 (2009): 17–40.

Jeauneau, Edouard. "Jean de Salisbury et la lecture des philosophes." In *The World of John of Salisbury,* ed. Wilks. 77–108

———. *Rethinking the School of Chartres.* Trans. Claude Paul Desmarais. Toronto: University of Toronto Press, 2009.

Johnston, Mark D. *The Evangelical Rhetoric of Ramon Llull: Lay Learning and Piety in the Christian West Around 1300.* Oxford: Oxford University Press, 1999.

Jolivet, Jean. *Abélard, ou la philosophie dans le langage: Présentation, choix de textes, bibliographie.* Fribourg: Éditions Universitaires, 1994.

———. *Arts du langage et théologie chez Abélard.* Paris: J. Vrin, 1982.

———. *La théologie d'Abélard.* Paris: Cerf, 1997.

Jolivet, Jean and Alain de Libera, eds. *Gilbert de Poitiers et ses contemporains.* Naples: Bibliopolis, 1987.

Jones, Paul H. *Christ's Eucharistic Presence: A History of the Doctrine.* New York: Lang, 1994.

Jordan, William Chester. "Adolescence and Conversion in the Middle Ages: A Research Agenda." In *Jews and Christians in Twelfth-Century Europe,* ed. Signer and Van Engen. 77–93.

———. *The French Monarchy and the Jews: From Philip Augustus to the Last Capetians.* Philadelphia: University of Pennsylvania Press, 1989.

———. *Louis IX and the Challenge of the Crusade: A Study in Rulership.* Princeton, N.J.: Princeton University Press, 1979.

————. "Marian Devotion and the Talmud Trial of 1240." In *Religionsgespräche im Mittelalter*. ed. Bernard Lewis and Friedrich Niewöhner. Wiesbaden: Harrassowitz, 1992. 61–76.

Jorissen, Hans. *Die Entfaltung der Transsubstantionslehre bis zum Beginn der Hochscholastik*, Münsterische Beiträge zur Theologie 28/1. Münster: Aschendorffsche Verlagsbuchhandlung, 1965.

Justice, Steven. "The Authority of Ritual in the *Jeu d'Adam*." *Speculum* 62, 4 (1987): 851–64.

Kahn, Charles H. *Plato and the Socratic Dialogue: The Philosophical Use of a Literary Form*. Cambridge: Cambridge University Press, 1996.

Kantorowicz, Hermann. "The Quaestiones of the Glossators." *Tijdschrift voor Rechtsgeschiedenis* 16 (1939): 1–67.

————. "The Questiones Disputatae of the Glossators." *Revue d'Histoire du Droit* 16 (1939): 1–67.

————. *Studies in the Glossators of the Roman Law*. Darmstadt: Scientia, 1969.

Karras, Ruth Mazo. *From Boys to Men: Formations of Masculinity in Late Medieval Europe*. Philadelphia: University of Pennsylvania Press, 2003.

Keats-Rohan, K. S. B. "John of Salisbury and Education in Twelfth-Century Paris from the Account of his *Metalogicon*." *History of Universities* 16 (1986–87): 1–45.

Kenny, Anthony. *Medieval Philosophy*. Oxford: Oxford University Press, 2005.

Kirkman, Andrew. *The Cultural Life of the Early Polyphonic Mass: Medieval Context to Modern Revival*. Cambridge: Cambridge University Press, 2010.

Klibansky, Raymond. "Peter Abailard and Bernard of Clairvaux: A Letter by Abailard." *Medieval and Renaissance Studies* 5 (1961): 1–27.

————. "Standing on the Shoulders of Giants." *Isis* 71 (1936): 147–49.

Knapp, Janet. "Polyphony at Notre Dame of Paris." *The New Oxford History of Music*. Vol. 2, *The Early Middle Ages to 1300*, ed. Richard Crocker and David Hiley. Oxford: Oxford University Press, 1990. 557–635.

Krauss, Samuel and William Horbury. *The Jewish-Christian Controversy from the Earliest Times to 1789*. Tübingen: Mohr, 1995.

Kretzmann, N., A. Kenny, and Jan Pinborg, eds. *The Cambridge History of Later Medieval Philosophy*. *Cambridge: Cambridge University Press, 1982.*

Kruger, Steven F. *Dreaming in the Middle Ages*. Cambridge: Cambridge University Press, 1992.

————. *The Spectral Jew: Conversion and Embodiment in Medieval Europe*. Minneapolis: University of Minnesota Press, 2006.

Kuchenbuch, Ludolf. "Ordnungsverhalten im grundherrlichen Schriftgut vom 9. zum 12. Jahrhundert." In *Dialektik und Rhetorik*, ed. Fried. 175–268.

Kuttner, Stephan. *Harmony from Dissonance: An Interpretation of Medieval Canon Law*. Latrobe, Pa.: Archabbey Press, 1960.

————. *Repertorium der Kanonistik*. Vatican City: Biblioteca Apostolica Vaticana, 1937.

————. "The Revival of Jurisprudence." In *Renaissance and Renewal in the Twelfth Century*, ed. Constable and Benson. 299–323.

Kuttner, Stephan and António García y García. "A New Eyewitness Account of the Fourth Lateran Council." *Traditio* 20 (1964): 115–78.

Ladner, R. "*L'ordo praedicatorum* avant l'ordre des prêcheurs." In *Saint Dominique: L'idée, l'homme et l'oeuvre*, ed. Pierre Mandonnet and M.-H. Vicaire. Vol. 2. Paris: Desclée de Brouwer, 1938. 11–68.

Laing, Margaret. *Catalogue of Sources for a Linguistic Atlas of Early Medieval English*. Cambridge: Brewer, 1993.

Landau, Peter. "The Development of Law." In *The New Cambridge Medieval History IV: c. 1025–c. 1198, Part I*, ed. David Luscombe and Jonathan Riley-Smith. Cambridge: Cambridge University Press, 2004. 113–47.

Landgraf, Artur. "Notes de critique textuelle sur les *Sentences* de Pierre Lombard." *Recherche de Théologie Ancienne et Médiévale* 2 (1930): 80–99.

Långfors, Arthur, Alfred Jeanroy, and L. Bandin, eds. *Receuil général des jeux-partis français*. Paris: Champion, 1926.

Langmuir, Gavin I. *History, Religion, and Antisemitism*. Berkeley: University of California Press, 1990.

———. "Majority Historians and Post-Biblical Jews." *Journal of the History of Ideas* 27 (1966): 343–64.

———. *Toward a Definition of Antisemitism*. Berkeley: University of California Press, 1990.

Lasker, Daniel J. *Jewish Philosophical Polemics Against Christianity in the Middle Ages*. 2nd ed. Portland, Ore.: Littman Library of Jewish Civilization, 2007.

Lavis, Georges. "Le jeu-parti français: Jeu de refutation, d'opposition et de concession." *Medioevo Romanzo* 16 (1991): 21–128.

Lawn, Brian. *The Rise and Decline of the Scholastic "Quaestio Disputata": With Special Emphasis on Its Use in the Teaching of Medicine and Science*. Leiden: Brill, 1993.

Le Goff, Jacques. *The Birth of Purgatory*. Trans. Arthur Goldhammer. Chicago: University of Chicago Press, 1986.

———. *Intellectuals in the Middle Ages*. Trans. Teresa Lavender Fagan. Oxford: Blackwell, 1993.

———. *The Medieval Imagination*. Trans. Arthur Goldhammer. Chicago: University of Chicago Press, 1992.

———. "Quelle conscience l'université médiévale a-t-elle d'elle-même?" In *Beiträge zum Berufsbewusstsein des Mittelalterlichen Menschen*, ed. Paul Wilpert. Miscellanea Medievalia 3. Berlin: De Gruyter, 1964: 15–29.

Leclercq, Jean. "La récréation et le colloque dans la tradition monastique." *Revue d'Ascétique et de mystique* 43 (1967): 3–20.

Lees, Jay T. *Anselm of Havelberg: Deeds into Words in the Twelfth Century*. Leiden: Brill, 1998.

Leonardi, Claudio. "Intellectual Life." In *The New Cambridge Medieval History*. Vol. 2, *c. 900–c. 1024*. Ed. Timothy Reuter. Cambridge: Cambridge University Press, 2000. 186–211.

Lerer, Seth. *Boethius and Dialogue: Literary Method in the Consolation of Philosophy*. Princeton, N.J.: Princeton University Press, 1985.

Lesne, Émile. *Les écoles, de la fin du VIIIe siècle à la fin du XIIe*. Vol. 5, *Histoire de la propriété ecclésiastique en France*. Lille: Économat, 1940.

Liebeschütz, Hans. "The Significance of Judaism in Abelard's *Dialogus*." *Journal of Jewish Studies* 12 (1961): 1–18.

Liebman, Charles J. *The Old French Psalter Commentary: Contribution to a Critical Study of the Text Attributed to Simon of Tournai*. Canandaigua, N.Y.: Humphrey Press, 1982.

Lim, Richard. *Public Disputation, Power, and Social Order in Late Antiquity*. Berkeley: University of California Press, 1995.

Lipton, Sara. *Images of Intolerance: The Representations of Jews and Judaism in the Bible Moralisée*. Berkeley: University of California Press 1999.

Little, A. G. and F. Pelster. *Oxford Theology and Theologians, c. A.D. 1282–1302*. Oxford: Clarendon, 1934.

Little, Edward F. "Bernard and Abelard at the Council of Sens." In *Bernard of Clairvaux: Studies Presented to Dom Jean Leclerq*, ed. M. Basil Pennington. Washington, D.C.: Cistercian Publications, 1973. 55–71.

———. "Relations Between St. Bernard and Abelard Before 1139." In *St. Bernard of Clairvaux*, ed. M. Basil Pennington. Kalamazoo, Mich.: Cistercian Publications, 1977. 155–68.

Ljubovic, Amir. *The Works in Logic by Bosnian Authors in Arabic*. Leiden: Brill, 2008.

Loeb, Isidore. *La controverse sur le Talmud sous Saint Louis*. Paris, 1881.

Logan, Donald F. *A History of the Church in the Middle Ages*. London: Routledge, 2002.

Lohr, Charles H. "The Medieval Reception of Aristotle." *CHLMP*, ed. Kretzmann et al. 80–98.

———. "Ramon Llull and Thirteenth-Century Religious Dialogue." In *Diálogo filosófico-religioso entre cristianismo, judaísmo e islamismo durante la Edad Media en la Península Iberica*, ed. Horacio Santiago-Otero. Turnhout: Brepols, 1994. 117–29.

Long, Alex. "Plato's Dialogues and a Common Rationale for Dialogue Form." In *The End of Dialogue in Antiquity*, ed. Goldhill. 45–59.

Lottin, Odon. "L'influence littéraire du chancelier Philippe." In *Psychologie et morale aux XIIe et XIIIe siècles*. 6 vols. Louvain: Abbaye de Mont-César, Gembloux, Duculot, 1948–1960. 6:149–69.

Lowden, John. *The Making of the Bibles Moralisées*. 2 vols. University Park: Pennsylvania State University Press, 2000.

Luchesi, Giovanni. "Per una Vita di San Pier Damiani." In *San Pier Damiano nel IX Centenario della Morte* (1072–1972). 4 vols. Cesena: Centro studi e ricerche sulla antica provincia ecclesiastica ravennate, 1972–78. 1:13–180; 2:13–160.

Luscombe, David E. "John of Salisbury in Recent Scholarship." In *The World of John of Salisbury*, ed. Wilks. 21–37

———. *The School of Peter Abelard*. Cambridge: Cambridge University Press, 1969.

———. "St. Anselm and Abelard." *Anselm Studies* 1 (1983): 207–29.

———. "St. Anselm and Abelard: A Restatement." In *Saint Anselm*, ed. Viola and Van Fleteren. 1983. 445–60.

Luscombe, David E. and G. R. Evans, eds. *Anselm: Aosta, Bec and Canterbury: Papers in Commemoration of the Nine-Hundredth Anniversary of Anselm's Enthronement as Archbishop, 25 September 1093*. Sheffield: Sheffield Academic Press, 1996.

Maccoby, Hyam. *Judaism on Trial: Jewish-Christian Public Disputations in the Middle Ages*. Oxford: Littman Library of Jewish Civilization, 1982.

Macdonald, A. J. *Berengar and the Reform of Sacramental Doctrine*. London, 1930.

Madec, G. "L'historicité des Dialogues de Cassiciacum." *Revue Théologique Augustiniene* 32 (1986): 207–31.

Makdisi, George. "The Scholastic Method in Medieval Education: An Inquiry into Its Origins in Law and Theology." *Speculum* 49, 4 (1974): 640–61.

Makdisi, John A. "The Islamic Origins of the Common Law." *North Carolina Law Review* 77, 15 (June 1999): 1635–1739.

Mandonnet, Pierre and M.-H. Vicaire, eds. *Saint Dominique: L'idée, l'homme et l'oeuvre*. 2 vols. Paris: Desclée de Brouwer, 1938.

Marenbon, John. *Aristotelian Logic, Platonism, and the Context of Early Medieval Philosophy in the West*. Variorum Collected Studies Series. Aldershot: Ashgate, 2000.

———. *Early Medieval Philosophy (480–1150): An Introduction*. London: Routledge, 1988.

——— *From the Circle of Alcuin to the School of Auxerre: Logic, Theology, and Philosophy in the Early Middle Ages*. Cambridge: Cambridge University Press, 1981.

———. "Gilbert of Poitiers." In *A History of Western Philosophy in the Twelfth Century*, ed. Dronke. 328–52.

———. "Glosses and Commentaries on the *Categories* and *De interpretatione* Before Abelard." In *Dialektik und Rhetorik*, ed. Fried. 21–43.

———. "Logic at the Turn of the Twelfth Century: A Synthesis." In *Arts du langage et théologie aux confins des XIe–XIIe siècles*, ed. Rosier-Catach. 181–218.

———. "Medieval Latin Commentaries and Glosses on Aristotelian Logical Texts Before c. 1150 A.D." In *Glosses and Commentaries on Aristotelian Logical Texts: The Syriac, Arabic and Medieval Latin Traditions*, ed. Charles Burnett. London: Warburg Institute, 1993. 77–127.

———. *The Philosophy of Peter Abelard*. Cambridge: Cambridge University Press, 1997.

Marsh, David. "Dialogue and Discussion in the Renaissance." In *The Cambridge History of Literary Criticism*. Vol. 3, *The Renaissance*, ed. Glyn P. Norton. Cambridge: Cambridge University Press, 1999. 265–70.

———. *The Quattrocento Dialogue: Classical Tradition and Humanist Innovation*. Cambridge, Mass.: Harvard University Press, 1980.

Martin, Christopher J. "Logic." In *The Cambridge Companion to Abelard*, ed. Brower and Guilfoy. 158–99.

———. "A Note on the Attribution of the *Literal Glosses* to in Paris, BnF, lat. 13368 to Peter Abelard." in *Arts du langague*, ed. Rosier-Catach. 605–46.

Martin, Hervé. *Mentalités médiévales, XIe–XVe siècle*. Paris: PUF, 1996.

Martin, John D. "Dramatized Disputations: Late Medieval German Dramatizations of Jewish-Christian Religious Disputations, Church Policy, and Local Social Climates." *Medieval Encounters* 8, 2–3 (2002): 209–27.

Matlock, Wendy A. "Law and Violence in *The Owl and the Nightingale*." *Journal of English and Germanic Philology* 109 (2010): 446–67.

Matter, E. Ann. *The Voice of My Beloved: The Song of Songs in Western Medieval Christianity*. Philadelphia: University of Pennsylvania Press, 1990.

McCabe, Mary Margaret. "Plato's Ways of Writing." In *The Oxford Handbook of Plato*, ed. Gail Fine. Oxford: Oxford University Press, 2008. 88–113.

McKitterick, Rosamond, ed. *Carolingian Culture: Emulation and Innovation*. Cambridge: Cambridge University Press, 1994.

———. *The Carolingians and the Written Word*. Cambridge: Cambridge University Press, 1994.

———, ed, *The Uses of Literacy in Early Medieval Europe*. Cambridge: Cambridge University Press, 1990.

McSheffrey, Shannon. "Place, Space, and Situation: Public and Private in the Making of Marriage in Late-Medieval London." *Speculum* 79, 4 (2004): 960–90.

Mehl, Dieter. "*The Owl and the Nightingale*: Mündlichkeit und Schriftlichkeit im Streigespräch." In *Mündlichkeit und Schriftlichkeit im englischen Mittelalter*, ed. Willi Erzgräber and Sabine Volk. ScriptOralia 5. Tübingen: G. Narr, 1988. 75–84.

Melve, Leidulf. *Inventing the Public Sphere: The Public Debate during the Investiture Conflict (c. 1030–1122)*. 2 vols. Leiden: Brill, 2007.

———. "'The Revolt of the Medievalists': New Directions in Recent Research on the Twelfth-Century Renaissance." *Journal of Medieval History* 32, 3 (2006): 231–52.

Merback, Mitchell B., ed. *Beyond the Yellow Badge: Anti-Judaism and Antisemitism in Medieval and Early Modern Visual Culture*. Leiden: Brill, 2007.

Merchavia, Chen. *The Church Versus Talmudic and Midrashic Literature, 500–1248* [Hebrew]. Jerusalem: Bialik Institute, 1970.

Merton, Robert. *On The Shoulders of Giants: A Shandean Postscript.* Chicago: University of Chicago Press, 1993 [1965].

Mews, Constant J. *Abelard and Heloise.* Great Medieval Thinkers. Oxford: Oxford University Press, 2005.

———. "Abelard and Heloise on Jews and *Hebraica Veritas.*" In *Christian Attitudes Toward the Jews,* ed. Frassetto. 83–108.

———. "The Council of Sens (1141): Abelard, Bernard, and the Fear of Social Upheaval." *Speculum* 77, 2 (2002): 342–82.

———. "Discussing Love: The *Epistolae duorum amantium* and Abelard's *Sic et Non.*" *Journal of Medieval Latin* 19 (2009): 130–47.

———. "The Lists of Heresies Imputed to Peter Abelard." *Revue Bénédictine* 95 (1985): 77–108.

———. "Peter Abelard and the Enigma of Dialogue." In *Beyond the Persecuting Society: Religious Toleration Before the Enlightenment,* ed. John Christian Laursen and Cary J. Nederman. Philadelphia: University of Pennsylvania Press, 1998. 25–52.

———. "Peter Abelard on Dialectic, Rhetoric, and the Principles of Argument." In *Rhetoric and Renewal in the Latin West 1100–1540: Essays in Honour of John O. Ward,* ed. Constant J. Mews, Cary J. Nederman, and Rodney M. Thompson. Turnhout: Brepols, 2003. 37–53.

———. "The *Sententie* of Peter Abelard." *Recherches de Théologie Ancienne et Médiévale* 53 (1986): 130–83.

———. "St. Anselm and Roscelin: Some New Texts and Their Implications. I. The *De Incarnatione Verbi* and the *Disputatio inter Christianum et Gentilem.*" *Archives d'Histoire Doctrinale et Littéraire du Moyen Âge* 58 (1991): 55–98.

Meyer, Paul. "Henri d'Andeli et le chancelier Philippe." *Romania* 1 (1872): 190–215.

Miethke, Jürgen. "Die Kirzche und die Universitäten im 13. Jahrhundert." In *Schulen und Studium im sozialen Wandel des hohen und späten Mittelalters,* ed. Johannes Fried. Sigmaringen: Thorbecke, 1986. 285–320.

Minio-Paluello, L. "The *Ars Disserendi* of Adam of Balsham." In *Medieval and Renaissance Studies,* vol. 3, ed. Richard Hunt and Raymond Klibansky. London: Warburg Institute, 1954. 116–69.

———, ed. *Twelfth-Century Logic: Texts and Studies.* 2 vols. Rome: Storia e Letteratura, 1956–59.

Minnis, A.-J. *Medieval Theory of Authorship: Scholastic Literary Attitudes in the Later Middle Ages.* 2nd ed. Philadelphia: University of Pennsylvania Press, 2009.

Minnis, A.-J., A. B. Scott, and David Wallace, eds. *Medieval Literary Theory and Criticism, c. 1100–1375: The Commentary-Tradition.* Oxford: Clarendon, 1988.

Montuori, Mario, ed. *The Socratic Problem: The History—The Solutions.* Amsterdam: J. C. Gieben, 1992.

Moore, John C. *Pope Innocent III (1160/61–1216): To Root Up and to Plant.* Leiden: Brill, 2003.

———, ed. *Pope Innocent III and His World.* Aldershot: Ashgate, 1999.

Moore, R. I. "Antisemitism and the Birth of Europe." In *Christianity and Judaism,* ed. Diana Wood. Oxford: Blackwell. 1992. 33–57.

———. *The Formation of a Persecuting Society, 950–1250.* Oxford: Blackwell, 1987.

Moore, Rebecca. *Jews and Christians in the Life and Thought of Hugh of Saint Victor.* Atlanta: Scholar's Press, 1998.

Moran, Dermot. *The Philosophy of John Scottus Eriugena: A Study of Idealism in the Middle Ages.* Cambridge: Cambridge University Press, 1989.

Morey, Dom Adrian. *Bartholomew of Exeter, Bishop and Canonist: A Study in the Twelfth Century.* Cambridge: Cambridge University Press, 1937.

Morrison, Karl F. "Anselm of Havelberg: Play and the Dilemma of Historical Progress." In *Religion, Culture and Society in the Early Middle Ages: Studies in Honor of Richard E. Sullivan*, ed. Thomas F. X. Noble and John J. Contreni. Kalamazoo, Mich.: Medieval Institute Publications, 1987. 219–56.

———. *Conversion and Text: The Cases of Augustine of Hippo, Herman-Judah, and Constantine Tsatsos*. Charlottesville: University Press of Virginia, 1992.

Morrow, Kara Ann. "Disputation in Stone: Jews Imagined on the St. Stephen Portal of Paris Cathedral." In *Beyond the Yellow Badge*, ed. Merback. 63–86.

Mostert, Marco and P. S. Barnwell, eds. *Medieval Legal Process: Physical, Spoken and Written Performance in the Middle Ages*. Turnhout: Brepols, 2011.

Mulchahey, M. Michèle. *"First the Bow is Bent in Study": Dominican Education Before 1350*. Toronto: Pontifical Institute of Mediaeval Studies, 1998.

Müller, Wolfgang P. "The Recovery of Justinian's Digest in the Middle Ages." *Bulletin of Medieval Canon Law* 20 (1990): 1–29.

Mundill, Robert R. *England's Jewish Solution: Experiment and Expulsion, 1262–1290*. Cambridge: Cambridge University Press, 2002.

Münster-Swendsen, Mia. "The Model of Scholastic Mastery in Northern Europe c. 970–1200." In *Teaching and Learning*, ed. Vaughn and Rubenstein. 307–42.

Murphy, James J. "Rhetoric and Dialectic in *The Owl and the Nightingale*." In *Medieval Eloquence: Studies in the Theory and Practice of Medieval Rhetoric*, ed. James J. Murphy. Berkeley: University of California Press, 1978. 198–230.

———. *Rhetoric in the Middle Ages: A History of Rhetorical Theory from St. Augustine to the Renaissance*. Berkeley: University of California Press, 1974.

Murray, Alexander. *Reason and Society in the Middle Ages*. Oxford: Clarendon, 1978.

Neff, Amy. "The *Dialogus Beatae Mariae et Anselmi de Passione Domini*: Toward an Attribution." *Miscellanea Francescana* 86 (1986): 105–8.

Nightingale, Andrea Wilson. *Genres in Dialogue: Plato and the Construct of Philosophy*. Cambridge: Cambridge University Press, 1995.

Nirenberg, David. *Anti-Judaism: the Western Tradition*. New York: Norton, 2013.

———. *Communities of Violence: Persecution of Minorities in the Middle Ages*. Princeton, N.J.: Princeton University Press, 1996.

Noble, Thomas F. X. and John Van Engen, eds. *European Transformations: The Long Twelfth Century*. Notre Dame, Ind.: University of Notre Dame Press, 2012.

Novikoff, Alex J. "Anselm, Dialogue, and the Rise of Scholastic Disputation." *Speculum* 86, 2 (2011): 387–418.

———. "From Dialogue to Disputation in the Age of Archbishop Rodrigo Jiménez de Rada." *Journal of Medieval Iberian Studies* 4, 1 (2012): 95–100.

———. "Reason and Natural Law in the Disputational Writings of Peter Alfonsi, Peter Abelard, and Yehuda Halevi." In *Christian Attitudes Towards the Jews*, ed Frassetto. 109–36.

———. "The Renaissance of the Twelfth Century Before Haskins." *Haskins Society Journal* 16 (2005): 104–16.

———. "Toward a Cultural History of Scholastic Disputation." *American Historical Review* 117, 2 (2012): 331–64.

Oakley, Francis. *Omnipotence, Covenant, and Order: An Excursion in the History of Ideas from Abelard to Leibniz*. Ithaca, N.Y.: Cornell University Press, 1984.

O'Callaghan, Joseph F. *Reconquest and Crusade in Medieval Spain*. Philadelphia: University of Pennsylvania Press, 2003.

Ong, Walter. *Fighting for Life: Contest, Sexuality, and Consciousness*. Ithaca, N.Y.: Cornell University Press, 1981.

———. *Rhetoric, Romance, and Technology: Studies in the Interaction of Expression and Culture*. Ithaca, N.Y.: Cornell University Press, 1990.

Ortoll i Martín, Ernest. "Algunas consideraciones sobre la iglesia de Santa Caterina de Barcelona." *Locus Amoenus* 2 (1996): 47–63.

Paetow, Louis. *The Battle of the Seven Arts: A French Poem by Henri d'Andeli, Trouvère of the Thirteenth Century*. Memoirs of the University of California 4, 1. Berkeley: University of California Press, 1914.

Page, Christopher. *The Owl and the Nightingale: Musical Life and Ideas in France 1100–1300*. Berkeley: University of California Press, 1990.

———. "A Treatise on Musicians from c. 1400: The *Tractatulus de differentiis et gradibus cantorum* by Arnulf de St Ghislain." *Journal of the Royal Musical Association* 45 (1992): 1–21.

Panofsky, Erwin. *Gothic Architecture and Scholasticism*. Latrobe, Pa.: Archabbey Press, 1951.

Paratore, Ettore. "Cicerone attraverso i secoli." In Luigi Alfonsi et al., *Marco Tullio Cicerone*. Florence: Instituto di studi Roamni, 1961. 237–244.

Patton, Pamela. *Art of Estrangement: Redefining Jews in Reconquest Spain*. University Park: Pennsylvania States University Press, 2012.

Payne, Thomas B. "Aurelianis *civitas*: Student Unrest in Medieval France and a Conductus by Philip the Chancellor." *Speculum* 75, 3 (2000): 589–614.

———. "Philip the Chancellor and the Conductus Prosula: 'Motetish' Works from the School of Notre Dame." In *Music in Medieval Europe: Studies in Honour of Bryan Gillingham*, ed. Terence Bailey and Alma Santosuosso. Aldershot: Ashgate, 2007. 220–38.

———. "Poetry, Politics, and Polyphony: Philip the Chancellor's Contribution to the Music of the Notre Dame School." 5 vols. Ph.D. dissertation, University of Chicago, 1991.

Pedersen, Olaf. *The First Universities: Studium Generale and the Origins of University Education in Europe*. Trans. R. North. Cambridge: Cambridge University Press, 2003.

Pelikan, Jaroslav. *The Emergence of the Catholic Tradition (100–600)*. The Christian Tradition: History of the Development of Doctrine 1. Chicago: University of Chicago Press, 1971.

Peters, Edward. *Inquisition*. New York: The Free Press, 1988.

Peterson, Joan. *The Dialogues of Gregory the Great in Their Late Antique Cultural Background*. Toronto: Pontifical Institute of Medieval Studies, 1984.

Pflaum, Hiram. "Der allegorische Streit zwischen Synagoge und Kirchse in der europäischen Dichtung des Mittelalters." *Archivum Romanicum* 18 (1934): 234–340.

———. "Poems of Religious Disputations in the Middle Ages (in Hebrew)." *Tarbiz* 2, 4 (1931): 443–47.

Pick, Lucy K. *Conflict and Coexistence: Archbishop Rodrigo and the Muslims and Jews of Medieval Spain*. Ann Arbor: University of Michigan Press (2004).

Piron, Sylvain. "Franciscan *Quodlibeta* in Southern *Studia* and at Paris, 1280–1300." In *Theological Quodlibeta in the Middle Ages: The Thirteenth Century*, ed. Chris Schabel. Leiden: Brill, 2006. 403–38.

Poirrier, Philippe. *Les enjeux de l'histoire culturelle*. Paris: Seuil, 2004.

Poole, Reginald Lane. *Illustrations of the History of Medieval Thought and Learning*. London: Society for Promoting Christian Knowledge, 1880.

Pop, Démètre. *La défense du pape Formose*. Paris: J. Gabalda, 1933.

Porée, A. A. *Histoire de l'abbeye du Bec*. 2 vols. Évreux: Charles Hérissy, 1901.

Post, Gaines. "Parisian Masters as a Corporation, 1200–1246." In idem, *Studies in Medieval Legal Thought: Public Law and the State, 1100–1322*. Princeton, N.J.: Princeton University Press, 1964. 27–60.

Pouchet, Jean-Robert, O.S.B. *La rectitudo chez Saint Anselme: Un itinéraire augustinien de l'âme à Dieu*. Paris: Études Augustiniennes, 1964.

Powicke, F. M. *Stephen Langton*. Oxford: Clarendon, 1997 [1927].

Račiūnatitė-Vyčinienė, Davia. *Sutartinès: Lithuanian Polyphonic Songs*. Trans. Vijole Arbas. Vilnius: VAGA, 2002.

Radding, Charles M. *The Origins of Medieval Jurisprudence: Pavia and Bologna, 850–1150*. New Haven, Conn.: Yale University Press, 1988.

———. *A World Made by Men: Cognition and Society, 400–1200*. Chapel Hill: University of North Carolina Press, 1985.

Radding, Charles M. and William W. Clark. *Medieval Architecture, Medieval Learning: Builders and Masters in the Age of Romanesque and Gothic*. New Haven, Conn.: Yale University Press, 1992.

Radding, Charles M. and Francis Newton. *Theology, Rhetoric, and Politics in the Eucharistic Controversy, 1078–1079: Alberic of Monte Cassino Against Berengar of Tours*. New York: Columbia University Press, 2003.

Ranft, Patricia. *The Theology of Work: Peter Damian and the Medieval Religious Renewal Movement*. New York: Palgrave Macmillan, 2006.

Rashdall, Hastings. *The Universities of Europe in the Middle Ages*. Ed. F. M. Powicke and A. B. Emden. 3 vols. Oxford: Oxford University Press, 1936.

Reale, Nancy M. "Rhetorical Strategies in *The Owl and the Nightingale*." *Philological Quarterly* 63 (1984): 417–29.

Reed, Thomas L., Jr. *Middle English Debate Poetry and the Aesthetics of Irresolution*. Columbia: University of Missouri Press, 1990.

Reinhart, Klaus and Horacio Santiago-Otero. "Pedro Alfonso. Obras y Bibliografía." In *Estudios sobre Pedro Alfonso de Huesca*, ed. María Jesús Lacarra. Huesca: Instituto de Estudios Altoaragoneses, 1996. 19–44.

Reinink, J. and H. L. J. Vanstiphout, eds. *Dispute Poems and Dialogues in the Ancient and Mediaeval Near East: Forms and Types of Literary Debates in Semitic and Related Literatures*. Leuven: Peeters, 1991.

Rembaum, Joel E. "The Talmud and the Popes: Reflections on the Talmud Trials of the 1240's." *Viator* 13 (1982): 202–23.

Resnick, Irven M. *Divine Power and Possibility in St. Peter Damian's* De Divina Omnipotentia. Leiden: Brill, 1992.

Rey-Flaud, Henri. *Pour une dramaturgie du moyen âge*. Paris: Presses Universitaires de Paris, 1980.

Riché, Pierre. "La vie scolaire et la vie pédagogique au Bec au temps de Lanfranc et de Saint Anselme." In *Les mutations socio-culturelles*, ed. Foreville. 213–27.

Riley-Smith, Jonathan. "Christian Violence and the Crusades." In *Religious Violence Between Christians and Jews: Medieval Roots, Modern Perspectives*, ed. Anna Sapir Abulafia. New York: Palgrave, 2002. 3–20.

Rillon, Anne-Zoé. "Convaincre et émouvoir: Les conduits monodiques de Philippe le Chancelier, un médium pour la predication?" *La place de la musique dans la culture médiévale*, ed. Cullin. 99–113.

Rizek-Pfister, Cornelia. "Die hermeneutischen Prinzipien in Abaelards *Sic et non*." *Freiburger Zeitschrift für Philosophie und Theologie* 47 (2000): 484–501.

Robinson, J. Armitage. *Gilbert Crispin, Abbot of Westminster: A Study of the Abbey Under Norman Rule.* Notes and Documents Relating to Westminster Abbey 3. Cambridge: Cambrudge University Press, 1911.

Robson, Michael. *The Franciscans in the Middle Ages.* Woodbridge: Boydell, 2006.

Roesner, Edward H. "Notre Dame Polyphony." In *The Cambridge History of Medieval Music.* Forthcoming.

Rolfe, John C. *Cicero and His Influence.* Boston: Marshall Jones, 1923.

Rolker, Christof. *Canon Law and the Letters of Ivo of Chartres.* Cambridge: Cambridge University Press, 2010.

Ronquist, E. C. "Learning and Teaching in Twelfth-Century Dialogues." *Res Publica Litterarum* 13 (1990): 239–56.

Rose, Paul Lawrence. "When Was the Talmud Burnt at Paris? A Critical Examination of the Christian and Jewish Sources and a New Dating: June 1241." *Journal of Jewish Studies* 62 (2011): 324–39.

Rosenthal, Judah M. "A Religious Disputation Between a Jew Called Menahem and the Convert Pablo Christiani [Hebrew]." In *Hagut Ivrit ba'Amerika: Studies in Jewish Themes by Contemporary American Scholars,* vol. 3, ed. Menahem Zohori et al. Tel Aviv: Brit Ivrit Olamit, Yavneh Publishing House, 1974. 61–74.

Rosier-Catach, Irène, ed. *Arts du langage et théologie aux confins des XIe-XIIe siècles: Texts, maîtres, débats.* Turnhout: Brepols, 2011.

Rospocher, Massimo, ed. *Beyond the Public Sphere: Opinions, Publics, Spaces in Early Modern Europe.* Bologna: Società editrice il Mulino, 2012.

Rowe, Christopher. *Plato and the Art of Philosophical Writing.* Cambridge: Cambridge University Press, 2007.

Rowe, Nina. *The Jew, the Cathedral and the Medieval City: Synagoga and Ecclesia in the Thirteenth Century.* Cambridge: Cambridge University Press, 2011.

———. "Rethinking Ecclesia and Synagoga." In *Gothic Art and Thought in the Later Medieval Period,* ed. Hourihane. 264–91.

Rubin, Miri. *Corpus Christi: The Eucharist in Late Medieval Culture.* Cambridge: Cambridge University Press, 1991.

Ruch, Michel. *Le préambule dans les oeuvres philosophiques de Cicéron: Essai sur la genèse et l'art du dialogue.* Paris: Belles Lettres, 1958.

Rudnick, Ulrich. *Das System des Johannes Scottus Eriugena: Eine theologisch-philosophische Studie zu seinem Werk.* Frankfurt: Peter Lang, 1990.

Rüegg, Walter. "Themes." In *A History of the University in Europe,* ed. De Ridder-Symoens. 3–34.

Russel, Theodore N. "Anselm of Havelberg and the Union of the Churches." *Kleronomia* 10 (1978): 85–120.

Rutledge, S. "The Literary, Cultural, and Historical Background of Tacitus' *Dialogus de oratoribus.*" Ph.D. dissertation: Brown University, 1996.

Saenger, Paul. *Space Between Words: The Origins of Silent Reading.* Stanford, Calif.: Stanford University Press, 1997.

Saltzstein, Jennifer. "Cleric-Trouvères and the *Jeux-Partis* of Medieval Arras." *Viator* 43 (2012): 147–63.

Sanders, E. H. "The Medieval Motet." In *Gattungen der Musik in Einzeldarstellungen: Gedenkschrift Leo Schrade, erst Folge,* ed. Wulf Arlt, Ernst Lichtenhahn, and Hans W. Oesch. Berlin: Francke, 1973. 497–573.

Sauerländer, Willibald. "Reims und Bamberg: Zu Art und Umfang der Übernahmen." *Zeitschrift der Kunstgeschichte* 39 (1976): 167–92.

Sayre, Kenneth M. *Plato's Literary Garden: How to Read a Platonic Dialogue*. Notre Dame, Ind.: University of Notre Dame Press, 1995.

Scheindlin, Raymond P. *The Song of Distant Love: Judah Halevi's Pilgrimage*. Oxford: Oxford University Press, 2007.

Schmitt, Jean-Claude. *The Conversion of Herman the Jew: Autobiography, History, and Fiction in the Twelfth Century*. Trans. Alex J. Novikoff. Philadelphia: University of Pennsylvania Press, 2010.

Schneyer, Johannes B. *Die Sittenkritik in den Predigten Philipps des Kanzlers*. Beiträge zur Geschichte der Philosophie und Theologie des Mittelalters 39, 4. Münster: Aschendorffs Verlagsbuchhandlung, 1962.

Schofield, Malcom. "Ciceronian Dialogue." In *The End of Dialogue in Antiquity*, ed Goldhill. 63–84.

Schreckenberg, Heinz. *Die christlichen Adversus-Judaeos-Texte und ihr literarisches und historisches Umfeld (1.–11. Jh.)*. Frankfurt: Peter Lang, 1990.

———. *Die christlichen Adversus-Judaeos-Texte (11.–13. Jh)*. Frankfurt: Peter Lang, 1991.

———. *The Jews in Christian Art*. New York: Continuum, 1996.

Schreiner, Susan. *Where Shall Wisdom Be Found? Calvin's Exegesis of Job from Medieval and Modern Perspectives*. Chicago: University of Chicago Press, 1994.

Serper, Arié. "Le débat entre synagogue et église au XIIIe siècle." *Revue des Études Juives* 123 (1964): 307–33.

Sharpe, Richard. "Anselm as Author: Publishing in the Late Eleventh Century." *Journal of Medieval Latin* 19 (2009): 1–87.

Shatzmiller, Joseph. *La deuxième controverse de Paris: Un chapitre dans la polémique entre chrétiens et juifs au Moyen Âge*. Paris: Peeters, 1994.

Shear, Adam. *The Kuzari and the Shaping of Jewish Identity, 1167–1900*. Cambridge: Cambridge University Press, 2008.

Sherwood, Jessie. "Thibaut de Sezanne & the Disputation of the Jews Against the Christians." Unpublished essay, http://jessiecsherwood.files.wordpress.com/2010/11/disputation-of -the-jews-aga inst-the-christians.pdf.

Shryock, Andrew and Daniel Lord Smail, eds. *Deep History: The Architecture of Past and Present*. Berkeley: University of California Pres, 2012.

Sieben, Herman-Joseph. *Die Konzilsidee des Lateinischen Mittelalters (847–1378)*. Paderborn: Schöning, 1984.

Signer, Michael and John Van Engen, eds. *Jews and Christians in Twelfth-Century Europe*. Notre Dame, Ind.: University of Notre Dame Press, 2001.

Smail, Daniel Lord. *The Consumption of Justice: Emotions, Publicity, and Legal Culture in Marseille, 1264–1423*. Ithaca, N.Y.: Cornell University Press, 2003.

———. *On Deep History and the Brain*. Berkeley: University of California Press, 2008.

Smalley, Beryl. *Historians of the Middle Ages*. London: Thames and Hudson, 1974.

———. *The Study of the Bible in the Middle Ages*. 3rd ed. Oxford: Blackwell, 1983.

Snyder, Jon R. *Writing the Scene of Speaking: Theories of Dialogue in the Late Italian Renaissance*. Stanford, Calif.: Stanford University Press, 1989.

Solterer, Helen. *The Master and Minerva: Disputing Women in French Medieval Culture*. Berkeley: University of California Press, 1995.

Somerville, Robert. "The Case Against Berengar of Tours: A New Text." *Studi Gregoriani* 9 (1972): 55–75.

Somerville, Robert and Bruce C. Brasington. *Prefaces to Canon Law Books in Latin Christianity: Selected Translations, 500–1245.* New Haven, Conn.: Yale University Press, 1998.

Sot, Michel, Jean-Patrice Boudet, and Anita Guerreau-Jalabert. *Histoire culturelle de la France.* Vol. 1, *Le Moyen Âge.* Paris: Seuil, 1997.

Southern, Richard W. "The Relationship Between Anselm's Thought and His Life at Bec and Canterbury." In *Saint Anselm,* ed. Viola and Van Fleteren. 9–26.

———. *Saint Anselm: A Portrait in a Landscape.* Cambridge: Cambridge University Press, 1990.

———. *Saint Anselm and His Biographer: A Study of Monastic Life and Thought, 1059–c. 1130.* Cambridge: Cambridge University Press, 1963.

———. *Scholastic Humanism and the Unification of Europe.* 2 vols. London: Blackwell, 1995.

———. "St. Anselm and Gilbert Crispin, Abbot of Westminster." *Mediaeval and Renaissance Studies* 3 (1954): 80–98.

———. "St. Anselm of Canterbury: His Mission of Reconciliation." In *Anselm: Aosta, Bec and Canterbury,* ed. Luscombe and Evans. 17–35.

Speer, Andreas. "Ratione duce: Die naturphilosophischen Dialoge des Adelard von Bath und des Wilhelm von Conches." In *Gespräche Lesen,* ed. Jacobi. 199–229.

Spiegel, Gabrielle M. *The Past as Text: The Theory and Practice of Medieval Historiography.* Baltimore: Johns Hopkins University Press, 1997.

———. "History, Historicism, and the Social Logic of the Text in the Middle Ages." *Speculum* 65, 1 (1990): 59–86.

Stein, Siegfried. "A Disputation on Moneylending Between Jews and Gentiles in Me'ir b. Simeons Milhemeth Miswah (Narbonne, 13th Cent.)." *Journal of Jewish Studies* 10 (1959): 45–61.

Stevens, John. "Medieval Song." In *The Early Middle Ages to 1300,* ed. Richard Crocker and David Hiley. Oxford: Oxford University Press, 1990. 357–451.

Stock, Brian. *Augustine the Reader: Meditation, Self-Knowledge, and the Ethics of Interpretation.* Cambridge, Mass.: Harvard University Press, 1996.

———. *The Implications of Literacy: Written Languages and Models of Interpretation in the 11th and 12th Centuries.* Princeton, N.J.: Princeton University Press, 1987.

Strickland, Debra Higgs. *Saracens, Demons, and Jews: Making Monsters in Medieval Art.* Princeton, N.J.: Princeton University Press, 2003.

Stump, Eleonore. *Dialectic and Its Place in the Development of Medieval Logic.* Ithaca, N.Y.: Cornell University Press, 1989.

Suchier, Walther. *L'Enfant Sage (Das Gésprach das Kaisers Hadrian mit dem klugen Kinde Epitus).* Gesellschaft für Romanische Literatur 24. Dresden: Niemeyer, 1910.

Sweeney, Eileen. *Anselm of Canterbury and the Desire for the Word.* Washington, D.C.: Catholic University Press of America, 2012.

———. "Anselm und der Dialog: Distanz und Versöhnung." In *Gespräche lesen,* ed. Jacobi. 101–24.

Symes, Carol. *A Common Stage: Theater and Public Life in Medieval Arras.* Ithaca, N.Y.: Cornell University Press, 2007.

———. "Out in the Open, in Arras: Sightlines, Soundscapes, and the Shaping of a Medieval Public Sphere." In *Cities, Texts, and Social Networks, 400–1500: Experiences and Perceptions of Medieval Urban Space,* ed. Caroline J. Goodson, Anne E. Lester, and Carol Symes. Aldershot: Ashgate, 2010. 279–302.

———. "When We Talk About Modernity." *American Historical Review* 116, 3 (2011): 715–26.

Szpiech, Ryan. *Conversion and Narrative: Reading and Religious Authority in Medieval Polemic.* Philadelphia: University of Pennsylvania Press, 2012.

Tachau, Katherine H. "What Has Gothic to Do with Scholasticism?" In *Gothic Art and Thought in the Later Medieval Period*, ed. Hourihane. 14–34.

Taruskin, Richard. *Music from the Earliest Notation to the Sixteenth Century*. Oxford: Oxford University Press, 2005.

Taylor, A. O. *The Medieval Mind*. Cambridge, Mass.: Harvard University Press, 1959.

Taylor, Andrew. "A Second Ajax: Peter Abelard and the Violence of Dialectic." In *The Tongues of the Fathers: Gender and Ideology in Twelfth-Century Latin*, ed. David Townsend and Andrew Taylor. Philadelphia: University of Pennsylvania Press, 1998. 14–34.

Teske, Roland J. "William of Auvergne." In *A Companion to Philosophy in the Middle Ages*, ed. Jorge J. E. Gracia and Timothy B. Noone. Oxford: Blackwell, 2002. 680–87.

Thorndike, Lynn. "The Survival of Mediaeval Intellectual Interests into Early Modern Times." *Speculum* 2, 2 (1927): 147–59.

Thurot, Charles. *De l'organisation de l'enseignement dans l'université de Paris*. Paris: Dezobry, Magdeleine, 1850.

Tolan, John. *Petrus Alfonsi and His Medieval Readers*. Gainsville: University Press of Florida, 1993.

Torrell, Jean-Pierre. *Aquinas's Summa: Background, Structure, and Reception*. Trans. Benedict Guevin, O.S.B. Washington, D.C.: Catholic University of America Press, 2005.

———. *Saint Thomas Aquinas*. Trans. Robert Royal. Washington, D.C.: Catholic University of America Press, 2005.

Tyler, Stephen A. "Ode to Dialog on the Occasion of the Un-for-seen." In *The Interpretation of Dialogue*, ed. Tullio Maranhão. Chicago: University of Chicago Press, 1990. 292–300.

Valente, Luisa. *Phantasia contrarietas: Contraddizioni scritturali, discorso teologico e arti del linguaggio nel "De tropis loquendi" di Pietro Cantore (d. 1197)*. Florence: Olschki, 1997.

Valois, Noël. *Guillaume d'Auvergne, Éveque de Paris (1228–1249): Sa vie et ses ouvrages*. Paris: Picard, 1880.

Van Engen, John, ed. *Learning Institutionalized: Teaching in the Medieval University*. Notre Dame, Ind.: University of Notre Dame Press, 2000.

———. "Letters, Schools, and Written Culture in the Eleventh and Twelfth Centuries." In *Dialektik und Rhetorik*, ed. Fried. 97–132.

———. *Rupert of Deutz*. Berkeley: University of California Press, 1983.

———. "The Twelfth Century: Reading, Reason, and Revolt in a World of Custom." In *European Transformations*, ed. Noble and Van Engen. 17–44.

Van Koningsveld, P. Sj. "Historische betrekkingen tussen moslims en christenen." In *Petrus Alfonsi, een 12de eeuwse schakel tussen en Christendom in Spanje*, ed. P. Sj. van Koningsveld. Nijmegen: Nederlandse Vereniging voor de Studie van het Midden-Oosten en de Islam, 1982. 127–46.

Van Riel, Gerd, Carlos Steel, and James McEvoy, eds. *Iohannes Scottus Eriugena: The Bible and Hermeneutics*. Leuven: Leuven University Press, 1996.

Van't Spijker, Ineke. *Fictions of the Inner Life: Religious Literature and Formation of the Self in the Eleventh and Twelfth Centuries*. Turnhout: Brepols, 2004.

Vaughn, M. F. "The Prophets of the Anglo-Norman 'Adam'." *Traditio* 39 (1983): 81–114.

Vaughn, Sally N. *The Abbey of Bec and the Anglo-Norman State, 1034–1136*. Woodbridge: Boydell, 1981.

———. "'Among These Authors Are the Men of Bec': Historical Writing Among the Monks of Bec." In *The Uses of History: Proceedings of the Illinois Medieval Association Annual Meeting*, ed. Allen J. Frantzen. Essays in Medieval Studies 17. Morgantown: West Virginia University Press, 2001. 1–18.

———. "Anselm, Lanfranc, and the School of Bec: Searching for the Students of Bec." In *The Culture of Christendom: Essays in Commemoration of Denis L. T. Bethell*, ed. Marc A. Meyer. London: Hambledon, 1993.

———. *Anselm of Bec and Robert of Meulan: The Innocence of the Dove and the Wisdom of the Serpent*. Berkeley: University of California Press, 1987.

———. "Anselm of Bec: The Pattern of His Teaching." In *Teaching and Learning*, ed. Vaughn and Rubenstein. 99–128.

———. "The Concept of Law at the Abbey of Bec, 1034–1136: How Law and Legal Concepts Were Described, Taught and Practiced at Bec in the Time of Lanfranc and Anselm." In *Law and Learning in the Middle Ages*, ed. Vogt and Münster-Swendsen. 167–80.

———. "Saint Anselm and His Students Writing About Love: A Theological Foundation for the Rise of Romantic Love in Europe." *Journal of the History of Sexuality* 19 (2010): 54–73.

———. *St. Anselm and the Handmaidens of God: A Study of Anselm's Correspondence with Women*. Utrecht Studies in Medieval Literacy 7. Turnhout: Brepols, 2002.

Vaughn, Sally N. and Jay Rubenstein, eds. *Teaching and Learning in Northern Europe, 1000–1200*. Studies in the Early Middle Ages 8. Turnhout: Brepols, 2006.

Verbaal, Wim. "Sens: une victoire d'écrivain: Les deux visages du process d'Abélard." In *Pierre Abélard: Colloque International de Nantes*, ed. Jean Jolivet and Henri Habrias. Rennes: Presses Universitaires de Rennes, 2003. 77–89.

Verger, Jacques. "La musique et le son chez Vincent de Beauvais et les encyclopédistes du XIIIe siècle." In *La place de la musique*, ed. Cullin. 71–85.

———. "A propos de la naissance de l'université de Paris: Contexte social, enjeu politique, portée intellectuelle." In *Schulen und Studium im Sozialen Wandel des Hohen und Späten Mittelalters*, ed. Johannes Fried. Sigmaringen: Thorbecke, 1986. 69–96.

Vicaire, Marie-Humbert. *Saint Dominic and His Times*. Trans. Kathleen Pond. New York: McGraw-Hill, 1964.

Vinay, Gustavo. "La commedia latina del secolo XII." *Studi Medievali* 18 (1952): 209–71.

Viola, Coloman and Frederick Van Fleteren, eds. *Saint Anselm: A Thinker for Yesterday and Today*. Texts and Studies in Religion 90. Lewiston, N.Y.: Edwin Mellen, 2002.

Visser, Sandra and Thomas Williams. *Anselm*. Oxford: Oxford University Press, 2008.

Vitz, Evelyn Birge. *Medieval Narrative and Modern Narratology: Subjects and Objects of Desire*. New York: New York University Press, 1989.

Von Harnack, Adolf. *History of Dogma*. London: Williams and Norgate, 1899.

Von Moos, Peter. "Les *Collationes* d'Abélard et la 'question juive' au XIIe siècle." *Journal des Savants* 2 (1999): 449–89.

———. "Le dialogue Latin au Moyen Âge: L'exemple d'Evrard d'Ypres." *Annales: Économies, Sociétés, Civilisations* 44 (1989): 993–1028.

———. "Gespräche, Dialogform und Dialog nach älterer Theorie." In *Gattungen mittealterlicher Schriftlichkeit*, ed. Barbara Frank, Thomas Haye, and Doris Tophinke. ScriptOralia 99. Tübingen: G. Narr, 1997. 235–60.

———. "Literatur- und bildungsgeschichtliche Aspekte der Dialogform im lateinischen Mittelalter: Der *Dialogus Ratii* des Eberhard von Ypern zwischen theologischer *disputatio* und Scholaren-Komödie." In *Tradition und Wertung: Festschrift für Franz Brunhölzl sum 65. Geburtstag*, ed. Günter Bern et al. Sigmaringen: Thorbecke, 1989. 165–209.

———. *"Öffentlich" und "privat" im Mittelalter: Zu einem Problem historischer Begriffsbildung*. Heidelberg: Universitätsverlag Winter, 2004.

Vogt, Helle and Mia Münster-Swendsen, ed. *Law and Learning in the Middle Ages: Proceedings of the Second Carlsberg Academy Conference on Medieval Legal History 2005.* Copenhagen: DJØF, 2006.

Vose, Robin. *Dominicans, Muslims, and Jews in the Medieval Crown of Aragon.* Cambridge, Cambridge University Press, 2009.

Wallach, Luitpold. *Alcuin and Charlemagne: Studies in Carolingian History and Culture.* Ithaca, N.Y.: Cornell University Press, 1959.

Ward, John O. *Ciceronian Rhetoric in Treatise, Scholion, and Commentary.* Turnhout: Brepols, 1995.

———. "From Marginal Gloss to *Catena* Commentary: The Eleventh-Century Origins of a Rhetorical Teaching Tradition in the Medieval West." *Parergon* 13, 2 (1996): 109–20.

———. "Quintilian and the Rhetorical Revolution of the Middle Ages." *Rhetorica* 13, 3 (1995): 231–84.

Ward, John O. and Karin Margareta Fredborg. "Rhetoric in the Time of William of Champeaux." In *Arts du langage*, ed. Rosier-Catach. 219–34.

Warichez, Joseph. *Étienne de Tournai et son temps, 1128–1203.* Paris: Casterman, 1937.

Warner, George F. and Julius P. Gilson. *Catalogue of Western Manuscripts in the Old Royal and King's Collections.* London: British Museum, 1921.

Watkins, Priscilla D. "Lanfranc at Caen: Teaching by Example." In *Teaching and Learning*, ed. Vaughn and Rubenstein. 71–97.

Watson, Nicholas. "Censorship and Cultural Change in Late-Medieval England: Vernacular Theology, the Oxford Translation Debate, and Arundel's Constitutions of 1409." *Speculum* 70, 4 (1995): 822–64.

Wei, John. "Gratian and the School of Laon." *Traditio* 64 (2009): 279–322.

Weijers, Olga. *La "disputatio" à la faculté des arts de Paris (1200–1350 environ): Esquisse d'une typologie.* Turnhout: Brepols, 1995.

———. *La disputatio dans les Facultés des arts au moyen âge.* Turnhout: Brepols, 2002.

———. *Terminologie des universités au XIIIe siècle.* Rome: Edizioni dell'Ateneo, 1987.

Weisheipl, James A., O.P. *Friar Thomas d'Aquino: His Life, Thought, and Work.* New York: Doubleday, 1974.

Wenzel, Edith. *"Do worden die Judden alle geschant": Rolle und Funktion der Juden in spätmittelalterlichen Speilen.* Munich: Fink, 1992.

Wetherbee, Winthrop. *Platonism and Poetry in the Twelfth Century: The Literary Influence of the School of Chartres.* Princeton, N.J.: Princeton University Press, 1972.

Whitbread, Leslie G. "Conrad of Hirsau as Literary Critic." *Speculum* 47, 2 (1972): 234–45.

Wilks, Michael, ed. *The World of John of Salisbury.* Oxford: Blackwell, 1994.

Williams, A. Lukyn. *Adversus Judaeos: A Bird's-Eye View of Christian Apologiae Until the Renaissance.* Cambridge: Cambridge University Press, 1935.

Wilson, K. J. *Incomplete Fictions: The Formation of English Renaissance Dialogue.* Washington, D.C.: Catholic University of America Press, 1985.

Winroth, Anders. *The Making of Gratian's Decretum.* Cambridge: Cambridge University Press, 2000.

———. "The Teaching of Law in the Twelfth Century." In *Law and Learning in the Middle Ages*, ed. Vogt and Münster-Swendsen. 41–62.

Winterbottom, Michael. "Schoolroom and Courtroom." In *Rhetoric Revalued: Papers from the International Society for the History of Rhetoric*, ed. Brian Vickers. Binghamton, N.Y.: Center for Medieval and Renaissance Texts and Studies, 1982. 59–70.

Wippel, J. F. "Quodlibetical Questions, Chiefly in Theology Faculties." In *LQD*, ed. Bazàn, Wippel, Fransen, and Jacquart. 153–222.

Witt, Michael A. "*The Owl and the Nightingale* and English Law Court Procedure of the Twelfth and Thirteenth Centuries." *Chaucer Review* 16 (1982): 282–92.

Woolf, Jeffrey R. "Maimonides Revised: The Case of the *Sefer Miswot Gadol.*" *Harvard Theological Review* 90, 2 (1997): 175–203.

———. "Some Polemical Emphases in the *Sefer Miswot Gadol* of Rabbi Moses of Coucy." *Jewish Quarterly Review* 89, 1–2 (1998): 81–100.

Wright, Craig. *Music and Ceremony at Notre Dame of Paris, 500–1550.* Cambridge: Cambridge University Press, 1989.

Yonah, R. Avi. "Career Trends of Parisian Masters of Theology, 1200–1320." *History of Universities* 6 (1986–87): 47–64.

Young, Karl. "Ordo prophetarum." *Transactions of the Wisconsin Academy of Sciences, Arts and Letters* 20 (1921): 1–81.

Yrjönsuuri, Mikko, ed. *Medieval Formal Logic: Obligations, Insolubles, and Consequences.* Dordrecht: Kluwer, 2010.

Zerbi, Pietro. *"Philosophi" e Logici": Un ventennio di incontri e scontri: Soissons, Sens, Cluny (1121–1141).* Rome: Nella sede dell'Istituto, Palazzo Borromini, 2002.

Ziolkowski, Jan M. *Solomon and Marcolf.* Harvard Studies in Medieval Latin. Cambridge, Mass.: Harvard University Press, 2008.

Zonta, Mauro. *Hebrew Scholasticism in the Fifteenth Century: A History and Sourcebook.* Dordrecht: Springer, 2006.

Zumthor, Paul. *La lettre et la voix: De la "littérature médiévale".* Paris: Seuil, 1987.

# Index of Works

Note: Only those titles that appear in the body of the book are listed. Additional works are cited in the notes. Known or presumed authors are listed parenthetically.

# GENERAL INDEX

Note: Authors before 1500 are listed by first name. Names in bold type also appear in the Index of Works.

Rhetoric, 5, 10–15, 20, 22, 23, 26, 29, 32, 33, 36, 38, 43, 64, 101, 104, 106, 123, 148, 158, 159, 166, 180, 193, 213, 231n6, 235n101, 245n19, 253n151; and Abelard, 84, 90. *See also* Trivium
Robert de Sorbon, 193
Robert Holcot, 131, 258n68
Robert of Courson, 100, 138–40, 156, 260n29
**Robert of Melun**, 93
**Rodrigo Jiménez de Rada**, 202–4
Rogerius, 95
Romanesque, 34
Rome, 18, 36–37, 84, 98, 140, 156, 165, 196, 217, 237n22, 250n99
Roscelin of Compiégne, 78
Rue du Fouarre, 143, 197
**Rupert of Deutz**, 56, 66, 70–72, 96

Sabbath, 191
Saenger, Paul, 24
Saltzstein, Jennifer, 152–54
Samuel ben Solomon of Château Thierry, 194
Saturn, 27–28
Saul, 205
Schofield, Malcolm, 12Scholasticism, 1–3, 7, 8, 33, 34, 92, 118, 123, 126, 133, 147, 180, 219, 222, 228, 252n142, 273n102
Schreckenberg, Heinz, 173
Scientific Revolution, 134
Scripture, 14–17, 30–31, 39, 51–53, 67, 72–73, 83, 87–89, 101, 134–36, 148, 151, 163, 167, 188, 203, 216–17. *See also* New Testament; Old Testament
Sens, 84
Sephardic Jews, 201–3
Sergius III, 28
Serper, Arié, 213
Sharpe, Richard, 35–36, 45
Sicily, 207, 274n121
Sigebert of Gembloux, 39
Siger of Brabant, 170
Simon of Tournai, 136–38, 141–44
Socrates, 8–9, 57, 108–10, 120
Soissons, 27, 78, 81, 84
*Sola ratione*, 42, 177
*Sola scriptura*, 177
Solomon, 27–28, 119–20
Solterer, Helen, 151
Southern, Richard W., 34, 40, 43, 49, 54
Spain, 158, 176, 180, 200–202, 205, 208, 268n2, 269n15

St. Catherine's (Convent of Santa Caterina), 201, 207–8, 211, 274n109, 275nn130, 132. *See also* Barcelona
St. Gallen, 107
St. Jacques, 208
St. Paul, 39, 60, 156, 237n24
St. Peter, 156
St. Stephen Portal (Notre Dame Cathedral), 63, 78, 100, 155, 179, 195. *See also* Iconography of disputation
St. Victor (School), 63, 189, 203. *See also* Paris
Stein, Siegfried, 200
Stephen Langton, 100, 134–35, 188, 253n150
Stephen VI, 28
Strasbourg Cathedral, 213
*Studia generale*, 134, 138, 161, 165
*Summulae*, 137–38
Symes, Carol, 144, 153
Synagoga, 174, 212–14, 276n148

Tacitus, 15, 232n28
Talmud, 173, 182, 191–204, 206, 211–14, 273n92
Talmud Trial, 7, 190–93, 197, 272n80, 273n93
Taruskin, Richard, 147, 153, 155
Tau, 49
*Tenso*, 152
*Testimonia*, 189
Theobald of Bec, 187
Theoduin of Liége, 37
**Thibaut of Sézanne**, 197–98
Thierry of Chartres, 109, 111
**Thomas Aquinas**, 143, 160, 163–68, 170, 227, 265n130, 266n36, 267n141
Thomas Becket, 100, 110, 187
Thomas of Cantimpré, 137, 150–51
**Thomas of Morigny**, 83–84, 250n95
Toledo, 63, 202–4, 270n34
Tortosa, 184, 218
Toulouse, 156
Tours, 36–37
Trinity, 30–31, 78, 85, 136, 188, 213–14, 217, 248n73
Trivium, 32, 64, 107, 110, 113, 120, 121, 123, 141, 226. *See also* Liberal Arts
Tunisia, 207

Umiliati, 156
University, 1–6, 8, 61, 89, 91, 94, 107, 113, 121, 124, 132, 134, 137, 149, 153, 155, 156, 157, 160, 169, 171, 222–24, 227–28, 230n11, 252n132,

260n29, 261n33, 262n53, 266n133; of Paris,
122, 133, 136, 139–46, 148, 190, 194, 196–97,
204, 207, 260n23; of Bologna, 138–39,
260n21; and Dominicans, 160–68. *See also*
Scholasticism
Urban II, 45

Valencia, 207
Valente, Luisa, 101
Vespers, 120
Victorine, 75, 188
Vienne, 195
Vincent of Beauvais, 144, 182
Virgil, 68
Virgin Birth, 149, 179–80, 216–17
*Vita apostolica*, 159
**Vital of Blois**, 118–20
Von Moos, Peter, 116–17, 239n50
Vose, Robin, 201

Wala of Corbie, 26
Waldensians, 156, 158
Walter de Cornut of Sens, 194
Walter of Berwick, 217
**Walter of Châtillon**, 66, 111, 121, 186, 194

Ward, John O., 64
Watson, Nicholas, 212
Weijers, Olga, 141
Weisheipl, James, 165
Westminster, 36, 52–55, 224
William of Auvergne, 150, 194
William of Champagne, 186
**William of Champeaux**, 63, 78, 79, 177
William of Moerbeke, 11
William of Ockham, 131, 145
William of Saint-Amour, 164
**William of St. Thierry**, 75, 82–84, 110, 226,
250n96
William of Syracuse, 69
William Rufus, 45
William the Conqueror, 48
Winroth, Anders, 91, 93
Würzburg, 63

Yehiel ben Joseph, 193–95, 199, 272n85
**Yehuda Halevi**, 119, 201–2
Ypres, 114, 117–18, 229n7

Zeno of Elea, 9
Zumthor, Paul, 100

## ACKNOWLEDGMENTS

This book is about the rise of scholastic disputation and its importance in the cultural history of the western tradition, yet I must concede that it is the academic culture of dialogue I inhabit to which I am most indebted. Over the years, a great many scholars, friends, colleagues, and editors have given generous amounts of their time and wisdom to me and to my work. It is my sincere pleasure to thank as many of them as I can.

My first debt of gratitude is to my teachers. Edward Peters has over the years provided me with guidance and mentorship of the highest and most compassionate order. He encouraged my pursuit of the vast and fissiparous topic of this book even when others (myself included) had grave doubts about it, and he has continued to be magnificently supportive of all my endeavors. Jill Claster and Norman Cantor turned me onto medieval intellectual history and Matthew Kempshall introduced me to the world of medieval political thought. Richard Fletcher introduced me to the extraordinary riches of medieval Spain; I still mourn his passing. Anna Sapir Abulafia offered me guidance and inspiration on the subject of Jewish-Christian relations and there is much in this project that will undoubtedly reveal my sustained debt to her own scholarship in the field. At one institution or another I benefited from productive conversations with a range of outstanding scholars who have, knowingly or unknowingly, deeply impacted my work: David Abulafia, Charles Burnett, Carmen Cardelle de Hartmann, Roger Chartier, Rita Copeland, Brian Copenhaver, Antonio Feros, Patrick Geary, Alan C. Kors, John Marenbon, Ann Matter, Benjamin Nathans, Calvin Normore, David Ruderman, Jonathan Steinberg, and Tom Waldman.

The University of Pennsylvania Press is to be congratulated for having procured such wonderfully insightful reviewers. In particular, Dan Hobbins revealed his identity to me as one of the readers and has since become a steadfast and valued supporter of both my scholarship and my career. His sensitive reading of the entire manuscript has done much to improve it. Jerry Singerman, senior humanities editor at the Penn Press, took an early interest in my work and has shown more forbearance than I deserve by expertly shepherding this book from submission to publication. For constructive feedback on the portion of Chapter 5 that deals with medieval music and polyphony, I am especially grateful to Edward Roesner, Tom Payne, Margot Fassler, and Jennifer Saltzstein. Carol Symes read and commented on Chapter 5 and has proved to be a cherished intellectual companion in rethinking the medieval public sphere. A special mention must be made of James J. Murphy, who wrote a detailed and enthusiastic letter to me after reading an article I published in *Speculum* in 2011. He has been a remarkable wellspring of encouragement and support for virtually all aspects of this project. Finally, Tony Grafton read and commented on an early version of my work with great acumen and also provided me with some heroic advice at a critical juncture in my career.

For the past five years I have had the great fortune of teaching in the History Department at Rhodes College. The support of my chairs, Tim Huebner and Lynn Zastoupil, of the Dean's office, of the Cap-Mellon junior sabbatical program, of the Faculty Development Committee, of the Spence Wilson International Travel Grant, and of all my colleagues in the department has been critical in bringing this project to completion. The cost of the images for this book was generously paid for by funds from the Rhodes College History Department and the Dean's office. The Marco Institute of Medieval Studies at the University of Tennessee-Knoxville awarded me a Lindsay Young visiting fellowship in the summer of 2009, where much of Chapter 2 was written. My participation in a 2012 NEH Summer Institute in Barcelona, "Networks of Knowledge," under the direction of Brian Catlos and Sharon Kinoshita allowed me to focus on materials associated with medieval Barcelona and the Barcelona Disputation of 1263. I am deeply grateful to all these persons and organizations for supporting my work.

This book appears as I transition to New York City to take a position at Fordham University, opposite the very Lincoln Center where I spent formative years in my musical education. Among the many compelling reasons for returning to the city where I was born and raised is the love and support of the two people who made my life as a transatlantic medievalist possible in the first place. As a small token of my love and appreciation, I dedicate this book to my parents, Albert and Danièle.

An earlier version of Chapter 2 was published in *Speculum* 86, 2 (2011): 387–418. The revised version appears here by permission. Portions of the introduction and other chapters were published in the *American Historical Review* 117, 2 (2012): 331–64, and also appear with the permission of the editors.